JOURNEY TO THE HORIZO

Escape & Evasion during World War II

Hans Onderwater MBE and Brian Lissette
Journey to the Horizon; Escape and Evasion during World War II.

© Hans Onderwater 1985 (Dutch), 2020 (English).

First published in 1984 by Hollandia Publishers, Baarn, Netherlands
ISBN 906 045 208 9

English edition in 2021 by

 **Nedvision**

Nedvision Publishing, Assen, Netherlands
nedvision.com   info@nedvision.com
ISBN 978 908 308 6019

Cover design & insert layout: Dick van der Zee

Hans Onderwater MBE
Brian Lissette

JOURNEY TO THE HORIZON
Escape & Evasion during World War II

Dedicated to the heroes of the Comète Line, who risked and sometimes lost their lives to help down airmen, fleeing soldiers and resistance members to evade capture.

Dedicated to the airmen who dared to run for freedom, to those who endured captivity and hardship and those who gave their lives for the freedom of others.

Dedicated to the families who had to endure so much fear, anxiety and sadness while their loved ones failed to return from their missions.

CONTENTS.

12. APPENDICES.

FOREWORD
by Patricia Willis née Giles, widow of Major Don Kenyon Willis USAF

In March 1982 Patricia Willis came to the Netherlands to see where her husband landed in April 1944 and to meet several people in the Netherlands and Belgium who were instrumental in his successful evasion. Before she returned to Florida, she wrote:

'It is with deep felt gratitude that I write these few lines as a foreword to the story of the successful escape of my husband Donald Kenyon Willis and his four comrades. They covered four countries before they returned to England. Although as time goes by it was not a very long span, at the time it happened during the war it was an eternity. I will never forget the day when I was informed that Don was missing in action. In spite of my confidence in Donald, I felt the chill of fear when I was left alone with the knowledge that there was only a slim chance of him returning safely to Britain. I cannot describe how I felt when I was called to the phone in the hospital where I worked. I still hear that voice saying to me: 'Hi, Pat, it's me, I'm home again.'

I knew little about Don's Journey to the Horizon until Hans Onderwater contacted me and told me what he was doing.' Little by little, a jigsaw puzzle formed into a fascinating story when I heard about the heroism of simple people in the occupied countries and five men on the run.

Hans has written many books about the history of his country The Netherlands during the Second World War, yet I do not think that any manuscript has taken so much effort and time as this story. I met Hans when I flew to Holland and he took me with him to meet the people who risked their lives to help my husband and so many other escapees. I will always cherish the first time I embraced old 'Mother' Kuppens in Oud-Gastel, who, with her husband had been the first to give shelter to my husband. They did this with their sons living in the house. My meeting with Yvonne Bienfait in Mons, Belgium will be a treasure in my mind as long as I live. Yvonne, a nurse like I, is one of the most courageous women I have ever met.

Hans travelled the long route Don and his friends took to reach freedom. During the second Journey to the Horizon Hans met as many eyewitnesses as possible. Now his story ends with a truthful reconstruction of an incredible evasion. To me it is impossible to express my gratitude to all the people who once risked their lives to help men like my husband. I cannot tell them how grateful I am, for they gave me back the best thing I have: the man I loved with all my heart. That is why he felt so strongly that he had to come back to me. His return to England and his continuing battle for our mutual freedom makes him my hero.

We were given many happy years until Don fell ill and died. Though I miss him a lot he stays in my memory as the man who gave me a wonderful life. I consider this book a tribute to all the people of the resistance and to the soldiers who tried everything to return to England to continue the war against the common enemy rather than to surrender.'

Patricia J. Willis

Patricia Willis née Giles.

FOREWORD

By Glynis Spencer, Angela Barnes, and Amanda Burrows, daughters of Pilot Officer Len 'Barney' Barnes MBE RAF

On March 15th 2020 we received a phone call 'out of the blue'. It was from Hans Onderwater in connection with the rewriting of a book he had originally written in 1985. The narrative recounted the passage of five brave aircrew in 1944, of which our father Pilot Officer Leonard Barnes was one, and their hazardous journey to safety and freedom across the Pyrenees.

They were guided by the selfless and courageous members of the Comète Line. As 'Reis naar de Horizon' was written in Dutch we were unable to comprehend it. However, it was a book we cherished dearly and recognised its importance as a treasured family archive. What was so amazing is that Hans' call came on the anniversary of our father's Lancaster bomber crashing in France on March 15th 1944! exactly 76 years later!

Hans has a lifelong interest in military history and is the author of many successful books on this subject. This particular project has been ongoing for nearly forty years, a testament to his perseverance in documenting these remarkable events. Now in collaboration with Brian Lissette a more detailed and informative edition is published. Brian has spent more than twenty years researching his uncle's wartime story, Warrant Officer Leslie Lissette RNZAF, who features in the original version. Their shared interest, research and dedication to bringing these stories of determination and bravery to print has culminated in this moving tribute to each and every one of those involved.

We can learn so much from these stories and how seemingly 'ordinary' folk could show such great courage, commitment, resilience and comradeship. Indeed, they were 'extraordinary'!

We feel so honoured and moved to have been asked to write this foreword and our sincere and utmost gratitude goes to Hans and Brian for allowing these stories to live on.

Glynis Spencer   Angela Barnes   Amanda Burrows

A SILK MAP, PART OF THE ESCAPE KIT.

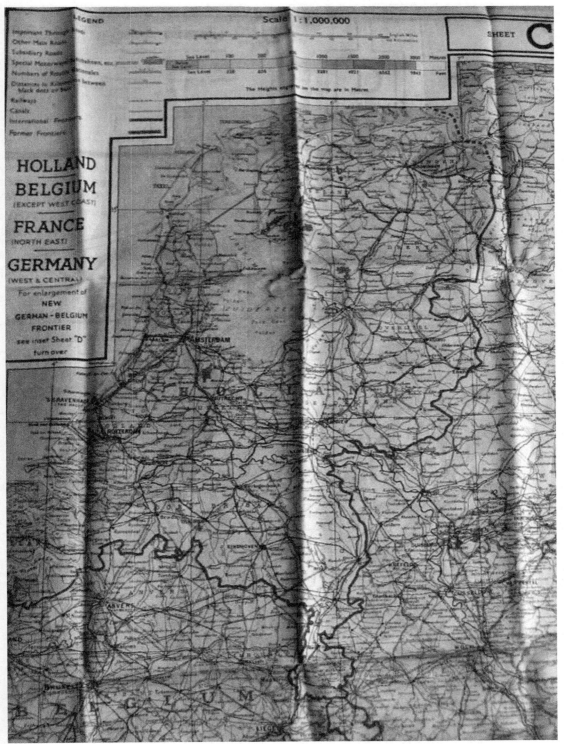

Holland and part of Belgium; One of the many silk escape maps. (HO)

ESCAPE AND EVASION LINES TO GIBRALTAR.

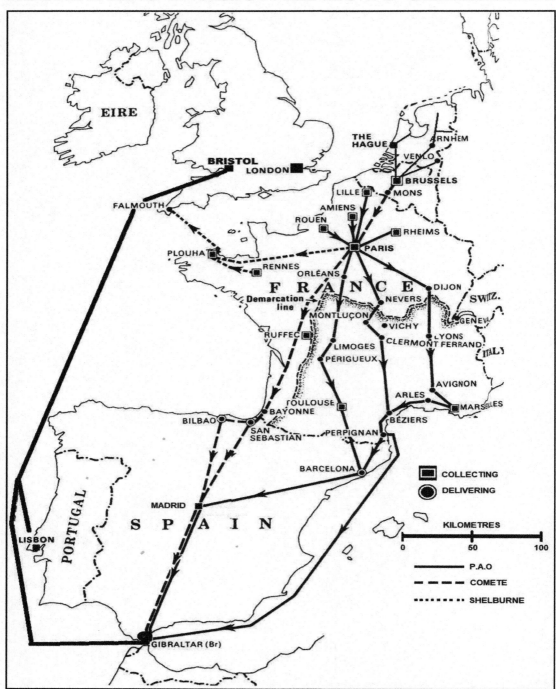

The different escape routes to Gibraltar, used by allied soldiers and aviators to return to Great Britain from the occupied territories. Comète ran all the way through occupied territory while the PAO line partly went through Vichy France, the non-occupied part of the country. Shelburne was the shortest and most dangerous route, as the escapers had to pass the Atlantic Wall, the German defence line along the coast of Europe, heavily fortified and well-guarded and patrolled (via Philippe d'Albert-Lake).

THE JOURNEY THROUGH OCCUPIED EUROPE.

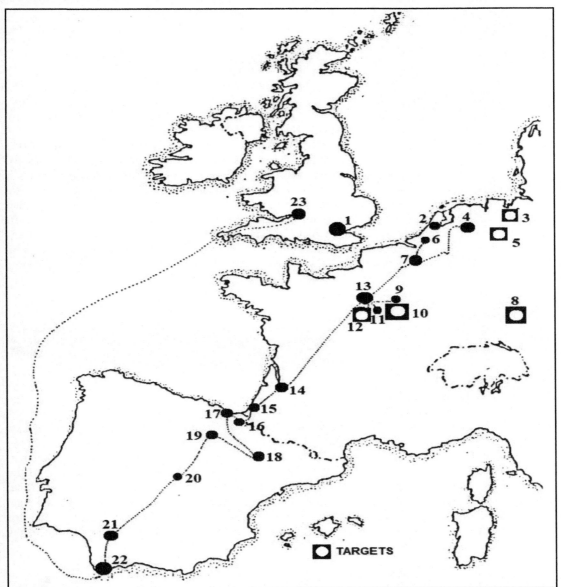

1.) London; 2.) Amsterdam; 3.) Bremen 13 November 1943; 4.) LtCol Hubbard lands near Mariënberg, Holland, by parachute; 5.) Gutersloh, Droop Snoot attack by P-38 Lightnings on 10 April 1944; 6.) Maj Willis makes a forced landing near Oud-Gastel, Holland on return from Gutersloh; 7.) In Brussels: evading military collected by members of Comète; 8.) Stuttgart 15/16 March1944; 9.) P/O Barnes lands by parachute at Dravigny, France; 10.) Mailly-le-Camp, France 3/4 May 44; 11.) Sgts Emeny and Pittwood land by parachute near Rossières; 12.) Etampes-Mondesir, France. USAAF strafing attack 27 April 1944. 2Lt Cornett lands near Arrancourt; 13.) Paris: major collection centre for evaders; 14.) Bordeaux; 15.) Bayonne, last town before trek through the Pyrenees into Spain; 16.) Pamplona, Spain; end of the evasion; 17.) San Sebastian, resort where enemies meet; 18.) Zaragoza, where aircrew are entertained by the Spanish Air Force; 19.) Alhama de Aragon; internment camp for refugees; 20.) Madrid, seats of the British and American legations; 21.) Seville; 22.) Gibraltar, haven of freedom and start of the last leg home; 23.) Whitchurch, Bristol; home after a successful evasion. (HO)

THE TRAVELLERS.

Lieutenant-Colonel Thomas Harvey 'Speed' Hubbard USAAF.
American fighter pilot. Serial 0-380248, HQ 355 FG. Station: Steeple Morden. Flew in P-47D2 Thunderbolt 42-7944 'Lil' Jo', 13 November 1943. Landed by parachute at Mariënberg, the Netherlands. Evaded capture via Dutch resistance. Continued his journey in the Netherlands and Belgium. When in Antwerp, hidden by Miss Nelly Rosiers. Went to Brussels and to Paris, helped by the Comète Line. Like Barnes, Willis, Cornett and Emeny, he reached the Pyrenees. Entered Spain 4 June and briefly interned in Pamplona and Alhama de Aragon. The Spanish handed him over to American embassy. Hubbard left the Continent via Gibraltar. Returned to England 28 June 1944. After the war he returned to Antwerp and married Miss Rosiers, who became Mrs. Hubbard. Continued a career in the USAF and aviation. Died in 1983, buried at Greenwood Memorial Park and Mausoleum in Fort Worth, Tarrant County, Texas. His wife Nelly died in 1987 and rests by his side.

Pilot Officer Leonard Alfred 'Barney' Barnes RAF.
British pilot. Serial 168998. RAFVR No.5 Group Bomber Command. No.630 Squadron. Station: East Kirkby. Shot down in the night of 15/16 March 1944 flying Lancaster ND530, P-Peter to Stuttgart. Crew: Flying Officer Geisler (Nav), Sergeants Walker Fl/Eng), Gregg (BA), Overholt (MUG), Plowman (Wop/AG) and Fox (RAG). Barnes landed by parachute near Dravigny. Found by a member of the resistance. First hidden in Fère-en-Tardenois. From there, to Paris to be handled by the Comète Line. With Hubbard, Willis, Cornett and Emeny taken to the border between France and Spain. On 4/5 June 1944, Plt Off Barnes entered Spain and after a brief internment by Spanish was handed to diplomats of the British embassy. Departed by plane from Gibraltar. Arrived in England 25 June 1944. Some of his crew members managed to evade capture as well. Barnes died in 1988.

Major Donald Kenyon 'Willy' Willis USAAF.
American fighter pilot. Serial 0-889159. Tactics Evaluation Officer HQ 67th Fighter Wing. Walcott Hall near Stamford. Willis took off from Kingscliffe to evaluate the Droop Snoot mission of 10 April 1944, in a borrowed aircraft. Willis landed P-38J Lightning serial number 42-68077, KI-X, 20 Fighter Group, 55 Fighter Squadron at Oud-Gastel in Holland. After landing Dutch patriots hid him and gave him shelter while German soldiers searched the area. Due to his fast departure, it was impossible to destroy the

aircraft and a German officer photographed it. In the meantime, Willis walked from Oud-Gastel to the Dutch-Belgian border. For days, he evaded on his own and reached Antwerp, where a Belgian resistance member saw him. He was passed to the Comète Line and spent time in Belgium before being moved to Paris. Don Willis travelled south with Hubbard, Barnes, Cornett and Emeny. He entered Spain on 6 June and after a brief internment in Pamplona and Alhama de Aragon, was handed to US embassy officials and travelled to Gibraltar. Arrived in England 28 June 1944. Willis flew as a pilot during the Winter War in Finland, during the German invasion of Norway in the Norwegian Naval Air Force and in the RAF Eagle Squadron, before joining the USAAF. After a long career in the USAF, Don Willis went back to sea. Suffering from Alzheimer's Disease he died in April 1977.

2nd Lieutenant Jack 'Jacko' Donald Cornett USAAF.
American fighter pilot. Serial 0-816632. 375 FS. 361 FG. Bottisham. P-47D Thunderbolt, 42-75219, E2-G. His aircraft was hit by Flak while he was strafing Étampes-Mondésir France on 27 April 1944. He landed near Arrancourt, south of Paris. Evading capture for a few days, he was found and taken to a safe house. First the local resistance checked Cornett's credentials and once satisfied took him under their wings. He went to Paris and was handed over to the Comète Line. With four others, he travelled to the Basque region of France and crossed the border on 6 June 1944. After a few days of internment in Pamplona, he went to Alma de Aragon and Madrid. American embassy officials arranged for transport to Gibraltar. He reached England on 30 June 1944. He retired a Lieutenant Colonel in the USAF and died in September 1986.

Sergeant Ronald Thomas 'Curly' Emeny RAF.
British air gunner, Serial 138167 RAFVR No.5 Group. Bomber Command No.207 Squadron. Station RAF Spilsby. Mid-upper gunner in Lancaster ND556, EM-F for Freddie. Shot down during the raid against Mailly-le-Camp, a Panzer training facility in France on 3/4 May 1944. The crew were: Warrant Officer Lissette (pilot), Flight Sergeant Pittwood (Nav), Sergeants Wesley (B/A), King (Wop/AG), Stockford (Fl/Eng) Ellis (RAG) and Emeny (MUG). Emeny was severely burned, and with the help of Pittwood hiding in a crypt near Rossières. The local resistance found them. Pittwood was taken to Paris and lost contact with Emeny. Due to his burns, Emeny had to stay behind until he had recovered or died, for which a grave had already been dug. Once he was fit, the resistance took him to Paris, where he met four other airmen with whom he was to continue south. From Paris he travelled to Bayonne by train, escorted by two members of Comète. During the night of 5/6 June, he and his four friends crossed into Spain and were briefly interned until the British embassy moved him and the other Briton Len Barnes to Madrid and Gibraltar. He left by aircraft and landed in England on 25 June 1944. Emeny AFM dedicated his retired life to the East Kirkby Aviation Museum. He died on 8th December 2001, leaving his wife Jess and family: Ron served twice on No.207. He had a long career in the RAF and told any number of stories of causing consternation among the local brass when senior officers he had known in their early days spotted him during visits.

THE LANCASTERS AND THE CREWS.

Lancaster ND530, LE-P for Peter, 15/16 March 1944.
No.5 Group Bomber Command. No.630 Squadron. East Kirkby, target Stuttgart.
Pilot Officer L. A. Barnes, Pilot 168998 (Evaded, escaped to Spain).
Sergeant K. A. Walker, Flight Engineer 1583707 (Evaded, hidden by French family)
Sergeant J. H. Overholt RCAF, Mid Upper Gunner R/197141 (Killed, buried St. Gilles).[1]
Sergeant T. A. Fox, Rear Gunner 1433606 (Killed, buried St. Gilles).
Flying Officer M. Geisler, Navigator 151194 (PoW 4140, Stalag Luft 1, Barth).
Sergeant M. E. Gregg, Bomb Aimer 1576438 (PoW 3816, Stalag Luft 1, Barth).
Sergeant G. E. Plowman, Wireless Operator 1333979 (PoW 3198, Stalag 357, Fallingbostel).
All were RAF, except for Sergeant Overholt, who was RCAF.

L.A.Barnes   *K.A.Walker*   *G.E.Plowman*   *T.A.Fox*   *M.Geisler*   *M.E.Gregg*   *J.H.Overholt*

Lancaster ND556, EM-F for Freddie. 03/04 May 1944.
No.5 Group Bomber Command No.207 Squadron. RAF Spilsby, target Mailly-le-Camp.
Warrant Officer L. H. Lissette RNZAF, Pilot 391011 (Killed, buried Chaintreaux).[2]
Sergeant R. Ellis, Rear Gunner 537642 (Killed, buried Chaintreaux).
Sergeant N. J. Stockford, Flight Engineer 673915 (Evaded, escaped to Spain).
Sergeant P. N. King, Wireless Operator 1580576 (Evaded, escaped to Spain).
Flight Sergeant J. Pittwood, Navigator 1219454 (Evaded, escaped to Spain).
Sergeant R. T. Emeny, Mid Upper Gunner 1383167 (Evaded, escaped to Spain).
Sergeant L. Wesley, Bomb Aimer 1581817 (PoW 8122, Buchenwald, Stalag Luft 3 Sagan).
All were RAF, except for Warrant Officer Lissette, who was RNZAF.

L.H.Lissette   *N.J.Stockford*   *P.N.King*   *R.Ellis*   *J.Pittwood*   *L.Wesley*   *R.T.Emeny*

---

[1] *Sgt (A/G) Fox Thomas Austin, RAFVR 1433606; Sgt (A/G) Overholt, James Henry, RCAF R/197141. Aged 20. Son of George Henry Overholt and of Irene Alberta Overholt (nee MacDonald), of Eastwood, Ontario, Canada. Died 16/03/1944. 630 Sqn.*
[2] *W/O (Pilot) Lissette Leslie Harry, RNZAF 391011. Aged 26. Son of Harry and Ellen Georgina (Nellie) Lissette, of Pakowhai, Hawke's Bay, New Zealand, Service Number 537642; Sgt Ronald Ellis RAF 537642. Aged 25. Husband of Kathleen Ellis, of Duns Tew, Oxfordshire. Died 04/05/1944. 207 Sqn.*

INTRODUCTION.

Many airmen were captured moments after they landed, dazzled, or wounded, not sure where they were, often very scared. The Germans were keen to capture aircrew; it was in their interest to catch as many PoWs[3] as possible. Helping downed flyers or fleeing soldiers was an extremely dangerous matter. Anyone trying to help them faced severe penalties, like death by execution or slow death in a concentration camp. Therefore, one needed exceptional courage to assist airmen. In addition, as an airman, one needed the same courage to decide to try to evade capture.

The way back to England was long and arduous, full of great danger and very uncertain, a long exhausting journey to Spain, Switzerland or Sweden. The title of the book is Journey to the Horizon for a good reason. It tells the fascinating story of the escape from Occupied Europe of five allied aircrew that abandoned their aircraft after it crashed or came down by forced landing. With great bravery and a lot of luck, they made contact with men and women of the resistance in the Netherlands, Belgium and France. Supposed to be protected by the Geneva Convention, they took great risk in changing their uniforms for civilian clothing and lay their lives in the hands of people they do not know at all. The Germans threatened captured evaders in civilian clothing with instant execution for espionage, unless they revealed the names, addresses and routes they had heard or seen.

While the book tells the story of the last five evaders to cross the Pyrenees, it also gives details about their lives between 1940 and today. In 1982 Hans Onderwater wrote the Dutch version of this book. However, in the years after its publication more and more information was found about these men, their fellow crewmembers and the men who fought with them in Finland, Norway, Great Britain and elsewhere. Consequently, we also followed the histories of particular aircraft that were flown during these times.

The plaque remembering the help given to downed aircrew at Koekelberg and the badges of the RAFES, AFEES and the Comète Line. (HO)

During the journey from Holland, Belgium and France to Spain, the five were unknown to each other: Hubbard was a seasoned regular Air Corps officer, Willis an adventurer and a pilot, Barnes a young RAF Volunteer Reserve pilot of the lowest officer rank. Jack Cornett was a greenhorn USAAF fighter pilot. Ron Emeny was an RAFVR machine gunner. They were three Americans and two Britons; four pilots and an air gunner. On their own at first, and slowly moving to their mutual safe house in Paris they became a team. Their journey could end every day, for treason and bad luck was all around them. They were 'clipped winged airmen' who avoided enemy capture and reached the relative safety of Spain, crossing the border just before D-Day. Though they denied the qualification I considered them heroes, like the men and women who helped them.

Their story stands for that of hundreds of allied soldiers who did not give up and surrendered or waited for their captors. They were the men who decided to put their trust in unknown people of all jobs and trades: teachers, nurses, policemen, wealthy, middle class and poor, simple workers and scholars. People

---

[3] *In this book will use the term PoW(s) for Prisoner(s) of War. Others use the letters PoW, P/W or PoW.*

who often had no idea of the risks of committing resistance and people who knew that the things they did to fight the enemy would cost them their lives and livelihood. Their Journey to the Horizon would have been impossible without the self-sacrifice and bravery of resistance fighters in the Netherlands, Belgium and France. Some were not members of a group, others belonged to other resistance organizations, but the majority of the heroes in this story were members of Comète, a superbly organized evasion line.

The Travellers were the last allied soldiers to cross the Pyrenees. After D-Day, 6 June 1944, aircrews were told to stay where they landed, hide, keep their heads down and wait for the allied armies to liberate them. The five, however, came down in a time when no allied troops had landed on the Continent yet. They had the choice between capture and the relative safety of a PoW camp, or put their destiny into the hands of people they did not know and hardly spoke their language. They decided to try to return home and undertake the Journey to the Horizon.

During this perilous journey, their fate was in the hands of ordinary people who before the war would not have thought of getting involved in illegal activities with such deadly risks. Their sole aim was to foil the enemy's plans by helping unknown young men to stay outside a PoW camp. They risked their lives because they loathed National Socialism and all it stood for, such were the men and women of the Comète Line, one of the bravest organisations in the history of the resistance during World War 2.

The last five who crossed the Pyrenees one day before D-Day.

The Comète line ran from Brussels through Belgium and France to the Basque Country at the Franco-Spanish border. Separate lines ran from the north of the Netherlands into Belgium where they connected with Comète. Of course, the Germans were aware of the existence of escape lines. In their battle against members of these resistance groups, they showed no mercy whatsoever. Helped by traitors, using infiltrators, brutal torture and terror, they sometimes virtually destroyed escape lines. If arrested a resistance fighter expected suffering and death. The lucky ones were shot; the majority succumbed from torture during dreadful Gestapo interrogations or in concentration camps. Yet, in spite of terrible retribution, Comète picked up the pieces, then re-grouped and continued its work.

On 4 June 1944, two days before the allied troops landed on the beaches of Normandy, a Basque guide and five exhausted men struggled in the Pyrenees. They were the last airmen to escape to Spain via Comète. After the allies landed, Comète established well-hidden camps in remote forests, where young Britons, Americans, Canadians and other allied military waited for their comrades to reach and liberate them. Living in relative safety, closely guarded by Comète, they still had to look out for the Germans until allied columns arrived. This book cannot tell the whole story of Comète. Colonel Gilbert Renault, better known by his resistance name Rémy, has already done this. I commend this excellent trilogy to anyone who wants to read the breath-taking story of men and women of all social classes, joined together in a common struggle: Keep them out of German hands.

The main character in this book is Donald Kenyon Willis. A naval rating, a soldier, a furniture salesman, a sailor, an alcohol smuggler or 'ridge runner', a mercenary in Finland, a brave volunteer in the Norwegian Naval Flying Corps and in the RAF, and an officer in the United States Air Force. He was a man who knew how to live. After the war, he stayed in the United States Air Force, retired early and became a quartermaster at sea. Sadly, I never had the privilege of meeting him. Shortly before I started my research, Willis died of Alzheimer's disease. Until the last moment his wife Patricia, the soul mate he met in England during the war, took care of him. She shared her memories with me and gave me free access to the documents, the photographs and the other materials she had. Pat Willis came to the Netherlands to meet some of the people who helped her husband and to thank them half a century later.

Hubbard, Willis, Barnes. Cornett and Emeny are just five men of the hundreds of braves who did not wait to be captured, but tried to make their way home. Others like Stockford, King, Pittwood and Walker used other means to stay free. Those who had the bad luck of being captured like Geisler, Gregg, Plowman and Wesley made the best of it, ensuring that thousands of German troops had to stay home to guard the prisoners, rather than to go to the front and fight.
Wesley's suffering is especially poignant, as he was caught in civilian clothes, treated as a spy and ended up in the infamous Buchenwald concentration camp. We remember the ones who died and where buried in France: Overholt, Fox, Ellis and Lissette. We especially remember the bravery of 'skipper' Les Lissette who stayed at the controls to allow his crew to take to their parachutes, giving his life when it was his turn to jump.

Research took me to Canada, Belgium, France, Great Britain, Germany, Gibraltar, New Zealand, Netherlands, Norway, Finland, Spain and the United States of America. Everywhere I went I met amazing kindness. Archivists spent many hours with me, going through hundreds of documents. Were it not for their help I doubt if I had been able to complete my reconstruction of the Journey to the Horizon? The highlight of it all was a six week trip that started in the east of the Netherlands that took us through Belgium, France and Spain, meeting many brave people who once dealt with the five evaders. We stayed with Pat Willis in Ocala, Florida. We met Len and Merville Barnes in Whitstable in Kent. Ron and Jessie Emeny received us with amazing hospitality. I owe them all a very big thank you.

It was difficult to reconstruct events, as many genuine members of the resistance were reticent and reluctant to speak about their activities during the war. For the great majority one thing seems to be very, very important: 'Never speak about yourself.' That is why they all returned to their pre-war jobs once the war was over. They went into the antique business, returned to their family farm or carpenter shop, the printing business or continued to nurse the sick. It was an honour and a pleasure to meet all these people. Their frankness and patience helped me to continue whenever I thought my story have entered a dead-end street.

The bravery of the members of Comète is remembered in the National Basilica at Koekelberg, a suburb of Brussels. The Comète Line badge in the bottom right-hand of the window represents a falling plane; the star represents those in the Comète line which aided Allied evaders and escapers, especially airmen, to get back. The window was unveiled in October 1953 by Prince Albert, later King Albert II. It was paid for with money received by the Belgian government in exile from the British Government, some of which went to university scholarships, some towards the window. It was designed by a Belgian artist, Anto Carte (1886-1954). Beneath the window is the Royal Air Forces Escaping Society plaque. On 21st June 1981, this plaque was dedicated to the countless brave men and women of enemy occupied countries who, during World War II (1939-1945), without thought of danger to themselves, helped a staggering 2803 aircrew to evade capture and return to the United Kingdom. They were members of the Royal Air Force, Commonwealth air forces and the United States (Army) Air Force and of squadrons representing the occupied nations to escape and return to their country and so continue the struggle for freedom.

Many paid with their lives; many more endured the degradation of concentration camps. Their names are remembered in equal honour with those who were spared to fight a longer battle. To mark its debt of gratitude, the Royal Air Forces Escaping Society erected a memorial as a lasting tribute and also to serve as an inspiration to future generations. The plaque, designed and created by Elizabeth Harrison, Secretary of the Royal Air Forces Escaping Society, shows an airman who parachuted out and is now being walked away by helpers. The plaque is also in Saint Clement Danes RAF Church London, the RAF Museum Hendon, the War Museums in Ottawa, Canada and Canberra, Australia, the Army Museum at the Hôtel des Invalides in Paris, and the War Museum Overloon, Netherlands.

There still is a strong bond between the helpers and the helped. The AFEES in the USA and the RAFES in Britain and the Commonwealth maintained lifelong friendships. In the East Kirkby Museum is a special room for the men who did not sit down but ran for freedom. It was the great achievement of Ron Emeny to ensure that the bravery of the helpers was never forgotten. One of the wartime escapees once said to me: 'Having experienced what these people so unselfishly did for me under those circumstances, I know the true meaning of everlasting friendship.' It explained the invisible thread that links the people who made contrails in the skies to those who kept an invisible trail on the ground below.

Brian Lissette and Hans Onderwater at work in New Zealand.

We are also aware of the anxiety and despair among the families when they received the dreaded news that a loved one had 'not returned from operations', followed by hopes and fears and the final information that these men were missing, killed in action or taken prisoner. We dedicated part of the book to these relatives by showing letters that were written during trying times.

There are too many people to be thanked. Please allow me to make a few exceptions. First, I thank the allied officers, who were such a tremendous support when I worked on this book. They are Air Marshal Philip Sturley MBE RAF, Colonel Allen Ryals USAF, air force attaché at the US Embassy in the Hague, Lieutenant-Colonel John Young RS, military and air attaché at the British Embassy the Hague, Captain Per Brekke RNN, defence attaché at the Norwegian Embassy in The Hague. They spent many hours reading and discussing this manuscript with me.

I am in debt to five brave men, and their next of kin for their patience and their support in our attempt to write a true story: Messrs. Len Barnes MBE, Jack Cornett, Ron Emeny, Tom Hubbard and Don Willis. Sadly, all five men have since died. Their next of kin gave tremendous support. Len Barnes and Ron Emeny became friends after the war and often travelled to France together, meeting their friends who risked all to hide them from the enemy. Len devoted his time to the RAFES, Ron worked to preserve the memory of the Lancaster, working as a volunteer at the East Kirkby Air Museum. My sincere thanks are for Patricia Willis, who helped, supported and came to Holland. How can I even forget her? As you will read, Donald Willis had a son by his second wife. Stewart Willis was a great help, even when information was not easy for him to digest. Thank you very much, Stewart!!

I also must mention my friend Peter Groenveld, who reproduced thousands of photographs. The quality of the many illustrations says enough about his skill as a professional photographer. Finally, yet importantly, I want to thank my wife Marjoan and my children Gerdy and Mark-Johan for allowing me to 'abuse' family holidays for research purposes. Without their patience and acceptance, this book would never have been written.

Meeting Brian Lissette in Mount Maunganui during a holiday to New Zealand in February and March 2020 was the icing on the cake. We enjoyed the hospitality of Brian and Jean Lissette, exchanging information about the crash and death of Brian's uncle, the late Warrant Officer Leslie Lissette. We decided to make this English copy of the book a joint venture and add the story of the Lissette crew in chapters 7 and 8 to show the reader how horrifying the fate of the crew of as stricken aircraft could be. Brian and Jean Lissette became friends of Hans and Marjoan Onderwater, giving a happy twist to this book, the result of almost forty years of painstaking research, study and interpretation of official documents, interviews with many eyewitnesses and participants as well as the study of books by other authors. A lot of new photographs were obtained via people and institutes mentioned in the final acknowledgement.

The memories of people who were involved in this journey sometimes differ from the official documents. It was amazing how many photographs and documents, even artifacts, are still in private homes.

The time passed since 1944 has been an issue. Almost everyone who played an active role in this book has since died. Therefor the interviews, correspondence, country walks and gatherings are still cherished as major sources of personal experiences. The documents, photographs and maps illustrate the stories perfectly. However, in later years memories and passed on stories became part of a somewhat imagined reality. On the other hand, some events must have had quite an impact and thus became a focal point in the memory of a frightening part of their lives and that of those who came after them.

It gives a great pleasure to know that through our investigations family members of airmen, who previously did not know each other, have now connected and are in touch. They exchange stories and photographs, they write messages and, in a way, reunited as the crews did when they served in the RAF. Their generosity in sending us all the private letters written by the airmen, their gallant helpers and the friends at home were a treasury full of emotional information about days of despair and utter delight.

We have tried to compare the stories with available documents. We tried to find confirmation of stories that were not in official documents. Consequently, interpretations of events and views expressed by next of kin are now the sole responsibility of the authors. Efforts have been made to trace all keepers of copyright; the authors were not in all cases able to trace those persons. Anyone who claims to hold the copyright of illustrations in this book is kindly requested to submit his evidence to the author through his publisher.

Hans J.G. Onderwater MBE
researcher and author

Brian Lissette
researcher and co-author

1. A VIOLIN FOR FINLAND.

Soviet demands.

The conflict between Russia and Finland, generally referred to as the Winter War, lasted from 30 November 1939 to 13 March 1940. First the Soviets tried to use diplomacy to reach their goal. On 5 October 1939, the Soviets invited Finnish representatives to come to Moscow to discuss what they called political questions. Finland sent J. K. Paasikivi to the meeting. One week later he met Stalin and Molotov to discuss land questions on the Finnish/Russian border. The Soviets said that to be able to defend the approach to Leningrad, they needed the Finnish islands in the Gulf of Finland, including Suursaari Island, to be handed over; they also wanted to lease Hanko as a military base and to establish a garrison of 5,000 men there. Finally, they demanded Finnish territory on the Soviet border to be ceded to Moscow.

In return, Stalin offered land in Karelia and the right to fortify the Aaland Islands. He explained his requirements in terms of defending parts of Russia, Leningrad or Murmansk, from attack. He said: 'We cannot do anything about geography, nor can you. Since Leningrad cannot be moved away, the frontier must be further off.' Paasikivi returned to Helsinki to discuss Stalin's demands with the Finnish government. The Finns were suspicious of anything required by the Soviet leader. Relations between the Soviet Union and Finland had been fraught for many decades and nearly everyone in Finland saw Stalin's demands as an attempt by Russia to regain authority over Finland.

By the end of November 1939, war between Finland and Russia was unavoidable. At the outbreak of this war the Finnish army was small. The country had a population of 4,000,000 people and could muster a small professional army. Finland also had a peacetime conscript army, which was boosted each year by an annual intake of men. There was a reserve, which all conscripts passed into after one year's service. At the beginning of the war, Finland had a small air force, with only 114 combat planes fit for duty. Missions were limited, and fighter aircraft were used to repel Soviet bombers. Strategic bombing doubled as opportunities for military reconnaissance. Old-fashioned and few in number, these aircraft offered little or no support for Finnish ground troops.

In spite of losses, the number of planes in the Finnish Air Force rose by over 50% by the end of the war. The Finns received shipments of British, French, Italian, Swedish and American aircraft. Compared to the vast potential resources of the Red Army, the Finnish Army still was a dwarf. But the Finns were a freedom loving people with a strong sense of independence after ages of foreign domination, they were very tough at the negotiation table. Sick and tired of what they called the Finnish obstructions, the Russians decided to show muscle by instructing their troops to provoke border incidents. It worked against them! During one on 26th November, no less than 28 Soviets were killed near Manaila, however not by Finnish fire. Soviet artillery caused the losses through bad mathematics! In spite of the failures of their commanders, this was what the Soviets waited for. Two days later, in a furious comment, the Pravda demanded revenge for the massacre of Manaila. The Politburo cancelled the Tartu Treaty and broke off diplomatic relations with Finland.

Mannerheim takes command.

It was the moment when Baron Carl Gustaf Emil Mannerheim [4] became the leader of the Finnish forces. Mannerheim had made a career in the Imperial Russian Army, rising to the rank of lieutenant general. He also had a prominent place in the ceremonies for Tsar Nicholas II's coronation and later had several private meetings with the Tsar. After the Bolshevik revolution, Finland suffered from a civil war between the pro-Bolshevik 'Reds' and the 'Whites', who were the troops of the Senate of Finland, supported by troops of the German Empire. Mannerheim was appointed the military chief of the Whites. Twenty years

---

[4] *Finnish military leader and later President (4 Jun 1867– 27Jan 1951) Regent of Finland (1918–19), commander-in-chief of Finland's defence forces during World War II, Marshal of Finland, and the sixth president (1944–46).*

later, Mannerheim was asked to successfully lead the defence of Finland as commander-in-chief of the country's armed forces. He wanted the peacetime army to act as a covering force to delay any attack until the reservists get to the front. He knew that the army was short of equipment, including uniforms and modern artillery. In November 1939 they had only 112 decent anti-tank guns. The means of producing modern weaponry was short of the standards of the western countries. Basic things such as ammunition could not be produced in large quantities. The army's communication system was basic, relying in part on runners. So, from whatever angle the Finnish army was looked at, it seemed an easy victim for the Russians. However, in one sense the Finnish Army was in an excellent position to defend its nation. Finnish troops were trained to use their own terrain to their advantage. Finnish troops were well suited to the forests and snow-covered regions of Finland and they knew the lay of the land. Finnish ski troops were highly mobile and well trained. However, these men were used to working in small units and large-scale manoeuvres were alien not only to them but also to the officers. No money had been spent in Finland prior to 1939 for many large-scale military training exercises. However, as it became more and more obvious that a conflict with the Russians was likely, patriotism took a firm hold and no one was prepared to tolerate a Russian invasion of his homeland. The Finnish navy was small and the air force only had 100 planes; some of these were useless in battle.

Left: Marshal Baron Carl Gustaf Emil Mannerheim. Centre: with nurses of the Women's Volunteer Corps. Right: The result of 'bread' being dropped by the Soviet air force on Helsinki (MoDF)

The Russian army was completely different. In September 1939, Russia had committed men to the Polish campaign and ignoring the Polish situation, Stalin believed his troops to be excellent. With 1,250,000 men in the regular army, there were many more Stalin can call on. For the Winter War, Russia used 45 divisions. Each division had 18,000 men; so, by that reckoning Russia used 810,000 men; nearly 25% of the whole of Finland's population. In fact, for the whole duration of the war, the Russians used 1,200,000 men in some form of military capacity. They deployed 1,500 tanks and 3,000 planes.

Whereas the Finnish army had difficulty supplying troops with ammunition, the Soviet forces had an almost unlimited supply and a vastly superior system of communication. The Russians, however, had two major weaknesses. It was used to war games on large expanses of open ground. The snow-covered forests of Finland were a different matter and the Russians were to find that they are frequently confined to the areas around roads, as many of their men were not used to Finland's terrain and the majority of their vehicles were unable to go off road. Their tactics developed during training did not include such terrain.

The Soviet Army had another fundamental weakness: its command structure was so rigid that field commanders did not make a decision without the approval of a higher officer who usually had to get permission from a political commissar to agree that his tactics were correct. Such a set-up created important delays in decision making. Therefore, the Red Army was a dinosaur hindered by both the geography of Finland and its rigidity in terms of decision making. Whereas Blitzkrieg was designed to incorporate all aspects of Germany's army and air force, each part of the Russian army acted as a separate entity. Whether this was a result of the purges in the military, which decimated its officer corps or the result of a fear of taking a decision that is unacceptable to higher authorities is difficult to know: it was a combination of both.

The Red Army was ill-equipped for a long winter war. White camouflage clothing had not been issued and vehicles simply could not cope with the cold. The winter of 39-40 was particularly severe. The Russians were forced to fight on a small front despite the sheer size of the Russian-Finnish border. Many parts of the 600 miles border were simply impassable, so the Finns had a good idea as to the route any Russian force might take in the initial stages of an invasion. The Russian air force was limited for flying time; it could barely help the army as the days were short during the winter months. When they flew, the Russians took heavy casualties, losing 800 planes, over 25% of their planes used in the war. Finnish High Command saw that the weak spot was in the Karelian Isthmus, south-west of Lake Ladoga. This area had been fortified with mine fields, trenches, barbwires and obstacles. Concrete emplacements had been built but they were rare with each emplacement having little ability to give any other covering fire.

Left: March 1940 a Finnish Bristol Blenheim Mk. IV bomber of No. 44 Squadron is being refuelled at its air base on a frozen lake in Tikkakoski. Right: The Brewster Buffalo Mk1s of the FAF proved very successful.

Soviet POWs with their captors: showing how visible the Red Army was compared to the camouflaged defenders, who knew the terrain they fought in. (Sotamuseo)

In no way could the line compare to the Maginot Line in France. However, the Karelian Isthmus had to be held, as its loss would give Russia a direct line to Helsinki, less than 200 miles to the west. This was the situation in which Finland found itself; yet there was no thought whatsoever of giving in to Soviet demands. Then followed a carefully planned increase of incidents. Stalin knew that Germany concentrated on the further occupation of Poland under the protection of the Russian-German demarcation line in the east of Poland. They needed no further excuse. In the early hours of 1 December 1939, Soviet troops crossed the border into Finland. Convinced that Finland was no match for the mighty Soviet forces Stalin expected to reach his goals within a few days. The day before declaring war, the Soviets sent bombers to Helsinki. Bombs fell, killing innocent victims. On 1st December's Pravda, the Soviets angrily protested that the Finns used guns against Russian aircraft that carried 'baskets full of bread for the starving population of these towns.' In the Finnish papers a request appeared: 'Please, no more bread', referring to the bombers as bakery vans! Finland could not accept this aggression. All reserves were mobilized and within a few days, a small army of 33,000 became a vast mass of almost half a million determined men and women. Finnish fighter pilots often flew their motley collection of planes into Soviet formations that outnumbered them 10 or even 20 times. Finnish fighters shot down a confirmed 200 Soviet aircraft, while losing 62 of their own. Finnish anti-aircraft guns downed more than 300 enemy aircraft. Often, a Finnish forward air base consisted of a frozen lake, a windsock, a telephone set and some tents. Air-raid warnings were given by Finnish women organised by the Lotta Svärd, women's volunteer organisation that took over many of the para-military duties from the men.

Foreign volunteers and adventurers assemble in Finland.
The largest foreign contingent came from neighbouring Sweden, with some 8,760 volunteers. The Swedish Volunteer Corps, Swedes, Norwegians (727) and Danes (1,010), fought on the northern front at Salla. A Swedish unit of Gloster Gladiators, named 'Flight Regiment 19' also participated. Swedish anti-air batteries with Bofors 40 mm (1.6 inch) guns were responsible for air defence in northern Finland and the city of Turku. Volunteers also arrived from Hungary, Italy and Estonia. Some 350 American nationals of Finnish background volunteered, and 210 other nationalities arrived in Finland before the war ended. In total, Finland received 12,000 volunteers, 50 of whom died during the war. The British actor Christopher Lee volunteered but did not face combat. Sweden was officially non-belligerent during the war, so the Corps was under Finnish command. The Swedes were in the front lines in the northern Salla area starting from 28 February, 1940. The strong Nordic unity was symbolized in their 'four brother hands' insignia, representing Finland, Sweden, Norway, and Denmark.

There was an outcry in Sweden to help the Finns. On posters it said: Finland's case is ours. For a disrupting fight, join the volunteers'. Soon the first volunteers arrived in Tornio and were welcomed by the Finns. The commanding officer of the Swedish Volunteer Corps was Ernst Linder (right) with Carl August Ehrensvärd (left) as his chief of staff in Tornio. Right: the 'Four Brothers Hand' insignia. (Sotamuseo)

The League of Nations had voted in favour of Finland. The Red representatives were outraged by this support and interrupted the meeting, claiming they are accused of waging a war that did not exist. Consequently, the Soviet Union was expelled from the League. It was very sad that the diplomats in Geneva were unable to do more than write long declarations. A few countries decided that much more was needed. Great Britain sent a number of Blenheim bombers to join the Finnish Air Force. A Finnish Air Bureau was opened to allow British nationals to go to Finland to do humanitarian work.

Apart from genuine volunteers many adventurers headed for Finland, eager to make their mark, get publicity or enjoy the situation. We will read about them in this chapter. People like American 'Pioneer Negro Aviator and Colonel' Hubert Fauntleroy Julian alias Black Hawk, and Spanish Colonel Nicolas Beres, aka Alfonso Reyes, found their ways into Finland. They are sent away as soon as their real personality and behaviour was known better. Colonel Beres for example was sent abroad using some pretext already at the end of February 1940. The Afro-American aviator Captain Julian stayed in Finland until June 1940. His and Beres' Finnish military ranks were then cancelled but Julian refused to hand over his Finnish Air Force uniform. He was tried when he returned to the States. The Finns later cleared the unpaid bills!
Who was this man, who was eager to get publicity, but who also acted as a champion of black pride? Hubert Fauntleroy Julian knew how to catch the front pages. He was born in Port of Spain, Trinidad, in 1897, the son of a cocoa plantation manager. He went to Canada in 1914, where he claimed he learned to fly and served as an officer in the Royal Canadian Air Force. In 1921 he patented Airplane Safety Appliance, a combination parachute/propeller. He emigrated from Montreal to Harlem in New York in

1921. His first flight above Harlem was during the 1922 UNIA Convention[5], when he flew over the parade in a plane with UNIA slogans. Although he never succeeded to cross the Atlantic as planned, he became a celebrity. In 1931 Emperor Haile Selassie invited him to Ethiopia to take part in his coronation ceremonies. He impressed the Emperor with his skills as a parachutist, landing within a few feet of his throne during a ceremony, a feat that won him Ethiopian citizenship and a position in the air force. He had less success as a pilot, crashing the Emperor's favourite aeroplane, after which he quickly returned to Harlem.

American aviator Hubert Fauntleroy Julian served as commander of the tiny air force of Ethiopia. He wore uniforms he designed himself and appointed himself to colonel. Though he was hailed as a black hero because he commanded the three-aircraft air force of Abyssinia during the Italian invasion, many saw him as a poser.

During the Italian invasion of Ethiopia in 1935, Julian returned to Ethiopia to aid in the defence of Selassie's government. He was put in command of the Imperial Ethiopian Air Force, which at the time consisted of three planes. Returning to the States, he was temporarily detained at Ellis Island over the question of his nationality British or Ethiopian. After getting into a fistfight with fellow African-American aviator John C. Robinson, Julian was ordered to leave the country. After the United States entered the war in 1941, Julian volunteered to train with the 99th Pursuit Squadron, the later famous Tuskegee Airmen. He was politely turned down. He was remembered as a colourful man with a non-regulation Colonel's uniform, despite not holding that rank in the Army Air Forces, being discharged before his graduation.

A famous pilot in Finland was Russian born Prince Emanuel Galitzine. Born in 1918, he came to Finland using the assumed name Edward M. Graham and flew in the Winter War as a 2nd Lieutenant in Flying Squadron 32. His contract in Finland ended by the end of 1940 and he travelled back to Canada and Britain to join the RAF. He became famous for flying combat at extreme altitudes. On 12 September 1942, he attacked a Junkers 86R long-range high-altitude reconnaissance-bomber at 13.000 meters in a high altitude Spitfire Mk. IX. This became known as the highest-level aerial battle of the 2nd World War. The Finns not only employed pilots but also technicians. Foreign technical volunteers came straight to flying units although their quality and experience varied. Experienced Italian Fiat mechanics of Captain Pelli did excellent work in keeping new troublesome Fiat G-50 fighters in the air during the last days of the Winter War. Pelli studied Finnish during his leisure time trying to improve communication between Finnish and Italian mechanics! Many Danish, Swedish, Norwegian, French mechanics and engineers

---

[5] *The Universal Negro Improvement Association was a black nationalist fraternal organization founded by Marcus Garvey, a Jamaican immigrant to the United States. It enjoyed its greatest strength in the 1920s, and was influential prior to Garvey's deportation to Jamaica in 1927. After that its prestige and influence declined, but it had a strong influence on African-American history and development. The organization was founded to work for the advancement of people of African ancestry around the world. The broad mission of the UNIA led to the establishment of numerous auxiliary components.*

also worked in Finland. Totally outnumbered by the Soviet aircraft, the brave Finns defended their country. Their tiny Air Force had old aircraft, Fokker C-VE and C-X biplanes, Fokker D-XXI fighters and other types like Bristol Blenheims 1F and IV, Bristol Bulldogs, Blackburn Rippons IIF and some Heinkel He-115 floatplanes: all slow and lightly armed. The Soviet Politburo seemed right: Finland would soon be wiped off the map.

Russian Prince In Ottawa Waiting To Fight In R.A.F.

Prince Emmanuel Galitzine. 22-Year-Old Scion of Russian Noble Family, Also Fought in Russo-Finnish War.

Prince Emmanuel Galitzine, 22-0-year-old son of Prince Vladimir, head of one of the oldest families of the Russian nobility, is in Ottawa awaiting acceptance by the British Air Mission here of his application to enlist in the Royal Air Force. He believes he will be accepted as a result of his previous training, not only in the R.A.F., but also with the Finnish Air Force, with which he served during the Russo-Finnish war.

Prince Emmanuel, who is staying at the Windsor Hotel, told a Citizen reporter that his enlistment first in the Royal Air Force in 1938 and in the latter part of 1939 was allowed his discharge in order to go to Finland to join the air force of that country. The war between Russia and Finland was then being fought, but before the prince had completed his training in Finland peace between the two countries was reached.

However, he remained with the Finnish Air Force for some time after the war ended and after he was given his discharge it was some time before he was able to leave the country, due to the difficulty of obtaining passage on a ship to any of the countries to which he wanted to go. Eventu-

ally, he was able to get a booking on a boat to New York. Just how he was able to do this, the prince said he preferred not to say. On arrival in New York he planned to come to Ottawa with the intention of applying for re-enlistment in the Royal Air Force.

Met Leslie Thatcher

Prince Emmanuel said when he was at the base in England for volunteers for the Finnish forces he met a Canadian, who was popularly known as "Butch" and who was well liked by all his comrades.

"Was Butch Leslie Thatcher of Ottawa?" the prince was asked.

"Now that you remind me, I believe that was Butch's name. I recall that he said his father was a member of the Ottawa police force."

The Citizen reporter told the prince that Leslie Thatcher is the

son of Detective William Thatcher. The prince said he was glad to hear of young Thatcher's eventual safe return to England, that he had rejoined the Canadian army overseas and had been decorated for distinguished service by the

Norwegian government.

Prince Emmanuel looks like a typical young Englishman. He went to England at the age of one year with his family following the collapse of the White Russian forces in 1919. He was educated at an English public school and later studied at Konigsberg University in Germany, where he learned to speak German fluently. His family is still in England, where his father, Prince Vladimir, is an interpreter with the British Intelligence Service. He has a brother, a lieutenant, in the Royal Navy, and another brother, a second lieutenant in the Welsh Guards.

While Prince Emmanuel thinks Ottawa is an attractive city and likes the people here he has met, he is eager to get back to England and active service with the Royal Air Force.

PRINCE EMMANUEL

Top left:
A Finnish Fokker D-XXI fighter, flown by Prince Galitzine in Finland.

Top right: Prince Galitzine in RAF uniform.

Left: The article in the Canadian Ottawa Citizen of 31 March 1941, about Emmanuel Galitzine and his epic fight with a Junkers Ju-86R high altitude recce aircraft at over 45,000 feet

Below: a Junkers Ju-86R and the Spitfire he flew. (INP/MoDF/OC)

Let us help these poor Finns; foreign volunteers, two of them Americans!!

On 18 February 1940, an American arrived in Tornio, a town at the northern shore of the Gulf of Bothnia. At the border he filled in the documents that give him temporary access to the country. His name was Donald Kenyan Willis, born 7 August 1911 in Westfork, Indiana. On his immigration card, he gave pilot as his profession. Why did this 29-year-old American join the battle? We found little information in the Finnish archives. The reason might be that the authorities wanted to keep silent about earlier activities. We read about it in 1944, when his story was told to the authors of 'The First of the Many', a book about the participation of Americans in the war against Germany before the USA got involved: 'I talked to many of the Eagles, sopped up their stories, and then began to ask the question to which I have not yet found a universal answer: Why did you go to war before your country did? I like this one best: it is the story of Don Willis from Leavenworth, Kansas, a Captain in the 8th Air Force, married to an English girl. One evening, out in Chicago, he heard a man play the violin in a nightclub, and the music the man made with his fiddle was beautiful. Don talked and drank with this man late into the evening, and early into the morning. The man came from Finland, and they were at war with Russia. Don decided that any country that could produce men who could make music like his new friend, must be a helluva fine

25

country. He went to Finland, joined their air force, and fought wing to wing with the Finns. Just like that. It was not idealism. He will call you an idiot or a liar if you say it was. It was just that 'this guy with the fiddle made such damned beautiful music and he was a Finn. He fought with the Finns until Germany muscled in on the war. Then Don decided that something was wrong, so he joined the Norwegian Air Force.' He does not know why he did, but he did. Norway fell and he came to England and joined the RAF. And then, along with all the others, he joined the USAAF.

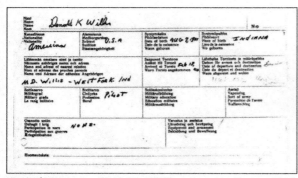

On 18th February 1940 Don Willis arrived in Tornio, Finland. To ensure his direct acceptance into the Finnish Air Force, he gave 'Pilot' as his regular job. During his service in the FAF, he flew Bristol Bulldogs over Karelia. He had to look for Russian armoured columns and report to base to enable Finnish bombers to attack. It was a dangerous job, for often Willis flew alone, trusting on his compass and map reading skills. (PW/MoDF).

It was many years later when Willis' widow Patricia, visited the Netherlands, that she revealed the reason for Don's decision to go to Finland[6]. Willis had lived an adventurous life. After his father died in 1927, 16-year-old Donald joined the United States Navy. However, after a while he found that this was not where he wanted to be and he deserted. The Navy was not happy with his decision, so he was brought back and posted 600 miles away on the Yangtze River in China. After two years, Willis returned to High School, graduating in 1929. First, he tried to earn money by selling radios. As this did not bring any money, Donald returned to Indiana to work with his mother on the farm. This too failed to appeal to him, so he joined the Army and was based at Hawaii for two years. He left the army and for a while became a ridge-runner, a whiskey smuggler, which was to become the name of his Spitfire in the RAF.

In 1934, he got a job as an assistant purser on a passenger ship sailing from New York to Buenos Aires in South America. During one of his voyages, he met a young woman and they married[7]. Donald Willis and his new wife started a small factory, producing high quality furniture. Don personally visited his customers and as a result the business flourished. He was such good friends with his employees that no one felt the need to join the Union. The wages were high and the labour situation was excellent. Several times Union representatives visited the plant to make Willis' workers to join them. Every time Willis denied them access to the plant. Then the Union declared a ban on the factory and it caused production to fall. With his marriage deteriorating, in a collapsing business with no timber, customers or money Willis ran away again. Left with only his car, and drove to New York, where he met the Finnish violin player mentioned earlier. With his commercial ideals destroyed, he decided to put his car on a ship to Finland, travel to that country and forget the USA.

Besides there was another reason why he left the USA. His son Stewart Willis, born as the child of the marriage between Willis and a Scottish girl, told us what happened and revealed what his mother told him before she died: 'My father was married to Kitty Alexander, closely related to the Alexander's

---

[6] *Her and Stewart's memories differ. Stewart heard it from his mother and Patricia calls Don her source.*
[7] *His first wife was Catherine 'Kitty' Alexander. In 1938, they had a son, Daniel. In February 1940 Willis arrived in Finland.*

department stores in New York and part of high society there. They lived at Doolittle Mills in Indiana where dad, related to the Doolittles, was part of the timber business supplying wood to furniture makers. Kitty though that she was better than everybody else as dad said. She expected him to dress for dinner. He got fed up with it and drove to New York[8] for a bit of fun, ending up drunk on a Finnish freighter with his car. He and Kitty had a son, Daniel who went to California, but we cannot find him. It is possible that Dad did not know about him but I am in touch with a cousin who remembers Auntie Kitty. Dad never divorced Kitty[9]. If you look at a map you will see that Southern Indiana is a long distance from New York. A hell of a long way for a night out, so there is more to this story than dad told me. He also ran away to sea and was thrown out of the US Navy for being under-age and been in the US Merchant Navy, and a ridge runner before returning to Doolittle Mills.[10]

One American volunteer was former bush pilot and adventurer David 'Simpson' Bondurant. At the end of the 1st World War, he was a pilot in France.

The other American Willis met in Finland was David Simpson Bondurant from Cairo, Illinois. Decades later his grandson researched his grandfather's career. He wrote: 'My name is David Bondurant. I am the grandson of Simpson Bondurant. He moved to Canada after World War 1 and pioneered the North. He trained pilots while in Amherst, Nova Scotia. He married my grandmother in 1946. He was 53, she was 18. I never met the man but I would like to learn more as I lost my father Lt Colonel David C. Bondurant in a ski accident.'

'He was an interesting man, much older than the other fliers, an experienced aviator. He flew as a bush pilot in Canada and Alaska. At the end of World War One, he flew with famous American aviators like Eddie Rickenbacker. After the war, he was a commercial flyer, doing barnstorming and stunt flying before coming to Canada in 1922. He did a lot of bush flying for Canadian Airways in Northern Quebec and Labrador, and then flew as an airmail pilot on the new Montreal-Toronto airmail route, setting a speed record for mail planes on 21 March 1929.

Angry about the American decision not to involve itself into European troubles, Bondurant sailed to Scotland, hoping for a flying job with the RAF. Turned down because of his age he boarded a ship to Norway. Bondurant travelled from Narvik to Sweden by train and reported to the Finnish Embassy in Stockholm. The Finns did not turn him down, for every skilled instructor was welcome. Five days after his arrival in Finland, he was teaching young men to fly. Every now and then he even put in a reconnaissance mission. Bondurant was a happy man. Frankly, for him the war was godsend[11]. A lot of his exploits are only described in his own papers, now held by the Canadian Directorate of History and Heritage.

---

[8] *Before going bankrupt in 1992, Alexander's was a department store chain that at its peak included 16 stores.*
[9] *Willis married four times: American Kitty Alexander, Canadian Mary Kathleen Krouse, Scottish Martha McNicol and South African Patricia Giles.*
[10] *Doolittle Mills is a community in Oil Township, Perry County, Indiana.*

In one of his papers, it reads: 'served as bomber pilot between 22 February and 1 April 1940. When the fighting ended, he moved to Norway. He flew captured German seaplanes [12] on raids against 6,000 Nazi troops, entrenched near Narvik. As the situation deteriorated, he escaped to the Shetlands and tried to join the Royal Air Force Volunteer Reserve, but was turned down. 'He therefore requested permission to return to Canada. This permission was given and Bondurant, now well aware that he would not fly combat accepted an officer of the Canadian Car and Foundry to work for them. The company planned to open a plant in Amherst, Nova Scotia, where the intended to build aircraft. Bondurant became their chief test pilot. He got the job and on 14 August 1941 tested the company's first aircraft, an Avro Anson. He flew many other types like Hawker Hurricanes, Fleets, Harvards, Ansons and Mosquitos. In fact, he was quite verbal in suggesting that Mosquitos be built at Amherst as well. On 29 September 1943 he flew an Anson V. It was the 1,000th machine produced at Amherst and Bondurant's 1,000th test flight there. His record was 1,000 test flights in 1,000 days, for which he was given a presentation. When he left CC&F in September 1945, he had flown 1,650 aircraft without an incident or accident. He died in 1959.'

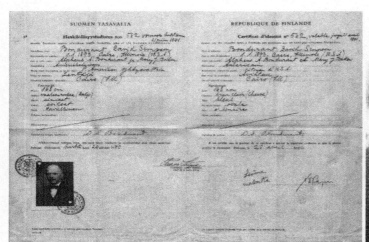 

Arriving in Finland he was given a Finnish ID saying he was a pilot. He soon joined the FAF as an instructor. On the photograph we see fellow-American Charles Doran, Finnish pilot Safari Histone, David Bondurant, and two Finnish pilots, Nauru Rimpivaara and Yrjö Hammarén. (NAUS, MoDF).

On 22 February 1940, Willis signed a contract as a volunteer in the Finnish Air Force. Legally he was a mercenary. The contract was valid for the duration of hostilities. First, he was a corporal and sent to the 2nd Air Regiment, where he got military pilot training on Bristol Bulldog biplanes [13]. Only a few weeks later he flew his first mission. During the Winter War, foreign flying personnel (except the Swedes in their own unit F19) were taken into Supplement Flying Regiment 2 (SFR2). There his pilot skills were tested and some extra training was given at the Supplement Flying Squadron at Parola. Most volunteers had no combat experience, although a few experienced pilots had been in action in the Spanish Civil War or in Abyssinia or even in World War 1. Fighting spirit varied but was generally good. Keen to show their skills many volunteers were killed in action or in aerial or land accidents because planes were new to them and conditions were hard in the winter of 1940.

---

[11] *Finnish documents say: 'Captain David S. Bondurant is recorded on the roll list of Lentorykinentt 4 (Flight Regiment 4), the only bomber regiment in the FAF. He may have flown sorties in Blenheims. He was released from his contract 24 March 1940.'*

[12] *There are no Norwegian records of Bondurant flying one of the German aircraft captured by the Norwegians.*

[13] *Jr Cpl Donald K. Willis received flight training at the FAF College and signed a contract on 22 Feb 1940.'*

Documents of Bondurant's time in Finland and Norway. Top left his service record of the Finnish Air Force, centre of his promotion to Captain. On 3rd May 1940 Bondurant received orders to proceed to Tromsø to join the Norwegian Forces. Interestingly the document has the same date and signature as the one that Willis was given. We think that they travelled together. The other documents allowed Bondurant to leave Norway and go to the United Kingdom. HM Consul in Tromsø wrote a document to allow Bondurant to contact the RAF. (NAUS/MoDF/ DHH/IOOF).

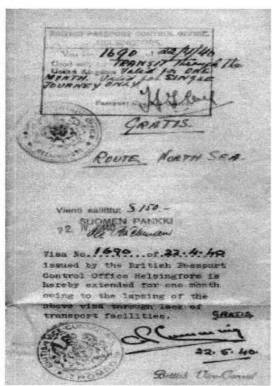

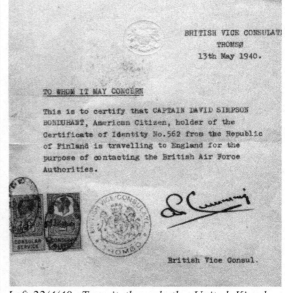

Left:22/4/40. Transit through the United Kingdom valid for only one month. Valid for single journey only. It was the document that allowed the passage from Finland to Norway and England.Top: Bondurant's travel permit to go from Finland to England 'for the purpose of contacting the British Air Force Authorities.

'Left: 'Permitted to land at Glasgow on 6.5.40 on condition that the holder registers at once with the Police, and reports to 50, Queen Anne's Gate London SW1, and is subject to any further conditions as may thereafter be imposed...

'Below: We know little about Simpson Bondurant after leaving CCF. He died at 66 and was buried in Charleston.

We know Willis did not engage much in combat against the Soviets air force. He mainly flew reconnaissance missions over Karelia. Yet he was one of thousands of volunteers who joined the Finns on the ground and in the air, everyone for his own reasons, but well aware of the dangers and the risk of being captured by the Soviets and being executed as a spy or a mercenary. Let us return to the Winter War in Finland. Willis and a Briton calling himself Peter Farragut flew operations in a Danish Volunteer Unit. It was risky to fly single low-level missions, to report the advance of Russian troops. We know little of Farragut; his real name was Macalister and that his social background might have been the reason why he concealed his identity in Finland. Being of a wealthy family, with a great dislike for communism, he felt obliged to do his part. Being the son of a capitalist, he may have wanted to keep his true identity hidden. On 13 March 1940 Finland and the Soviets signed an armistice. Though staying independent, Finland had to allow the Soviets to occupy large parts of the country. It brought the Finns dangerously close to further co-operation with Nazi Germany.

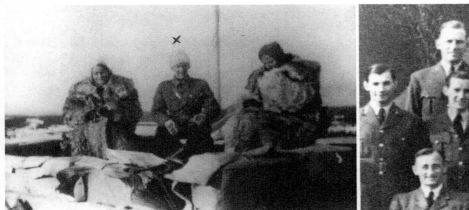

After the Soviet attack on Finland, volunteers of all nationalities joined the Finnish forces. One of them was a Briton called Peter Macalister, who served as Peter Farragut. (Helen Ambrose-Macalister)

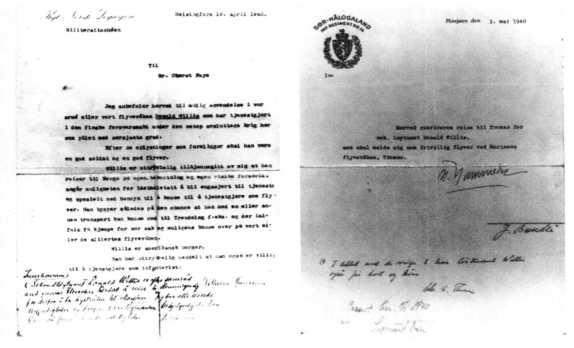

These documents helped Willis to travel north and cross the border with Norway to reach the northern town of Honningsvåg, northwest of Kirkenes and still rather close to the border between Norway and the Soviets. Once he arrived, Willis went to Tromsø to report as a volunteer pilot in the Norwegian Naval Air Service. (PW).

At the end of hostilities between the Soviet Union and Finland, Farragut and many others left the country. Some moved to Norway to fight there until they returned to England. Farragut is said to have flown there too, working closely with members of British Intelligence, though there is little evidence of his intelligence activities. The official British records state that he was killed flying a Wellington with No. 12 Squadron RAF during the night of 2/3 July 1942 [14]. The crew took part in a raid against Bremen. It was the first attack since October 1941. Fires raged in Bremen. Warehouses, a pier and a German destroyer were destroyed. No less than 83 people were killed, 29 seriously and 229 slightly injured. The RAF, however, suffered heavy losses as well. Eleven bombers were shot down. One of the aircraft lost was the Wellington of Peter Macalister and his crew. All crewmembers were lost and their bodies recorded as missing. Only wireless operator Flight Sergeant Crocker has a known grave. The names are mentioned at Runnymede along thousands of airmen who are still missing in action.

For Willis and Bondurant, the time had come to leave. There was a fair chance that, if captured by the Russians, they would be shot as mercenaries. They reached the Norwegian Embassy in Helsinki to offer their services to the country that had been at war with Germany since 9 April. On 19 April they received visas for Norway from the Norwegian military attaché, with a letter saying that they were good soldiers and experienced pilots who served in war conditions. Colonel Hansteen added in his own handwriting that Willis wanted to serve as an infantryman.

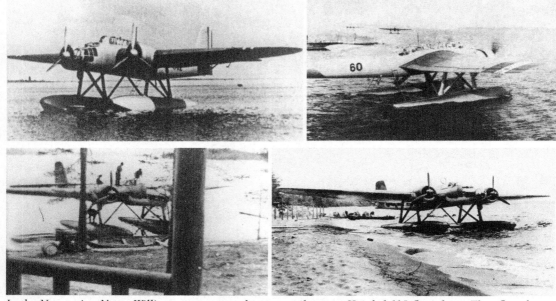

In the Norwegian Navy, Willis was a gunner, then a co-pilot on a Heinkel 115 floatplane. They flew daring attacks against German troops. The Norwegians operated from the many fjords. Heinkel He-115 F50 escaped to Finland. After landing the aircraft was confiscated by the Finns. Then they put it to good use. It flew a lot of secret operations far behind Soviet lines dropping crack troops and picking them up again after their mission. The aircraft remained operational until 1941 (NNA/MoDF)

[14] *Wellington W5419, No.12 Squadron, 020741. FTR Bremen. F/L William Bethune Baxter 39213 RAF. 27. Pilot. Panel 29. Son of Ferdinand & Amelia Aytone Baxter, Chelsea, London. P/O Peter Donald Macalister 60081 RAFVR. Co-pilot. Served as Farragut in Finland & Norway. 24. Panel 33. Son of Sir George Ian Macalister KT MA & Lady Macalister, Tonbridge Kent. Husband of Mabel Macalister. His brother John Edmund Seaton also died on service. F/S Glyn Davies Mansel 561305 RAF. 30. Panel 37. Son of David John & Sarah Mansel of Ogmore Vale Glamorgan. Sgt Philip Ivan Ferebee 550178 RAF. 22 yrs. Panel 43. Son of Ernest & Florence M. Ferebee of Worcester. F/S Edward Francis Porter 542209 RAFVR. 21 yrs. Panel 37. Son of Mr. & Mrs. J. Porter of Glasgow. All remembered at Runnymede. F/S Bryan Crocker 747874 RAFVR. Wireless Operator. 21 yrs. Grave 7C9 Sage War Cemetery, Oldenburg. Son of Frank & Ellen Crocker, Manor Park, Essex.*

Fleeing Finland; going to Norway.

They made their way by car, train and dog sledge, and on 26 April they reached Kirkenes in the north of Norway. Here they reported to Colonel Faye, the local commander. This officer, bewildered about the two Americans, so very keen to join him in battle, contacted General Fleischer. He added to the earlier letter of the Norwegian military attaché in Helsinki: 'After consultations with General Fleischer I order Second Lieutenant Willis to travel to Honningsvåg and to proceed by coaster to Mosjöen. I request all Norwegian authorities and civilians to help the Lieutenant to reach his destination. Kirkenes 26th April 1940.' Peter Farragut aka Macalister also returned to Great Britain. An entry in the Operations Record Book of No.8 Air Gunners School, Evanton, records the arrival of one of the He115s: 'May 2nd 1940, 'A Norwegian Heinkel 115, No.52, belonging to the Norwegian Air Force, but which had been captured by the Germans, arrived at Meikle Ferry stolen from the Germans by Lieutenant Hakon Offendal (pilot, Norway), Fenrick P.Riktoen (Norway), G.Haugen (mechanic, Norway), and British Lieutenants Giles Owbridge and Peter Farragut. Having been shot at by British Ack-Ack they landed with only one of two engines running. They had served with the Norwegian Hardanger Air Group after fleeing Finland, where they had done voluntary service. They also brought with them a bundle of German Air Force publications and a German Officer's diary. An Intelligence Officer took possession of these.'

On 3 May, a week after arriving in Mosjöen, Willis travelled to the south. In his pocket was a letter of recommendation from the commander of the 14th Infantry Regiment 'Orland'. The letter said that the Norwegians were quite willing to accept foreigners in the struggle against the Germans. They signed him on as an officer in the forces. The letter read: '2nd Lieutenant Willis has orders to travel to Tromsø to report as a voluntary pilot in the Naval Air Service. Willis and his three companions will receive free lodging and food.' The bottom of the letter reads: 'Arrived here 5 May 1940.'

In the battles at Narvik Willes was an air gunner in the He-115 of Lieutenant Hans Andreas Bugge (HB/NF)

All over Norway war was raging. Having recovered from the surprise of German landings at Oslo Airport and the sudden appearance of German vessels in harbours, the small Norwegian Army fought at its best. Though hopelessly outnumbered, fighting with old weapons and equipment the soldiers bravely faced the Germans. The German navy suffered heavy losses after Norwegian shore batteries sank the cruiser Blücher. Norwegian Air Force and Naval Air Service attacked, helped by RAF aircraft, Gloster Gladiator biplanes and Royal Navy Skuas. Norwegian Heinkel He-115 floatplanes attacked the German cruisers Köln and Konigsberg. British, French and Polish forces landed to support the Norwegians desperately trying to prevent the Germans from using the Narvik railway to the rich iron ore mines of Sweden. Most of the naval missions were around Narvik, where the Germans tried to get a foothold. The first raid was on 3 May by three He-115 aircraft, led by Lieutenant Jorgensen. They bombed German paratroopers near Laigastlind. The aircraft attacked from only 750 feet to ensure a complete surprise. They were successful, for when the Germans saw the He115s they took them for their own and held their fire. The Norwegian troops, however, shot with everything they had at their own aircraft returning to base.

During the following days, the Norwegian naval aircraft attacked several times. According to the flight administration, one of the crewmembers was Don Willis, as we saw in the diary of a Norwegian naval pilot, Hans Andreas Bugge, captain of a Heinkel He-115 floatplane. Willis served with the 2nd Naval Air Detachment in Tromsø. For the American this twin-engine float plane was a challenge. The German-built Heinkel He-115A-2: bomber and a torpedo plane had two 960hp BMW-132K engines. It could reach a maximum speed of 300 km p/h at 1,000 m. Its maximum range was 2,800 km and the armament consisted of 2 flexible machine guns, 1 fixed forward and 2 fixed guns firing backwards. Its bomb load was 1,250 kg bombs or one 45 cm torpedo. It had a crew of 3. Twelve He115A-2 had been ordered by Norwegian Navy but before April 1940 only six had been delivered. They were used by the navy as bombers, reconnaissance and torpedo planes. They got the numbers F50, F52, F54, F56, F58 and F60.

Conform the orders all Norwegian aircrew left their country and took their aircraft with them to Great Britain, to Sweden and to Finland. There the handed their Heinkel He-115s to officers of the RAF.(NNA/IOA)

Willis' first commanding officer was Captain Edwin Manshaus, who wrote: 'Willis was a relatively small man, quiet, yet very eager to fly against the Germans. I believe that he was not interested in politics. He mainly wanted to fight. It seemed that he had experience, as he had flown against the Russians. We made him an air gunner, as he had no hours on floatplanes, especially on a larger type like the He-115. He took part in several sorties against the Germans. On 11 May Bugge attacked German positions. Three aircraft dropped two 500 lbs bombs from 750 feet. Again, they caused much damage and made many casualties among the invaders.

On 29th May Bugge lead a formation against German positions near Narvik. In the book 'Norges Sjökrig 1940-1945', Captain Scheen wrote: 'May 29, was a bad day for the Germans, when three Norwegian Heinkel float planes, led by Lieutenant Hans-Andreas Bugge successfully attacked the German positions not far from the Ofoten railway. They bombed the enemy east of Narvik and fought off a German fighter that tried to intercept them. The fighter caught fire and was seen to go down in flames. They claimed it as destroyed.'

'When Willis arrived with us, it was 4th May and things did not look good. We were in the middle of the battles at Narvik. The allies were fighting hard and seemed to succeed in capturing the town. Many other positions had been evacuated. Our slow twin-engine naval bombers, He-115 floatplanes, operated at treetop level. To our advantage, it was a German-built aircraft and the Germans seemed very hesitant to open fire upon us. Needless to say, we used this to the fullest. Willis was a brave man. We had only three aircraft and he was part of the crew that consisted of Bugge, Björneby and Batalden. They flew daily and sometimes two or three times a day.'

Don Willis in the thick of it.

The last raid of Norwegian aircraft was flown on 6 June. In the evening three Heinkel He115s and two army bombers, all commanded by Bugge, took off to attack positions at Grenseroys. They returned at 2230 hours. In spite of the courage of Bugge and his men, the hit-and-run attacks only annoyed the Germans. Bombing was done without good aiming equipment from extreme low level. Two days later 6th Division asked for air support. Again, Bugge led the three Heinkel He115s and two old Fokker army aircraft. Their brief was to attack the ammunition dumps the Germans had built at Rundjfellet, 3 miles north of Bjørnfell railway station. No results were observed and the formation had to leave in a hurry. All landed safely.' It took until 10 September 1940 before Bugge was able to write a report of his flights

After a long and dangerous flight along a long stretch of the Norwegian coast and then across the Atlantic, Lieutenant Bugge and 2nd Lieutenant Willis arrived in the Shetlands. As Don Willis was a citizen of a neutral country and could be seen as a mercenary, it was recognised as an ally and consequently received a document that certified he could continue his duty until further notice. (HB/PW).

M.A.E.E. Royal Air Force
HELENSBURGH.

This is to certify that the bearer Donald Willis arrived at this Unit on duty with Norwegian Aviation Officers, p.m. Sunday June 9th 1940, and has so remained up to and including the present day Friday June 21st 1940.

It is understood that Mr. Willis is liable to continue on this duty until further notice.

F/Lt.
Adjutant,
for Group Captain, Commanding
M.A.E.E., Helensburgh.

21st June,1940.

against invading Germans and the events that took him and his fellow-countrymen to the Shetlands, to Scotland and finally to Canada: 'In addition to the report dated 6th August 1940, I hereby take the liberty to send a report on my service as Commander of the Navy's Air Group at Skjervoy and later the Navy's Air Group at Helensburgh, Scotland. 'From 1st until 22nd May, I served at the Navy's Air station in Tromsø. Here I examined, and made some tests with two aircraft, F62 and F64, which had been stolen from the Germans. The testing included its Lotgo bombsight, releasing mechanisms, plus captured German 250 and 50kg bombs with electric detonators. I made a setting up and firing trials with German 2cm Flak. I participated in bombing sorties with three He-115 aircraft against German positions north of Narvik on 11 May.'

'I flew transport missions in Toms and the Finnmark. I was based in Skjervoy from 22 May until 7 June, with two Heinkel He115s. By order of HQ 3rd Flying Unit, I lead bombing sorties against German positions on Bjernefjell on 29 May (3 He-115), 31 May and 7 June (2 He-115). The sorties southwards went as far as Bardufoss, where we were accompanied by British Gladiator fighters for protection against German aircraft. On each mission, I had a scout in the aircraft, an officer from the Army Air Force. The bombs were dropped from 700-800 meters above the ground. The bombs were 250 kgs and 50 kgs. The first 250 kgs bombs were the ones that hang on F62 and F64, the German He115s the Norwegians had captured and put to good us, when they were taken over from the Germans. Later we dropped 250 kgs bombs (bought from Germany). Each of them exploded. The bombs were dropped on positions given by Army Defence Command. I could not observe any damage, but I received a report later that it had a good effect. It is unknown whether this was directly or morally.' Soon it was clear that further operations would only lead to loss of valuable aircraft. The only option left was to keep as much equipment and personnel out of the hands of the Germans. One of the consequences was that many officers who were to leave the country would also leave their families behind. It was also possible that the separation would be definite.

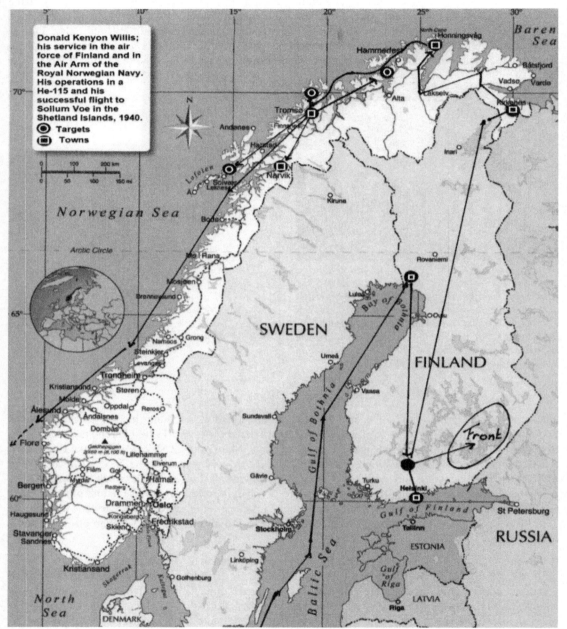

This map of the war over Finland and Norway shows Willis' activities from his arrival in Tornioon, his training in Parola, and the area of some of his reconnaissance flights in old Bristol Bulldogs over the front in Karelia. Then we follow his escape, partially by dog sledge, to Kirkenes, his flights as an air gunner on Heinkel He-115s of the Norwegian Navy and his evasion to the Shetlands. (HO)

The Day Report for 8 June 1940 reads: 'Only five He115s remained. At 1630, they received orders to leave the country immediately after a cease-fire has been agreed with the enemy. They took off from Skervöy and flew to the British Shetland Islands to prevent the aircraft from falling into the hands of the Germans. One of the aircraft was under command of Lieutenant Brinch. Due to navigational problems, he made an emergency landing near Svino lighthouse. The crew sank their aircraft. A second aircraft, flown by Lieutenant Skavhaugen, suffered engine trouble shortly after take-off. The captain considered it impossible to cross the sea to the Shetlands, so Skavhaugen decided to enter Swedish air space and seek refuge in Finland, where he landed later that day. The crew was interned for a while and the aircraft taken over by the Finns, who gave it Finnish markings. Lieutenants Bugge, Jörgensen and Stansberg flew the other three aircraft. They reached Sollum Voe in the Shetlands without difficulties. They landed at 23:00 hours. Bugge's crew consisted of Lieutenants Diesen and Björneby, Quartermaster Odd Batalden, Flight Engineer Jensen and Volunteer-Lieutenant Willis USA.' For the time being many Norwegian aircrews and their machines were sent to Britain. There was little they could do to help the British. Most of the time they walked through Glasgow, frustrated. Thanks to his command of the language, the British gave Don Willis a temporary administrative job, as was written in a document signed by the Adjutant of the Officer Commanding RAF Helensburgh: 'This is to certify that the bearer Donald Willis arrived at this unit with Norwegian aviation officers, p.m. Sunday 9th June 1940, and has so remained up to and including the present day Friday June 21st 1940. It is understood that Mr. Willis is liable to continue on this duty until further notice.'

1&2. The four Norwegian He-115A-2s that escaped to England were taken into the R.A.F. and given standard British markings and serial numbers. This is BV186 with black underside paint for night operations. British added eight machine guns in wings, four firing to the rear and utilized He-115 for transporting agents to North Africa.

It was not long before the Norwegian He-115s were painted as Royal Air Force machines. British test pilots were to find out what was to be the best way to make use of these German aircraft. Many sorties were flown, always escorted by a familiar RAF aeroplane, just in case trigger happy anti-aircraft gunners would have a go at it in anger.

To Britain with the aircraft; the Norwegian retrospective.

'Just after the last bombing sortie (6/7 June) the flying group of F64 and F58 received an order by phone at noon from 3rd Flying Unit to fly to England. Then we received the order to leave the country immediately and take all serviceable aircraft with us. A specific explanation of this order was impossible to obtain. The aircraft left Skjervøy at 1620 hrs. We flew off-shore to Röst. From there the course was set for Statt where we made landfall, and flew further for the Shetlands. An officer was also onboard; Lieutenant Diesen, who had just arrived after two MF 11s had reached the Shetlands. He guided us to

Voe, where the planes landed at 2230 hrs. We landed entered the harbour on the surface. We were told later that the British crew at the AA artillery had been blamed for not firing at our aircraft. We received a warm welcome. The next morning F56 arrived from Tromsø. This aircraft had been with F54, which sadly disappeared in heavy fog north of the Shetlands. Later we heard that it had flown to Svinoy where the crew sank the aircraft and rowed ashore. On 9 June 1940 I received orders from the Commander of Sullom Voe to fly to Helensburgh Experimental Establishment. An RAF pilot joined us as a navigator. 'We departed from Sullom Voe at 1640 hrs with F64, F56 and F58. Flew west of Scotland and landed in Helensburgh at 2000 hrs. In Helensburgh, we met several of the pilots who earlier had flown directly from the Western Norway to Scotland.'

Flight Lieutenant John Iverach (centre) was one of the pilots responsible for evaluating the He-115 as a suitable aircraft for Coastal Command. He flew from Rhu near Helensburgh. The Luftwaffe photographed the air base in May 1941

As mentioned, He-115 was inspected by a number of RAF officers. Here we see Flight Lieutenant Middleton and Flying Officer Fleming of No.201 Squadron during a test flight. During the invasion of Norway this particular He-115 '52' had attacked the German cruisers Köln and Konigsberg. The crew flew to Meikle ferry ending their flight in Invergordon. Later this was one of two Heinkels to fly covert operations in the Mediterranean from Malta with German markings. On the left photo we see John Iverach (left) with Pilot Officer Harold Hirst. Later Hirst died in a Catalina crash. Right: John Iverach (far right, holding coat) comes ashore at Rhu Hangars from a sortie in a Helensburgh Heinkel, moored top right on this picture. On the left we see a Coastal Command Catalina.

Bugge remembered: 'Heinkel aircraft F52 was also stationed in Helensburgh. I took over the command of four aircraft and seventeen pilots and mechanics. They were taken to Helensburgh. 'While negotiations were going on in London about the use of the Heinkel aircraft, the group in Helensburgh was busy with maintenance and repairs of the aircraft, physical training, communications exercises and so on. Gradually more personnel joined, so finally we were 22 personnel. The four escaped aircraft were reformed into the Norwegian Helensburgh Group under my command. Soon after arriving in Britain the now exiled Norwegian Nygaardsvold Cabinet made plans to use the four He-115 aircraft to perform leaflet dropping missions over Norway. The leaflet mission was to deliver a declaration to the Norwegian people, stating the Norwegian authorities were re-established in the United Kingdom and rejected any Nazi German overtures for a German–Norwegian peace deal. 'All four Norwegian He-115s were ordered from Helensburgh to Scapa Flow on 3 July 1940 to carry out the mission, although one had to return to

Helensburgh due to engine problems. The three He-115s assembled at Scapa Flow were ordered to fly to Norway and drop the declaration over the cities of Oslo, Bergen and Trondheim. Shortly before the mission was to get under way the British Air Ministry intervened and stopped the expedition, insisting that such an undertaking would be suicidal to attempt with the slow flying He-115s.

Three days later, the aircraft returned to Helensburgh. In British service, the three received new serial numbers, BV184, BV185 and BV187. However, the English authorities denied any flights to Norway and we had to return to Helensburgh. On 19th July, the crew left for Glasgow. Here we boarded 'Iris', by which we sailed to Canada. There we were put under the order of the Navy Commander. One pilot and two mechanics stayed in Helensburgh to look after the aircraft. Four weeks later we arrived in Canada.'

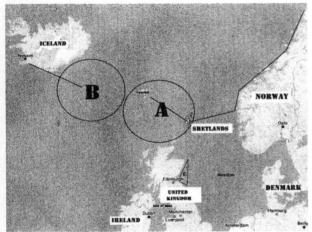

After they successfully flew from Norway to the Shetland Islands the Norwegian He115s briefly flew patrols between Sollum Voe and the Faroër Islands (A). For a brief period, they patrolled the eastern coast of Scotland. They then were posted to Canada for the creation of a new Norwegian Air Force. The Norwegians then flew long patrols between Iceland and the Faroër Islands.

Once the aircraft and become part of No.1477 Flight, RAF, the Norwegians also operated from Woodhaven on the River Tay. Most of the time they flew coastal and sea patrols (Gerd Garnes)

For a while the four Norwegian Heinkels were moored in Helensburgh harbour. Neither RAF nor the RNAS had spare parts for these enemy-built aircraft. Then the British finally found employment for the floatplanes. In June 1941, the aircraft were handed to Scottish Aviation Service to be made airworthy again. They were painted in RAF colours with British markings and serial numbers, BV184, BV185, BV186 and BV187. Two became part of the Norwegian Navy in exile. They had been captured in 1940 from the Germans and got the number F62 and F64. F62 was a German naval aircraft, M2+EH of 1./Kü.Fl.Gr.106, the 1st Squadron of Coastal Flying Group 106, flown by Lt.z.S. Joachim Vogler, who made a forced landing 13th April at the Sola See-Bodö.F64 had also been part of 1./Kü.Fl.Gr.106. They were taken into Norwegian service and based at Tromsö at the end of April. Further aircraft, F52 and F58, had been based at Bergen and F60 at Stavanger. The rest operated from Tromsö. Heinkels F52 and F58 escaped from southern Norway on 1 and 2 May. F52 flew to Scotland and F58 to northern Norway. As mentioned earlier, F56, F58 and F64 escaped from Northern Norway to Shetland just before the Norwegian surrender, and at least two of them continued to serve in the Allied forces. F54 failed to reach Shetland and returned to Norway, where it was lost. F50 got engine trouble and flew to Finland. F62 was not airworthy and in Tromsö where it was captured after the surrender. F60 was confiscated by the Germans near Stavanger.

Unable to service the aircraft properly to fly for Coastal Command the RAF destroyed them. Lack of spares forced them to finally scrap them at Stanraer.

The Norwegian He-115s that fled to Finland were first interned and then handed over to the Finnish air force, which used them for covert operation behind the Soviet lines. The ones sent to Malta to fly secret missions over the coast of North Africa, were both lost in action. (IQA/IWM /NNM).

Norwegian-British-German floatplanes??

Three of the Norwegian He-115s (F.56, F.58 and F.64) were subsequently used in covert operations off Norway and in the Mediterranean Sea with Norwegian crews. BV184 was attacked and damaged by two Polish Spitfire fighters over the Bay of Biscay in the spring of 1942, while co-operating with French fishing boats and later lost in a refuelling fire in the UK. BV185 was later destroyed in an Italian air raid on Kalafrana, Malta after flying just one clandestine operation to North Africa. BV187 flew several missions on the North African coast from its base in Malta before being destroyed by two German Bf 109s. The two sent to Malta were used for secret operations with German markings. Painted in green and light blue and with German markings they flew from Kalafrana, carrying British and Free French agents to Vichy-France and Algeria.

Although it was not easy to obtain information about the covert operations, we know that two aircraft were lost. One was destroyed in a Luftwaffe attack in Tunisia where it was moored. On a Maltese website we found some more information about the fate of one of the two 'SOE He-115s': '22 September 1941 Malta. Free French air crew killed on spy mission.

The Heinkel 115 used for clandestine operations from Malta crashed today with the loss of the crew and one passenger. The Heinkel which has been at Kalafrana since June took off just after midnight for its latest secret mission, but appears to have got into difficulties and was forced to make an emergency landing on the sea, some 20 miles off the coast of Malta.

The crew of No.431 Flight[15] have been named as Free French Flight Sergeant Georges Blaize, 31067 RAF (FFAF), pilot and Sergeant Raoul Gatien, 31011 RAF (FFAF), Flight Engineer. Also, on board and acting as observer was Fleet Air Arm Sub Lieutenant Reginald Drake[16], who was on the high speed launch from Malta set out to search for the stricken aircraft. They found wreckage strewn over the sea and the bodies of Drake and Blaize. There was no trace of Gatien. The spy plane had taken off from Kalafrana Bay at 00.05 hrs, but faced some difficulties, and was forced to alight on the sea. It was broken up by rough seas and high waves and subsequently lost at sea. The aircraft was ex #58 of the Norwegian Navy, registered BV185. The Heinkel was the second aircraft to be lost on Special Operations from Malta. The island's Governor and Commander in Chief referred to the Heinkel as the only aircraft based on the Island dedicated to the service of the Defence Security Officer. The Heinkel carried German markings. It was stored under cover at Kalafrana[17] and used only at night.'

SOE He-115 (BV185) at a hangar in Kalafrana shortly after its arrival in Malta on June 23, 1941. Pierre Blaize with his brother Georges (r), who was killed on 22 September 1941 serving with the Free French forces in Malta. The other Free Frenchman who died was Sergeant Raoul Gratien. Blaize and Gratien flew BV185.

Another interesting article appeared in the Times of Malta of 15 March 2004 by Ray Polidano, the director general of the Malta Aviation Museum Foundation, entitled 'Aviation Museum on the hunt': 'The Malta Aviation Museum is trying to track down fishermen who, it is thought, left the old jetty at Marfa some time ago cluttered with debris which turned out to be aircraft wreckage. The fishermen are being sought because their help is needed to pinpoint where the aircraft remains were found. The remains were an unusual Christmas present for the members of the Malta Aviation Museum Foundation, for that is when the foundation was informed about the debris at the Marfa jetty. Trawling fishermen, it is thought, had probably dragged up the wreckage in their nets, forcing them to call at the nearest jetty to get rid of it. It turned out that the wreckage was a strut which joins the fuselage of an aircraft to a float, and to have belonged to a Heinkel 115 floatplane. There was the added possibility that the wreckage was part of a particular Heinkel floatplane, the BV185 which had been lost during the 2nd World War, 23 miles north of Malta. The wreckage from the He-115 is at the Aviation Museum, Ta' Qali.

The connection of the Heinkels with Malta came about during WWII when the planes were used in a number of 'clandestine operations'. Most of these cloak-and-dagger activities involved the dropping of agents, or picking them up from, beyond enemy lines. For some odd reason the British authorities had chosen to make use of several Heinkel 115 floatplanes that had originated in Norway. During and after the fighting in Norway following the German invasion on April 9, 1940, four He115s of the Norwegian Naval Air Force escaped to Britain. The first, serial no. F.52, arrived at Dornoch in Scotland on May 2,

---

[15] *No. 431 (General Recce) Flight, briefly re-designated as No.1431 Flight RAF at Malta became No. 69 Squadron. In April 1944 when the Squadron returned to the UK.*
[16] *Sub-Lieutenant (A) Drake Reginald George. Died 22/09/1941. HMS Grebe Royal Navy. Commemorated at Lee-on-Solent Memorial Bay 1, Panel 7, Hampshire, United Kingdom.*
[17] *According to a study by French Colonel Henri Lafont*

after fighting ceased in southern Norway. The other three came from northern Norway. Eventually all four aircraft were sold by the Norwegian government to the Royal Air Force.' 'BV185, BV186 and BV187 were specially modified for clandestine missions. Extra fuel tanks were installed, much of the glazed panelling of the cockpit sections was removed and as defensive armament eight 0.303' Browning machine-guns were installed in the wings, four firing aft.

These clandestine operations were carried out from Kalafrana with aircraft and personnel operating under the name of 'Z Flight', under the control of Colonel Ede, the Defence Security Officer at Malta. During the night of June 23, 1941, the Heinkel 115 floatplane BV185, piloted by Norwegian Lieutenant Haakon Offerdal, arrived at Malta from the UK and was hurriedly parked in a hangar at Kalafrana, where it was kept under strict security. This was to be the first of the Heinkel 115s to come to Malta. During the night of 8/9 July, enemy bombs dropped on Kalafrana damaged the Heinkel, which sprang a petrol leak that necessitated repairs.

The two Blaize brothers are remembered in their hometown Saint Leocadie near Perpignan. HMS Daedalus at Lee-on-the-Solent was the principal base of the Fleet Air Arm and the site of the memorial to the men of the service who died during the Second World War. The Memorial is dedicated to the 1,400 Fleet Air Arm personnel who have no known grave but the sea. Sub Lieutenant Drake is also remembered here.

The Heinkel flew for the first time following repairs during the morning of September 3 but carried out its first operation on September 18. A few days later, on the night of September 21 and 22, the Heinkel was lost. A Fairey Swordfish biplane, flown by Flt Lt Moore, spotted the wreckage 23 miles north of Malta. The Heinkel crew, made up of Flt Sgts Blaize and Gatien, and Sub Lt Roy Drake FAA as observer were lost. Frederick Galea, a member of the Aviation Museum has written extensively on clandestine operations from the former RAF Station Kalafrana, in his book CALL-OUT - a wartime diary of air/sea rescue operations from Malta.'

Alastair McKenzie, journalist/editor, wrote on 3 July, 2017 in his website Mechtraveller, under the title Malta Mystery. Here is an interesting and puzzling piece of history that I stumbled across recently. It makes me think it might be time for a return visit to Malta! I came across the anecdote in Stuart R. Scott's 1996 book: Battle-axe Blenheims – 105 squadron RAF at war 1940-41. In Chapter 13 he writes about the life in Malta where 105 Squadron were stationed in the early part of the war. The airfield was at Luqa where the airport is now. Their barracks and mess were down at Marsaxlokk Bay where seaplanes used to be based, and where they used to swim from the seaplane slipway. Inside the hanger next to the slipway was kept a captured German Heinkel He-115 floatplane in matt black camouflage.

One of the 105 Squadron aircrew, Ron Scholefield, is quoted: 'From time to time we saw two quite mysterious characters in the bar of the mess. They were older than us presumably; looking back I think they were in their thirties. Both of them wore the ubiquitous khaki shirt and shorts. One wore an army sergeant's stripes on his arm, but no regimental badges of any kind. The other just wore a khaki shirt and shorts with nothing on them at all. They used to come in and were very friendly but talked rather guardedly about going over to North Africa from time to time, and having lots of contacts over there. They would not answer any questions about how they got there, or what they did when they were there, except that they had a lot of friends and they went from time to time and brought back information.'

'This went on for quite a long time, and then one evening the German seaplane was wheeled out of the hanger, the first time we had seen it moved. It was taken down to the bottom of the slipway and launched. These two chaps came along and got into it, started up the engines, taxied around and eventually faced towards the exit to the harbour and took off. We watched the take-off and the seaplane disappearing into the distance. When it was almost out of sight, it suddenly turned into a bright flash of light, and presumably exploded. It was very mysterious for we never heard anything more about it, whether it had been shot down, whether it had been sabotaged, or whether there was an accident; the only thing we knew was that we never saw the two men again.'

Heinkel He-115 plane on a crane, ca.1940. A burning Short Sunderland in Kalafrana Bay, Malta (BuA/IWM)

Searching the Internet, we found some information about the other 'Maltese Heinkel' as given by aviation-safety.net: Date: 05 Feb 1942. Time: 11:10. Type: Heinkel He-115 A-2 Owner and operator: Z Flight Royal Air Force (Z Flt RAF). Registration: BV187. Fatalities: 0/Occupants: 0. Aircraft damage: Written off (damaged beyond repair) Location: Kalafrana seaplane base Malta. Phase: Standing Nature: Military. Narrative: 'Seven He-115A-2 served in the Royal Norwegian Navy Air Service when Germans invaded Norway in April 1940 and four flew to Britain before the fall of the country. Three (bearing the codes F.56, F.58 and F.64) were used in covert operations with Norwegian crews off Norway and in the Mediterranean Sea [18]. In British service, the three received new serial numbers: BV184, BV185 and BV187. The He-115 BV187 flew several missions on the North African coast with Z Flight RAF from its base in Malta before finally being attacked at 1110 hrs on 5 February 1942 by two German Bf 109s that carried out a surprise strafe of Kalafrana seaplane base, Malta. The He-115 was caught at its moorings, set alight and damaged beyond repair. Plt Off McKay, a witness, reported that the German fighters were flying at least 400 mph when they attacked and that Bofors AA guns opened up but did not touch them. The AA gunners claimed hits on one of the attackers.

To Canada.
Norway and Great Britain agreed that the Norwegian fliers had to undergo training before they could be declared operational. Canada was safe and there was enough space and equipment to help the Norwegians. Therefore, they prepared to cross the Atlantic. As mentioned earlier by Captain Bugge, the Iris left Scotland on 9th July 1940 for the long voyage to Canada. The Norwegian naval personnel went there to build a camp, to train old and future members of the Norwegian Air Force and Navy in exile and prepare for battle against the Germans. Don Willis joined the Norwegians across the Atlantic. His destination was Camp Little Norway near Island Airport, Toronto. There Norwegian military staff started to build a new air force with Col. Oscar Klingenberg as head of the training schools and Georg Unger

---

[18] *The Maltese He-115 were flown by French crews, who knew the North African coast from flights with the French.*

Vetlesen and Thor Solberg to deal with US aircraft manufacturers handling the procurement orders for military equipment

The greatest need revolved around the requirement for more combat pilots, necessitating placing orders in summer 1940 for 36 Fairchild PT-19s as a basic training aircraft. 24 Northrop N-3PBs and 35 Curtiss Hawk 75-A8s already on order were sent to Canada along with a further order for 36 new aircraft as advanced trainers. Air defence forces were divided between Army and Naval Air Corps, with both services retaining their own commanding officers. The 'Little Norway' camp was officially opened on 10 November 1940, located in the bay area of Toronto, on the shores of Lake Ontario.

Toronto Airport was renamed Camp Little Norway. Today it is a modern airport one the same island.

We know little about Willis' stay in Canada. His flying logbook mentions that he flew 05.15 hours in the Curtiss fighter. This led us to believe that he was with his Norwegian friends for a while. It was not until 2014 that we found evidence of Willis' posting to Canada. Frankly, we have been unable to find out how much, of even if Willis paid for his perjury and his bigamy. We know that he 'got away with it'. His transfer to the RAF meant that his way and that of the Norwegians separated. After his arrival in Canada, the Norwegian government Bugge to the United States as a member of an aircraft purchasing party. They bought Northrop N-3PB aircraft. Bugge was promoted to command it and took the Squadron to Iceland.

Our source was an unexpected one, an article in the June 20, 1941 Cass City Chronicle, where a report of a court case against Don Willis in the City of Toronto was described. The article said: 'He Served 3 flags, Ready for the RAF, Jailed for Bigamy' and 'Canadian Judge Is Puzzled Over Rare Case, Gives Him 9 Months. Veteran of service under three flags and applicant for enlistment under a fourth, Donald Willis, 27, was sentenced to nine months in reformatory for perjury and bigamy, with probable deportation to the United States to follow. Willis, who served in the United States army in Hawaii, and later fought for Finland and Norway, and who was awaiting enlistment in the Royal Air Force, admitted having married a Toronto girl in Hamilton, but pleading that he believed his first wife Kathleen Krause, whom he married in New York in 1937, had divorced him. Willis testified he enlisted in the United States army at the age of 17. He admitted serving 14 months in Alcatraz prison for assault. He stated that upon Russia's invasion of Finland a year ago, he enlisted in the Finnish air force, serving there until the end of the campaign. 'Later he made he made his way to Norway and served in the air force there with Cdr Hans Bugge, now in command of the Norwegian aviators training in Toronto. After the collapse of the Norwegian campaign, Willis flew with Bugge to England in a captured German plane. Later he came to Canada, trained with the Royal Norwegian Air Force and received an honourable discharge to permit him to qualify for a commission in the British or Royal Canadian Air Force. Willis also testified that on arriving in Canada he was informed that his first wife had launched divorce proceedings against him and that he had assumed that he was free to remarry. I don't know what to do with this man', Judge Klein commented'.'

He Served 3 Flags, Ready for the RAF, Jailed for Bigamy

Canadian Judge Is Puzzled Over Rare Case, Gives Him 9 Months.

TORONTO.—Veteran of service under three flags and applicant for enlistment under a fourth, Donald Willis, 27, was sentenced to nine months in reformatory for perjury and bigamy, with probable deportation to the United States to follow.

Willis, who served in the United States army in Hawaii, and later fought for Finland and Norway, and who was awaiting enlistment in the Royal Air force, admitted having married a Toronto girl in Hamilton, but pleading that he believed his first wife, Mary Kathleen Krouse, whom he married in New York in 1937, had divorced him.

Willis testified that he enlisted in the United States army at the age of 17. He admitted serving 14 months in Alcatraz prison for assault.

Fought With Norse.

He stated that upon Russia's invasion of Finland a year ago he enlisted in the Finnish air force, serving there until the end of the campaign. Later he made his way to Norway and served in the air force there with Commander Hans Bugge, now in command of Norwegian aviators training in Toronto.

After collapse of the Norwegian campaign, Willis flew with Bugge to England in a captured German plane. Later he came to Canada, trained with the Royal Norwegian air force and received an honorable discharge to permit him to qualify for a commission in the British or Canadian air force.

Willis testified that on arriving in Canada he was informed that his first wife had launched divorce proceedings against him and that he had assumed he was free to remarry.

"I don't know what to do with this man," Judge Otto Klein commented. "He has a remarkable record."

"He is a man of restless disposition, enterprising, energetic, and of such a mentality that he would not inquire too closely into what was best for him," E. G. Black, defense counsel, pleaded. "But his motives were right, and he has always been on the right side. He is the impulsive type."

Crown Disagrees.

W. O. Gibson, crown prosecutor, stated that he did not agree with the defense estimate of Willis' character.

"He left Kathleen Krouse to go to Finland," the Crown added. "I believe he used the same means to attract this Toronto young woman, as he did to lure the young woman who became his first wife."

"Everybody loves a soldier," Judge Klein observed — "nine months!"

After arriving in Helensburgh Don Willis was accepted as a member of the new Norwegian air force. He followed them to Canada. While the Norwegians trained at Camp Little Norway, not far from Toronto, Willis had to appear in court. The charge was bigamy and the judgement was nine months. On 25 August, less than two months later, Willis was back in Britain. The entire article about his day in court can be read on this page.

'He has a remarkable record. He is a man of restless disposition, enterprising, energetic, and of such a mentality that he would not inquire too closely into what was best for him. E.G. Black, defence counsel, pleaded. 'But his motives were right, and he has always been on the right side. He is the impulsive type.' W.O. Gibson, crown prosecutor, stated that he did not agree with the defence estimate of Willis' character. 'He left Kathleen Krouse to go to Finland', the crown added, 'I believe he used the same means to attract this Toronto young woman, as he did to lure the young woman who became his first wife. Everybody loves a soldier', Judge Klein said, 'nine months.' And that was all for marriage number two…'

On 25 April 1941 Hans-Andreas Bugge and his crewmembers Staale Haukland Pedersen and Fridjof Glór Whist took off to fly a recce sortie between Iceland and the Faroes Islands. With Bugge overdue and no news received of an emergency landing, it was soon clear that he and his men were lost in the ice-cold seas. The Norwegian Naval History reads: 'On 25 April a simple celebration was prepared, but it had to be cancelled since the Squadron's popular boss Captain Bugge and his crew Petty Officers Whist and Pedersen have disappeared. They were on a search for a submarine. The mystery of their loss was never solved. It was assumed that they had an engine problem. A forced landing in the high seas was as good as impossible. This was a blow for the Squadron as they treasured Bugge and his crew as a boss and as friends.' In Norway, his wife Hanne and their two daughters waited for news. They stayed behind when he flew to England. The last time she heard from him was when he contacted her from the USA.

It was not until 1945, when the Norwegians return to their liberated country, that she heard that her husband disappeared between Iceland and the Faröer Islands, never to return home. Most of Willis' Norwegian friends did not survive the war.

Sub Lieutenant Von Hanno, Quartermaster Batalden and Rating Hansen were killed in an accident off the coast of Iceland in Northrop N-3PB G-24 of 330 Squadron on 30 July 1941 Björneby was luckier.

He survived the war to return to Norway as the commander of No.333 (RNOAF) Squadron. Brinch became OC No.330 Squadron from 30 April to 12 September 1942. Diesen survived as a captain, while Jensen's track was lost in the mists of time. Much was owed by Norwegians to Wilhelm von Tangen Hansteen.

Hans Andreas Bugge was put in charge of Camp Little Norway near Toronto, where Norwegians were trained to become pilots. They flew obsolete Hawk 75A7 fighters. (CCC/Hanne Bugge).

From 1937 to 1941 he had been the Norwegian military attaché to Helsinki. He worked for stronger Norwegian support for Finland during the Winter War. After a short period in Stockholm, he was promoted directly from Major to Major General in 1942 and appointed Commander in Chief of the Norwegian Armed Forces. He held this position until 1944 when Crown Prince Olav was made Commander in Chief, and Hansteen served as Deputy Commander for the rest of World War II. He continued his distinguished military career serving as commander of the Norwegian forces in Germany from 1946, commander of the Norwegian Army from 1948 and commander of NATO forces in Norway from 1951. He retired in 1966 and died 1980 in Oslo.

On 24 August 1941, two months after being sentenced to Willis arrived in England for further pilot training. Being close to the USA he never crossed the border. It should also be remembered that the United States had not yet entered the war. They were not encouraging its citizens to join the British forces. Norwegians, however, were most welcome to join the RAF in their own Norwegian units. RAF Woodhaven on the River Tay opened in February 1942 as the base for 1477 Flight, Royal Norwegian Air Force, and the Catalina flying boats would become a familiar sight on the Tay for the next three years. The Norwegians, like their compatriots crewing submarines operating from Dundee, had all escaped from occupied Norway, many of them making hazardous passages across the North Sea in small boats so they could take the fight back to the enemy. No.1477 Flight was absorbed into a new, much larger unit, No.333 Squadron in May 1943 with one flight continuing to operate the Catalinas out of Woodhaven and another, operating from Leuchars, equipped with Mosquito fighter-bombers.

The squadron was tasked with hunting down U-boats operating from bases in occupied Norway against the Atlantic convoy routes and attacking enemy shipping convoys off the Norwegian coast. Finn Lambrechts, the first commander and his flight engineer, Hans Ronningen, had flown the northern route of the Norwegian Airline DNL before they escaped from the Germans, as many others did by a variety of routes finally leading to Britain Commander Lambrechts had observed that German defences were weak along the coast of Heligoland so that it would be possible to put agents ashore to watch and report on German coastal shipping. His proposal to form a unit was supported by the Norwegians and received the approval of Coastal Command. Woodhaven was chosen as the base because of its relatively isolated location which served the need for secrecy, and Catalinas, designed for anti-submarine warfare and convoy escort duties were chosen for the work. Norwegians from all over the world provided the ground crews, flight engineers and other staff needed. Some eager Americans joined the Royal Canadian Air Force and asked for a transfer into the RAF as soon as they completed their training.

After the squadron's formation in 1941 at RAF Reykjavik, Iceland it flew Northrop N-3PBs on convoy escort, anti-submarine patrols, anti-shipping sorties and other operations across the North East Atlantic. At the end of the war the squadron was disbanded by the RAF on 21 November 1945 and transferred to Norwegian control as No. 330 Squadron RNoAF whose squadron number and markings they retain to this day.(NNA)

Soon the first American volunteers arrived in Great Britain to fight against Germany, many of them as members of the Eagle Squadrons. For the Norwegians, the road to battle would be longer. Willis and Bondurant went their own ways. They lost contact and while Willis worked hard to earn a commission in the RAF, Bondurant stayed in Canada, having been told that he was too old to fight the war. It was not until much later that Galdwell Hill, a reporter of Associated press, wrote an article about the short period when both Willis and Bondurant served in the air forces of two Scandinavian nations. It is a different story than the one Bondurant told after he returned home in the 'Flying story of Crawford major told by AP Correspondent':

Thus, was created the rather odd picture of two Americans in the Norwegian air force landing in German bombers in the Shetland Islands. It was a tricky business of setting down German bombers on English territory but they made it and explanations straightened the affair out after considerable difficulty and checking up. Though we have no evidence that Bondurant and Willis knew each other in Finland, documents give reason to assume that the briefly met in Norway before Willis became and airman in the Royal Norwegian Naval Air Arm.

Top: Hans Andreas Bugge in front of a He-115 of the Norwegian Air Service.Wilhelm von Tangen Hansteen built the new Norwegian air force

Elizabeth Muriel Gregory 'Elsie' MacGill, lived from 27 March 1905 to 4 November 1980). She was known as the 'Queen of the Hurricanes'. She was first woman in the world with an aeronautical engineering degree as well as the first woman in Canada to receive a bachelor's degree in electrical engineering.

She worked as an aeronautical engineer during the Second World War and did much to make Canada a powerhouse of aircraft construction during her years at Canadian Car and Foundry in Fort William in Ontario. During the war a comic book was written to tell about their contribution to military aviation. (Wikipedia).

It is possible that Bondurant returned to Canadian Car and Foundry as they also manufactured aircraft for the Canadian market. With the war now on, Canadian Car & Foundry and its Chief Engineer Mrs. Elsie MacGill, were contracted by the Royal Air Force to produce the Hurricane (Marks X, XI and XII). Refinements introduced by MacGill on the Hurricane included skis and de-icing gear. When the production of the Hurricane was complete in 1943, CC&F's workforce of 4,500 (half of them women) had built over 1,400 aircraft, about 10% of all Hurricanes built.

Canadian Car and Foundry (CC&F), also variously known as Canadian Car & Foundry or more familiarly as Can Car, manufactured buses, railroad rolling stock and later aircraft for the Canadian market. CC&F history goes back to 1897, but the main company was established in 1909 from an amalgamation of several companies and later became part of Hawker Siddeley Canada through the purchase by A.V. Roe Canada in 1957. Today the remaining factories are part of Bombardier Transportation Canada.

Later during the war, following the success of the Hurricane contract, CC&F sought out and received a production order for the Curtiss SB2C Helldiver. Eventually, 834 Helldivers were produced in various versions. Some of the dive-bombers were sent directly to the Royal Navy under Lend-Lease arrangements. CC&F also built the North American AT-6 Texan/Harvard under licence, many of the aircraft being supplied to European air forces to train post war military pilots. The work of Canadian women building fighter and bomber aircraft at the plant during the Second World War is documented in the 1999 National Film Board of Canada documentary film Rosies of the North Today. The remaining factories were part of Bombardier Transportation Canada. Bondurant returned to Cairo for a short time and then went to Canada to become a test pilot, a job which he still does with credit to himself and satisfaction to his Canadian employers. Bondurant stayed in Canada and the United States during the entire war, making an important contribution to the air forces by ferrying aircraft from the factories to troops. For Bondurant the fighting war had come to an end. After the events in Canada Willis joined the RAF and for Willis, however, becoming a member of the Royal Air Force meant that he would be in the middle of a bloody air war.

Yellow coloured Harvards and Cessna Cranses were used to training single and multi-engine pilots.

Canada and the Air Training plan.

With Britain a battlefield, and also lacking the space for an extensive scheme for pilot training Canada was chosen as the primary location for this purpose because of its ideal weather, wide open spaces suitable for flight and navigation training – sometimes on a large scale, ample supplies of fuel, industrial facilities for the production of trainer aircraft, parts and supplies, the lack of any threat from either the Luftwaffe or Japanese fighter aircraft and its relative proximity to both the European and Pacific theatres. For initial training biplanes, as one example of the wide range of American and British aircraft designs used for Canadian-based training facilities, pilots might have started their initial flight training on both British and Canadian-produced examples of the Tiger Moth, the Boeing Stearman from the nearby United States, or even the indigenously designed and produced Fleet Finch biplane. The government agreed in December 1939 to join the British Commonwealth Air Training Plan, operate its bases in Canada, and pick up a large proportion of the costs. Events turned the scheme into a huge operation, one that cost Canada $1.6 billion of a total cost of $2.2 billion, and employed 104,000 Canadians in airbases across the land[20].

The W.L.M. King government saw involvement in the BCATP as a means of keeping Canadians at home, but more importantly, it eased demands for a large expeditionary force and buried the politically divisive issue of overseas conscription. Negotiating the agreement and agreeing upon aspects of involvement was notably difficult. Canada agreed to accept most of the costs of the plan but in return insisted British pronouncement that air training would be Canada's primary war effort. Yet another negotiation point was the British expectation that the RAF would absorb Canadian air training graduates without restrictions, as in World War One, and distribute them across the RAF. W.L.M. King demanded that Canadian airmen be identified as members of the RCAF with distinct uniforms and shoulder badges.

---

[20] *Steven Haytee: History of the Creation of the British Commonwealth Air Training Plan*

The RCAF would run the plan in Canada, but to satisfy RAF concerns, Robert Leckie, a senior RAF commander (at the time in charge of RAF squadrons in Malta) and a Canadian, was posted to Ottawa as Director of Training. From 1940 he directed BCATP training.

At its height of the British Commonwealth Air Training Plan, 131,533 Allied pilots and aircrew were trained in Canada, 72,835 of which were Canadian. At the plan's high point in late 1943, an organisation of over 100,000 administrative personnel operated 107 schools and 184 other supporting units at 231 locations all across Canada. Infrastructure development including erecting some 8,300 buildings of which 700 were hangars or of hangar-type construction. Fuel storage totalling more than 26 million US gallons (98,000 m3) was installed along with 300 miles of water mains and a similar length of sewer mains laid, involving 2,000,000 cubic yards of excavation. A total of 100 sewage treatment and disposal plants and 120 water pumping stations were completed; and more than 2,000 miles of main power lines and 535 miles of underground electrical cable placed, servicing a total connected electrical power load of over 80,700 horsepower.

An instructor and his student with North American Harvard II aircraft at Uplands. This Cairn at Mossbank remembers the ones 'who did not make it'. Canadian Prime Minister William Lyon Mackenzie King with British Prime Minister Winston Churchill, 1941.

The Air Training facilities in Canada became the most important source of new aircrew for the Commonwealth air forces with Initial Training Schools, Elementary Flying Training Schools, Service Flying Training Schools, Air Observer Schools, Bombing and Gunnery Schools, Air Navigation Schools, Wireless Schools, a Naval Air Gunner School, Flight Engineers' School, General Reconnaissance Schools, Operational Training Units, a Central Flying School, a Central Navigation School, an Instrument Navigation School, Flying Instructor Schools, many Relief landing fields, Groundcrew training facilities and Support facilities

In late 1944, the Air Ministry announced the winding-up of the plan since the Commonwealth air forces had long had a surplus of air crews. At the conclusion of the war, over 167,000 students, including over 50,000 pilots, had trained in Canada under the program from May 1940 to March 1945. While the majority of those who successfully completed the program went on to serve in the RAF, over half (72,835) of the 131,553 graduates were Canadians. One of these 167,000 students was an American, Donald Kenyon Willis, who was somewhat in a rush to return to Blighty…

In 1943 his adventures in Scandinavia were published in a newspaper:
'It a feature story written for Associated Press about Captain Don Willis of Crawford, Indiana, who started flying for the Finns, joined the Norwegians, flew German planes from Norway to England joined the RAF and is now with American forces defending the English coast. The story contained a reference to Simpson Bondurant of Cairo, who won a reputation as a flyer in World War II, and had been a test pilot in Canada for the past two years. He was a brother of Dr. Flint Bondurant and Lonnie Bondurant of this city. Major Bondurant came out of the last war as a captain. After spending a few months with

relatives in Cairo, he became a commercial pilot and flew many cargoes into the remote wildness of Canada for various gold mining companies. During the Winter War, Bondurant joined the Finnish forces, and it was there that Willis first met him. They both flew fighter planes for the Finns for a time, and when the Finns surrendered, Willis and Bondurant got away in a car to Norway and joined the Norwegian naval forces. There they flew captured German naval bombers near Narvik for a long time, making daily attacks on about 6,000 Germans strongly entrenched on a hill. One night they heard on the radio that the Norwegian king had landed safely in England. The Germans hit Norway hard in about four different places at the same time and matters got rather confused and complicated. The commander of the outfit in which Bondurant and Willis were flying said that the King of Norway was in England, he did not know who they were fighting for, and ordered them to take off for the British Isles.'

Crawford Countian Bombed Nazis While Flying a German Plane

A U. S. Fighter Station In England, May 13 (AP)—Capt. Don Willis of Crawford County, Indiana, an Eighth Air Force fighter pilot, is probably one of the few aviators who have flown German planes while fighting for the Allies in this war.

He also has the distinction of having fought for four countries in this war—Finland, Norway, England and the United States—and of having gotten into the war in the first place by posing as a Finn, although he looks about as Yankee as Wendell Willkie.

Worked In Louisville.

Willis was working in Louisville but got bored and went to New York on a vacation, checked in at a hotel, and—

"In the bar this guy, a Finn, starts telling me about Finland and their fights with the Russians.

"He brought out his violin, and started playing sad Finnish music. He began to cry, and I began to cry, and pretty soon he decided I should join the Finnish Air Corps.

"The next day we went to the Finnish Embassy. He tells them a sad story about how I am really a Finn although I live in America and talk like a guy from Crawford County, Indiana.

"When he tells them I am also

one of the best pilots in America, the guy at the embassy says yes, I do look like a Finn, don't I, and gives me a passport.

"In Finland I flew with a Danish outfit. There was an American major there named Bondurant, from Cairo, Ill. He had quite a reputation in the last war . . ."

Willis is laconic about his experiences with the Finns. When they surrendered, he and Bondurant got away in a car to Norway and joined the naval air force. His squadron consisted of nine captured German Heinkel 115 seaplane bombers, which were handy in offensive work against Germans.

Bombed Germans.

"There were about 6,000 Germans surrounded on a hill near Narvik for a long time," he recalls. "They wouldn't surrender, and we bombed them regularly, but I don't think they ever fired a shot at us in anger because of our Heinkel 115's.

"We heard on the radio one night that the Norwegian King

CAPT. DON WILLIS.
From a photo made while he was flying in Norway.

had landed safely in England. The Germans hit Norway in about four places at once and things were pretty disorganized. Our commander said if the Government was in England, he didn't know who we were fighting for. He told us to take off for the British Isles."

So you had the curious picture

of an American in the Norwegian Air Force landing with a squadron of German planes in the Shetland Islands.

Escorts Flying Forts.

"They took a pretty dim view of us coming in there in Heinkels, but we finally got cleared and I joined the R.A.F." With the Eagle Squadron he transferred over to the U. S. Air Force last September.

He now has a total of eighty-two operations over enemy territory to his credit, but doesn't make much of it. "As a matter of fact, I don't think I ever knocked an enemy plane down," he says casually. "This fighting doesn't happen the way people think it does. It isn't that exciting."

In the Eagle Squadron, his unit concentrated on enemy shipping. "We drove those small German boats right out of the Channel. A squadron of fighters can lick a destroyer easily. Sooner or later someone hits a steam pipe or something vital. The thing stops, and you have it."

Now he is one of the fliers who have been escorting the Fortresses and Liberators in their raids on Europe. He thinks the American bombers are great stuff, and, as a fighter, that their claims of enemy victims are not excessive.

In 1943 the adventures of Donald Willis appeared in a newspaper. It told the reader in some detail of Don Willis' flying and his exploits in the Winter war in Finland, in Norway and in England. (PW).

2. EAGLES FOR ENGLAND.

A new job for Don Willis.

With Willis' return to Britain a new chapter in his life was to start. A chapter full of adventure, danger, and new marriage. Having shown sufficiently that he was a qualified and operational pilot Don Willis finally was given the opportunity to join the Royal Air Force. On 25 August 1941 he was declared physically fit for all air duties. Four days later, on 29 August, he made a first flight as a cadet-pilot of No.8 Elementary Flying Training School in Reading, west of London. His first aircraft were the De Havilland Tiger Moth and the Miles Magister. But apparently, he showed his instructor a thing or two. He needed seven days to prove his abilities as a pilot. His logbook showed that his first solo was one week later when he took off in Magister P6423. He was accepted as a Pilot Officer on probation in the General Duties Branch of the RAF Volunteer Reserve, serial number 105136.

Tiger Moths and a Magister as used at No. 8 Elementary Flying Training School at Woodley, Berkshire (IWM).

His duties were to last as it says, 'until the end of hostilities'. Don Willis had become an officer and a gentleman. Nevertheless, he had to start at the bottom of the ladder. Three months later, on 1 December 1941, Willis arrived at No.5 Secondary Flying Training School, where he flew the Miles Masters I and II and the Hawker Hurricane. Yet, it was not until 4 April 1942 that he controlled that superb aircraft, the Spitfire. In his logbook he wrote: 'First solo on the Spit. What a bird!' In spite of being a qualified pilot and not withstanding his previous experiences in the air war over Finland and Norway, the RAF wanted him to start from the bottom. He stayed with No.5 SFTS for five months. When he left on 30 April 1942, he had logged 6.10 hours on the Magister, 21.45 on the Spitfire I and 6.10 hours on the Spitfire II. His instructors considered Pilot Officer Willis a good navigator and an above average pilot. Now he was ready for the last step before becoming operational. Whilst at No. 61 OTU [21] his good results were again noticed. Don Willis logged a further 50.15 Spitfire hours.

On 1 June 1942, Pilot Officer Donald Willis was declared combat-ready. He was to a group of young Americans who lived and fought near Southend, at RAF Rochford. Proudly wearing the American Eagle on their left sleeve, they are known as No. 121 'Eagle' Squadron. Soon his new wife Martha followed him. His Scottish born son Stewart wrote many years later: 'My mother Martha McNicol and her family lived at Helensburgh and she was at university at Saint Andrews from which she graduated with an MA. They were married at a church in St Andrews. I believe that they were married after he returned from training in Canada because there was a period when she worked in the Land Army in Scotland after university and before becoming a teacher. They moved to England where she was working as a teacher, a job she hated. Just before she died Mum told me that, because of her degree she had been approached and asked if she would like to do war work. Not only did Mum hate waiting around for news of Dad's death on a daily basis, but she was bored to tears by her teaching job. One day as she sat in front of the class rocking her chair on its back legs she tipped over backward and landed on the floor. Owing to the

---

[21] *OTU: Operational training Unit.*

shortage of material, she was wearing no underwear, which made her hugely popular with the boys in the class. She accepted the offer of war work and was told to say that she had been offered a teaching job elsewhere. Much later she said that she went to work at Bletchley Park. She worked in Hut 6, the naval hut where the Enigma codes were first broken. Plainly she could not tell Donald and had she done so she would have been shot.'

Much of Don Willis' career in the RAF could be reconstructed via the Operations Record Book of No. 121 'Eagle' Squadron. On 6 June 1942 it said: 'In the early afternoon four sections took part in a Blitz Exercise with the army near Chelmsford. At 1530 hours, twelve pilots left for Martlesham Heath. From there they carried out a Circus Operation in co-operation with Boston bombers. The target was Flushing. We flew over it between 15,000 and 20,000 feet and returned via Blankenberge. No enemy aircraft were sighted and all pilots landed safely at 1925 hours. Today Pilot Officer Daley received the Distinguished Flying Cross. This morning Pilot Officer Willis arrived from No. 61 OTU to reinforce the Squadron. In the Finnish-Russian War, he flew with the Finnish Air Force and later joined the Norwegian Air Force during the German invasion of that country. After having escaped from Norway when the country was forced to surrender, he came to this country and joined our Air Force less than a year ago. He has excellent reviews from his OTU.'

Once he was declared fit for all aircrew duties Don Willis went through the rigorous training to qualify as a fighter pilot. He proved himself a good pilot. In spite of his experience as a private pilot as well as under battle conditions, he had to begin at the bottom: Elementary Flying Training School. His training took from 28 August 1941 to 2 June 1942, when he was posted to No.121 Eagle Squadron. However before joining the Squadron Pilot Officer Donald Kenyon Willis married a Scottish girl. (Patricia Willis/Stewart Willis)

Only two days after his arrival at RAF Rochford near the town of Southend Willis was sent into battle. On 8 June Spitfire MkVbs took off with orders to attack the area around Saint Omer in France and caused as much damage as possible. It was a successful day for Flight Lieutenant Jack Mooney. With his No.2, Pilot Officer Gene Fetrow, he led his Flight over the Channel into France. The battle area was over Saint Omer and Lille in Northern France. Fetrow remembered: 'We were looking for trouble. We roamed the skies between 5,000 and 6,000 feet. There was perfect cloud cover and flying from one cloud to the other we looked for enemy aircraft. Suddenly I saw six Focke-Wulf Fw190s coming up through the clouds below us. They flew away from us and apparently had not seen us. We both dived down and completely surprised them. I saw smoke coming from Jack Mooney's guns while he roared down. He shot down two Fw190s in one long volley. I also tried to aim at one but the Jerry managed to disappear into the clouds. I lost him. Around that moment our CO told us to come home. Jack was the hero of the day. By the way, Mahon shot down two Fw190s as well.' Willis also took part in the raid. In his scribbled handwriting he wrote in his logbook: 'I was badly mauled by a German who scared the hell out of me.

I ran with my tail between my legs. This was my first test. AV-X survived the test but my self-confidence is a lot less now.' As a newcomer Don Willis had no aircraft of his own. Every sortie he flew a different airplane. On 14 June it was AD199 and BL597 and the next day BL597 on a convoy escort. On 21 June he got an old aircraft, P8589, to escort bombers on their way to Dunkirk. He used this aircraft again the following day. On 23 June Willis flew an attack against Ostend and Dunkirk, Belgium. Again, he was at the controls of P8589. When the pilots flew home one of the newcomers almost killed himself by badly executing a flying manoeuvre. While closing formation the Spitfire of Pilot Officer Osborne hit the wing of the pilot on his port side. He lost control and spiralled down. With the greatest difficulty Osborne managed to regain control when he was almost at sea level. Being too low now, the Spitfire hit the water with a great splash and disappeared. To the amazement of all Osborne climbed out alive. On 26 June Willis finally got his own Spitfire, BM590. It was named Olga. Don promptly changed the name to Ridge Runner in memory of his wild days as a whiskey smuggler in the USA. Most of the time Willis flew sweeps[22] against German airfields along the Channel coast.

Left: Willis flew BM590, AV-R. He changed the name from Olga to Ridge Runner, remembering the runs he made in the Caribbean as a smuggler. Right: Preparing for a mission. Front left is the Commanding Officer of No.121 'Eagle' Squadron British Squadron Leader Hugh Kennard. Proudly displaying his British Distinguished Flying Cross is American Flying Officer Jim Dailey, with Willis looking over his shoulder. The officer with a pipe is Adjutant Brown. In the background the famous American reporter Quentin Reynolds. (ESA)

Another beautiful picture of Willis flying AV-R over Kent. Don in front of his aircraft (1942) (PW).

Meet the Rafwaffe; German aircraft in RAF uniform...

At the end of the day something interesting happened at Debden. Two strange birds landed at the airfield. They were a Heinkel He-111 bomber and a Messerschmitt Bf-110 fighter of the Luftwaffe. They had been captured, repaired and taken over for evaluation by the RAF 'Flying Circus', a unit that flew from one base to another to give air crew the opportunity to see some enemy aircraft at close quarters. One after the other the American pilots took off to fly mock attacks against the German aircraft. Some of those present were invited to fly as a passenger in the German aircraft. Willis found a place in the belly

---

[22] *Sweeps: Sudden attacks by a number of aircraft against ground targets.*

turret of the Heinkel 111. His diary said: 'Today I flew in what looked like the bath of an He111 bomber. No place for me! Then I was allowed to fly in a Me110. Extremely heavy on the controls! Manoeuvrability zero. This is a bloody useless aircraft!!' How different had it been if he had been allowed to fly a Focke Wulf Fw190, a much respected adversary. Anyway, it gave the pilots some idea of what the Germans were flying. What Willis called the Flying Circus, was in fact a very imported small unit within the RAF. It was called No.1426 (Enemy Aircraft) Flight and nicknamed 'the Rafwaffe.' It had been formed to evaluate all captured enemy aircraft and demonstrate their characteristics to Allied pilots. During the more than three years the Flight was in existence, it was able to give their aircrew at least some idea of the capabilities, and, more important, the weak spots of the enemy aircraft. The Flight met with many maintenance difficulties, due to the lack of spares and maintenance details. Tools and equipment had to be specially made and all engine and airframe spares had to be obtained from unserviceable and crashed aircraft.

On 2 June 1942 Don Willis joined No.121 'Eagle' Squadron. It turned out to be a hot month, with a frightening experience on the 8th with a first encounter over Saint Omer. He wrote: 'Saw F/L Mooney shoot down 2 FW190s by Lille. 190s were flying South, we jumped them, we were at 18,000 ft they were about 8,000 ft... etc.' On 16 June he reported that Mooney was missing on a fighter sweep (Rhubarb) near Ostend in Spitfire Mk Vb W3841 16-6-42. He was later declared killed in Action (KIA). (PW)

It was also necessary to assemble aircraft that had never been in Great Britain and about which little was known from a maintenance point of view. The unit was formed at RAF Station Duxford at the end of 1941. Four pilots were posted for eleven days for flying experience on mainly German aircraft. All the pilots had been Maintenance unit test pilots. The aircraft were allotted to the flight early in December that year. The first one was the Heinkel He111, followed by a Messerschmitt 109 and a Junkers 88. The first tour of RAF stations commenced in February 1942 and the demonstrations were carried out at Lakenheath, Watton, Coltishall, Bircham Newton, Docking, Sutton Bridge and Wittering. A second tour commenced in April 1942 and flying demonstrations were carried out until the flight returned to Duxford on 18 April. A further 6 tours followed up to December 1942 visiting different regions of the United Kingdom.

On 27 February, the same day the pilots had a chance to get to know some of their adversary's aircraft, Willis flew four missions, during one of which Luftwaffe Lieutenant Hermann Thiessen in his Fw190 of 8./JG26 was killed: '26 February: Aircraft of our Group escorted Ventura's attacking Dunkirk. 27 February: Took off twice as part of escort for RAF Ventura's again attacking Dunkirk. Two Jerries chased me. I they missed. I ran like hell. 1.30 hours each. Flew AV-R. Jerries missed me.' On 4 March Willis flew a patrol over Northern France: 'Saw a Jerry go down. He was going home for dinner. 'On 7th March he wrote: 'Weather Lousy.' Of course, we do not know how much profit Willis had from his brief contact with the Rafwaffe. We do know that 1426 (EAC) Flight did further tours, one of them to Debden and photographic duties, before it proceeded to RAF Digby on 27 May 1943 and was inspected by Their Majesties the King and Queen. The tenth tour commenced on 6 November 1943 and visited USAAF Stations Goxhill and Grafton Underwood. These demonstration flights were not without danger. Whilst landing at Polebrook on 10 November, the He111 crashed killing the pilot Flying Officer Barr and six members of the ground crew, and injuring four other ground crew who were travelling as passengers on the aircraft . The tour was then cancelled and the flight returned to Collyweston. The Flight continued its work almost until the end of the war. On 21 January 1945, official notification was received of the disbandment of the Rafwaffe or No.1426 (EAC) Flight as it was called, with effect from 17th January 1945.

Two aircraft of the 'Rafwaffe.' Top left the FW190, a fighter aircraft that was quite able to deal with allied pilots. Right a Ju-88, which cause havoc as a bomber and as a night fighter against RAF bombers. (RAFM)

The Yanks are coming.

On 4 July 1942 the first Americans directly from the USA took part in a mission against the Germans. Captain Charles Kegelman and crew flew one of twelve Bostons of No.226 Squadron RAF against marshalling yards at the Belgian town of Hazebrouck. They were the first crew of Americans of VIII Bomber Command to take part in a bomber operations. Their hosts were 226 Squadron at Swanton Morley. 1st Lieutenant Dorton was navigator/bombardier, Sergeants Cunningham and Golay were the other crew members. Kegelman received the Distinguished Flying Cross for the 8th Air Force's first bombing action over Europe. In the citation is said a.o.: 'The right propeller of his Douglas Boston was shot away by flak while. Further ground fire caused damage to his right wing, and the engine caught fire. Kegelman's aircraft lost altitude and even bounced off the ground. While flying away from the target on one engine Kegelman opened fire on a flak tower, he then limped back to Britain, by flying home at water-level.'

One of the Eagle Squadron pilots flying escort for the bombers under command of Squadron Leader Hugh Kennard, was Pilot Officer Willis. The raid was uneventful. The Operations Record Book said: 'Engagements with enemy took place, but no results.' Five days later a new attack followed, now by six Bostons of the USAAC 15th Bomb Squadron, together with six British Bostons. The targets this time were fields in Holland. Two Americans flew to De Koog, one crew to Bergen, one to Valkenburg and one to Haamstede. It was a costly raid for the Americans. Two aircraft were lost, one was so badly damaged that it had to be written off, while a fourth was slightly damaged by flak. It showed the newcomers what the Eagles already knew: the war in Europe is not easy to win! On 11 July General Spaatz pinned the Distinguished Service Cross on Kegelman's uniform for his 'excellent airmanship' in bringing back his badly damaged Boston on 4 July. Lieutenant Dorton was also decorated while Sergeants Cunningham and Golay of Kegelman's crew also got the DSC. Kegelman was promoted to Major.

On 13 July Willis escaped death. It was no German fighter that almost killed him. It was his own fault. Gene Fetrow, who flew that day with Willis as his wingman, remembered: 'It was my 51st mission. Don Willis flew slightly above me. Suddenly he turned over and started a long dive down. As his speed increased his aircraft levelled and started to climb again. Everyone was yelling through the radio, but Don did not answer. At the top of his climb the aircraft stalled and again down he went. This time we all thought we have seen the last of Willy. Thank God the boys of JG26 stayed at Abbeville that day, for if they had been around Don would have bought it. At 12,000 feet Don regained control one way or the other. He was mumbling over the radio and slowly joined us in a gentle climb. We decided to go home. After we landed Don told us that his oxygen pipe had disconnected without him noticing it.'

Eagle Squadron pilots waiting to 'scramble', to run to their aircraft and attack the approaching enemy. Don Willis is seated in the second chair on the right, with his omnipresent black cigar. The transfer of the Eagle squadrons from the RAF into the USAAF not only meant an improvement of pay. The Eagles had to change into USAAF uniforms. They were however allowed to keep the RAF wing over the right pocket of their uniform jackets. From left to right Don Willis, Sel Edner [23] and Sandy Saunders. Sel Edner was tortured to death by Greek communist guerrillas after his aircraft crashed there on 22 January 1946. (ESA)

'He remembered absolutely nothing of his dives and climbs. He said that suddenly the sea seemed to be awfully close. We all laughed and for a while Willy had a hard life, for anytime he wanted something we said: 'Mind your oxygen, old timer.' Some suggested he would better to take bicycle lessons or apply as a WAAF-driver. Jim Daley said he could do with a batman. Don's reaction was the same as ever; he got one of those black cigars from his pocket, lit the thing, ordered a beer and spoiled the air with his black cigar. Later rumours said that Willy always triple-checked his oxygen before he closed the cockpit.' Two days later Don Willis flew a sweep against Le Touquet in France. The pilots encountered JG26 [24], known as the Yellow Noses or Abbeville Boys for the yellow painted noses of the Messerschmitt Bf109 fighters with which they fly from Abbeville. That day one of the top RAF pilots, Wing Commander 'Paddy' Finucane DSO DFC [25] was hit and crashed into the Channel, not able to escape from his Spitfire.

After 32 victories his war was over. John Campbell, one of the few Eagles transferred to the Far East who spent three years in a Japanese PoW camp, wrote: 'We were milling around with three Squadrons, Nos.121, 165 and Paddy's 602. Suddenly Fw190s came out of the sun. They caught us by surprise. Paddy went down before he knew what hit him. He disappeared into the sea. It was awful. It was one of the moments when suddenly and without warning friends disappeared. The next day their lockers would be emptied, their personal belonging would be sent to the family or would be locked up until better times. Many aircrews refrained from close friendships. As one of them once said: 'You do not want to involve yourself too much with someone who will die before you know it. We lived by the day. We played hard and drank hard; we wanted to enjoy life as long as we had it.'

---

[23] *See Appendix for detailed information about this remarkable officer and his gruesome death in Greece.*
[24] *JG: Jagd Geschwader: Hunt (Fighter) Squadron*
[25] *Wing Commander Brendan Eamonn Fergus Finucane, RAF 41276. Died 15/07/1942, age 21 602 Squadron. DSO, DFC & 2 Bars. Remembered Runnymede. Son of Thomas Andrew and Florence Louise Finucane, of Richmond, Surrey.*

However, sometimes there was great excitement when a squadron was successful. During the last week of July, the Eagles successfully attacked Berck-sur-Mer and Abbeville. Hugh Kennard made a forced landing at Lympne and the squadron destroyed seven Germans in a day. The 4th of August 1942 was a turning point in Don Willis' life. Over North Western France and the Channel there were dogfights between American and German Eagles. One of them was Donald Willis. That morning he had seen the Medical Officer complaining of a headache. He thought he had caught a cold. Doctor Laing examined him and knew what a sinus condition can do to pilot. He shook his head and told Willy to take some well-deserved rest until he had fully recovered. Laing suggested that he stayed on the ground. The answer was: 'Hell, no, Doc, I will fly. That is why I am here and that is what I am going to do.' All too soon 'Ridge Runner' was airborne and engaged in a dogfight, reaching its peak with Willis on the tail of a German FW190 fighter. The German tried to escape by diving steeply to the ground. Willis pushed his controls forward and followed. The intense pressure on his eardrums, now very vulnerable as a result of his cold, caused extreme pain. Nevertheless, Willis stayed in the air until it was time for him to land. Almost fainting, sick with pain he tried to reach the airfield. With great difficulty he managed to land at North Weald. He switched the engine off and stayed in the cockpit, his head forward. Ground crew rushed to the aircraft to lift him out of the narrow space. Later that day, while the pilots were having tea, his eardrum ruptured.

After their raid against Hazebrouck Kegelman and his crew 1st Lieutenant Dorton, Sergeants Golay and Cunningham were decorated by General Spaatz. Kegelman was promoted to major before the ceremony. (AMB)

Willis was admitted to Halton Hospital. Dizzy with pain and very tired (according to his logbook he had flown three sorties that day) he walked through the long hospital corridor supported by two medics. A nurse came in to help him. Her name was Patricia Giles, a young South African, who came to England before the outbreak of the war. Like many girls she took up nursing to help casualties of war. In the hospital Willis fell in love with the young nurse. Seeing the pilot, she offered to take him over from the medics. However, before she could reach him, he fell, vomiting all over her spotless white uniform. 'Gee, nurse, I'm sorry,' he said, willingly allowing her to take off his flying clothes and put him into a bed. The nurse felt sorry for him and treated him very kindly. It was to be the beginning of a third relationship. Willis' Scottish son Stewart recalled what his mother Martha [26] then Willis' third wife later told him: 'Mum said that she arrived at the hospital only to find a young nurse sitting on my father's knee, at which point she got violently sick. There was an open and rather straightforward exchange of words between my mother and the nurse, to put it mildly. Later it turned out she was a South African volunteer and that her name was Pat.' Being married to Martha Don decided also to enjoy life with Pat. He stayed married to Martha and shared his free time between two ladies. After the war in 1947 Don and Patricia married in Mexico. No trace was ever found of any divorce documents. But that is another story, to be told later. Upon his return Willis was given administrative duties for the time being. One of his friends recalled that Willy raised hell and was a pest until the day he was allowed to fly again. In a

---

[26] *At that time, he was married to Martha Catherine McNicol, with whom he had a son, Stewart, as late as in 1946...*

cloud of smoke coming from the black cigars he constantly had with him, he was fumigating at the powers that be, stating that he could fly and that he would fly!!!

In August 1942 Willis received his promotion to Flying Officer in the RAF. A month later he had to relinquish his commission because of his appointment as an officer in the United States Army Air Corps. The United States' entry into the war in Europe had many consequences for the American volunteers in the RAF. No longer were they mercenaries or adventurers; they formed the core of what was to become the most powerful air force ever to fly from the United Kingdom. The Eagle Squadrons were renamed 4th Fighter Group; the aircraft still being Spitfires. There was another change now that they became American officers: their pay was much higher than it had ever been in the RAF. From now on the former Eagles happily occupied the Savoy Hotel in the Strand, London. Besides, they got large quantities of good cold American beer and honest whiskey!

Wing Commander 'Paddy' Finucane DSO DFC disappeared on 15 July 1942. Don Willis flew with No. 121 'Eagle' Squadron that day.

On 29 September 1942, the three Eagle squadrons were officially transferred from the RAF to the Eighth Air Force of the United States Army Air Forces, with the American pilots becoming officers in the USAAF. The Eagle pilots had earned 12 Distinguished Flying Crosses and one Distinguished Service Order. Only four of the 34 original Eagle pilots were still present when the squadrons joined the USAAF. Typical were the fates of the eight original pilots in the third squadron: Four died during training, one was disqualified, two died in combat, and one became a prisoner of war. About 100 Eagle pilots had been killed, were missing or were prisoners.

Negotiations regarding the transfer between the Eagle Squadrons, the USAAF and the RAF had to resolve a number of issues. The RAF wanted some compensation for losing three front-line squadrons in which they had heavily invested. Determining what rank each pilot would assume in the USAAF also had to be negotiated, with most being given a rank equivalent to their RAF rank. For example, a flight lieutenant became a USAAF captain, while a wing commander became a lieutenant colonel. None of the Eagle Squadron pilots had previously served in the USAAF and did not have US pilot wings. As such, it was decided that they be awarded USAAF pilot wings upon their transfer. Due to their insistence, the Eagle Squadron pilots who transferred to the USAAF 4th Fighter Group were permitted to retain their RAF wings, reduced in size, on the opposite side of their uniform to their new USAAF pilots wings.

Major General Carl Spaatz, head of the USAAF in Europe, wanted to spread the experience of the Eagles amongst various new US fighter squadrons, but the pilots of the three Eagle Squadrons wanted to stay together. The 71, 121, and 133 Squadrons were renamed by the USAAF as the 334th, 335th and 336th Fighter Squadrons and transferred as complete units, retaining their Spitfires until P-47 Thunderbolts became available in January 1943. The 4th Fighter Group flew Spitfires until its conversion to P-47s was completed in April 1943. All three units had switched to the P-51 Mustang by the second half of March

1944. The 4th Fighter Wing, along with the 334th, 335th and 336th Fighter Squadrons, exist today as F-15E Strike Eagle units at Seymour Johnson Air Force Base in Goldsboro, North Carolina and are part of the Ninth Air Force.

Left: Pilot Officer Gene Fetrow, one of Willis' friends, in RAF uniform. Together they flew dangerous low-level missions over Northern France. When they became American Army flyers the Eagles kept their trusted Spitfires. On the right we see Lieutenant Donald Young leaning against 'Ridge Runner', the Spitfire of Willis (ESA, DY).

When he transferred to the 8th US Air Force Don Willis was an experienced fighter pilot. He had logged 219 hours in the Spitfire, of which 200 were Roadsteads, Ramrods, Spoofs, Rodeos and Rhubarbs. On 18 September General Spaatz sent a message to Air Chief Marshal Sir Charles Portal, the Chief of the Air Staff RAF: 'I want to express my appreciation and that of all the Americans who once were part of the Eagle Squadrons, for the message you gave them through me. Although I was not able to meet all of them, I have noticed that they are excellent young men, able to carry the heavy responsibilities given them when they still flew with the Royal Air Force and which has been given to them again with their entry into the 8th Air Force. The 8thAF is proud to see such men come. Although they will now fly under a different command, their transition will have no consequence whatsoever for the common goal of the United Nations. I have passed your message to the Eagle-pilots and even though I know that they very are happy to have returned to their own ranks they will never forget their ties with your air force. I wish to thank you personally for the brilliant co-operation to ensure a smooth transition of these men. Everything possible has been done to make this transfer a successful one and at the same time continue normal operational flying without diminishing the effectiveness of this group in which both you and I are so deeply interested.'

Now Willis was an American officer. In a telegram it said that he is commissioned for the duration of the war and six months after and that he was to report to the Commander in Chief of the 8th Air Force. It meant that he had to cut his ties with his English ground crew and the people he worked and fought with since he entered the RAF. He received a second telegram: 'The Secretary of War has instructed your Commander to inform you that the President has appointed you a temporary First Lieutenant in the US Army, with effect of 23rd September 1942. The President can terminate this commission at any time. Your number is 0885159 and your rank is with effect from 23rd September 1942. You are to keep this letter as a proof of your commission.'

On 29th September, the Eagle Squadrons were formally disbanded during an official ceremony at Debden. Commander in Chief of RAF Fighter Command, Air Chief Marshal Sir Sholto Douglas, handed the units to the new Commander, Major-General Carl Spaatz. With the ceremony being the best proof of excellent Anglo-American relations in war, all are expected to do their best to make the event a memorable occasion.

With American participation in the war in Europe, public opinion in the USA wanted to be informed about the men over there. Life Magazine of 2nd November 1942 was the first to publish a long article about the men who once flew with the RAF: 'The American fliers of the RAF's Eagle Squadrons, which have begun fighting ten months before Pearl Harbor, were taken into the US Army Air Forces on

September 29th. There were three squadrons, numbered by the British 71st, 121st and 133rd, averaging 28 pilots to a squadron. Only four of the original 34 pilots were on hand. 100 men were missing killed in action or by accident, or prisoners of the Axis. Half a dozen came down over Europe just a few days before because of bad icing on the wings.' There were very mixed feelings indeed about this shocking disaster, so briefly mentioned by Life. In fact, it was No.133 Squadron's worst loss of the war. On 26th September twelve Spitfires of No.133 Squadron took off from Great Stamford at 1600 hrs. They first flew to Bolt Head for refuelling, after which they were to join with B-17s of 92nd, 97th and 301st Bomb Groups. The bombers were briefed to attack airfields in Brittany. After this the fighters were supposed strafe German targets.

Donald Willis and Patricia Giles, the South African nurse he met in hospital and who became his 4th wife. Don wears his USAAF uniform. They look at the old RAF uniform, with the RAF pilot's wing and the Eagle badge on the left arm, showing that the owner is an American pilot, in the RAF.

The Eagle Squadron badge shown on the photo left was given to the author when Patricia finally visited Holland to see the places of Don's evasion and meet the people who were involved in Willis' Journey to the Horizon.

Sadly, everything went wrong that day. First 301st Bomb Group was recalled because they could not find the escorting fighters. Then clouds obscured 97th Bomb Group from bombing; they miscalculated a tail wind and finally turned back over the Bay of Biscay. Lack of fuel caused eleven aircraft of No. 133 Squadron to come down in the Brest area, unable to return to England[27]. Four pilots were killed: Flying Officers Neville, Ryerson, Smith and Pilot Officer Baker. Six men became prisoners: Flight Lieutenants Cook, Jackson, Brettell, and Flying Officers Middleton and Sperry. For Brettell his captivity was to end tragically as after the Great Escape from Stalag Luft III the Gestapo murdered him. Only one of the pilots, 2nd Lt. Robert Smith, escaped to Spain. The catastrophe led to a great controversy with the poor weather forecaster being blamed in the end. In the Operations Record Book they wrote: 'Whoever the thick-headed, incompetent son of a bitch is can now take credit for twelve Spitfires. He should have received the Iron Cross and a pension from the Third Reich.'

However, the report of Life continued: 'They liked what British Air Chief Marshal Sholto Douglas said to them in farewell: 'The US Army Air Forces' gain is very much the RAF's loss. The loss to the Luftwaffe will no doubt continue as before. Of the 73½ enemy aircraft destroyed 41 have been claimed by the Senior Eagle Squadron No.71, a record, which I understand, the other two squadrons are determined not to remain unchallenged for long. Goodbye and thank you, Eagle Squadrons and good hunting to you, Squadrons of the 8th U.S. Air Force.'

Life of a pilot was stressful. One moment he flew in enemy fire in a burst of adrenaline, two hours later he relaxed in a bar or a pub, enjoying himself with friends. Next day there was the ten-second moment of terror and fear, followed by a completely uneventful one-hour sortie with nothing but empty sky around. Death was always around the corner, and it seemed as if aircrews were able to switch off the moment they landed, were debriefed and left for their evening pleasure.

---

[27] *It was the worst loss of the unit during its existence.*

You are now in the United States Army Air Force.

Debden became American station 356. The Squadrons, renamed 334th, 335th and 336th Fighter Squadrons formed 4th Pursuit Group; their proud name remained The Eagles. Commanding Officer was Colonel Edward W. Anderson, with Wing Commander Raymond M.B. Duke-Woolley in operational control of the Group for the next two months. The British ground crew stayed on to teach their new American colleagues the good and bad habits of the Spit. Soon Americans were seen roaring through the skies, now with bright white stars in a blue circle on the fuselages of the aircraft.

For Willis daily routine changed little. He now wore the USAAF olive drab uniform with the 8th Air Force badge on his left arm. The only difference was the RAF wing on his right breast, showing his connection with the RAF. Maybe 'Life' was right when it said: 'The Eagle Squadrons have become a legend of glory in the United States. Some part of their generous courage was indicated in the movie Eagle Squadron. But like the Lafayette Escadrille[28] the Eagles hated publicity[29]. We are no soldiers of fortune, one said. We are a lot of hometown boys trying to make good in big time. They collected no less than twelve Distinguished Flying Crosses and one Distinguished Service Order.

In their first raid as US Air Force pilots, they triumphantly shot down four more Focke-Wulf 190s.' On 9 October, 4th Fighter Group flew Circus 224. Led by Duke-Woolley they took off from Debden. Some were briefed to attack Euvermont, Fecoup and Abbeville while the main force escorted B17s and B24s to Lille, Courtrai, Roubaix and the airfield of Saint Omer. One German aircraft of JG26 was shot down, the pilot, Unteroffizier Hager, was killed. One month later 4th Fighter Group flew another mission. This time they were to escort Bostons to Le Havre. First the Americans flew to Tangmere to refuel. Over Selsey Bill fighters and bombers met. When arriving over Le Havre, thick clouds obscured the target. To prevent the bombs from killing innocent French civilians the whole formation flew to Honfleur, the secondary target. The aircrews were quite upset to see Honfleur was also under clouds. All the pilots returned very frustrated. Willis wrote: 'Targets completely obscured; no way to hit anything, returned home.'

The next day they tried again. Pressured to accomplish a successful mission they crossed the Channel for a second time, determined to show their British counterparts that the United States Army Air Corps was a force to be reckoned with. This time eighteen Bostons and their Spitfire escorts successfully attacked the French port. No German aircraft showed up and all RAF aircraft returned undamaged. The American High Command was satisfied. Four days later Major Jim Daley lead eleven Spitfires, patrolling along the Belgian coast. At the end of that day Don Willis noted: 'Heavy Flak. Attacked three Flak ships off the Dutch coast.' On 19th November Willis claimed an enemy aircraft when 335th Fighter Squadron attacked Souburgh airfield near Flushing in Holland. Having circled over the field the Spitfires were attacked by four Fw190s. After a short encounter over the Scheldt Estuary Willis shot one down. In his logbook he said: 'Rhubarb, 4 Fw190s off Flushing. I got one.' But the Fw190 was credited to another pilot, Frank Smolinski[30]. The Germans were very annoyed by these attacks. It was reported in the highest echelons of the German forces. The German High Command War Diary for 19 November 1942 said: 'between 13:10 and 15:35 hrs. ± 20 Spitfires attacked between Cap Griz Nez and the Scheldt estuary. They machine-gunned and dropped individual bombs on military establishments.'

On 6 December 36 Spitfires escorted Fortresses and Liberators, while eight others were looking for German shipping trying to sail through the Channel and on the North Sea. The Operations Narrative of 4th Fighter Group said: 'Wing Commander Duke-Woolley was up front again when he covered the retreat of the Fortresses that had bombed Lille. The mission was from 1155 to 1325 hours. After we had passed

---

[28] *American volunteer Squadron in the French air force during World War one.*
[29] *Most Eagle Squadron members detested this particular movie.*
[30] *Frank Smolinski was killed on 3 April 1943 when he attempted to take off from RAF Sawbridgeworth in a P-47 Thunderbolt when the engine of 41-6181, WD-B suddenly ceased and the aircraft crashed in flames.*

Cap Griz Nez at 1223, the Group shuttled between Griz Nez and Gravelines where we saw B17s at some 20,000-23,000 feet. Enemy aircraft, about 12,000 at 28,000 feet trailed them. When we approached the Channel six Fw190s were spotted in pairs over Calais between 15,000 and 25,000 feet. Over the Channel two more Fw190s were seen. Fetrow attacked one and damaged it, after which he shot down an unidentified aircraft[31].

Top left: Donald Willis in the cockpit of Spitfire 'Ridge Runner' AV-R. The nose art shows the now famous smuggler carrying a full whiskey barrel on his shoulder, chased by a customs officer or a cop. Interestingly the aircraft still has the AV-R letters of the RAF days. The British roundel has been replaced by an American white star on a blue roundel with a yellow ring.

There were at least three aircraft with the name Ridge Runner. Ridge Runner III was a North American P-51 Mustang, serial number 44-72308 WD-A of 4th Fighter Group flown by Major McKennon in March 1945. It is thought it also was the last fighter with this name. (PW/AC)

Don Willis flew this mission too. Contrary to the other report he saw little or no action. In his logbook for that day, we read: 'Ridge Runner, 1.35 hours, escort Forts, 30,000 ft, and contrails.'

On 12 December he flew no less than three missions on one day. First, he participated in 'Circus 242' under command of Major Gregory Gus Daymond, an ex-Eagle like Willis. Their target was the Abbeville aerodrome. Over the coastal town of Hastings, the Spitfires were to be joined by twelve B-24 Liberator bombers and six B17s. The 18 bombers never showed up, so Daymond decided to attack Abbeville with the fighters only. On their flight home they spotted the bombers, slightly overdue. Later that day Willis carried out two anti-shipping patrols. Early 1943 the main task of 4th Fighter Group was to fly anti-shipping patrols, a dull job, yet all pilots had to be incredibly careful as German fighters often lurked high in the sky. In the waters of the Channel and the coastal waters of the North Sea were dangerous Flak Ships, former fishing vessels, carrying a tremendous array of weaponry. If you were hit over the sea, especially in the early months, with the water temperature freezing, ditching meant certain death. Many pilots who reached the sea alive perished in the ice-cold water while their comrades desperately circled overhead, trying to guide a Walrus amphibian or a launch to the man below. It was excessively frustrating to see men die in the water and be unable to do anything. Therefore, bomber escorts were a welcome change of operations. Willis wrote: 'It's good to know that one has a chance to go down over enemy territory. I would hate to ditch. At least, when you come down on the earth you can run for it.'

---

[31] *Two Fw190s of 1./JG26, flown by Lieutenant Friedrich Count Iberacker and Obergefreiter Erich Eschke, both killed.*

On 13th January, during an escort mission, Willis' Spitfire developed engine problems. With a rough running Merlin, Willis reached Tangmere and made a rough, but successful landing. It was one of many lucky escapes. A fortnight later twelve Ventura's were detailed to bomb the airfield of Ursel near Bruges in the west of Belgium. Spitfires of 335th Fighter Squadron escorted them. Lieutenant Boocke, one of the fighter pilots, was hit by Flak and had to ditch. Fortunately, a British destroyer was in the area and Boocke landed in the sea, right alongside the vessel.

On 24 February 1943 Willis got a medal. In Aeroplane the caption read: 'General Hunter of the 8th USAAF Fighter Command decorating one of his pilots who served with an Eagle Squadron. AM Sir Trafford Leigh-Mallory KCB DSO, AOCiC Fighter Command, looks on. This particular pilot flew Bulldogs in the Finnish-Russian War, Heinkel He-115s for Norway in the German attack in April, 1940, and flew Spitfires in the RAF.' The following day is again was 'business as usual'. One of the last photographs of Don Willis is his trusted Spitfire. Soon the Group changed to a new aircraft, the Thunderbolt.

On 5 February Willis passed through the eye of a needle during one of his anti-shipping patrols. Led by Bill Kelly, Willis and four others took off from Debden. In his combat report Willis wrote: 'At 1055 hrs. we took off from Debden. While flying along the Dutch coast we spotted a convoy, about two miles off the coast near Noordwijk, Holland. The convoy consisted of three Flak ships, converted whalers, a destroyer and about ten freighters. They sailed in line astern with three Flak ships leading. The freighters were coasters of between 600 and 1800 tons. They were steaming at a speed of about six knots. Our aircraft flew in a loose Vic-formation of three pairs. We flew at zero feet. We approached from the southwest on the port side of the leading ships. At a distance of 1-2 miles, we turned to the right. Captain Kelly turned left, attacking the first ship in a right hand turn. He was hit during this attack. He turned climbing to the left and headed for the Dutch coast while white smoke came from his aircraft. The fire from the ships was extremely fierce. I attacked the second Flak ship and opened fire when I was 150 yards away from it. This ship was still firing at Captain Kelly. I was hit several times as was reported by Lieutenants Young and Ellington. The guns of the enemy ship were silenced. A grenade in the port wing hit my aircraft when I commenced my attack. I headed for home, and landed at Martlesham at 1245 hrs.' In spite of this eventful attack, Willis flew another patrol the next day, and on 10, 12 and 13 February. On 19 February Willis and twenty-two other pilots, led by Major Don Blakeslee flew to St. Omer. That day he discovered what fear was, when he got into a fierce dog fight with FW190s. Safely back at Debden Willis scribbled in his diary: 'We were surprised, outnumbered and outrun by over thirty Fw190s. These are dangerous machines. They out-climb, out-turn and out-dive us. They were all over the place and shot us up pretty badly. We ran like hell and got away with minor scratches on our aircraft.'

THE STARS AND STRIPES   Saturday, April 3, 1943
Vol 3 No. 136

...iolin Sent the Captain to War

Veteran of 4 Forces Scorns Merriwell Role in Air

By Andrew A. Rooney
Stars and Stripes Staff Writer

A USAAF FIGHTER STATION, England, Apr. 2—There is a quiet, likeable little guy with blue eyes from Crawford County, Indiana, walking around this airfield who doesn't care whether anyone ever knows he fought with the Finns and the Norwegians or not.

"There's been a lot of cheap publicity about guys like me—we're just working here." That's how he feels about it.

He's Don Willis, promoted to captain last week after six months in the American air force, and is one of those honest, efficient Eagle Squadron men who did a job over England before the spotlight was turned on the outfit.

Capt. Willis doesn't tell his story in the manner of the fantastic type of American he is. He's pretty matter of fact about it.

"Not much story," he says. "Sounds kind of foolish but it all started in Louisville. A guy that drove for me—what the hell was his name? Well, Louisville got dull so we shoved off for Chicago, only 300 miles away.

"We were having such a good time that we decided to take our party to New York. We checked in at a hotel in New York and that's how I got in the Finnish air force.

"In the bar, this guy, a Finn, starts telling me about Finland and their fights with the Russians.

Both Start Crying

"He brought out his violin, started playing sad Finnish music. He began to cry and I began to cry, and pretty soon he decided that I should join the Finnish air corps.

"He was with another Finn who had money he made bringing marble to America. There was a boat sailing for Finland in three days and he agreed to pay my way.

"The next day we went to the Finnish Embassy. He tells them a sad story about how I am really a Finn although I live in America and talk like a guy from Crawford County, Indiana.

"When he tells him that I am also one of the best pilots in America, the guy at the Embassy says that yes, I do look like a Finn, don't I, and gives me a passport.

"In Finland I flew with a Danish outfit. There was an American major there, name Bondurant. I think we were the only two guys to get into the air with the Finnish air force.

"Bondurant was from Cairo, Ill., had quite a reputation in the last war. He was the first graduate of Kelly Field; in the first class anyway. He wanted one more fling."

After the Finns surrendered, the commander of his outfit gave his car and a stack of visas and passports to Maj. Bondurant and Capt. Willis, and they drove from Helsinki to Norway, where Willis joined the Norwegian Navy.

Norway was short of planes, and Willis was used as a rear gunner rather than a pilot. Later he acted as co-pilot.

He explains that the squadron he was with in Norway was an ideal one for bombing Germans, because it was made up of nine captured German Heinkel 115s, seaplane bombers.

"There were about 6,000 Germans surrounded on a hill near Narvik for a long while," Capt. Willis recalls. "Hill number 144. They wouldn't surrender and we bombed them regularly, but I don't think the Germans ever fired a shot at us in anger because of our Heinkel 115s.

Ordered to Britain

"That got to be a regular mail run. We flew over, dropped our bombs and came back without having a shot fired at us.

"We heard on the radio one night that the Norwegian King had landed safely in England. Our commander said if the government was in England he didn't know who we were fighting for. The Germans hit Norway in about four places at once and things were pretty disorganized. He told us to take off for the British Isles."

Capt. Willis interrupted his story long enough to pay his respects to the Finns and the Norwegians. He thinks the Norwegians make the best pilots in the world. They are intelligent, they work hard, and the records show that they are excellent navigators.

The Norwegian squadron of German bombers left Norway and landed in the Shetland Islands.

"They took a pretty dim view of us coming in there in Heinkels," Willis says, "but we finally got cleared and I joined the RAF."

That was Capt. Willis' third air force. His fourth came when the Eagle Squadron was transferred to the USAAF last September.

During the period from April, 1940, when he joined the Norwegian Navy, up to last week he has taken part in 82 operations over enemy territory. He doesn't count the number of times he has been on operational flights that didn't take him over enemy territory.

The way Willis tells his story won't keep the kids he and his pretty English wife have sitting still on his lap. He makes no fantastic claims about the number of planes he has shot down.

"As a matter of fact, I don't think I ever knocked one down," he says. "This fighting doesn't happen the way people think it does. It isn't that exciting."

Capt. Willis says that much of the work the old Eagle Squadron did was not against enemy planes but against small shipping in the channel.

"We drove those small German boats out of the channel. A squadron of fighters can lick a destroyer easily. Sooner or later someone hits a steam-pipe or something vital. The thing stops and you have it."

Willis and the other men of the ex-Eagle Squadron, plus a lot of newcomers, have been accompanying the Forts and Libs, and they are sold on the American heavy bombers. They don't think the claims of the gunners are exaggerated.

Capt. Don Willis in an American Group Spitfire.

In April 1943 Stars and Stripes magazine told the story about Don Willis' service in four different air forces. David Bondurant, who flew in Finland at the same time as Don Willis during the Winter War, was named in this article too. (S&S)

That same day Don received a letter written by General Eaker, CiC VIII Fighter Command, saying: 'Donald K. Willis, 0-885159, 1st Lieutenant, 4th Fighter Group, Army Air Corps, US Army. For exceptional courage while serving as a pilot in a Spitfire Squadron, during ten operations over enemy-occupied European Continent on 14, 21 October, 9 ,10 19, 28 November, 3, 6, 12 December 1942 and 13 January 1943. The courage and airmanship of Lieutenant Willis shown during these operations give great credit to him and the Forces of the United States of America.' On 24 February at 1100 hours, 1st Lieutenant Don Willis and eleven other pilots stood to attention to receive the Air Medal from General Hunter [32]. Air Marshal Sir Trafford Leigh-Mallory, the old boss of the former Eagles was present as a guest of honour.

---

[32] Robert Boock, Pete Peterson, Oscar Coen, Stan Anderson (ex-71 Squadron), Roy Evans, Don Willis, Bob Patterson (ex-121 Squadron) and Carl Milley, Leroy Gover, George Mirsch, Glenn Smart and Robert Smith (ex-133 Squadron).

3. MY NAME IS MONTGOMERY.

The three Musketeers arrive in Europe from the Pacific.

On 13 November 1943 no less than three attacks were planned against the port of Bremen and its surrounding industrial areas. 272 heavy bombers, escorted by 390 fighters, carried out only one of the planned attacks. One of the pilots taking part in this mission was Lieutenant Colonel Thomas H. Hubbard. He was nicknamed 'Speed' for his slow Texan drawl and his quiet attitude. Flying his P-47 D with the name 'Lil' Jo' he was a seasoned warrior.

Before coming to Europe with his friends Cummings and Dix (calling themselves the Three Musketeers) he had seen a lot of combat. They flew both fighters and bombers in various commands prior to the outbreak of World War II. On 7th December 1941, when the Japanese navy surprised the Americans at Pearl Harbour, Hubbard was stationed at Clark Field, in the Philippine Islands with the 28th Bomber Squadron. There he saw combat against the Japanese. After spending two months on Bataan, he joined a task force that went to New Caledonia. Hubbard flew P-40 Tomahawks in Java, then P-400/P-39s. He also flew bombers, like Boeing B-17E no.41-2668 from Port Moresby, New Guinea to Garbutt Field in Australia on June 25, 1942. He flew 35 missions in P-39 aircraft in the Pacific Theatre. Major Hubbard was awarded the Silver Star for Gallantry in Action while serving in support of the US Marine Corps near Guadalcanal, Solomon Island, during October 6-14, 1942. He returned to the United States and was assigned to the 355th Fighter Group as deputy commander. When Cummings took command of the 355th he took Hubbard and Dix with him. They organised and trained the 354th, 357th and 358th Fighter Squadrons in the US before departing for England in July, 1943.

Major Thomas Hubbard (right) waiting to be decorated with a Silver Star[33] by Major General Willard Harmon in 1942 while serving on the Solomon Islands. On the right we see Hubbard wearing the Silver Star. (S&S)

13 November 1943; a bad day.

The mission of 13 November 1943 started under a bad omen. At about 11:00 Hubbard took off to join and protect the bombers to Bremen. During aerial assembly two B17s, one of 384th Bomb Group and one of 305th Bomb Group collided in mid-air, killing a total of 17 people. A B-17 of 388th Bomb Group had to be abandoned on fire near East Wrexham. Two B17s of 385th Bomb Group collided over the North Sea. One crashed into the sea, while the pilot ditched the other. Fortunately, the crews were rescued. Two B24s of 389th Bomb Group collided during the bomb run. Of almost 300 bombers, only 143 attacked the enemy. Yet the plan of attack looked particularly good. The first wave followed a course leading them to the island of Helgoland. Then they were to fly south, past Bremen and then turn north for their attack, after which the bombers were to go west again via Holland, with the relative safety of the Zuiderzee and head back for home. A second wave was ordered to fly north first and then turn southeast to attack the city from the north. This wave too, was to return via the same route as the first wave.

---

[33] *The Silver Star Medal was authorized by Congress for the U.S. Navy on 7 August 1942 for presentation to personnel for gallantry in action not warranting the award of a Medal of Honour or Navy Cross.*

It looked a sound plan in theory; the debriefing, however, revealed what really took place! Bad weather caused part of the 1st Bomb Division force to return to their bases before they completed their rendezvous over the North Sea. This and some bad navigation widely scattered the whole force causing B17s of 95th Bomb Group, 385th Bomb Group and 390th Bomb Group to attack targets of opportunity, while eight Liberators of 93rd Bomb Group dropped bombs on Helgoland. Some of the crews dropped their bombs as far away as Flensburg near the Danish border and Kiel on the Baltic Sea. German reactions against the attacks differed completely from previous experiences. No less than 300 German fighters were waiting over Bremen.

Steeple Morden in 1947. Before a mission discussing tactics. Colonel Claude E. Putnam, the Group Commander, briefs Lieutenant Colonel William J. Cummings of. Lieutenant Colonel Tom Hubbard and Major Gerald Dix of. Hubbard, Cummins and Dix were known as the Three Musketeers. (IWM/USAFHRC)

They did not attack very aggressively, they dealt with stragglers and escorting fighters. Most of the aircraft the Luftwaffe sent up were the Bf109s and Fw190s but there were also sightings of Bf110s, Me210s, Ju87s, Ju88s and Do217s. Some crews thought they had seen a new type of fighter, reporting two unidentified fighters, with noses longer than the Bf109 and wings further to the tail. The thought they were Italian Macchi 205s [34]. Other crews claimed having seen two P47s operated by the enemy and flying inside a small group of Fw190s. One of these P47s was shot down. The adverse weather conditions made flying difficult for the Liberators. The Germans attacked from cloud cover into which they disappeared again before the American fighters could reach them. Using contrails as a safe approach enabled them to make attacks from behind. Even in the target area, some German aircraft braved their own anti-aircraft defences. Both single and twin-engine aircraft were used to fire rockets between the bombers from about 1000 yards astern. At the same time, other groups of German fighters flew courses parallel to the bombers, suddenly making sharp turns firing rockets simultaneously from 1000 yards. Bf110s came as close as 500 yards but broke off their attacks once the gunners of the bombers started firing their .50 calibre guns. The P-38 Lightnings escorting the bombers all the way reported screens of enemy aircraft from 15,000 to 34,000 feet. The single engine fighters attacked the American fighters and

---

[34] *The Macchi C.205 was an Italian fighter aircraft built by the Aeronautica Macchi. It was built around the powerful Daimler-Benz DB 605 engine. With a top speed of some 640 km/h (400 mph) and equipped with a pair of 20 mm cannon as well as 12.7 mm Breda machine guns it was highly respected by Allied and Axis pilots alike. Widely regarded as one of the best Italian aircraft of World War II, it proved to be extremely effective, destroying a large number of Allied bombers. It was a match for the P-51D Mustang on equal terms, which encouraged the Luftwaffe to use a number of these aircraft to equip one Gruppe.*

tried to lure the P-38s away from the bombers. Other German aircraft, twin-engine mostly, went for the bombers, in well-coordinated attacks being flown from different directions at the same time. In a report after the 13 November attack one remark seemed to prove that, just like the allies had done in North Africa [35], the Germans used American aircraft to fight the Americans. A secret report read: 'Through secret channels we have obtained a photograph of a B-17 with German markings and swastikas. This aircraft may have fallen into enemy hands some time ago. On top of the fuselage are aerials, not common to the B-17. We think it is used as a flying command post.'

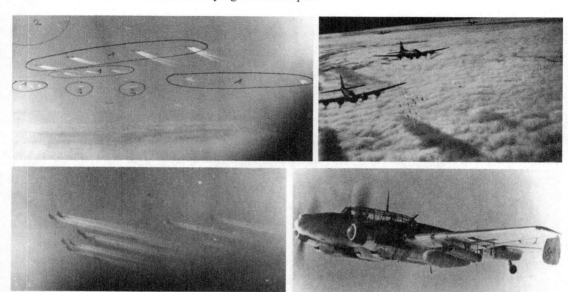

Left: III./ZG26 Feldwebel (Sergeant) Wabersich took these photographs from his gunner's position in the back of the cockpit of a Bf110. At 27,000 feet he saw many Bf110s (1) and Bf109s (2) heading for the Flying Fortresses of the 8th USAAF. Formations of bombers, escorted by fighters, in German air space.
Top: The B17s attacked Bremen through the clouds. In 1943 there was little chance bombs would hit their targets. At the post-mission debriefing some airmen reported having seen Bf110s with rocket launchers under both their wings, flying near formations and attacking stragglers. (USAFHRC)

Meanwhile, people in eastern Netherlands watched the dogfights. The first fighters were seen flying from west to east between 1115 and 1145 hours. They were Thunderbolts, flying ahead of the main formation. Sometime later bombers were visible, some under cover of escorting fighters. That day many aircraft were seen to be in serious trouble. One of them was B-24 no. 42-7650 of 44th Bomb Group, known as the Flying Eightballs. Coming from Shipdham it struggled back on two engines, which eventually caused the pilot to crash land near the village of Schoterzijl near Lemmer. Earlier American and German fighters clashed in the area over the Dutch-German border. At about 1215, dogfights took place over Mariënberg and Ommen. They lasted barely 15 minutes before all was silent again. The bombers were seen flying back to England. Columns of smoke on the ground revealed where aircraft had crashed and people had died. Near the town of Ommen, according to a report of the local LBD (Luchtbeschermingsdienst or Air Protection Service), more aircraft had crashed. The LBD chief and the mayor of Ommen hurried to the place where the smoke rose. Arriving at Arriën, they found the area sealed off by the police. Bits of a B-17 bomber were everywhere. The wreckage covered such a vast area that it was thought that the B-17 had exploded in mid-air. The Dutch police, searching for victims, found the body of a crewmember, and somewhat later they found another mutilated body. In the wreckage the body of a third man was found. There were no survivors.

---

[35] *Remember the use of the Norwegian Heinkel He-115 floatplanes by SOE.*

After a short discussion the authorities decided that the area must put under guard until the arrival of the Wehrmacht. Both the Mayor and LBD-commander then drove to Vilsteren. Locals had reported a crash near the Laar Bridge over the Regge River[36]. Here the NAD, a Nazi paramilitary workforce of the Dutch, had sealed off the area. The aircraft, an American fighter, was totally destroyed. There was no trace of the pilot. The two officials returned to Ommen to report their findings to the 'Polizeioffizier beim Beauftragten' the highest-ranking German police official in Overijssel province, the Town Commander in Zwolle and in The Hague to the National Air Raid Inspectorate. A few hours later a message came that an American airman had been found in the hamlet of Beerze, in the home of widow Meulman. The LBD-chief, accompanied by the mayor and Sergeant J. van Zanten of the police drove to Beerze.

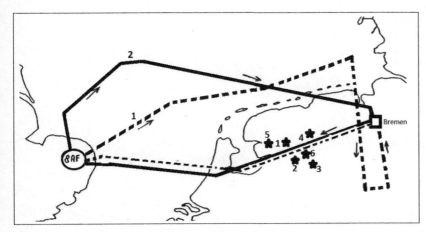

The mission against Bremen of 13 Nov 1943. The plan was to send two bomb groups to the target: Force 1 flew north east to Heligoland Island, turned south and after a turn north attacked Bremen from the south. Force 2 flew further north at first, then south east and attacked from the north to fly home trip as Force 1. Numbers 1, 2, 3, 4, 5, 6 show the aircraft crashes. (HO)

In the kitchen of Mrs. Meulman they found an American, with a broken ankle waiting for the police. All he said was: 'I was in a B-17 crew and I am from Boston'[37]. When asked about the fate of his crew he shrugged his shoulders and refused to say anything more. Accompanied by three Dutchmen he was taken to the police station at Ommen. The next day, on 14th November, some people of Arriën found bodies. Now seven had been found and one was a prisoner. Further searches were abandoned. On 13 November many more people saw the fighting in the sky. At Hardenberg Sergeant De Jong of the Bergentheim Police saw fighters trying to shoot each other down. Then people rushed to him saying that parachutes were coming down. De Jong and Officer Van Mildert quickly went to the village of Mariënberg. On a piece of land near the house of farmhand Hendrik Wijnholt, they found someone, still in his harness, bleeding and unconscious. A doctor named Post, who lived in Bergentheim arrived and after examining the man said that he had severe brain concussions and a possible spinal damage. An ambulance soon arrived as well and took the man to Hardenberg hospital. It was revealed that he too was part of the crew of the B-17 that crashed near Arriën. Later the local police received a message that a second parachutist had landed. Two officers were dispatched. They heard that the man had landed around 1300 hrs. His parachute was found, but there was no trace of the owner. All people could tell the police was that the man disappeared into a southerly direction, probably heading for the town of Vriezenveen. So, there was little else for the police officers but to write a report, that in spite of investigations it had not been possible to find the parachutist. The aerial combat caused havoc on the ground. Few people really felt sorry when they heard that an American fighter strafed the NAD-camp and fired at the barracks and the men running for cover. One of them, Arbeitsmann Bult[38], was hit in the thigh. Besides, one of the P47s dropped its

---

[36] *Lieutenant Lamphier got killed in his Thunderbolt P-47 42-8626 of 355 Fighter Group.*
[37] *Staff Sergeant Francis Joseph Ferrick. He was a waist gunner and came from Roxbury near Boston, MA.*
[38] *During the war, the Germans organized a semi-military work force like the one they had in Germany. Many unemployed Dutch people joined the force to get work, at first unaware of its Nazi-background. Later in the war, these men were armed and used for armed non-combat duties. The Dutch government considered these people collaborators.*

belly-tank on the camp. Having no idea what it was, the Arbeitsmänner mistook it for a bomb, forcing everyone to take cover and wait for soldiers of the Wehrmacht to arrive and defuse the contraption!

In the meantime, the authorities wrote their report. Having no idea that the aircraft was B17G 42-37830 or knowing the identity of the crew, they only said that an enemy aircraft had been shot down. According to three American flyers, who witnessed the loss of the aircraft the B-17 collided with another Fortress and spun out of control. In a report, compiled by the Operations Officer of 96th Bomb Group other eyewitnesses gave a very different account of the events: 'Aircraft 42-37830, 2nd Lieutenant Henry Earl Marks Jr. and crew, are missing. Contrary reports say that the aircraft was hit in the tail by German anti-aircraft guns and got lost in the clouds after it dropped its bombs. Other reports say that it was attacked by enemy aircraft and exploded as a result. We believe the first report to be true. Statements were made as well about missiles being fired from the ground. They looked like rockets with smoking tails or contrails behind them. Three crews also reported loud explosions at 24,000 feet. The projectiles came from the ground and have a grey smoke tail. After the explosions, clouds were seen that looked like the tentacles of an octopus.'

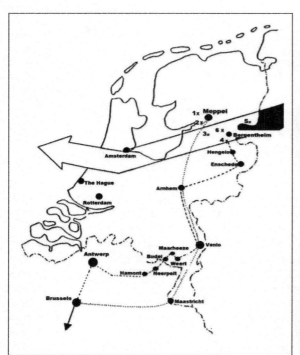

The wreck of another crashed Thunderbolt. Hubbard kept his Browning until they arrived in Spain.

Losses at the return of the attack on Bremen. 1.) B-24 Liberator 42-7650, 44th BG. 2.) B-24 Liberator 42-7483, 392nd BG. 3.) B-17 Flying Fortress 42-27830, 96th BG. 4.) Thunderbolt 42-7944, 355th Fighter Group (Hubbard) 5.) Bf109 Messerschmitt 15344, 6./JG11. 6.) P-47 Thunderbolt 42-8626, 355th FG. A B-24 Liberator and a B-17 Flying Fort crashed south of The Hague. ----- evasion route Lt Col Tom Hubbard ...... evasion route of Lts Ferrari and Roberts.(HO/USAFHRC).

The Operations Officer did not know at that time that seven crewmembers of B-24 42-37830 have been killed: Marks, Cress, Ehrlich, Wren, Fuhrman, Bowen and O'Rourke. Neither did he realize the ferocity of the battles high in the skies over the Netherlands and Northern Germany. At about the same time another bomber was in serious trouble. It was B-24 Liberator 42-7483 of 392nd Bomb Group [39]. The aircraft carried a crew of ten. The name of the pilot was Lieutenant Isaac Marx. It is quite a coincident that it sounds a lot like that of the pilot of 42-37830 (Marks). In the early afternoon, the aircraft and

---

[39] *For the story of this aircraft and crew see appendix 'Escape and Evasion.'*

24 others of the Group have joined up with 33 B24s of 44th Bomb Group, part of 14th Combat Wing of 2nd Bomb Division. For the first time the Liberators flew formations of twelve aircraft, believing that this could give the bombers the best mutual protection. Yet 42-7483 was one of the four aircraft 392nd Bomb Group lost that day. Six aircraft of the Group return to base in a bad state.

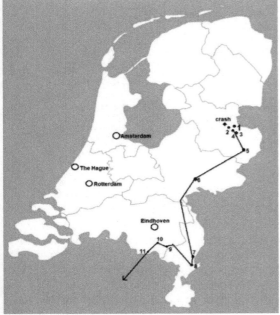

Tom 'Speed' Hubbard's journey from his landing to his passage of the Dutch-Belgian border, from where he was taken to Antwerp by the Belgian group of the escape line.

At the square, the crash site of P-47D 42-7944, WR-P 'Lil' Jo'.

The evasion route:
1. *Mariënberg   (13-16 Nov),*
2. *Laarbrug   (16 Nov),*
3. *Sibculo   (16-29 Nov),*
4. *Bergentheim (29 Nov-2 Dec),*
5. *Hengelo   (2-4 Dec),*
6. *Arnhem   (4-6 Dec),*
7. *Venlo   (6-11 Dec),*
8. *Horne   (11 Dec),*
9. *Weert   (12 Dec),*
10. *Sterksel   (12-17 Dec),*
11. *Maarheeze   (17 Dec), the Belgian border. (HO)*

On this day, the Group loses no less than 40 young men. Among the pilots shot down were high-ranking officers, one of them Thomas H. 'Speed' Hubbard, a big Texan. He, too, was escorting bombers to and from Bremen. It is his 23rd mission over occupied territory. Whilst leading his squadron, the 357th Squadron of 355th Fighter Group in the defence against German Messerschmitt Bf-109 fighters something goes very wrong. In his Escape and Evasion report [40], Hubbard later wrote: My engine fell forward in its frame and I lost control. Turning away from the bombers, Hubbard bailed out at 25,000 feet. Afterwards he remembered trying to delay pulling the D-ring to avoid lack of oxygen at that altitude. Later he thought he pulled the ripcord at about 20,000 feet, because, he said: 'I lost consciousness until around 10,000 feet. It seemed but a short time before I hit the ground. I saw several people running towards me when I landed, about 50 feet from a farm. I was not even sure if I landed in Germany or the Netherlands.'

Tom Hubbard in Holland; the start of a 7 month journey.
'Three young men rushed up to me, one spoke some English - they were kind and explained that I was in Holland. I told them that I was very thirst due to my lack of oxygen. They took me inside the farm and gave me a large glass of milk. They also made me understand that I must take off my flying kit and change into a civilian suit. I was not to worry but to do exactly as I was told; they would take care of everything. In the meantime, a crowd gathered around the farm, which upset me considerably. I was then told to run and hide in the nearby forest, which I did. I found shelter under some bushes in a large ditch. Three policemen in civilian clothes arrived in the farm. One of them spoke English.'

Then Hubbard was guided into a field some 500 metres from the farm and told to stay there until he was collected. He continued in his E&E Report: 'Pretty soon I saw the first Germans arrived at the farm. They found my parachute, which for some reason had not been taken away. I saw the boy who first took the parachute from me after I landed, gesticulating wildly to the Germans endeavouring to lead them in

---

[40] *E&E 802*

a totally opposite direction from my hiding place. I thought I should make more distance between myself and the farm, so I took refuge in the tall grass of a trickling channel where the layer of water reached some 10 centimetres and stayed there till about 18:30, when I decided it was safe to return to the farm. There I met one of the young men I had spoken to before. He told me he was hiding here to escape forced labour in Germany. That evening he took me to a prepared hiding place some 3 miles from the farm.'

Republic P47D Thunderbolt of 355FG, similar to the aircraft Lieutenant-Colonel Thomas Hubbard flew on 13 November 1943. It was called Lil' Jo. The nose art of Hubbard's Thunderbolt. (USAFHRC)

Hubbard's Squadron had no idea what had happened to their commander. When the remaining aircraft of 355th Fighter Group landed at Steeple Morden, the Intelligence Officer conducted a debriefing. Pilots wrote statements about the mission. Many had bitter complaints about the fuel tank the Thunderbolts carried. They wondered what to do if German aircraft attacked. The drop tank made the P-47 sluggish as they produced a lot of drag. Some said they dropped the tanks the moment they spotted Germans, others wanted to keep the fuel as long as possible. Major 'Dixie' Dix said: 'All pilots will keep their tanks as long as possible. If German fighters are seen, the commander is to be warned and he will tell the pilots what to do. Fuel tanks are not to be dropped until the leader gives orders. Let us try to bring the tanks home if possible. However, as soon as your own safety is at stake, drop them[41].'

After debriefing Dix wrote a report about Hubbard: 'Location F-122 (Steeple Morden), 355th Group Headquarters. Airfield of departure Bungay, course 285. Task: Ramrod. Date: 13 Nov 1943, 12.15 hours, near Meppen in Germany. Cause of crash: Enemy action. Aircraft: P-47D2, serial number 42-7944. Engine 1xR-2800-21, serial 42-124877. Weapons: .50 calibre gun. Left 1)576369, 2)575812, 3)573860, 4) 576337 Right 1) 576411, 2)575833, 3)575860, 4)575818.
Camera serial nr. 42-31584. Cause: air combat. Pilot: Hubbard, Thomas H, Lieutenant-Colonel 0-380248 Witness; Meyers, Raymond B. Major 0-437037.' Meyers concluded: 'On 13 Nov 1943 while on a Ramrod mission over the German-Holland border I was leading 358th Fighter Squadron at 29,000 feet flying 270 degrees on the left side of the bomber formation, when I heard someone say: 'Speed (Lt. Col. Hubbard) Break.' I looked around and saw two ships in a dive, one a P-47. Then the left wing of the P-47 flew off and the pilot bailed out. His chute opened. The second aircraft broke off and went into the clouds. At this time, I got a glance of the aircraft and I believe it was a BF-109. The P-47 went down to about 20,000 ft. and then exploded[42].' As far as the returning pilots were concerned Lieutenant-Colonel 'Speed' Hubbard was a PoW now. Had he been lucky enough to survive being blown out of his aircraft, he might well be on his way to a PoW Camp. Not good, especially if he was injured. But fortunately, none of this was true; Hubbard was not only alive and well, but he was now in the hands of the Dutch resistance. The big Texan was now in civilian clothes, had shaved his Clark Gable moustache and looked

---

[41] *Many drop tanks came down in Holland during the war. Before people knew what they were, all approached with great caution, as many believed they were bombs. Later these tanks were used as washbasins, water tanks for animals etc. Some people used the fuel that was left inside for cooking.*
[42] *Statement of Witness, 14 November 1943 by Raymond Meyers, Major, Air Corps, CO 358th Fighter Squadron. This report differs from the report Hubbard himself wrote later.*

almost as a Dutchman. One thing, however, he refused: he was not going to hand over his .45 pistol at any cost. After some three days it was considered safe enough to take him to the south of the Netherlands. Everything was done in the utmost secrecy. Hubbard only knew his helper was called Hans. He handed him over to another member who took the Texan to Hengelo, Arnhem and Venlo. This escort never revealed his identity to the American. During this evasion Lieutenant Colonel Hubbard made many interesting intelligence observations, as he wrote in an appendix to his Escape and Evasion Report when he returned in England: 'In early December I saw a large airfield 1 km. East of Venlo. It was one of the largest and best in the area with a dummy field a few km. to the north of it. This dummy field has lights and a presentable runway which has been bombed several times, but not the main field itself, as it is well camouflaged with a monastery nearby.'

Left the house of Reverend Dijkhuis in Bergentheim where Hubbard began his long Journey to the Horizon. Right Zonnehoeve, the farm of the Smeenk family in Sicbulo, another hiding place for Hubbard. (AFEES)

From Venlo Hubbard was taken to Eindhoven. Once he was back in England he reported during his debriefing: 'The Philips factory at Eindhoven was being repaired and was almost ready to be put back in operation.' Hubbard's next stop was the town of Weert, not far from the border between Holland and Belgium. A young police officer by the name of Frans van Riel waited for the Texan. Frans had been in the resistance for quite some time. His uniform was a relatively good cover, though the Dutch police no longer had the confidence of the Germans. He planned to escort Hubbard to Maarheeze, at the Belgian border on bicycles. But there was a problem. It was not the first time the resistance fighters had to face this with Yanks:

Texans might be tremendously skilled equestrians, but riding bicycles turned out to be a different matter. Hubbard said there was no way he could ride a bike. As speed was essential, a quick solution had to be found. Frans van Riel decided that Hubbard would become a skilled cyclist at the shortest possible notice. Sweating he pushed the tall American from Weert to Maarheeze. Imagine, the large Texan, desperately trying to stay in the saddle with a Dutch helper as desperately trying to maintain speed. We could not reconstruct where Hubbard hid during the time he was in the area. Former members of the resistance are still reluctant to reveal too much about their experiences. But we know he stayed not far from Maarheeze, living with the Hendrikx family in their small farm. A wartime photograph showed him standing in front of it, with Frans van Riel, some other escapees and old Mrs. Hendrikx.

It must have been in a forest farm near the border, an area where main escapers met before crossing into Belgium, where brave people helped Frenchmen, Britons, Canadians, Russians, Poles and others. One of the resistance leaders in the border area was Hubert Peeters, who sold beer and lemonade to cafes and bars in the area. As a travelling salesman he drove a car without causing much suspicion. Peeters and his assistant Moors had already taken no less than twenty-three people across the border. Hubert Peeters and Vrolinkx, a Belgian customs officer, both had contact with the White Brigade, a resistance group in northern Belgium. In the town of Bree these Belgians had contact with a Dutch group called 'Luctor et Emergo' (I Struggle and Emerge). Once Hubbard arrived in Belgium his identity was checked again. The Belgians did not want phony airmen. At the house of Mrs. Wijnen in Hamont the airmen were interrogated by asking questions only aircrew could answer. It was not easy for Hubbard as many questions referred to the RAF rather than the USAAF. Hubbard's answers survived over fifty years and are still available: Thomas H. Hubbard. Address in England: secret. Address in USA: Mrs. Fray F. Hubbard (mother), 108 Crestwood Drive, Fort Worth, Texas, USA. Born Dallas Texas, December 4 1911. Lieutenant Colonel pilot. Nr 0-380248. Aircraft: Thunderbolt. Target Bremen, 13th November 1943. Name of crew: none.'

Right: A unique photograph, in spite of its poor quality. It shows the courage of simple folk. Many Dutch patriots gave shelter to allied flyers. Standing from left to right: an unknown American pilot, Lt. Col. Tom Hubbard, a third and unknown American, Frans van Riel of the resistance and a fourth American. Seated in front are the women of the Hendrix family, who risked their lives for men they could not even speak to. Right: Norman Michie, Harold Shepherd and Thomas Hubbard while with the Bardoel family in Sterksel, December 1943. (FvR/AC)

Of the other 20 questions Hubbard could only say that Pilot Officer Prune was a character in Tee Emm Magazine. He was unable to answer questions about the RAF. However, he gave a brief report of his mission: 'Bailed out of aircraft at about 25,000 feet, left all switches on. I believe that the aircraft crashed, burned and was destroyed. The engine failed, a tremendous vibration set in and oil spread in great quantity over the aircraft. I landed safely in an open field near a farmhouse and as people from the house motioned me away, I concluded they were friends. I hid in the field until dark and then went back to the house to get warm. In a short time, a young man came who could speak English and took me to a safe place. From then on others who advanced me further to this area helped me. I was alone in the plane.' On 28 December 1943, after six weeks on the run, Hubbard was in the Belgian village of Kelpen. He had to wait until the resistance was satisfied about his identity. If he were an infiltrator he would be executed, if genuine, lives would be put at risk to help him. Since he was an important man, he must not fall into the hands of the enemy. The resistance decided to contact London directly by radio. Two Belgian agents, Bob Beckaert and Jacky Falaise were the links between underground and allied intelligence.

A day later Hubbard was declared safe. Now the wheels of the Belgian network started moving. Mrs. Anna Martens took Hubbard to Overpelt where he stayed with Lambert Spooren. Hubbard said later: 'I recall the names Overpelt and Neerpelt. In one of these towns, I was in the house of a shoemaker. I met his wife and little daughter. I remember that I was shocked to see how brave this simple family was. They risked their lives and that of the little girl to help me.' 'I made sure that I knew as little as possible. I never asked questions and I did exactly as I was told. I knew that if I were captured, I would be taken to a camp; these three people, however, would surely be executed. One morning, it had been snowing, I was suddenly told to prepare to leave the shoemaker and his family. Hubbard was taken to Antwerp, where Miss Nelly Rosiers took him under her wings[43]. As he could not stay in Antwerp too long Tom Hubbard was taken south. Much later he remembered: 'A guide came and took me by train to Brussels. I stayed there three months.'

---

[43] *After the War Hubbard married her and took her to Dallas, Texas.*

At the Bardoel farm in Sterksel, December 1943, standing left Mrs. Anna Bardoel van de Rijdt (grandma of Harrie Bardoel, Johanna and Forns (aunt and uncle), Willem Bardoel (grandfather) Harold Sheperd, Tom Hubbard, Toon, with his two sons Toon Jr. and Theo and Norman Michie. Front from left to right: Sjef, Jan and Kees, three Dutchmen, hiding for the Germans looking for forced labourers, and Fine, daughter of Anna and Willem. Right: a more recent image of the Bardoel farm in Sterksel. (AC).

Some monasteries along the border of Dutch and Belgian Brabant gave help to evading airmen. At times the monks escorted the Allied evaders, dressed up as monks from one country to the other. The increase of young monks, crossing the border in silence, did not seem to make the German guards suspicious. (Wikipedia)

On 4 January 1944, Hubbard was handed to members of Comète. Louis Berinx escorted him to the house of Paul Hellemans. Then everything seemed to go wrong. We have no idea what actually happened; in his letters to the author Hubbard remained vague and evasive. According to members of the Patriotic Militia, a resistance group in the Brussels suburb of Schaarbeek, closely related to Comète, Hubbard got suspicious. He decided not to reveal his identity. Hubbard said his name was Montgomery. We have no idea why; maybe the four months of travelling through enemy-occupied territory had made him extremely cautious. Maybe he observed things he did not like.

However, he broke the most important rule of a successful evasion: 'Put your faith in your helpers.' Intelligence sources in London of course were unable to verify this. Another worry for the helpers was a package that Hubbard (or Montgomery) carried under his shirt. He said it contained secret information for the Dutch in England. Further, he showed a .45 revolver and refused to part with it. However, the fact that he seemed to be a high-ranking officer made the Belgians reluctant to dispose of this tall American[44]. The group decided to isolate Hubbard for the time being by keeping him under strict surveillance in the house of the Goovaerts sisters.

The resistance knew the Germans dropped Abwehr agents, using captured parachutes and uniforms from prisoners. Some infiltrators were Germans with an American background. They caused horrible damage to the escape lines and were responsible for the death of hundreds of people. If the resistance managed to capture these agents, they were quickly killed and buried at locations that remain unknown even today.

---

[44] *A later report written by the people in the foothills of the Pyrenees also mentions the parcel and the .45.*

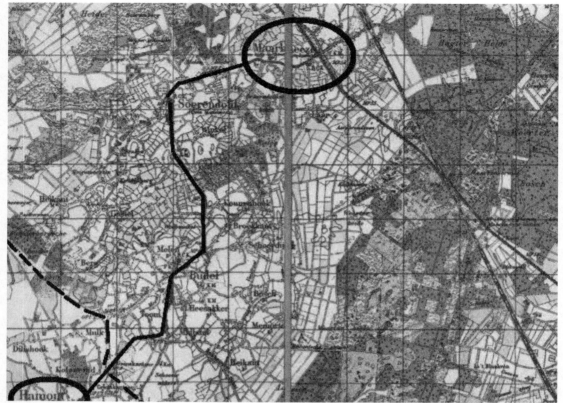

The last hurdle was an unobserved passage of the border between the village of Maarheze in Holland and the next reception in Hamont in Belgium. (HO)

Into Belgium.

No one could have blamed Comète if they had decided to kill Hubbard as well. We never found out how Comète checked Hubbard's identity, but after a few days they appeared satisfied with the American. A photographer called Duschène was sent for. He took pictures of Hubbard, to be used in his forged Belgian papers, supplied by a Doctor Warny. He then was taken to the house of Mr. Max Evrart, a Brussels coal merchant who lived at 24 Rue de la Station, Waterloo. During Hubbard's stay with Evrart the Gestapo arrested Louis Berinx. The group scattered and for some time Hubbard too went missing. With the greatest difficulty the members of Comète managed to find Hubbard again. They took him to the house of a man called L'Heureux and told him to wait. On 4 May he had to move again and was taken to the home of Yvonne Bienfait, a nurse, an active member of Comète under the alias 'Monique.' In her house Speed Hubbard met another American. It is Don Willis, who had been in occupied territory for exactly a month. According to a description by Yvonne Bienfait when she met Willis' widow in the Eighties, 'Willis was a relatively small man of the same age as Hubbard, who was a giant compared to the little major from Indiana. Willis was nervous, pacing the room saying repeatedly: 'I have to get back to my wife, I have to get back to my wife.'

4. AIRCRAFT FAILED TO RETURN.

Stuttgart; target for tonight.

Evening had fallen at RAF East Kirkby in Lincolnshire. On the airfield, people were hard at work. Big Lancasters of No.630 Squadron are prepared for a sortie against Germany. It was 15 March 1944. The four engine bombers waited to fly to Germany, and since this decision was made the station had turned into a beehive of activity. Ground crews were busy servicing the Lancasters. At the bomb dumps, armourers prepared the bombs. Incendiaries were packed into containers; larger bombs were mounted on trolleys, ready to go the aircraft. Armament crews fed thousands of .303 calibre cartridges into the belts. Huge Matador petrol trucks and smaller oil trucks were topped up. Carrying 2,500 and 450 gallons respectively they drove from one aircraft to the other. Instrument switches, plugs, bomb release mechanisms, everything was checked and checked again. At the same time, the Intelligence Officer was busy collecting all the available data he had about tonight's target. The Meteorological Officer prepared and revised his weather information, to make sure that his forecasts were right up-to-the-minute. Flying clothing was sorted out, escape kits were made ready while kitchens busily prepared the special 'pre-op' meals for the flying crews, who ironically called these 'the last supper.' Others prepare the flying rations of fruit, chocolate, chewing gum and flasks with coffee or tea. At Station Headquarters, the CO and his staff checked the latest information for the crews.

Len Barnes as a young airman, with the white flash showing accepted for flying training and during his time in the USA in front of a Vultee trainer. (AB)

Below: Aerial photo and map of East Kirkby in Lincolnshire. (IWM)

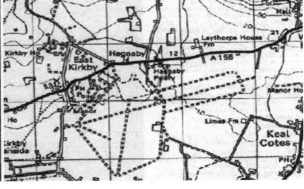

Everyone was busy. Everyone, but the air crew selected for tonight's raid; they sat together, played cards, read, wrote a letter or tried to break the tension by joking and laughing. Others sat in a corner and tried to get some sleep. Rumours about the target had spread already. One said it was Hamburg, he heard it from the ground crew, who heard it from someone at Station Headquarters. Another was sure it had to be the Ruhr as he heard that many incendiaries are loading into the bomb bays. Nobody really knew more than the hour of the briefing. First to be briefed were the navigators. Consequently, they would be the first to know the target. From the maps on the wall each navigator drew the course on his own. Then he calculated his flight plan. By the time the other crewmembers walked into the briefing room he had done most of his homework. All crews gathered in the briefing room, where they received the information needed to carry out their task. The sound of nervous laughter mixed with the humming of quiet voices, contemplating the chances for this night. One of the pilots was young Pilot Officer Leonard A. Barnes, 'Barney' to his crew. He celebrated his 24th birthday on 22 February, having joined the RAF four years earlier.

Left to right: P/O Barnes 1944,   Mr. Barnes 1990,   Sgt Walker 1944,   Mr. Walker 1990 (Barnes, Walker)

No.630 Squadron in May 1944. P/O Barnes and his crew could be in this picture.

With his aircraft and crew he was no longer a Rookie. He had a good and reliable crew. Though Barnes' navigator Flying Officer Giesler outranked his skipper, there was a friendly relationship between the officers. Barnes' other crew members were Sergeants: bomb aimer Gregg, flight engineer Walker, wireless operator Ploughman, the Canadian mid-upper gunner Overholt, and rear gunner Fox[45]. They trusted the Skipper with their lives.

When the Station Commander and Squadron Commanders walked in, all stood to attention. 'Be seated', said the Station Commander before revealing: 'As you see the target for tonight is Stuttgart.' Some crews were relieved, for there were far worse places to fly to. No one enjoyed flying to Berlin or the Ruhr area, where the Germans had massed their flak guns. In January and February the men flew a number of extremely difficult and dangerous missions. Twice they went to Berlin and once to Leipzig, deep inside the Reich. When, at the end of February and in early March, a few sorties were cancelled, very few crews felt bad about their mandatory rest from operations. Now all aircrew prepared for tonight's sortie.

---

[45] *The British give their crews different names: radio operator (US): wireless operator (UK); bombardier (US) bomb aimer (UK); tail gunner (US), rear air gunner (UK); top turret gunner US, mid-upper gunner UK.*

The final sortie.

After the briefing Barnes and his men got together for a last conference. All details were checked again until everyone knew exactly what to do. Then they all went out to the locker room. Kit and parachutes were collected; jokes were made with the WAAFs. Gunners got a helping hand to put on their unwieldy heated suits. Turrets were the worst places as far as the temperature was concerned. Especially rear gunners, who sometimes had their central panel removed for better vision, were in an almost Arctic environment with temperatures of minus 40° Celsius. Then they sat down and had a last cigarette before they were off to dispersal, where the Skipper checked the aircraft and signed for it. Many thought Stuttgart would be a piece of cake. Others had suspicions. One of them was Len Barnes. Len did not consider himself a suspicious man, but one little event made him nervous. While he prepared himself in the cockpit, he put a tiny teddy bear, a gift from his girlfriend Merville, at its regular place, on the compass. The little bear was to stay there until P for Peter had landed back at East Kirkby. Barnes and his crew were sure that this little mascot was the best good luck charm one could have. But, when he started the engines, the little teddy bear fell to the ground. 'I immediately took it for a bad omen', remembered Barnes, when asked about this sortie many years later. Strangely enough Merville also had a worrying experience that day. When she heard that Len was to fly that night, she decided to wear the RAF wing he had given her as a present. When she was at work, she bent to pick something up from the ground, and the wing fell on the floor. Merville wondered if anything bad was in store for the man who gave her this keepsake. At about 1700 hrs. the first crews of No. 630 Squadron were in the aircraft, waiting for the signal to start the four Merlin engines and taxi to the runway. An elaborate plan had been devised at Group HQ to make this mission a success.

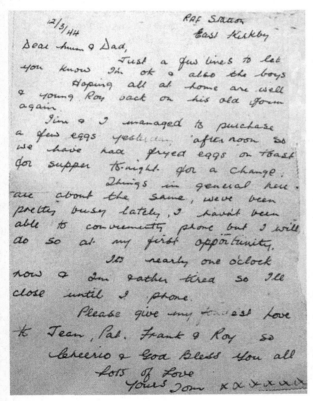

On 12 March 1944, only three days before he was killed, Sergeant Tom Fox, Rear Gunner of ND530 P-Peter, wrote a last letter from East Kirkby to his father and mother, writing:

'Dear Mum & Dad,
Just a few lines to let you know I'm OK and also the boys. Hoping all at home are well & young Roy back on his old form again.
Jim[46] and I managed to purchase a few eggs yesterday afternoon so we had fried eggs on toast for supper tonight for a change.
Things in general here are about the same, we have been pretty busy lately, I have not been able to conveniently phone but I will do so at my first opportunity.
It is nearly one o'clock now and I am rather tired so I will close until I phone.
Please give my fondest love
to Jean, Pat, Frank & Roy, so
cheerio and God Bless You all.
Lots of love.
Yours, Tom XXXXXX.'

---

[46] we suppose he speaks of his.

During the night of 15/16 March an immense fleet of aircraft were detailed to participate. Six Groups of Bomber Command sent aircraft. There were 266 Lancasters of No.1 and No.3 Group. Nos.4 and 6 Groups sent 230 Halifaxes, while No.5 and No.6 Groups had 235 Lancasters taking off. Pathfinders were to lead the bombers to the target and illuminate it sufficiently for it to be wiped out by the bombers. No less than 116 Lancasters and 16 Mosquitoes were available to show the way to the target. Ten other Mosquitoes were to carry out a diversionary attack against Munich, while other Mosquitoes had orders harass airfields Saint Trond, Venlo and Deelen. This way the RAF hoped to keep the feared German night fighter force occupied. If the experienced pilots of the Luftwaffe could not be beaten in the air, they might be destroyed before they took off. The weather forecast seemed to be in favour of the RAF. There would be a cloudless sky at first, but the closer the crews got to the target the heavier the clouds were expected to be. Some forecasters said that strong winds over the target might disperse the clouds, making it possible to bomb visually rather than by H2S[47]. It would make aiming a lot easier, but without the help of cloud cover the Lancasters would be spotted more easily by the enemy. Take-off was at 18:57 hours and Ken Rodbourn was the first take off in ND583[48]. Almost all squadron Lancasters followed and slowly disappeared in a south-easterly direction, with the following pilots at the controls:

JB546-A	: P/O J.S. Kilgour	ND527-O	: F/L W.H. Kellawa
ME650-B	: F/L J.C.W. Weller	ND530-P	: P/O L.A. Barnes
ND554-C	: P/O F.H.A. Watts	ND685-Q	: P/O A.W. Wilson RAAF
JB290-D	: W/O J. White	ND688-R	: S/L R.O. Calvert RNZAF
JB672-F	: P/O H.W. Hill	ND337-S	: F/L D. Roberts
JB288-H	: P/O A.G.G. Johnson	ME664-T	: F/S A.J. Perry RAAF
ND655-J	: F/O J.B. Nall	ND583-V	: P/O K. Rodbourn (first to take off)
ND531-K	: P/O H.C. Rogers	ND657-W	: P/O C.L.E. Allen (landed at Coningsby)
ND335-L	: F/L K.R. Ames	JB556-Y	: F/L G.H. Probert
ND686-M	: P/O K.W. Orchiston	RNZAFED944-Z	: P/O R.W. Bailey

In the end a total of 863 bombers took off to attack Stuttgart flying into adverse winds which delayed the opening of the attack. The German fighter controller split his force of night fighters unsure of Bomber Command intentions as the main force flew directly across France almost to the Swiss frontier before turning north-east towards Stuttgart. The night fighters did meet the main force however just before the target was reached and bombers began to fall. 630 Squadron, bombing between 23:15 and 23:29 hours from 20,000 to 23,000 feet believed that the Pathfinders were late but that their markers had been quite well placed based on their bombing photos which showed the River Neckar and railway lines. Some crews encountered moderate to light defences in the target area whilst others suffered heavier flak and some reported intense fighter activity from Strasbourg and on the line of withdrawal. David Roberts crew had the unnerving experience of seeing a bomber hit the sea on the outward journey and considered the bombing may have been scattered, 'Cab' Kellaway and Cliff Rogers noted large fires burning near the railway station and also east of the River Neckar whilst the crews of Ken Orchiston and Alan Wilson reported scattered fires.

Apart from Stuttgart there was an attack against the marshalling yards at Amiens. 140 aircraft were to fly this sortie. It had to force the Germans to divert at least some of their night fighters to this bomber force. Finally, yet importantly single Mosquitoes and pairs were to fly to the cities of Duisburg, Düsseldorf, Dortmund and Bochum. This distraction would draw more German night fighters away from the main attack. Seventeen Wellingtons were to fly to northern France and drop leaflets. A small force of night intruders would attempt to stir up German defences. Then the green light flashed. The heavy bombers took to the air, and their roaring engines struggled for altitude. After a long assembly 900 aircraft set course in a south-easterly direction. One of them was ND530, P for Peter. The flight to Stuttgart was rather uneventful. Here and there flashes of German anti-aircraft guns were visible. The relative quietness

---

[47] H2S (Home Sweet Home): a radar device that shows the ground and can be used to navigate and bomb.
[48] P. Sharpe 2018-2019 Squadron Association Website.

in the sky gave reason to think that the optimists had been right. Nevertheless, more than forty aircraft returned to England without attacking the target. There were many reasons. Engine problems, radio-interference, oil pressure, navigational errors and in one or two cases fear for what lay ahead.

Flying in a large but loose formation the bombers headed for their targets. Their route took them as far as the Swiss border. There they turned towards Stuttgart. During the inward flight there was little opposition from German night fighters, but a few miles south of the city the first combats began. Still untouched 'Peter' droned over Nancy then headed for Lake Boden at the border of Germany and Switzerland. From there it flew a northern course that took the aircraft over Stuttgart. In the distance the crews could see the searchlights trying to catch an aircraft. Exploding flak lit the skies. Target Indicators, known as Christmas trees, coloured lights dropped by Pathfinders, slowly floated down, illuminating a town in distress. As 'P for Peter' approached the city, the navigator, took over. Giesler, announced the course to fly with 'H'-hour, (the aircraft's time to bomb), Gregg, the bomb aimer, picked up the Target Indicators through his bombsight. Quietly he started guiding his skipper: 'Bomb Aimer to Skipper, Left, Left. Hold it. Right a bit. OK. Hold it. Open bomb doors. Keep her steady Skipper, steady, steady, OK, Steady, steady. He pressed his button that started the pattern of bombs from the Lancaster's belly. Gregg continued: 'Bombs gone, close bomb doors! Skipper to engineer, close bomb doors. Engineer to skipper; doors closing; Skipper to navigator, course for home please.' While the huge black doors closed, Gregg searched the empty bay to see if there were hang-ups: 'Bomb Aimer to skipper. All clear, let us go home.' 'Skipper to gunners; watch out for fighters; turning port !!!'

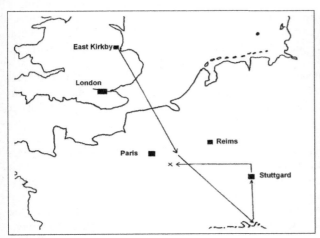

No.630 Squadron The route of ND530 P for Peter to Stuttgart and her crash. Today's monument for the crews that flew from East Kirby during WW2. (IWM, HO)

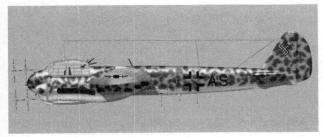

The Junkers Ju-88 night fighter, with radar arrays in de nose, machine guns and the so-called Schräge Musik' guns pointing slightly up and forward. Flying underneath a bomber it could easily finish a Lancaster in a few minutes. (Int)

Although the Germans had tried to hide the town under a thick layer of artificial smoke all bombs hit the target as planned. Large fires and explosions were seen. Barnes, and lonely rear gunner Sergeant Fox, who had a grandstand view of the old city from his confined turret, did not want to think of the people below. They were bloody Germans, who started all this themselves when they attacked the Poles.

But the attack failed to achieve the desired results. Adverse winds delayed the opening of the attack. These winds caused the Pathfinder markers to fall well short of the target, despite the clear weather conditions. Only the first bombs came down in the city centre, and 88 people were killed and 203 injured. It was 0013 hrs. before the people of Stuttgart heard the last bombers disappear westwards. There were large fires. The famous Akademie had been destroyed. Pilot Officer Barnes felt great relief while he turned this bomber for home. Nothing better than back to East Kirby. None of the crew could possibly know what fate had in store for them that night. In the darkness a Ju88 night fighter of III./NJG4 picked up the trail of P for Peter and tried to catch up with her. The German is armed with Schräge Musik, two guns, pointing up from the fuselage of the Ju88. It was a deadly weapon against bombers flying home unaware of the attacker. The Junkers approached the Lancaster until it flew about 100 feet below and 50 feet behind the bomber. While the crew of 'Peter' thought of home and a good cup of tea, the decisive moment arrived. The night fighter struck like lightning, its guns raking the bomber's fuselage. Immediately the oxygen supply system and hydraulics were damaged. Mid-upper gunner Overholt was killed instantly [49].

A Lancaster in serious trouble.
With the elimination of the hydraulics, necessary to operate the turrets, it was no longer possible to use the .303 machine guns effectively. Flying Officer Geisler was wounded badly and he was unable to navigate the aircraft home. Desperately Len Barnes tried to escape the enemy. But at 24,000 feet, another attack followed. This time the Junkers used its nose armament. In his cramped rear turret Sergeant Fox is helpless, dying in a hail of bullets [50]. Barnes tried to get away from the night fighter by making a corkscrew, a violent evasive manoeuvre to surprise the enemy and escape its fire. However, the flames streaming from 'Peter' made the Lancaster an easy target. The Junkers returned for the third time. Again, the Lancaster shivered while the shells exploded. The fourth attack finished the bomber, with the starboard engines both on fire.
Len Barnes knew that there was no chance of surviving this ordeal. The only thing was to save the rest of his men. Barnes ordered them to abandon the aircraft as long as it was possible. With his intercom out of service he could only shout and gesture to his crew. First Walker, Plowman, Gregg and Geisler bailed out.

Then, as soon as he knew that no one alive has remained on board, Barnes too bailed out. Many years later, when talking to the author, Barnes recalled: 'The last thing I remember is the blow I got when I hit the bomb aimer's device on my way out through the forward hatch. For a moment I must have lost consciousness. However, while tumbling through the cold air I came to my senses again and fell down earthwards with my parachute still closed.' After pulling the D-ring Barnes felt the painful jerk of the canopy opening. Slowly he floated to earth. In the air he could see 'Peter' exploding on impact about three miles away. The orange glow of the fire lit the hillside. It would not be long before the Germans would come to search the area for survivors or bodies. Then Barnes hit the ground. He landed near Dravigny in the Aisne department. The silence of the area was frightening. The only thing Barnes heard was the sound of engines; they were Lancasters and Halifaxes flying back to England.

Barnes' Lancaster 'P-Peter' (ND530) had been shot up by Oberleutnant Dietrich Schmidt of 8/NJG1 (8th Squadron of Night Fighter Group 1) who recorded his attack as having taken place approx. 00.56 hours at 6,300 metres altitude to the West of Reims, he crippled the Lancaster. The rest of the crew bailed out while ND530 crashed at St. Gilles (Marne) on the west bank of the River Ardre, ± 24 km west of Reims, 'Freddy' Fox and Jim Overholt the gunners are buried in St-Gilles Churchyard. George Plowman, a leather worker from London was captured wounded, Gregg, a Nottingham clerk, was also captured on 15 March. He was wounded in his hand and Malcolm Geisler a Manchester salesman, the third to be captured near Crugny. He was also wounded. Having recently celebrated his 24th birthday Len Barnes recalled that on their 5th operation 'P-Peter' was attacked from below, the hydraulics were shot away

_____
[49] *Sergeant James Henry Overholt, Royal Canadian Air Force, R/197141.*
[50] *Sergeant Thomas Austin Fox, Royal Air Force (Volunteer Reserve) 1433606.*

and both turrets put out of action. During continued attacks his gunners worked their guns manually but he believed that his rear gunner had been wounded and ordered him to jump out before going into a 360 mph dive to 12,000 feet to try to shake off the fighter. Realising that both starboard engines had been badly hit and were ablaze and the rudder controls badly damaged he repeated the order to his crew to jump out before attempting unsuccessfully to clear the nose escape hatch himself. After hitting the bomb sight he regained his senses tumbling through the night sky and pulled the ripcord.

Thomas Fox was called 'Freddie' Fox by his friend after the then famous British jockey Frederick Sidney Fox (1888-1945). He was a British Classic winner in his early twenties, but it was not until the last quarter of his thirty-year career that he had his greatest successes. He became the British flat racing Champion Jockey in 1930, making him one of only three jockeys to interrupt Gordon Richards' three decade run as champion and won two Derbies on Cameronian in 1931 and Bahram in 1935. He narrowly missed out on the British Triple Crown. He was ranked the 20th best jockey of the 20th century by Britain's industry paper, the Racing Post.

On the website of No.630 Squadron Fox was remembered by his younger brother Roy, who said: 'The following information was kindly passed on from Thomas Fox's brother Roy: 'Tom was my eldest brother and he was killed in March 1944 when he was 21 and I was 8. He was the eldest and I was the youngest of six children. I did not know Tom very well because he had joined the RAF in May 1941 when I was only 5 and I had always had more contact with my two sisters than our three older brothers. However, I know that he was very sporty, fit and strong. He was a keen amateur boxer and sparred with well-known Midland champions in the late 1930s. Tom left school at 14 and trained as a butcher under my father, who was a Master Butcher with a business in partnership with his brother in Stourbridge Market and a shop in Kinver. Tom went on to work for the famous local company of meat purveyors, sausage and pie manufacturers, Marsh & Baxter, before developing an interest in the Air Training Corps and leaving the meat trade to work at RAF Hartlebury.

He volunteered for war service and joined the RAF in May 1941, firstly as a motor cyclist and despatch rider before training for air crew and gaining promotion to Sergeant in August 1943. He wanted to be a pilot but at only 5 feet 1½ inches in height, he was considered too short and trained as a gunner. His regular letters to my sister, who was in her mid-teens at the time show him to be a very affectionate, caring and amazingly mature young man who enjoyed life and had many friends and interests. He worked very hard on courses to gain his promotions and showed great determination. He clearly understood the difficulties at home with businesses to run with my two other brothers also by this time having joined up, and with young children to look after and for all of my adult life I have wished I could have known him better. My father died within three years of Tom's death and I have often wondered how things would have been for our family if Tom had survived. In his letters he mentioned his fellow crew members: Canadian Jim Overholt and George Plowman. He also mentioned reaching the finals of the fly-weight division of an inter-squadron boxing tournament in March 1943. In letters he received he was often addressed as Freddie as were others with the surname Fox at that time, after the famous jockey of the 20s and 30s.'

P for Peter had done only seven sorties when it crashed: 30/01/44 Berlin, 15/02/44 Berlin, 19/02/44 Leipzig, 24/02/44 Schweinfurt, 25/02/44 Augsburg 01/03/44 Stuttgart and 15/03/44 Stuttgart again. A Gendarmerie report said the Lancaster crashed at Mont-sur-Courville, close to Saint-Gilles (Marne), 24 km west from Reims. A rough translation of this reports said: 'March 16, 1944 around one o'clock an English four engine plane was shot down on the territory of the commune of Mount-on-Courville (Marne) but close to the borders of the department of Aisne. Two bodies were discovered in the remains of the plane, scattered in the fields. The other crew members had escaped by parachute. One of the surviving crew who was slightly wounded, took refuge at the commune of Crugny (Canton of Fismes), while another was discovered towards Fere-en-Tardenois by the Feldgendarmerie of Chateau-Thierry.'

Barnes' aircraft was not the only one lost this night. 27 Lancasters and 10 Halifaxes were shot down. Two Lancasters made a forced landing in neutral Switzerland.

On 11th November 1942 James Henry Overholt joined the RCAF. He was a 19 year old worker in a munition factory who lived in Eastwood in Ontario. The bodies of Mid-Upper Gunner Sgt James Henry Overholt RCAF, age 20 bottom left) and Rear Gunner Sergeant Thomas Austin Fox, age 21,(bottom right) were buried after the Germans found them. (HO /Walker/JG)

Immediately after landing Len Barnes buried his parachute, his Mae West, harness and the tops of his flying boots. His whole body hurt and one eye was swollen. While he tried to figure out where he was, he smoked a cigarette, before setting off for the first leg of his escape. It was 0130 hrs. After about a mile he saw a second parachute hanging in a tree. Dragging it clear he buried it, but in the excitement of the moment he forgot to look for a name on the chute. Hence, he has no clue if this was one of his crew. Unaware of the fate of his fellow crewmembers, Flight Engineer Sergeant Kenneth Walker landed safely too. 'Being the Flight Engineer I stood in the aircraft next to the Skipper, in front of the bomb aimer and navigator. Therefore, I was the nearest to the forward escape hatch. It was my task to open the hatch in case of an emergency. It also meant that I would have to be the first to jump.' Walker landed in a small forest. His parachute draped over the treetops with Walker dangling underneath, there was still over ten feet between him and the French earth.

Finally, Walker managed to unlock his harness and hit the ground very hard. Then he ran away as fast as he could. Maybe, if he had waited a while, he might have joined his pilot when Barnes arrived on the scene, finding Walker's parachute dangling from the tree. As it was pitch dark between the trees Walker had great difficulty in getting away. Every time branches hit his face, he realised he had to evade capture. He hid his Mae West in the bushes and using the small compass from his escape kit he headed west, taking care to stay within the confines of the trees. When dawn broke Walker reached the edge of the forest. As it was dangerous to walk around in RAF uniform in broad daylight, Ken decided to hide for the time being. In front of him was a large plain with meadows and fields, without a living soul to see. Once he had got a hold of himself Walker decided to try and cross it, rather than stay here for the next twelve hours.

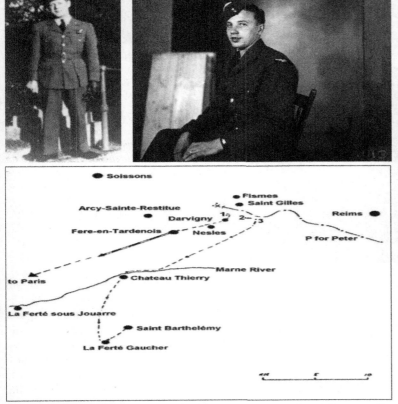

Top left: Flying Officer Geisler RAF. The centre picture shows Sergeant Overholt posing in his uniform with the white cap flash of an airman under training. His death was reported in the local newspaper. The last flight of ND530 P for Peter —•—•—•. The. X shows the crash site. 1. Landing of Pilot Officer Barnes. 2. Area where Geisler was captured. 3. Landing of Sgt Walker and his evasion. 4.Railway line Fere-en-Tardenois. 5. Ken Walker went into hiding on a farm in Saint Barthélemy The death of James Overholt was reported in the paper. As the family belonged to the Woodstock community, a loss like his made a deep impact in his hometown.

After a long walk he reached a little shack, in which French farmers kept their tools. Here Walker rested while he contemplated his next steps: 'I was alone. I was in RAF uniform. I spoke no French. I knew no one in the resistance. I had been told that the best way to evade capture was the go to Spain. I knew that it would be impossible to succeed if I did not find people who would be willing to take the risk helping me. On the other hand, the idea of being a captive of the Germans did not appeal to me either. There was no reason why I should not make it difficult for them to get me. So, I decided that this was what I was going to do: Walker was to walk to Spain.'

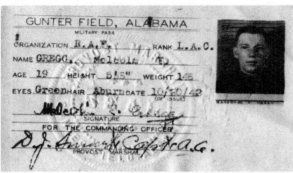

Clockwise: In August 1943 Leading Aircraftman Malcolm Gregg was posted to Gunter Field in Alabama to receive his training. After he finished this he went to England to become the bomb aimer in the crew of Len Barnes. Seated second from right bomb aimer Sergeant Malcolm Elliott 'Ginger' Gregg. He spent the rest of the war in Stalag Luft 1 Barth at the Baltic Sea. (PG/BL)

While Barnes and Walker started their escape, the Germans sent a platoon from nearby Fismes to find the remains of the shot down bomber. Upon arrival at the burnt out wreck of Peter, they found the bodies of Fox and Overholt. The next day the Germans returned with three captured crew members, Plowman, Geisler and Gregg. The prisoners were told to identify the two bodies. They told the Germans that the bodies were those of Sergeant Fox and Pilot Officer Barnes[51]. A German NCO wrote the details down and then allowed the villagers to bury the men at St. Gilles village cemetery, where their remains still rest today. The prisoners were then escorted away from the site. After a brief interrogation they were sent to Oberursel, where the Luftwaffe interrogated them further before locking them up in one of the many camps in Germany[52].

No. 630 Squadron also lost Lancaster III, ND583 (LE–V), attacked by Hauptmann Ludwig Meister of 1/NJG4 (1st Squadron of Night Fighter Group 4), who attacked at 01:30 hours, altitude 6,300 metres, west of Laon and out of control it crashed and exploded with great force at Besme near Bourguignon-sous-Courcy, 23 km north-west of Soissons. The entire crew were killed and after a hasty burial in shrouds by the Germans, were almost immediately reburied properly in coffins in the local churchyard by the

---

[51] *Barnes was trying to evade capture, so he needed time to put more distance between himself and the site of the crash!*

[52] *For more information on Oberursel see appendix G and H.*

French people. Meister was a Luftwaffe night fighter ace and this was his second victory of the night. The whole crew was killed:

Pilot Officer	Kenneth Rodbourne	169004	RAFVR Pilot	22
Sergeant	Albert Henry Wilkinson	1622716	RAFVR Navigator	20
Flight Sergeant	Leslie Hall,	1495938	RAFVR Mid Upper Gunner	23
Sergeant	Frank James Hobbs	1262633	RAFVR Wireless Operator/Air Gunner	35
Flight Sergeant	Ernest John Philipson	418299	RAAF Rear Air Gunner	25
Warrant Officer Class II	Alexander Mc Cowan Freeman	R/160030	RCAF Bomb Aimer	24
Sergeant	Richard John Harry Easter	1636431	RAFVR Flight Engineer	21

They rest in graves 1-7 at Bourguignon-sous-Soucy Churchyard, the only RAF casualties.

Left: The spot where F/O Geisler was arrested has changed little since 1944. The crash site of ND530 'P for Peter.' Right: When he visited the crash site, the author found various bits and pieces of Barnes' Lancaster. (HO)

Home in England; what happend to our boys?

In England ground crews and station personnel anxiously awaited the return of the bombers. It had been a dire night for the RAF. No less than 36 aircraft were missing, one of them being 'P for Peter.' When Barnes' aircraft was declared missing, his squadron commander had the task of informing the next of kin. A telegram arrived at the house of Walker's parents: 'I am very sorry to have to inform you that your son, 1583707 Sergeant Walker, has been missing since the night of 15/16 March. Please accept my feelings of sympathy. Letter follows. As long as no news has been received from the Air Ministry you are not to inform the press. Officer Commanding No. 630 Squadron.'

The next day Wing Commander Geat wrote a personal letter to his parents:
'With great sorrow I have to write you and confirm my telegram that your son, Sergeant Kenneth Arthur Walker, has not returned from operations during the night of 15/16 March 1944. He was the Flight Engineer in an aircraft, which took part in an attack against Stuttgart. As our aircraft maintain radio silence after take-off, it is impossible to say why his aircraft has not returned. Your son was an experienced Flight Engineer and a member of an excellent crew, which already carried out many successful sorties against the enemy. I have full confidence in the captain, Pilot Officer L.A. Barnes who will, as I know, do everything possible to ensure the safety of his crew. Of course, there is a possibility that the crew managed to abandon the aircraft and land safely in enemy territory. If this is the case, as we all hope, you will be informed through the International Red Cross in due course. Please allow me to express my sympathy and that of the members of the Squadron during the coming days. I would like to explain the reason for the request I put to you in my telegram. It intends unwanted publicity to prevent a possible attempt by your son to escape. It does not intend to withhold any information, but to ensure the safety of anyone missing. His personal belongings will be sent as soon as possible. All information regarding the missing crew and their aircraft will be forwarded to you via the Air Ministry. However, should you receive news through other channels, I would like to hear from you. If, in the meantime, there is anything I can do for you, please do not hesitate to let me know.'

In the days after the next of kin of the crew received the sad news of the crash of their sons' aircraft, they started to write letters to the other bereaved family members. This way they tried to support each other while hoping for news that was to tell them that their loved ones were still alive and well. Sadly, after a while they received the dreaded telegram of a confirmed death or a second letter by the Commanding officer of the Squadron. He might be able to tell them a little more about the mission the crew had participated in. First there would be hope that the boys were alive and well, a prisoner of war or a fugitive, hiding with French patriots. Today it is touching to read these letters more than 75 years later, after the authors managed to contact the next of kin, about sons or daughters, or more distant relatives, searches were made in attics, opening old boxes and reading letters and watching pictures of a long time ago. The letters often show the courage and resilience of those in England and the Commonwealth, waiting for news.

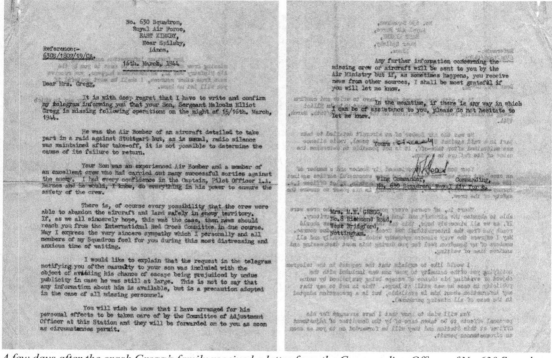

A few days after the crash Gregg's family received a letter from the Commanding Officer of No.630 Squadron. The situation was grave, but not hopeless, he said. (PG)

While the relatives and friends of hundreds of RAF aircrew had to face the fact that the worst may have happened to their loved ones, Barnes and Walker struggled to stay out of the hands of Germans and Milice [53]. With his wounded eye now virtually closed Barnes reached a hamlet. In the dark he found a cistern and washed his eye and his face. However, while he washed and drank from the water, he made too much noise. A dog in a nearby farm barked so ferociously that Barnes hurried away from the hamlet. After continuing to walk for almost an hour Len Barnes reached a farm near Cohan. His watch showed the time as 0530. In the distance he saw a farmer leading his horses towards the stables. Barnes waited until the farmer had gone into the house before daring to sneak into the barn. Exhausted and full of emotions the pilot hid in the hay and soon fell asleep.

Not until half past ten in the morning did the sunlight and the sound of people wake him up. Cautiously he crept out of the haystack to check on his map where he was. Suddenly he saw the farmer standing in

---

[53] *Milice: Vichy French para-military organization. The members of the Milice especially chased members of the resistance, Jews and allied aircrew. They were brutal and much hated by the French population.*

front of him. Barnes could do little else then say that he was a British pilot on the run. The man looked at Barnes, recognized the uniform and immediately knew that this stranger must be from the aircraft he heard and saw go down last night. He put a finger over his mouth and indicates to Barnes that he must get back into the hay. After a few minutes, the farmer returned, bringing a loaf of bread and a bottle of red wine. He washed Barnes' eye again and, while he said something in French, pointed at the haystack again. With a friendly smile the farmer left Barnes and disappeared. A little later two men entered the barn and showed Barnes his position on a map. At 1500 hours a young woman came into the barn. Speaking English with a French accent she interrogated the pilot. She told him what would happen if he was not who he claimed to be. The French had no mercy for infiltrators.

Further she wanted him to stay hidden for as long as it took, even if he had to wait for days. Under no circumstances was he to leave this spot. Barnes nodded; remembering what the Station Intelligence Officer had said: 'If you are met by the resistance, do exactly as they tell you. Do not question their plans, give them all they need to establish your identity. Their greatest fear is infiltration by the Germans. They will kill you if they are not sure about your identity. Do not argue with them. They are your only chance of success.' That evening a man came to see Barnes. The resistance was satisfied that he was an RAF officer and they were ready to take him under their wings. Having made sure that Barnes was a genuine fugitive he shook hands with the young Englishman, and gave him a beret and an overcoat. Then he produced something from under his coat that Barnes never expected to see: a bottle of the finest whisky! After a few drinks Len followed the Frenchman from a distance. With overcoat and beret he looked more or less a like a peasant. After an hour the men arrived at the door of a farm, called Le Reray. Somewhat secluded, close to the forest, this seemed to be a good place to hide the fugitive. The farmer was called Pierre Martin.

Letters sent by Mrs Barnes and Mr. and Mrs. Plowman after they had been informed of the crash of the aircraft with their sons had not returned.

Ken Walker also desperately tried to stay out of German hands. For days he walked south without any help. To feed himself he stole carrots and turnips from the fields. He drank water from ponds and streams, purified with the tablets from his escape kit. He still hoped to get in touch with members of the resistance but frankly, he believed the chance was very remote. During the first day of his escape, he met a French farmhand. The man spoke practically no English. Yet he felt that the young stranger was desperately looking for help. Producing some bread and wine from his haversack he shared it with Walker. When the Englishman showed him his silk escape map, the Frenchman pointed out where the fugitive was. He advised Walker to avoid towns and villages at all cost. And something must be done to disguise the flyer. With flying boots, RAF uniform and white woollen pullover Walker did not look like the average Frenchman. Without saying anything the Frenchman shared his meagre ration of bread, cheese and wine with the fugitive. He also gave him a jar with jam. Then the man stood up, said goodbye and left Ken.

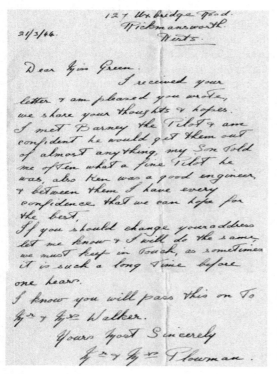

Top: The parents of Ken Walker received a letter from the RAF Benevolent Fund, expressing their regret and the chance that he had saved some money and telling them that financial support would be given. The parents of Plowman sent a letter saying how much the crew trusted their 'skipper' and how they 'hoped for the best'.

When evening fell Walker made a bed of grass, leaves and branches and camouflaged his hiding place as best as he could. The next morning, he set off for another day of walking. While Walker started the first part of his evasion, Len Barnes was still hiding at the farmhouse. Not long after dark a middle-aged Frenchman approached Barnes' hiding place. He asked Len to identify himself again. Ken Walker slowly moved south, to Spain, it was a terribly long way and Walker knew that he was very unlikely to make it without the help of the resistance. His first setback came at the end of the third day of his lone journey. When he tried to find a hiding place, he stumbled over some roots and fell flat on his face. The jam-jar breaks into pieces and covers Walker's white pullover with a large, red, sticky stain. During a very cold night with hardly any sleep, Walker came close to giving up and reporting himself to the nearest police station or German post. Yet he pressed on, using his map and compass, until he finally reached the bank of the river Marne. He spotted an angler, but was afraid to approach as the man was dressed in a green uniform and black boots. With no real food since yesterday morning and terribly thirsty Walker was very weak. He had only eaten a few raw Brussels sprouts and a Benzedrine tablet. When he approached a village at the riverside he found a small house. Desperate and exhausted Walker knocked on the door. After a while, a man opened it. Walker points at his uniform, especially his Flight Engineer's wing. The man turned his head back into the house and shouted something in French. Two other men came out of a room and gave Walker an amazed look. Soon a woman with her child joined the three.

The men pulled Walker's arm and took him into the kitchen. While they spoke French among each other the woman broke big lumps of bread and gave it to Walker. She brought out her food reserves, putting everything on the table, all the time pointing at her mouth and stomach. Meanwhile one of the men returned with a coat, a beret and a large razor blade. In no time Ken Walker looked like a fairly decent person again. Then the woman, with a very worried face, pointed at the red stain on Walker's white pullover, wanting to know how he had been wounded and tried to explain that she should bandage it.

The parents of sergeant Fox replied to a letter of sympathy written by the parents of Ken Walker

Top: *They had no idea that Sergeant Walker had found a hiding place at the farm of the Théveniault family in the village of Saint Barthelémy. This unique photo was made during his stay and shows Ken standing second from right with Mr. and Mrs. Théveniault, and family with Mrs. Terlet seated.*

Left: *A letter Mr. Greisler to Mr. and Mrs. Walker.*

For the first time the tension broke when Walker explained that it is strawberry jam! Almost hysterically the four French people and the Briton laughed as the woman took the pullover away for a wash. Shortly after midnight Walker left the house, grateful for what the good people had done for him. He passed the rest of the time in the forest, spending the night trying hard to find a safe place to cross the river. Following a railway, he reached another village. Again, he knocked on the door and once again simple people supplied him with a meal.

Having changed his identity Sergeant Walker became a French farmhand. Living as a member of the Théveniault family war seemed remote and life almost idyllic in the countryside. Provided with excellent papers Ken Walker was now a skilled worker, who could not be spared from the farm, not even to go and work in the German war industry. The Théveniault family had themselves photographed with Arthur Pierrot/Walker in the middle of a happy group of people. Years later Walker said: 'If there is one thing that will always stay in my mind, it is the bravery, the hospitality and the kindness of simple French people, working class folk like me. They never gave me away, they shared food with me and gave me clothing. They refused the money I carried in my escape kit. They were tremendously good to me.' Sometimes fear was noticeable; then people quickly handed over some food and locked their doors again. Most of the time Ken avoided contact to make sure that the people would not be compromised by his presence. In spite of the dangers, he had to endure Walker remembered funny incidents. He once got a shock when at night he walked into a group of cows, mistaking them for a German patrol. But after another cold night Walker decided to try and enter the city of Château-Thierry.

Left: On 16 March 1944 Sergeant Walker's parents got the sad news that their son was 'Missing from operations on the night of 15/16th March 1944. Right: On 11 September 1944 they received another telegram. This time it is was much better news: Ken had safely returned to the United Kingdom. (Walker)

A bit more daring than before he crossed the bridge and walked into town. Going through he saw German guards in front of the Ortskommandantur, the German Town Headquarters, their vehicles and the columns of infantry marching through the streets of Château-Thierry, singing German songs. He also saw how the French acted as if there are no Germans around. With all the enemy soldiers so near, Walker felt it was better to leave the town again and seek refuge in the country. Strolling out of Château Thierry he headed for the south. By now he had covered about thirty miles since he landed by parachute near Saint Gilles. He had no idea that he was not the only crewmember at large. After hours he saw a man chopping wood by the roadside. The man looked at Ken Walker without speaking merely pointing him in the direction of a nearby farm, then following Walker. Then he gestured that Walker must knock on the door. No sooner had he done this when the door opened and a woman looked at him. At the same time a tall man entered the corridor and addressed Walker in fluent English: 'OK, mate. Who are you, where do you come from, how did you get here, can you identify yourself?' Before Walker could answer the lady took him to the kitchen, helped him to take off his boots and washed his sore, blistered feet in warm water.

After Walker's answers appeared to have satisfied the tall guy, he took the phone and spoke in fluent French to someone on the other end. At the end of a long conversation, the man said to Walker: 'I will help you; you are in good hands here. Sleep, rest and stay away from the windows. Leave everything to me and get rid of your RAF stuff.' Then he left, closing the door. Soon Ken Walker was sound asleep in a white, soft bed. All the tensions of the last few days had exhausted him so much that all he wanted was to sleep and sleep and sleep. While he recovered, his hosts organized his further escape. Walker's identity was checked and confirmed. Now was the time to put the wheels of the resistance in motion. A day later a car arrived; with a brief handshake the driver, Mr. Reignier, met the host, and had a long talk. Then Walker was called and introduced to Reignier, who asked him to get dressed and take the road to the village of Saint Barthélemy. Reignier was to follow by car and pick Walker up, as if he was a hitch-hiker. Sitting in the back of Reignier's little truck Walker was taken to a garage, which belonged to Reignier. A few days later, his feet recovered, dressed in more suitable civilian clothing, Flight Engineer Sergeant Kenneth Arthur Walker RAF(VR), reached his destination. He arrived at the farm of the Théveniault family in Saint Barthélemy. From that moment on he was Arthur Pierrot, born in Nantes on 12 May 1923, farm labourer, deaf and mute. Life on the farm seemed as if there was no war.

The perfectly forged Carte d'Identité of Kenneth Walker, farmhand.
Name: Pierrot. First name(s): Arthur.
Profession: Farm hand.
Born 12 May 1923 Nantes.
Address: Place de l'Hotel de Ville at Laichaut.
Nationality: French.

Walker signed this ID card as all French people do, last name first, followed by his first name. His description says: Length: 1 meter 62 cm. Hair: Brown. Beard: None, Forehead: High, Eyes: Blue, Nose: Medium, Face: Round, Skin: White.
The card is numbered 301 and signed by the Deputy-Chief of Police, on 24th May 1944.

A town stamp and a 13 Francs seal make the ID Card official. At the bottom right side, we see two fingerprints of Ken Walker/Arthur Pierrot. It is interesting to know that Pierrot is the French word for Clown. Everyone knew that the deaf and mute farmhand Arthur Pierrot was not a Frenchman but an airman. After the war Ken returned to his hosts, as we will see later in this book.(Walker).

For ten days Pierre and his family shared their food and house with the Briton. The relative safety of the silence and quietness made Len almost believe that the war was far away. There are no Germans to be seen anywhere. Pierre Martin even took Barnes to the site of the crash. Yet the peace in which Len Barnes thought to be dwelling was deceptive. At night he heard the bombers, during the day saw fighters. The Germans were still looking for the two bodies missing after they had counted the dead and the prisoners. In ever decreasing circles they scoured the countryside. After their efforts met with failure, they decided to try again. At Le Reray the phone rang. The voice of an exited woman said that the Boches[54] had sent a special detail to Dravigny. No one knew why they returned, but they had dogs and they started from where the British bomber crashed a few days ago. Had one of the captured crew members said too much, or had there been a villager who could not keep mum? Martin decided that Le Reray was no longer safe.

During the late evening of 25 March, a guide lead Barnes through the fields to the cemetery of Nesles, a village near Fère-en-Tardenois. He told Barnes to stay there and wait. 'Someone will come to collect

---

[54] Boche: French equivalent of Jerry, Hun or Kraut.

you, wait and stay here!' The man disappeared in the darkness. Barnes was on his own again. It was almost midnight when Len noticed people at the cemetery. Dark figures moved between the head stones. Were the Germans on his heels? Then a French voice said: 'Allo, Tommy, where are you?' Len replied: 'Here!' A few men appeared from the dark, carrying Sten guns[55]. They were the Maquis, the French resistance. Their leader, a tall man, told Barnes to follow him and his men at a safe distance. The group sneaked through a narrow country lane. High in the sky they heard the sounds of aero engines. The RAF was on its way to a target. What would they have told his parents back home and how would Merville cope with the disappearance of her fiancé? Suddenly Barnes saw the men dive into a ditch for cover. Without hesitation the Englishman followed suit. Out of the darkness came the sound of field boots. A German patrol approached. Dead still the men waited for the enemy to pass. It was pointless to encounter the patrol. That would endanger the mission and besides, they knew that the Germans would carry out dreadful reprisals against a local village if soldiers were attacked. They waited until the sound of the knob-nailed boots disappeared. Then they continued the march until reaching Fère-en-Tardenois, where the leader of the group, Léon Coigné lived.

Léon Coigné, a French marine turned Maquisard.

The wall of the cemetery of Nesles, where Len Barnes met Léon Coigné. The Frenchman was hiding behind the wall help Barnes evade or to shoot and run away in case Len was a German agent (HO/Coigné).

Along the bank of a stream called l'Ourque stood a white house with a large garden. The garden was full of home-grown vegetables and potatoes. Chickens walked about, unaware of the day when they would end up in the pots of Mimi, Léon's wife. Four years ago, when the detested Germans had attacked France, as they did in 1914, Léon served in the navy as an aircraft mechanic. However, at the outbreak of the war he had done little work on aircraft. Sent to the front as an infantryman he killed a few Boches before the French surrendered. Coigné was furious, but like his comrades he had to accept captivity. Léon was a prisoner, but he escaped twice. He returned home and took up his old job as a plumber in a nearby factory. It looked as if for Léon Coigné the war was over. But at night there was another Léon. He ran a small resistance group called BOA[56].

At night they roamed through the fields to wait at drop zones for RAF aircraft with supplies, weapons, explosives and ammunition for the resistance. They carried out sabotage, blowing up railway bridges, telephone poles or switchboards. At times they assassinated collaborators or Germans who dared to leave the main roads, straying into the countryside. Some Germans and collaborators disappeared without a trace. Léon liked this best, for 'if there are no bodies, there are no reprisals', was his rule. The next morning tall, quiet Coigné would be back at work, always on time. No one knew of his nightly existence, no one knew of the regular radio contacts he had with London via a secret transmitter in nearby Arcy Sainte Restitue.

---

[55] *Sten guns: British made light machine guns, very popular by the resistance.*
[56] *BOA Base: Organization Aeriënne (Basis Air Organization)*

This was the man with whom Len Barnes had to stay. At first Léon was very suspicious about the identity of the young Briton who walked into his house all on a sudden, wearing a brown suit and a Basque beret. When they met again in 1974 through the services of French television Léon made a confession to Len: 'Mon ami, I was not at all pleased with your arrival. We were so busy doing our sabotage and collecting weapons from the air that we could do without you. Besides we had been warned about Germans counter agents, dressed like aircrew, speaking English fluently with British, Canadian or American accents. They told us that some of them had infiltrated the resistance and were waiting to frame us. Even if you were just a simple Frenchman, who got moved by the stories these people told and who had nothing whatsoever to do with the resistance, they would let you feed them and share your house, until they gave you away to their own people. We all knew what the Gestapo did to these people; they were executed and left behind at a street corner. I was not sure if you were a genuine Briton and I had already told my people to kill you if there was any doubt about your identity. I had instructed my people what do with you at the slightest suspicion. We already picked a place to bury you.'

Léon Coigné as a sailor 1939. The chimney where Coigné stayed for a week. The house in Fere-en-Tardenois looked exactly as in did in 1944. Len Barnes stayed in the attic, with an escape on both sides. (Coigné/HO).

Coigné had more than one reason to feel uneasy about aircrew. Before Len Barnes' arrival he hosted two Americans, crew of a bomber that had been hit over the Tardenois area. They maintained an irresponsible attitude. They scared Mimi and Léon to death by leaving the house without asking permission. They sang American songs in the garden at the top of their voices. They complained about the food, the home-grown tobacco and the wine. Finally, Léon moved them to a hideout in the forest. Two of his men had to stay with them to keep them from committing more mischief. Len Barnes is an entirely different man. He spent six weeks in Léon's house. Most of the time he sat in a chair, away from the window. He had no demands, helped in the house and kept the rules of his host. After a few weeks Léon and Mimi felt affection for the young pilot. As far as they were concerned, he could stay here until the war was over. But soon plans had to be changed. During the night of 8/9 May Léon and his men gathered a few miles out of town to await the arrival of a supply aircraft. Around midnight the rattling of machine guns was heard in the distance. The sound of the shooting even woke the people in La Cabane. Anything might have happened. When Léon failed to show up that night Mimi feared the worst.

The next morning their young daughter Christine found out what caused the uproar last night. After a successful drop, Léon and other members of BOA were returning home, tired but satisfied with the generous gifts from England. They were unaware that a German patrol had heard and seen the drop and waited in an ambush at the crossroads outside town. When the group reaches the crossing with the supplies, a hail of bullets hit them. Although the group tried to fight back they were no match for the Germans. In despair they dropped the baskets and containers and scattered. Immediately after the first rounds were fired Léon took cover in a shallow ditch. Then he quickly ran away. After a long run through the forest Léon found a hiding place inside the disused chimney of a factory.

While the Germans searched the village, Mimi was told where her husband was. With daughter Christine she took food to the factory leaving it for Léon, who dared not come out of his hiding place. He stayed there a whole week. Then the storm died down and the Germans seemed satisfied with the result of their action. Some of his friends were less fortunate. Surrounded, some wounded, they surrendered to the enemy. They are quickly rounded up, taken to prison and transported to Germany. The majority of them died in Neuengamme concentration camp. After this incident the Commander of BOA considered Coigné must leave the area. Léon was given orders to continue his work in another group. This meant that Len Barnes had to leave the house as well.

A wealthy family, called Lesguillier, was willing to help. A member of BOA, Madame Pinard, collected Barnes from La Cabane and took him to the Lesguillier house, where he met another escapee, a British airman by the name of Bill Jacks[57]. Madame Lesguillier was a bit nervous about her future with two allied airmen in her house. But Madame Pinard put her at ease: 'Do not worry, my dear. If the Germans shoot you for hiding one pilot, one more will not make any difference.' The Lesguilliers had made a hiding place at the far end of their huge back garden. It was a deep hole in the ground, covered with wood and camouflaged with earth and plants. Without a thorough search it was not possible to find the place. Barnes and Jacks stayed there for a week. Their guard was the Lesguillier son, who was hiding in order to avoid being sent to a German camp.

During the last week of May Barnes and Jacks were told that they must prepare to move elsewhere. Their stay in Fère-en-Tardenois was over; soon they would be on their way to Paris. In order not to cause any suspicion Jack, Barnes and the guide took the train to the French capital. The trip was quite uneventful until poor Bill Jacks bumped into a German officer. 'I'm so sorry', says Jacks without thinking. Barnes wished the earth could swallow him! The German however hardly looked at this stupid Frenchman and snarls: 'Mensch, sei vorsicht!' (Man be careful) and walked on.

When they arrived at the Gare de l'Est the guide from Fère-en-Tardenois disappeared into the crowd. Suddenly a complete stranger walked by, saying: 'Follow me' and took them to a house in the Trocadero area. Two days later Barnes and Jacks were separated again, as Bill was to travel south. Len moved to an apartment on the Rue Vanneau, not far from the Eiffel Tower. The house belonged to Philippe and Virginia d'Albert-Lake. Virginia was an American by birth, Philippe a Frenchman. They ran the house in a happy mood but with a strong arm. No less than twenty soldiers were hiding here. Virginia was cheerful indeed, but all the guests knew that they must obey her house rules to the letter.

A rank held no importance here. For instance, there was the Texan, a Lieutenant Colonel, who spent most of his time washing dishes after Virginia had prepared a meal for 'her children.' He had been shot down over Holland about five months ago and was still on the continent, waiting to be taken to Spain. Upon arrival Len Barnes was interrogated once more with the American staring at him. As the house was rather full, Philippe decided to make the best of things by asking questions while Barnes was seated in the lavatory. Fortunately, his answers satisfied tall Philippe. Once again, the only thing the lodgers were allowed to have was 'patience.' From time to time the men were allowed to take a walk in pairs with a guide. During one of these trips someone took photographs of the escapees. It all looked so peaceful if it was not for a German officer or soldier walking by or being photographed, having no idea that the 'Luftgangster' are also strolling around. Philippe and Virginia had taken this risk deliberately. It was impossible to keep the peace with all these men crowded together. They were all so full of energy, feeling terribly frustrated having to sit and do nothing. Most of the time everything went well.

---

[57] *Bill Jacks crossed the Franco-Spanish border on 26 March 1944. His companions were four American airmen: Julius Miller, Leslie Claude, Campbell Nelson and Meyles Sheppard.*

One day, however, one of the Americans had to run for his life when he strolled underneath the Eiffel Tower ignoring the consequent summons of the German guards. When he returned a few hours later, having been on his own and completely lost in the area, Philippe and Virginia decided that more care must be taken to avoid such silly and deadly incidents. During his time in the safe house Len Barnes also met another airman with whom he and Hubbard were to travel further south when the time was there. He was an American major, who had made a forced landing in Holland after his aircraft had been hit over Germany. His name was Don Willis and he seemed to be in a hurry to get back.

Run, run, run,
We now return to the events that started the continuing evasion to the Pyrenees of the other men. In Paris, in the safe house of Philippe and Virginia, Hubbard, Willis, Barnes and other evaders awaited developments. Two more very young airmen were due to arrive some weeks later. One was an American Second Lieutenant, Jack Cornett, who was seemingly incapable of coping with his unusual situation, the strains of which seemed to have made him totally oblivious of his surroundings and all the things happening around him. The second man was a British NCO, a Sergeant air gunner. His name was Ronald Emeny, and he still had the scars of burns, which he got when he bailed out of his aircraft. His was not fit enough to undertake the long journey to the Spanish border. It had been decided that he would have to wait until he was declared fit enough. Unaware of this, the four others waited until a decision was made about their departure. Philippe d'Albert-Lake had picked these five to form the next group that was to travel to the Spanish border in an attempt to reach freedom.

An American Lieutenant-Colonel, and an American Major, a young American 2nd Lieutenant, a British Pilot Officer and a British Sergeant waited for the last leg of their Journey to the Horizon. Hubbard had been on the run the longest time, Barnes had been a fugitive since mid-March. Ken Walker stayed with his brave hosts until the Americans liberate the area in August 1944. It was not until almost three months later, that Ken Walker's parents received a second telegram from the Royal Air Force. It was dated 9th November 1944. For six months, they had wondered in anxiety and fear about the whereabouts of their son. Like many parents, they had worried if he was dead or alive, a prisoner or an unknown flyer, buried in a corner of a cemetery in a remote village somewhere in France. We understand their joy when the telegram said that their son was alive and well, and had arrived unharmed home in the United Kingdom! What they did not know was that Ken's pilot Len Barnes by then was home in the United kingdom for some 6 months. With Len Barnes and the other fugitives departed to 'elsewhere', Léon Coigné returned to his nocturnal occupation of terrorist, as he would later call it with a smile. Again, it is quite interesting how the last weeks of occupation were spent in Fere-en-Tardenois.

On 29 August spearheads of General Patton's troops reached the Aisne area. On September 1, 1944 various resistance movements agreed to launch the slogan of general uprising. Throughout the city, from Friday evening, the Resistance attacked various designated objectives as well as the German convoys which set out for Belgium. At the same time Allied aircraft, on the prowl for Germany transport, attacked anything that moved or that was hiding, as the people of Fere-en-Tardenois found out. One day a German column was sheltering in the town. One of their vehicles had an engine problem and the retreating enemy wanted to make sure that they repaired it. Not known to them a message had been sent to Chateau-Thierry and after a couple of hours machine-gunned the convoy. One of the houses caught fire, and when the fire brigade arrived, they were threatened by the panicking German who screamed: 'Camerade brûle!'. One of the Germans had burned alive inside the vehicle. On 27 August, the Americans closed in on Fere-en-Tardenois. The first tanks of Patton's divisions were seen in the outskirts. Excited people rushed there to welcome the liberators. A large column was welcomed with flowers, kisses and bottles of wine and champagne. On the trucks and tanks were young Americans, who were happily handing out cigarettes, chewing gum and chocolate to the liberated men and women. Members of the various resistance groups started rounding up captured Germans, who were marched through the streets, while all kinds of abuses were shouted at them. Fortunately, both the Resistance and the Americans made sure that no physical harm was done to the hated enemies, who were now fearing the worst. Various websites give a vivid description of these last days, often illustrated by exiting images. Fere-en-Tardenois was finally free.

The last thing that had to be done was to temporarily bury the Americans who had been killed in de days before the liberation. They were laid to rest on the cemetery with the remains of the French soldiers killed during the Great War. A large part of the population attended the funerals. There was one last thing that was inevitable: the rounding up, judging and punishing of the collaborators and the girls who had been the lovers of German soldiers. There were no killings, but the poor girls were all humiliated and had their heads shaved as a token of their sins...

On 28 August 1944, units of the American Third Army under General Patton liberated Fere-en-Tardenois after RAF Spitfires strafed and bombed a German column trying to escape through the town. After the attack a destroyed 88m gun, one of the most feared pieces of German artillery is smouldering along the road, while the charred body of a German soldiers lies inside the armoured vehicle. A few hours later the Americans entered Fere-en-Tardenois.

The resistance with René Coigné in charge of one of the units, attacked the retreating Germans while the Americans supported the French Maquis. After Fere-en-Tardenois had been liberated the last Germans were rounded up by the Resistance and marched through the Rue Carnot in the town. The war was finally over for the people of Fere-en-Tardenois. (AFeT).

5. TELL MY WIFE I'M OK.

Flying a desk…

At the end of April 1943, Don Willis left 4th Fighter Group. He was posted to a unit that was to evaluate and improve American fighter tactics and to see if these tactics could be used to avoid the losses during dogfights over Occupied Europe. Being a staff officer now, Willis was not pleased. He said: 'I am here to fly a fighter, not a desk. I want to wear my flying kit and not my Pinks'.

Major Don Willis had to fly a desk and suddenly lost his major aim in life: flying aircraft on a daily basis. He made the best of his involvement in experiments with the P-38 Lightning as a bomber, leading the other aircraft with a bombardier flat in the Perspex, unarmed nose.
For Willis it was a compensation for loss of combat thrills. Here we see him behind his desk; a black cigar in his hand. (PW)

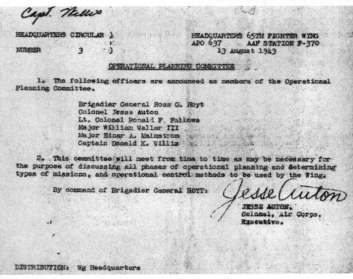

In August 1943 Captain Donald K. Willis became a member of a special 'Operational Planning Committee' of 65th Fighter Wing. Their main job was to discuss 'all phases of operational planning and determining types of missions, and operational control methods to be used by the Wing'.
Willis saw a glimmer of operational flying at the horizon, which came when he transferred to 67th Fighter Wing. (PW)

Don Willis had done a lot of writing to convince top brass that it was time to put Droop Snoot to the test. In February 1943, he wrote a report to Brigadier General Hunter, explaining his ideas. He was convinced that the enemy would get the scare of a lifetime when the P-38, called 'Gabelschwanzteufel' (Twin-Forked Devil), by the Germans, was used as a fighter-bomber. He pressed for speed and suggested putting bombs under the Lightnings as quickly as possible, sending them to strategical targets and then use the P-38, with its high speed of over 440 mph and murderous nose guns, with a 20mm gun and four .50cal machine guns, as a fighter. The General answered with a friendly letter, but at the same time he turned down the suggestion in a letter stamped 'Secret' saying: 'To 1st Lieutenant Donald K. Willis AAF Station F356 APO 637, US Army. Your splendidly prepared letter and chart of 24 February 1943, has been studied with great interest by me and the members of my staff, and it is with great regret that at this time difficulties present themselves, which force me to deny your request. In the first place we are doing all we can to get our new groups operational. Experienced personnel are very valuable to us. I would not wish to risk the loss of your services in your present capacity to carry out a special and individual project. Secondly, there are no P-38 aircraft available for this use by this Command and thirdly, at present our principal mission here is the protection of our bombardment aircraft. In the future we may wish to expand our operations to that of fighter-bomber. It may be interesting for you to know that the P-38 aircraft has proven itself highly effective in similar operations undertaken in the African theatre. I wish to commend you on your keenness and the time and thought put upon these suggestions to help carry the war to the Germans. (signed) Frank O'D. Hunter, Brigadier General USA, Commanding' To hear the story of Willis we jump to February 1944, when two officers from Michigan did the first tests with the Lockheed P-38 at the test facility of Lockheed in Langford Lodge in Northern Ireland. After two years working in secrecy, they were going to test the twin-boom fighter in a dual role: that of bomber and fighter. They had been working on the project for two years, and it was time to put it to the test.

Don Ostrander (left) and Cas Hough (right) realised the big potential and tested the abilities of the Droop Snoot P-38 Lightning. (HO)

Major General Don R. Ostrander was born 24th September 1914, in Stockbridge, Michigan. A West Point graduate he had first served in the cavalry. Like so many of his brother officers he realised that the future war would be fought much higher than horse back; the battlefield was to become the air. He lobbied General H.H. 'Hap' Arnold for a transfer to the Army Air Corps. Once Arnold granted his request, he went to the 709th Aviation Ordnance Company at Langley Field, Virginia. In October 1941, he was transferred to the 726th Aviation Ordnance Company at Selfridge Field near Mount Clemens, where he met and befriended Cass S. Hough. This officer was born on 4th October 1904 in Plymouth in the state of Michigan. His grandfather started the Daisy Manufacturing Company, makers of the famous Daisy air rifle, in 1886. He graduated from Culver Military Academy in 1921. He attended the University of Michigan, graduating in 1925. He joined the family business in 1926. He was commissioned into the Army Air Corps in 1938 and stationed at Selfridge Field, where he commanded a fighter squadron until he was transferred to England and the 8th Air Force in 1941. In May 1942 Ostrander was also transferred to England where he became the ordnance and armament officer for the 8th Air Force Interceptor Command. He and Hough renewed their acquaintance and began working closely together on ordnance projects.

Droop Snoot; a new concept.
The P-38J 'Droop Snoot' project was the brainchild of Ostrander and Hough. They came up with the idea of modifying the Lockheed P-38 Lightning fighter into a lead bomber. The advantages of using a fighter as a strategic bomber were three-fold: a much higher air speed to and from the target, much fewer crew members risked in the mission, and the squadron could serve as its own fighter escort. The Modified P-38J was equipped with a Plexiglas nose cone and fitted with a top-secret Norden bombsight and body armour replacing the machine guns and cannon. The bombardier rode in the nose cone and led the bombing run; when the lead P-38J dropped its payload, so did the entire squadron. The concept was so successful that the 8th Air Force immediately ordered three, then fifteen, Droop Snoot conversions.

A total of twenty-three P-38Js were modified at Langford Lodge. The 20th Fighter Group flew the first successful combat mission 10th April 1944, when a Droop Snoot bomber led forty-two other P-38J's on an attack against the Luftwaffe base at Gutersloh, Germany. Major Don Willis, as the Tactics Evaluation Officer for 67th Fighter Wing, flew along in a P-38 as an observer. In April 1944 he found out that he badly needed these skills when he had to land in Occupied Holland.

Don Willis wants to see how it works.
It was 0530 hrs. 10 April 1944 at Kingscliffe airfield in East Anglia. During the previous evening, the airfield was a beehive of activity. Mechanics prepared P-38 fighter-bombers for a mission. The aircraft looked vicious on their tricycle undercarriages. The P-38 was a powerful aircraft and the Group using the twin-engine P-38 was proud of it. Its armament was feared for the destruction it caused. The latest model P38J had excellent range, speed and manoeuvrability. With the nature of the air war changing, less P-38s were used as bomber escort duties. Today's mission was a special one. An officer from Headquarters 67th Fighter Wing arrived the evening before and spent all night preparing for the experiment. Now Major Donald K. Willis had a chance to make his point. He was convinced that the twin-engine P-38 Lightning was an excellent aircraft for a special job. Willis' idea had found notice with the top brass.

Photographs of 'Droop Snoot' P-38 Lightnings. In the nose, room has been made for a highly accurate but highly secret Norden bombsight, to be operated by a bombardier. It seems he had very slim chances of abandoning the aircraft in case of an emergency (USAFHRC)

After several test flights in late February 1944, the new configuration was declared operational. The second crewmember would be the heart and soul of the formation around the 'Droop Snoot.' Responsible for accurate simultaneous bombing, he had to be an experienced navigator and bombardier at the same time. Once near the target he was to navigate the entire formation. Then he would order the pilots to drop their two 500 pounders, or a single 1000 pounder. This was no job for rookies. The bombardier must be a man without fear, able to endure a mission cramped in the Perspex nose of a virtually defenceless aircraft. To give the Droop Snoot P-38 some protection, a white circle was painted around the noses of all P-38s, so that the Germans could not immediately see which aircraft was the defenceless one. The bombardier in charge of the 39 aircraft of 20th Fighter Group on 10 April was 1st Lieutenant Herschel Ezell, who had flown 25 missions as the bombardier of a B-17 Flying Fortress. Major Willis also flew the mission to see if these kinds of attacks were worthwhile. As the Tactics Evaluation Officer of 67th Fighter Wing, he rather flew than wrote. Not keen to sit behind a desk and wait for the result of his ideas, he borrowed KI-X of 5th Fighter Squadron to see for himself. Major Johnson was put in charge of the mission. Once the aircraft approached the target, the pilots must wait for Ezell's orders to release their bombs. The pilots had to stay on a steady course minutes before they bombed. They needed steel nerves, for there was always a chance that the Germans intercepted the heavily laden aircraft. However, there was a greater risk for the Droop Snoot Lightning: Without weapons in the nose, it was vulnerable. Willis enjoyed flying this Droop Snoot mission. At last, he was where he wanted to be, in the air, over enemy territory!

P38J 42-68077, KI-X, at its base Kingscliffe. The nose armament is clearly visible. The black triangle shows the aircraft is of the 20th Fighter Group. This was the aircraft Willis flew on 4 April 1944. One P-38 with a Plexiglas nose, a bombardier and a Norden bombsight would make all the difference and ensure accurate tactical bombing before the aircraft would behave itself as a fighter. (Pat Willis/USAFHRC)

At 0730 hours the Lightnings took off. They had orders to bomb Florennes airfield in Belgium, using the Droop Snoot method. Of 39 aircraft 29 carried bombs, while the remaining 10 protected the bombers until the bombing. Unfortunately, the mission was a failure. Heavy overcast shielded the airfield at Florennes from providing a clear target. Major Johnson decided that it was impossible to see the result of this attack. Therefore, he ordered the pilots to return to base and drop the bombs in the Channel. Their bombs splashed harmlessly into the water in a useless pattern. The fact that one pilot claimed to have shot down an enemy aircraft failed to satisfy the others. The Americans, however, did not give up. The same morning 51 P-38s of 55th Fighter Group took off from Nuthampstead to carry out another Droop Snoot attack. Again, not all Lightnings were equipped as bombers; 34 carried bombs, 17 others escorted them while 7 P-47 Thunderbolts of 353rd Fighter Group take off from Metfield as top cover. The target was Saint Dizier airfield. Again, bad weather spoiled the attack. The formation then flew to Coulommiers airfield where they dropped 17 tons of explosives.

At the same time P47s strafed Villaroche airfield. Unfortunately 55th Fighter Group lost two aircraft, though fighters claimed two German aircraft destroyed and one damaged. The same day a third mission was ordered, this time not to attack in France. The Lightnings were sent to Germany, the target being Gütersloh airfield. Major Willis prepared to join the Group. One of the pilots, Lieutenant Robert H. Riemensnider, recalled: 'I can remember no other instance of a member of the Staff of 67th Fighter Wing actually participating in a combat mission of one of our squadrons. Most of the time they would send memos and we would carry them out. Then we would write our reports, hand them in and hear nothing of it ever again. However, in this case the officer seemed very keen to see for himself. Rumour had it that he was a very experienced fellow. We heard many wild stories of his participation in the Russo-Finnish war and of his exploits in Norway in mid-1940. We knew that he had been an ex-Eagle squadron member. He was a relatively small man, who liked his Bourbon and smoked dreadful black cigars. He did not say much; he was more of a listener. I do not think he cared much for his present job, though he was never outspoken about it. One thing was clear: he wanted something to be tried and he wanted to see it first-hand. We liked that kind of attitude.'

A lethal thread: a formation of P-38 Lightnings on its way to a target. The Germans feared these 'Tail Forked Devils' as they called these fighter-bombers. One of these aircraft might very well be a Droop Snoot; not recognizable among the other aircraft. Willis took part in such a mission of 10 April 1944. (USAFHRC)

At 1330 hours Willis and the others climbed into one of 35 Lightnings. Led by Major McAuley the aircraft took off half an hour later. Over East Anglia 46 Thunderbolts of 359th Fighter Group joined them. However, soon after they set course for Germany, 8 Lightnings abandoned the mission due to all kinds of problems. Flying in formation, the P47s covering their top, the remaining Lightnings crossed Holland and continued east. When the formation approached Gütersloh, McAuley handed over to Ezell, who was in the small nose section of the Droop Snoot Lightning, looking through his bombsight. Now all the pilots had to do was to wait for the bomb aimer's order to drop. The moment the Norden bombsight indicated the target pin-point, Ezell called over the radio: 'Go!' With great precision 13 tons of bombs fell between hangars, offices, aircraft, vehicles and runways of Gütersloh. Then the Lightnings started the second part of the mission. Relieved of the bombs they were fighters, roaring down to strafe the airfield with their nose armament, before disappearing to high altitude. Joined by the P-47s the formation returned to England. This third mission had been remarkably successful.

Back at Headquarters Major Willis could prove that the use of the P-38 for fighter-bomber duties would add to the strength of the 8th Air Force. But it ended differently. When the formation flew over the Zuiderzee in Central Holland, the voice of Major Willis sounded over the radio, reporting he had been hit in his fuel lines and was quickly losing precious juice. Oil pressure has also dropped fast. He was not able to stay with the formation. 1st Lieutenant Arthur Rowley asked Willis his position but the pilot answered that he did not know. Then Major McAuley came on the air to tell Willis that he was south of the Zuiderzee. Willis, however, believed he was north of Rotterdam. Some of the P-38s went down to find Willis but were unable to trace him. Then they heard: 'I am crossing out over the sea. Will they fish me out if I go down?' There was still a long way to fly before the aircraft reached Kingscliffe. No RAF rescue launch dared to come so close to the enemy coast. From England it was impossible to get to Willis in time. Maybe a German launch would save him if he landed near the Dutch coast! Willis did not like the idea and replied: 'I think I won't make it.' A moment later he said that he was back over land but could not get any fuel pressure. Willis' last words were: 'I'm going down over enemy territory; tell my wife I'm OK.' That was the last they heard of the Major of 67th Fighter Wing, who flew for evaluation purposes only.

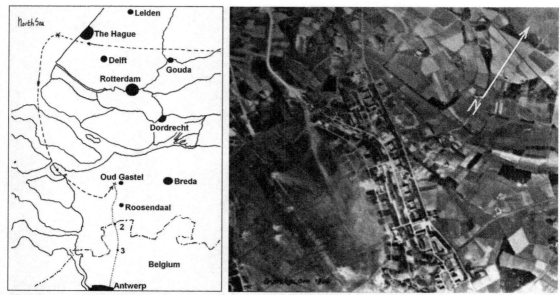

The last part of Don Willis' return flight, which ended in the south of the Netherlands. First Don tried to cross the North Sea to return to England. When this was impossible, he decided not to ditch the aircraft and risk capture by a German naval vessel before the British could snatch him away from the water. Therefore, he flew south and crossed the coast into Occupied Holland over the islands in the southwest of the country. He landed his P38 not far from a soccer-pitch north of the village of Oud-Gastel (1). After a few days with the Kuppens family he was taken to the Dutch-Belgian border at Essen (2). The Belgian resistance caught up with him north of Antwerp from where his further journey was organized. The next day a reconnaissance aircraft took this photograph of Gutersloh airfield to assess the damage (HO/NAUS).

Nothing better than a soccer match on Easter Monday.

April 10th 1944 was the second day of Easter in Holland. It was a national holiday and many people gathered at the soccer field of Oud-Gastel for an important match. On 28th March, the board of the Gastelsche Soccer Club decided that, a year late, the 10th anniversary was to be celebrated. It was to help people forget the misery of war for a few hours while watching a fair game against a worthy and strong opponent from a nearby town. The club diary: 'To celebrate the 10th anniversary a jubilee match will be played against Red-White from Sint Willibrord.' What was to be an enjoyable day with 90 minutes of the most popular sport in the Netherlands, turned into a brief time of great tension and amazing courage. But something was clearly wrong with it. While players attacked and defended and hundreds of spectators enjoyed the game, an aircraft approached in the distance. Flying extremely low over the soccer pitch came a large, twin-engine, silver bird. The engines made a strange sound and it looked as if it would not stay airborne much longer. The many spectators turned their heads towards the aircraft that seemed to prepare for landing.

Director Waalwijk of the Municipal Electricity Board of Oud-Gastel was also Head of the local Air Raid Warning Service. In his capacity as a director, he was one of the few who drove a car without having to fear the Germans commandeering it. He travelled a lot in the area, to see that nobody used power illegally and to ensure that the black-out rules were strictly kept. In reality he had arranged for secret power lines to farms to enable the farmers to use their mills to grind their wheat into flour and press their rape into oil. As Chief of the Luchtbeschermingsdienst (the Air Raid Warning Service) in this part of Holland, he had a direct responsibility to the German Town Commander in Roosendaal. He hated the Germans, but for the good cause Waalwijk was kind and courteous, always willing to be of service. Therefore, he often heard things that were not supposed to be heard. When anything of note happened Waalwijk took his job seriously. To make sure 'not to bother the Germans with trivialities', he always made an extensive enquiry before submitting a written report. Of course, this took a lot of time and often Waalwijk's reports arrived much too late for the Germans to take action. Sometimes they suspected Waalwijk of sabotage, but every time the Dutchman said that, as a civil servant, he must write reliable reports, which always takes time.

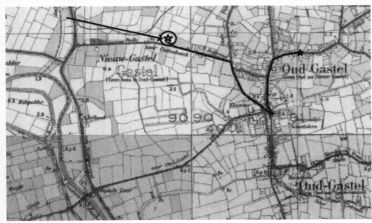

X-KI 42-68077 on the ground at Oud-Gastel. The port propeller has been torn off. There seems to be no damage to the aircraft itself. The Lightning has stopped just in front of the Bansloot, a ditch that would have caused the aircraft to break up if it had hit it.

On the right, we see the long road to town, the Rolleweg (HO/BuA From the crash site Willis was taken to the Kuppens house at the Meierstraat.

It was a good scheme and every time Waalwijk managed to slow down German reactions to any violation of law. The farmers appreciated Waalwijk's attitude, and many of them considered him a friend. When they slaughtered a pig, or if there was a little butter left, they remembered him. With the poor situation in Holland, it was nice to know people who had that little extra. This day Waalwijk and his wife were invited to call on a farmer Van Akkeren, who lived at the Zuiddijk, some distance from Oud-Gastel. Van Akkeren had promised the Waalwijks a good meal to show his appreciation. As this visit was not official, Mr. and Mrs. Waalwijk travelled by bicycle. Using a road through Koelstraat they headed for the country lane called the Rolleweg.

A visitor who wants to leave quickly.
They too had seen the aircraft coming over incredibly low with a rough engine. In the distance it had made a sharp turn, lost more height and flew straight at the couple. At hardly ten feet it roared over ploughed farmland. Terrified, the two Dutch people jumped off their bikes and took cover in a ditch.

They saw the pilot in the cockpit between the engines before the big aircraft hit the ground with a terrific crash. It bounced again, skidded over the flat Brabant clay, mud flying in all directions for about 300 yards, before coming to a halt, with its nose pointing towards Oud-Gastel, a few yards from a second wide ditch. Immediately the cockpit opened and a man jumped out. It was Major Donald Kenyon Willis. Wearing a yellow Mae West and a leather cap on his head he ran from his aircraft without even looking back, heading directly for the two Waalwijks, and asked them in English how to get to Belgium.

Without giving baffled Waalwijk a chance to answer, he rushed back to his aircraft, where he takes off his helmet, Mae West and flying overall[58]. He also retrieved what looks like a parcel from the inside of the cockpit, breaks it into two halves and stuffs it in his jacket. Then he runs back to the Waalwijks, jumps on the carrier of Waalwijk's bicycle and shouts what Mrs. Waalwijks will never forget: 'OK, let us go, go go!!' Mrs. Waalwijk speaks good English. She explains to Willis that he will never be able to escape that way. She points at an old tram carriage in a field used by the local farmers to tie down their cows during milking time. She says to the American: 'Hide inside the carriage and we will come back and help you.' Willis seemed to feel that the Waalwijks were patriots for he did exactly as he was told[59]. In the meantime, trusting that his wife does the right thing, Mr. Waalwijk raced back to Oud-Gastel, as quickly as he could. He knew where to go; to the house of Jan Kuppens, the clog maker, who is said to be in the resistance. Maybe they know what to do with the pilot. Meanwhile, the soccer pitch was virtually empty as all people hurried to the aircraft. There were no Germans yet, so maybe they could do something before they arrived. When they came near, they saw the aircraft was empty. One man found the flying helmet and put it under his coat. Another climbed on the wing and looked into the cockpit. He had no idea what all the clocks and gauges meant, but remembered many years later that some of the little lamps inside were still alight. A daring young chap even sat inside the cockpit and moved the butterfly-like controls[60].

The pilot was nowhere to be seen. Later, after his return to England Willis wrote in his Escape and Evasion Report[61]: 'I saw spectators and players run from the soccer field and at least 500 people gathering around the place where I touched down. Some of them had dropped their bicycles along the road, not far from the place where I was hiding. I went to the bicycles while they were climbing on my aircraft and took one that had a red coat tied to its carrier. I put the coat over my uniform and jumped on the bicycle. Then I rode off as fast as I could and caught up with a few cyclists who were heading away from the aircraft. We followed the road until it went up a dike then followed the dike and passed a few German soldiers who were watching the scene of the crash through binoculars. Other Germans ran, from what looked like an anti-aircraft battery, to the aircraft and started to chase the people away. I rode next to a woman who looked at me from the corner of her eyes several times, but who said nothing. She knew that I was not a local, but she never gave me away'[62]. Warned by Waalwijk, Jan Kuppens jumped on his bicycle too, taking an old raincoat with him. As Waalwijk had told him where to find the pilot, Kuppens rode directly to the carriage. But when he entered the Veerkensweg, a narrow lane that led to the carriage, he noticed movement in the bushes. Kuppens got off his bike and walked to the place where he saw the branches move. When barely ten yards from the spot a man stood up and Kuppens stared into the muzzle of a Browning pistol! Not speaking any English Kuppens put his fingers over his lips and tried to show the pilot that he had no ill intentions. After Willis left the scene of his forced landing, the first Germans arrived and began a search of the area. When they spotted a police officer among the spectators, they ordered him to act as their guide.

A long row of Germans walked through the farmland, looking in every ditch and behind every shed in the fields. They also searched the tram carriage; according to their report they found a bloody piece of

---

[58] *His flying overall now is with the Historical Circle of Oud-Gastel as is the steering wheel of the P-38.*
[59] *At that moment of course Willis' identity is not known.*
[60] *Unlike most fighter aircraft the P-38 did not have a stick but a 'spectacle grip' cantilevered control.*
[61] *See appendix.*
[62] *Willis 'story differs from the one told by the eyewitnesses in Oud-Gastel and by Mr. and Mrs. Waalwijk.*

bandage with English words on it, which they thought to be the pilot's. Willis however had long since vanished. The Germans were less than 500 yards away. For Kuppens Willis looked very odd. Over his uniform he had a civilian overcoat. Under his green trousers he had flying boots. On his face were still the marks of his oxygen mask visible. Kuppens pointed to the south, saying 'België' (Belgium in Dutch) and then shook his head. Within an hour the roads would be full of Germans trying to find the pilot. With gestures and simple Dutch words Kuppens succeeded in convincing Don Willis that he must stay where he is, put on the brown coat that Kuppens brought and get rid of the coat he is wearing. He makes the pilot understand to stay hidden for now. He will be back! Kuppens returned to his house and told his sons to come with him. Sjef, the eldest, went back to the hiding place with his father while Marinus followed a little later to make sure that no others were following.

Family Kuppens decided that to help a poor boy, scared and hungry was a duty as good Catholics. They have little to do with the Dutch resistance; like most of the people they try to survive in these dangerous times. Yet they hid Don Willis behind a pile of elm wood blocks, as Mr. Kuppens was a clog maker. 'Mother' as she is known, gave Willis a bowl of hot soup and thick buttered sandwiches with meat (Kuppens).

More than an hour had passed since Feldgendarmen [63], assisted by ordinary soldiers, arrived with dogs. They questioned people, who of course knew nothing. While the Germans searched the area, Kuppens, his son Sjef and Don Willis strolled back to the village of Oud-Gastel. The little town was and still is a typical Roman-Catholic community. It has a large cathedral, built in the late 19th century and looking far too big for its small parish. But the people of Oud-Gastel were good folk. They knew each other for many years. Members of the Dutch Nazi Party were treated with contempt. In this environment Don Willis stood a small chance of staying free. Kuppens led the way; Don followed from a distance, while Sjef, joined by Marinus, casually walked at the other side of the street slightly behind Willis. A brief moment of shock occurred when the group approached the house of the mayor in the main street. In front of the house was a German truck with a sentry. Without saying a word Marinus drew the attention of the German, standing still, walking back and walking towards the sentry once more.

Suspicious as he was in this close-knit community the German crossed the street, passed Willis and said to Marinus: 'Ausweis', schnell' (ID, quickly!). Marinus fumbled in his coat, pretending he could not find his ID card. By the time he had produced it, his father, Sjef and Don Willis disappeared around the corner near the church. From there it was a short walk to the small house where Jan Kuppens had his wooden shoe business. Mrs. Kuppens knew that Jan brought someone home. With the hospitality, for which all people from Braband Province are known, she prepared a pile of thick sandwiches, hot milk and a small piece of pork for the guest. Don however was so tense that he could hardly eat. He drank his milk and took a cigarette from Kuppens, made from home-grown tobacco that was kept the dry in the loft. 'Essen, Belgium, Essen', Willis said repeatedly. He wanted to leave as quickly as possible for he did not feel safe in the house with so many Germans around. Kuppens tried to explain to Don that he could not leave until it is dark.

---

[63] *German Military Police.*

Top left and right: Marinus Kuppens shows the place where Willis landed. The nearby road is the Rolleweg, Don Willis' escape route on a stolen bicycle. Oud-Gastel and Saint Laurentius church are hidden in the morning mist at the horizon. (HO)

This map from 1945 shows the global route Willis took the first days to walk from Oud-Gastel, via de outskirts of Roosendaal to the border post at Esschen, where he followed the road south to Kalmthout and then took the streetcar to the outskirts of Antwerp where he was recognised as a fugitive by a member of the resistance. (HO)

For the time being he kept the pilot in his shop, behind a large pile of willow wood for making clogs. Don stayed there until the early evening. When it was dark Kuppens told Willis to come out. Mother Kuppens had made more sandwiches, some apples and a small flask of coffee. She also gave Willis some Dutch money. Kuppens in the meantime drew a little sketch of the area between Oud-Gastel and the Dutch-Belgian border. He warned Willis to stay away from Roosendaal, where the Germans had a garrison. He drew Woensdrecht airfield on the map, and made sure that Willis did not enter this guarded and dangerous area. Then the moment had come for Willis to say goodbye to the Kuppens family.

It would not to be until 1985 that Willis' widow Patricia returned to the small house in the Meierstraat to meet old Mrs. Kuppens and thank her for her bravery. Since that fateful day in April Sjef had been killed in action as a soldier in the Dutch East Indies in 1947 and Mr. Kuppens had died as well. Although some time had passed since Willis left the village of Oud-Gastel, the Germans still looked for the pilot. Outraged by the sheer 'stupidity' of the villagers they decided to do a house-to-house search of the entire area around the site of Willis' forced landing. While Willis was gone the first German trucks enter Oud-Gastel. This search, called razzia[64], was causing grave problems for one of the townspeople. Interrogated by the Feldgendarmerie, a villager mentioned that he saw someone with a flying overall run away from the aircraft. When the Germans asked him if this was the pilot, the man said: 'No, it was Hoefsloot, the

---

[64] During a razzia, all people would be rounded up, regardless of age and sex. At a later stage some of them would be released. These razzias especially took place at the end of 1944 when most of the Dutch labour force had gone into hiding.

blacksmith from the Rijpenweg.' As removing enemy property was a profoundly serious offence the Germans immediately went to Hoefsloot's house. His neighbour was Mr. Waalwijk, who almost got a fit when the grey German police van stopped in front of his house. Had they seen him? Had anyone betrayed him?

There were collaborators in Oud-Gastel, as there were in every town and village in Holland. Waalwijk had taken precautions long ago. The nearby butcher Hagenaars had since put one of his ladders underneath the bedroom window of the Waalwijk house. He also prepared a hiding place in the slaughterhouse behind his shop. It is not the cleanest place, but in case of an emergency it might keep the Germans away if they came to Hagenaars. But it was too late for Waalwijk to leave the house. An escape through a bedroom window would arouse suspicion. Waalwijk decided to stay home and hope for the best. Hoefsloot however was put under arrest while Germans searched his house. They soon found the overall. 'Where is the pilot?', they shouted at poor Hoefsloot. The blacksmith swore that he

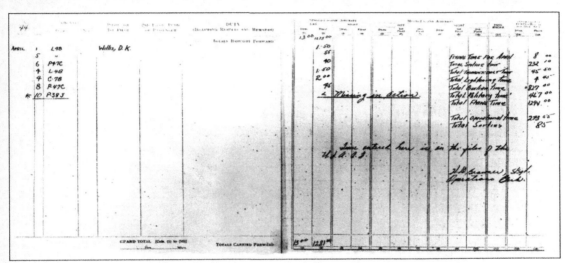

Don Willi's Logbook, saying 'April 10, P38J, missing in action.' (PW)

had no idea. He found the overall near a ditch and believed it to be a good garment for his work in the smithy; he had not thought much about it at the time, simply taking it with him. For some reason, the Germans accepted his explanation and after a stern warning they left the house and returned to their van with the overall as a prize.

In the darkness, with curfew on, Kuppens, Sjef and Don Willis left the house. After a two-hour walk Kuppens pointed east and said: 'Roosendaal.' Then he pointed to the south where the Belgian border was, shook hands with Willis and returned to Oud-Gastel. Followed by Sjef he soon disappeared into the darkness. Don Willis was on his own. Still dressed in parts of his uniform, wearing the coat that Kuppens had given him, he headed south. His journey would be dangerous, for Don Willis had no forged papers, no permit to be out at curfew, and did not speak Dutch. With his uniform as a 'security' for being recognized as an officer and not as a spy he moved through the countryside. His means of navigation were an escape kit compass, a silk map of Europe and the small map Jan Kuppens made for him.

This was how the disappeared pilot, as he was called in the report of the burgomaster of Oud-Gastel, headed for the border between Holland and Belgium. It was slow going with the border some 10 miles away. At midnight, two hours after saying goodbye to Kuppens, he was no further than Moerstraten, a hamlet about two miles west of Roosendaal, the town he had been told to avoid at all costs. Many ditches forced Willis to make detours. This made it doubly difficult to keep his general direction to the south. Late that night he reached barbed wire obstructions. Willis believed he has reached the border. He decided to look for shelter among the nearby trees and rest for a while. It was a lucky decision, for less than fifty yards away from him was a machinegun post! Three soldiers came walking along the path. They were the relief squad for those on duty. Willis dropped flat on his face and they passed him less than ten yards away. When the men had gone Willis made up his mind to follow the barbed wire away from the guard post. This took him further west than to the south. He found a haystack in an open space between two fields, crawled into the hay, ate two sandwiches, had some now cold coffee and was soon asleep.

ROLL OF HONOUR

Group Capt. P. C. Pickard, D.S.O., D.F.C.: Reported missing.

Wing Commander Patrick E. Hadow, youngest son of Mrs. Hadow and the late Rev. E. M. Hadow, of Uffington Vicarage: Reported missing since Dec., 1943.

Major Willis, U.S.A.A.F.: Reported missing from a recent mission. He is well-known in North Northamptonshire.

Graham Wallis, R.N.: Posted missing, believed killed.

Pte. Kenneth William Scott Brown, St. Ives: Killed on active service.

LISTS OF PHRASES

| FRENCH |
| DUTCH |
| GERMAN |
| SPANISH |

DUTCH

ENGLISH	DUTCH	ENGLISH	DUTCH
One	Een	Twenty	Twintig
Two	Twee	Thirty	Dertig
Three	Drie	Forty	Veertig
Four	Vier	Fifty	Vijftig
Five	Vijf	Sixty	Zestig
Six	Zes	Seventy	Zeventig
Seven	Zeven	Eighty	Tachtig
Eight	Acht	Ninety	Negentig
Nine	Negen	Hundred	Honderd
Ten	Tien	Five Hundred	Vijfhonderd
Eleven	Elf	Thousand	Duizend
Twelve	Twaalf		
Thirteen	Dertien	Monday	Maandag
Fourteen	Veertien	Tuesday	Dinsdag
Fifteen	Vijftien	Wednesday	Woensdag
Sixteen	Zestien	Thursday	Donderdag
Seventeen	Zeventien	Friday	Vrijdag
Eighteen	Achttien	Saturday	Zaterdag
Nineteen	Negentien	Sunday	Zondag
Minutes	Minuten	Week	Week
Hours	Uren	Fortnight	Twee weken
Day	Dag	Month	Maand
Night	Nacht	O'clock	Uur

ENGLISH	DUTCH
I am (we are)	Ik bent (wij zijn)
British; American	Engelsch; Amerikaan
Where am I?	Waar ben ik?
I am hungry; thirsty	Ik heb honger; dorst
Can you hide me?	Kunt U mij verbergen?
I need civilian clothes	Ik heb burgerkleeding noodig
How much do I owe you?	Hoeveel ben ik gij schuldig?
Are the enemy nearby?	Is de vijand dichtbij?
Where is the frontier?	Waar is de grens?
BELGIAN:	BELGISCH:
Where are the nearest British (American) troops?	Waar zijn de dichtst-bijzijnde Britsche (Amerikaansche) troepen?
Where can I cross this river?	Waar kan ik deze rivier oversteken?
Is this a safe way?	Is dit een veilige weg...?
Will you please get me a third class ticket to...?	Wilt U mij alstublieft een derde klas kaartje bezorgen naar...?
Is this the train (bus) for...?	Is dit de trein (bus) naar...?
Do I change (i.e. trains)?	Moet ik overstappen?
At what time does the train (bus) leave for...?	Hoe laat vertrekt de trein (bus) naar...?
Right; left; straight on	Rechtsch, linksch, rechtuid
Turn back, stop	Keer om; halt
Thank you; please	Dank U; Alstublieft
Yes; No	Ja; Neen
Good morning	Goedemorgen
Good afternoon	Goeden Middag
Evening; Night	Avond; Nacht
CONSULATE	Consulaat
Out of bounds	Verboden toegang
Forbidden	Verboden

When Willis failed to return from his mission the local paper mentioned his fate. Also mentioned is G/C Pickard, who led a group of Mosquitos on the Amiens raid, in which he was killed in action 18 February 1944. During his evasion aircrew carried a booklet with phrases that would help them communicate with locals. (IWM/PW)

Walking to Antwerp on the way to Spain.

The next morning the rising sun woke Willis up. The world looked so peaceful here. However, the American had no time to watch the sunrise. He had to continue his march and cross the border before it was easy to spot him in daylight. Barely five minutes later Willis met a young couple. They had seen him leave the haystack. Willis made himself known to them. The young man explained that Willis should return to his hiding place and wait. An hour later the youngster returned with food. He pointed out that Willis was heading for the town of Bergen op Zoom, instead of the Belgian border. The American should be extremely careful, for by going south now, he would end up at Woensdrecht airfield, which had a strong German garrison.

At about 8 o'clock Willis and his young companion were back on track. The boy took Willis around Roosendaal leaving him when they came to the spot where the road ran to Bergen op Zoom and to Antwerp. He warned Don to stay within sight of the road, but not too close, as there were regular patrols by Dutch police as well as by German soldiers to prevent sabotage by the resistance and to stop the smuggling that in this region. Following the road Willis reached the border after a three-mile walk. At the border was the village of Essen. In spite of its German name, it is Belgian territory. Crossing into Belgium west of Essen Don Willis wanted to avoid the airfield, further to the west, about three miles away. From Essen most of the small roads to Antwerp went through forests, all providing a better opportunity to remain unseen. In the afternoon Willis reached the edge of Essen. The first leg of his escape, only 15 miles, had taken him much more than 24 hours.

The next problem was to cross the border without being spotted by Dutch police, customs or German soldiers. Willis took a great risk by asking a woman if she spoke any English. She shook her head, but did not appear to be unfriendly. She understood that this stranger wanted to avoid uniforms at all costs. She pointed out that he must follow a forest road and hide when he reached the spot where people were working. The road was still on Dutch territory, but the farm workers were on Belgian soil. Don Willis' best chance was to wait until they finished working and then follow them, for they all go to Essen, where they lived. Willis stayed hidden until the evening fell. At about six o'clock the workers seemed to be ready to go home for they came together at one place. From a safe distance Willis followed them, until they disappeared via a back road to Essen. Willis did the same. Pausing briefly between the first houses, he saw the checkpoint ahead of him on the left. But the presence of German soldiers made it too dangerous to enter the village and find the address he had been given as a safe house when he was briefed at Kingscliffe.

He was now in Belgium, but he was stuck. For the rest of the evening of 12th April Willis followed the road to Antwerp. At midnight he found shelter in a small shack, where he had his last sandwich and some sweets from his escape kit. Knowing that he must keep his strength up, he slept for a few hours. The next day around five in the morning he left his hiding place to continue his long journey, staying away from villages to avoid people. German officers hunting with rifles twice crossed his path. Both times Willis managed to hide before they saw him. In the early evening of 13 April, after a long march, he reached the outskirts of Antwerp. He realized it would be impractical to try to walk around this city. So, Willis retraced his steps to find a suitable hiding place for the night and think about his plans for tomorrow. Again, he was lucky when he walked into a German anti-aircraft position. With angry shouts the German sentry chased the stranger away. With a sigh of relief Willis obeyed! It had been three days since he force-landed his aircraft and during these three days he had covered less than 25 miles. If he maintained this speed he would be back in England after the war.

After a cold and sleepless night in the open Willis went to a farmhouse, where at three in the morning the farmer got a shock when Don knocked on his door. He told the American to go away and come back when it is light. A quick survey showed Willis that there were no telephone lines leading to the farm, so there was no chance that the farmer warned the authorities. At about 5 o'clock he returned, and he found the farmer not helpful. Maybe he was too terrified to do more than give Willis bread and a bottle of beer, after which he closed the door, leaving Willis outside. Willis now realized that his only option was to walk into Antwerp and hope for the best. Casually strolling he followed street after street, using the beautiful cathedral of Antwerp as aiming point. Near the cathedral, not far from the Antwerp Quay, Willis passed a man, standing in the entrance door of a shop. Seeing the man look at him in a peculiar way the American decided to risk it all and enter the shop. The owner recognized Don as a fugitive and quickly invited him to follow him into a small back room. After Willis was seated the man said: 'America, Tommy?' Willis, not knowing quite what to do just bowed his head in silence. The man then reached for his wallet and handed 300 Belgian francs. He explained that it was safe to take the tram across the city. There were no controls on the trams as they do not leave the city boundaries.

Willis jumped on the one the man pointed out to take to the south of the town. Without being bothered by anyone Willis passed through, gratefully using his Belgian money for the fare. Success made Willis reckless. When he reached the south of Antwerp his attention was drawn by one of the many Belgian beer advertisements. Thirsty after a long day, he walked to a cafe and sat down in one of the chairs outside. When the patron asked him for his order, Willis mentioned the word that he had seen on one of the beer posters: 'Bock.' The proprietor looked at Don, said nothing, walked away and came back a few minutes later with a Bock beer. When Don finished his glass and looked for money to pay, the proprietor indicated that the American was to come in. He took Don into the living room. On the table were bread, beer and fried eggs. The proprietor, who could not speak any English, pointed at the food, then at his own mouth and his stomach. Willis understood this and ate with gusto! When he had finished his meal he tried to thank the man, but the landlord shook his head, put his hand on Willis' shoulder and said something. Willis did not understand it, but presumed that the man wished him well. After this kind reception at the café Don Willis felt he could cope with any problem, so, when he got lost in Antwerp, he decided to play it cool and take a train to Brussels.

Willis used the Antwerp tram to get through the town. (GAA)

Willis walked into the Zuid Station, the Southern Station, of Antwerp, hoping to catch a train to Brussels without arousing suspicion. When he entered the station, he walked to the ticket office and simply said: 'Brussels.' The Belgian at the ticket office immediately knew that this passenger was a foreigner. 'Who are you?' he said 'English?' Willis took the gamble and said 'Yes.' The Belgian walked to one of his colleagues, who looked at Willis and then took the man's place at the counter. 'Come', said the ticket clerk. Willis followed him out of the station, into town. They stopped at a house about five minutes from the station. Both men entered to be warmly welcomed by a Belgian who spoke fluent English. Although he had no connection with the resistance, he offered to help. Then suddenly, the telephone rang. After a short conversation in Flemish, the man put down the receiver and told Don: 'They know you are here, the Gendarmes are on their way.' Willis left the house within seconds. The ticket clerk followed him and took him to the outskirts of Antwerp, where he told Willis to take the tram to Boom. With a short goodbye to this good Belgian Willis boarded the tram. Late that afternoon Willis arrived in the town of Boom, halfway between Antwerp and Brussels. To get to Brussels he would have to cross the Rupel River.

Heading for Brussels.
Unfortunately German soldiers and Belgian Gendarmes had set up a checkpoint. Everyone wanting to pass the bridge had to show his ID card. Willis had no papers whatsoever. Moreover, he still carried his pistol under his shirt. Don decided to reconnoitre the bridge before making a decision. He saw that some people were allowed to cross the bridge without any check. They probably are locals or collaborators. Rather than hurrying Willis looked for a place to spend the night. The bridge across the Rupel River was particularly important to the Germans. They put a permanent guard at the bridge, no less than 54 soldiers of the 16th Sicherheits Regiment. The commander was a Belgian by the name of Oberleutnant Jozef Bolten. He came from the German-speaking part of eastern Belgium and did anything to find favour in the eyes of his German masters. The Belgians despised him. Upon his arrival at the bridge Bolten had requisitioned three houses where the Belgian bridge workers used to live. He had told them to leave everything behind and go. The middle house was taken over by Stabsfeldwebel Schreurs, also a Belgian of German origin. His suspicious eyes never missed a thing and people feared him. There was little else for Willis to do but wait, sleep and think of a plan. He found a quiet place to sleep in a derelict tool shed.

The next morning, it was 14 April, he slowly returned to the bridge. Again, the checkpoint is strongly manned, but this time something had changed. A small workforce had arrived. They were locals who had to do a job for the enemy. The men carried poles across the bridge. In the fields along the river, they planted the poles into holes in the ground to make sure that no allied parachutist or glider could land safely. It was one of the elaborate plans of the Germans to prevent an allied invasion. The workers walked on and off, every time crossing the bridge. The guards did not pay any attention to them, but allowed them to pass without checks.

Willis in the garden of the house of Philomene Hoofd. (PW)

On the right we see her with François Luykx. (AC)

Don Willis had a plan. It was dangerous, but it might work. While the Germans checked the identity of a woman Willis joined the workers. Though they all look at him, no one said a thing. Willis took a pole and put it over his shoulder. His face shielded by the pole he walked towards the German soldiers. They ignored him so he followed the group of workers to a place about 50 yards from the checkpoint. There, other workers were busy digging more holes into which their colleagues put their poles. The area, however, turned out to be guarded by a German soldier with a Schmeisser submachine gun. Had Willis put himself into a trap? Had his luck run out at last? No! Again, Lady Luck smiled at the lone escapee. An ice cream vendor came near, pushing his cart. Asked by one of the workers, the German allowed them to buy an ice cream. Again, Willis joined the gang, causing some confusion by presenting the vendor with a 100 Franc note. This made the German guard impatient. With a harsh voice he ordered the men to return to their job. While the soldier argued with those who have not yet been served, Willis casually walked from the checkpoint. Unnoticed by the soldiers and shielded by workers, whom had all gathered around the German, he slipped away between the bushes and then made a run for it. Fortune had been with Don Willis once again. The American walked for the rest of the day until he reached the village of Ruisbroek at the outskirts of Brussels.

For three days Willis wandered through the country, using his last money to buy some bread and, when necessary, stealing apples from orchards. On 18 April he reached the outskirts of Brussels. He looked like a tramp, not having had a chance to shave since he said goodbye to the kind café owner in Antwerp. In spite of his shabby appearance, he entered another café and ordered a beer. Corneel van der Wilt, the owner, immediately saw that there was something wrong with this stranger. When the American had finished his drink, he left the café. Corneel caught up with him. 'Do not look back', he whispered, 'Are you a pilot?' Willis admitted he was indeed one and on the run. 'Follow me, I will help you', was the answer. Willis followed, led by the man through the streets of Ruisbroek, a village near Brussels. After hiding Willis in a shed Corneel warned the chief of the local police. His name was Van den Bogaert, and he was a local resistance leader. Sadly, as he had two escaped soldiers in his house, he could not help. The police chief therefore saw a lady from the hamlet of Puurs, Mit van Geel, who owned a small lingerie shop. After a brief conversation it was agreed that the next morning at five, before the end of the curfew, the resistance would see Willis, check him out and decide what to do next.

At five in the morning, Miss Mit van Geel waited at a quiet spot along the Puurse Amer creek, for the people who sheltered Willis during the night. Minutes later the group from Ruisbroek arrived. The group counted four men, one of them Don Willis. The Reyntjes brothers and Corneel van der Wilt knew that they took a deadly risk trying to help a pilot staying out of Germans hands. Yet, like many of their compatriots, they felt that they had to do something to support the men who fought for their freedom. Miss Van Geel took the American by the arm and while they walked to Puurs village she casually asked Willis where he keeps his little compass. Willis remained silent, suspicious too about the strangers in whose hands he was now.

After fifteen minutes they arrived at the shop of the 42-year-old spinster. He was not the first airman to find a safe place with her. So far no one had been luckier than this officer. Many escapers who tried on their own were quickly captured. Often the Germans tortured them, as they could not believe the escapee had been all by himself for such a long time. Sometimes, after German interrogation aircrew collapsed and divulged all they knew about the people they had been with. This soon was followed by a German attack on a safe house. Anyone arrested then did not live much longer. The SD and SS showed no mercy. It remained a matter of pure luck if an escaper ended up with the resistance and got away safely. It was Don Willis' luck that he had fallen into the hands of the best-organized escape organisation in Western Europe: the Comète Line.

From that moment, he was no longer master of his own destiny; the resistance decided what to do with him and when. First, he was thoroughly investigated and his identity checked. Once the group was satisfied he was a genuine pilot Mit van Geel took him to a bridge over the Vliet River, at the border of the villages of Puurs and Oppuurs, where Willis was handed to another member of the resistance, Jan de Decker, the local blacksmith. This man was in charge of the resistance in the little town of Saint Amands. He took Don to Corneel Hoofd, leader of a section of the Secret Army, who hid Willis in a local house. There Don Willis was photographed in the orchard behind the house. And, though a big risk, he was also photographed with Philomene, Corneel Hoofd's wife. The photograph can be used as proof of the 'family life' of the holder of the Belgian ID card. While with this family Willis told them how much he longed to go to Britain. He said he misses his wife and wanted to go back to his unit to join the battle against the Germans: 'When I am back in England, I will come and see you again', he says. 'I will fly to Belgium and roar over your house. Don't worry, I know where it is.'

Meeting Monique, one of many nurses…
A few days later Willis left. Knowing the danger of long stays at safe houses, the resistance never kept airmen longer than a few days at the same spot. Van Saelen, another member of the Secret Army, took Willis to the house of Albert Snackaert at Breendonk. The American pilot was not aware that he stayed within two miles of the infamous Breendonk fortress, where many Belgian patriots are locked up to be tortured or killed. At Breendonk Don Willis met Constant Crab, who was in hiding for the Germans too. Crab was to take Willis to the next man of the resistance, Henri Maca, who lived in Schaarbeek, a suburb of Brussels. A second companion was Gaston Matthys of the Patriotic Militia and the Service 'EVA' of the 'Zero' resistance group, which was in direct contact with Comète, the organisation that transports escapers to Spain. For obvious reasons, the resistance was split up in cells, to make it more difficult to arrest the whole organisation. Willis' private escape, after days of luck in spite of many dangers, had come to an end at last! At first Willis was treated with the usual suspicion. His hosts found it impossible to believe that this officer had come all the way from the south of the Netherlands without papers, and what is more, without the help of any organisation. Henry Maca, who was responsible for Willis' well-being as well as for his temporary detention, did not know what to think of this American. Again, Willis was interrogated. Using a list of questions that only aircrew could answer, Maca and his friends tried to establish Willis' true identity[65]. But soon it turned out that a Willis is listed 'missing in action.' Personal information about his private life that Don had given to the interrogators was checked and proved true. Now that the Belgians were satisfied, they told Willis that it was time for him to learn another trick: patience and strict obedience to the rules made by his protectors. Maca took Willis to the house of a

---

[65] See Appendices for the Questionnaires that were used to clarify the identity of aircrew.

Belgian nurse, Yvonne Bienfait. He was to call her Monique. Single, she lived on her own. Monique was an exceptionally brave young woman who had sheltered many airmen as well as continuing her daily work as a nurse. She seemed to have no fear. Once she was hiding an American pilot, 2nd Lieutenant George Vogle. The young bombardier was one of a crew of ten. His aircraft had been on a mission to Leipzig on 22nd February 1944 when their B-17 Flying Fortress was hit and crashed some 10 miles south of the Belgian city of Liege.

The crew landed by parachute in the forest near Liege where soon three of the crew were taken prisoner by the Germans. They were Lieutenant John Stahl, pilot, Technical Sergeants Claude Keenbum Jr, the engineer/gunner and Howard Kallal, the radio operator. Seven crew members managed to evade capture. They were 2nd Lieutenants Vogle, Miller [66] and Chemosky and Staff Sergeants Engstrom, Johnson, Pyles and Pogodin. The Staff Sergeants all managed to escape to Switzerland. Vogle and Miller found each other and stayed together in Fraiture, Chemosky was on his own. Vogle and Miller were taken to Huy, a small town in the Ardennes, southwest of Liege. However, when their helpers suddenly took them to a new safe house, they had reason to believe that the Germans knew the place and keeping the building under surveillance. They were taken to another hiding place near the railway station.

On 22nd February both Americans left for Brussels by train. In the outskirts of the Belgian capital, they left the station and took tram to a church where they were to be picked up. There two men waited for them. One of the men spoke some English. The Americans were taken to the top of the building, where the concierge, a bald man, his wife and their two children are waiting. After a meal, a colonel of the Belgian army came to interrogate the Americans. He asked details about their unit, and other military information. Then he left and sometime later the men were brought in contact with the leader of the resistance. According to Vogle he was a Belgian who had worked in England for 10 years and who kept on walking around with his hands behind his back. He told them that after they left Brussels they would be taken to another town. Then Vogle and Miller returned to the church where two other men escorted them further. They were Georges and Albert. Finally, they were in the hands of the EVA-group, where Vogle and Miller stayed with Mr. Lheureux and Mrs. Demelenne from 23 February until 13 June 1944. There was a reason for that long stay of Vogle. He had to be taken to the house of Yvonne Bienfait in Schaerbeek, because of an acute appendicitis. He was rushed to the hospital where Yvonne worked and operated at once, then given a separate room, with a notice on the door, warning for a 'contagious disease.' Once recovered Yvonne took him home. As the American desperately wanted a walk, she walked arm-in-arm. However, upon reaching the Chaussée d'Ixelles, they were 'snapped' by a street photographer. Yvonne hastened to order a picture and the negative as well! No one saw that the two young people, strolling along casually and smiling at the photographer were in fact an American airman and a Belgian resistance fighter! When Willis arrived at Monique's house, he met a second lodger, a tall Texan, a Colonel, who had been with Monique for the last few days. His name was Thomas H. Hubbard, his friends called him Speed. He was on the run since parachuting over Holland in November 1943.

Vogle may have become one of their victims, for he does not appear on the list of successful evaders via Comète. Willis and Hubbard, however, were about to embark on the next leg of their evasion. In spite of the tension of staying alert every second of the day and night, there were moments of great fun. One day, Don Willis witnessed a weird incident during an American bombing attack of a target near Brussels. One of the participating B17s had been hit by flak and flew over Schaarbeek, its engines on fire. Members of the crew abandoned the aircraft. One of them landed in the middle of a garden, a few houses from the place where Don Willis was hiding and watching events from an attic window. The American dropped his harness and ran into the house. Almost immediately, a German dispatch rider arrived on the scene, stopped his motorbike, climbed over the hedge surrounding the garden and also entered the house. At that moment, the American hit him straight in the face. As the German fell down, the American jumped on the bike and roared off, leaving a cheering crowd and an outraged soldier behind [67].

---

[66] *Julius Miller and Elbert Pyles reached Spain via Comète.*
[67] *As described in Escape and Evasion Report No.800 by Major D. K. Willis USAAF.*

During his time in Brussels Willis saw and heard many other things. He saw the Germans marching through the streets. He witnessed the daily curfews. He heard sounds of aircraft engines and anti-aircraft guns, day and night. His hosts told him stories about the suffering of the Belgians. Yvonne told how the Germans rounded up and executed hostages at random, whenever members of the resistance attacked their enemy.

Top right: Two braves of Comète, Nurse Yvonne Bienfait and Gaston Matthys. As Monique, she sheltered many escaping airmen and escorted them to the next destination. Her uniform was a good cover. She was never arrested. Matthys not only helped airmen, he also took maps, photos, messages via the escape line to England. One photograph that was used for Willis forged papers. Lieutenant Vogle and Monique (Yvonne Bienfait) on a stroll in Brussels after Vogle had an appendix operation. Bottom left: Lieutenant Vogle 4th from right in the front row, with fellow evaders waiting for allied troops to liberate them. Bottom right: Sam Slavin and Enoch Bettley in the Place de la Brouckere in Brussels, They seem perfectly at ease with a German soldier walking with them. PW/AC)

Soon after his arrival in Brussels Willis heard how a force of 91 Fortresses dropped 200 tons of bombs on the city. On 8 May, he saw 57 American Liberators drop over 160 tons of bombs on Schaarbeek itself. Three days later 106 Flying Fortresses bombed Brussels, on 25 May a group of 99 B-17s again attacked the Belgian capital. Every time terrified citizens paid a horrific price when bombs missed the target and hit houses, hospitals or schools. Willis and Hubbard were told by their hosts that, if the Allies continued dropping bombs, apparently at random, the population would turn against them and fall for the trap, which had already been put in operation by the German propaganda machine. Matthys told them very bluntly: 'Listen. If this goes on, the people will lose faith. They are cursing your air forces. Something must be done to tell your people that this cannot go on.' That night a plan was made. Matthys wrote reports and made photographs of the damage. Official reports from the Brussels Air Raid Protection Service were copied. One evening Yvonne Bienfait took Hubbard and Willis into town, to see the damage with their own eyes. It was an unpleasant experience for the two Americans, who were deeply shocked and promised to take the documents with them as soon as they were cleared to continue their journey. Hubbard would carry the parcel under his clothes.

On 29 May 1944, four men boarded a train that left Brussels for the south. They were Hubbard, Willis and their two guides Matthys and Bolle. It was the next leg of the Journey to the Horizon.

Comète had to be extremely cautious. They had to be aware of counter intelligence like the Abwehr, the Geheime Feld Polizei, the Gestapo and the Sicherheitsdienst SD. Even more dangerous were traitors like Jacques Desoubrie, alias Jean Masson, Prosper Dezitter, Pierre Boulain, or Roger le Neveu. They worked for the Nazis, impersonating resistance fighters. It is shocking to find how they worked and how they became almost essential for their German masters. Over 70 RAF aircrew along with numerous USAAF flyers were led into Gestapo traps from the safe houses in Brussels. The total traced back to Dezitter's work runs into hundreds.

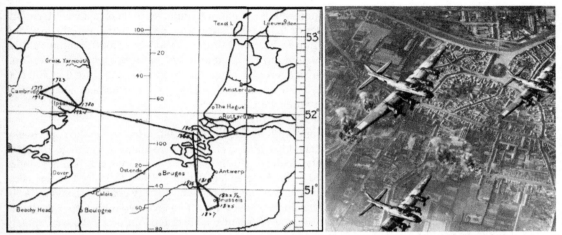

On 11 September 1944 both Hubbard and Willis witnessed an American attack on Brussels, which also caused collateral damage and loss of lives in nearby Lokeren. Hubbard reported on these tragedies when he returned

Treason in Belgium.[70]

During the period of Nazi occupation, many Belgians collaborated with their occupiers. There were pro-Nazi political organizations in both Flemish and Walloon communities before and during the war. The most significant were De Vlag, Verdinaso and Vlaams Nationaal Verbond in Flanders as well as the Catholic Rex movement in Wallonia. Each of these movements had subtly different ideologies, their own paramilitary forces and printed their own newspapers. These organisations encouraged Belgians to enlist into the German Army. On the whole, the Belgian administrative system was very pliant and became an instrument of collaboration. In a 2007 report by a Belgian research institute concluded that Belgium had offered 'maximum administrative collaboration' with the German occupation forces. The same report also commented on the apparently higher levels of collaboration in Flanders as part of an attempted integration into a 'German-Flemish New Order'. The towns of Brussels and Liège, the report added, 'remained [generally] patriotic-Belgian and decisively hostile to Germany'. The report also found that many Belgian authorities had been compliant, even active, in the deportation of Jews.

---

[70] *Wikipedia*

These traitors accounted for the arrest and the death of many airmen and members of the resistance. Jacques Desoubrie (left/top), Prosper Dezitter (left/centre), Roger le Neveu (left/right). (KMB/BuA)

Two units of the Waffen-SS, the Flemish Legion and the Walloon Legion, were recruited from Belgium during the occupation. Léon Degrelle, founder of the Rexist Party, was the commander of the Walloon Legion, which fought against the Soviet Union in Eastern Europe. A total of 15,000 Belgians in the 'divisions' (neither ever greater than brigade strength) fought on the Eastern Front where the Walloon Legion was nearly annihilated in the Korsun–Cherkassy Pocket in 1944. After the war, a total of 400,000 Belgians were investigated for collaboration. Of these, around 56,000 were prosecuted. The majority received prison sentences although several hundred were executed.

Leopold and his companions were liberated from captivity in early May 1945. Because of the controversy about his conduct during the war, Leopold III and his wife and children were unable to return to Belgium and spent the next six years in exile at Pregny-Chambésy near Geneva, Switzerland. A regency under his brother Prince Charles had been established by the Belgian legislature in 1944. In 1946, a commission of inquiry exonerated Leopold of treason. But controversy concerning his loyalty continued, and in 1950, a referendum was held about his future. Fifty-seven per cent of the voters favoured his return. The divide between Leopoldists and anti-Leopoldists ran along the lines of socialists and Walloons who were mostly opposed and Christian Democrats and Flemish who were more in favour of the King. The result was the coronation of Leopold's son Baudouin as the new King of the Belgians.

6. STRAFING.

Rooky on a mission.

With the Americans sending more Thunderbolts, Lightnings and Mustangs over Occupied Europe, they gained air superiority. Though the allies were still a long way from air supremacy, less Germans could use roads without soldiers sitting on the mudguards, scanning the skies for the allied fighters. The skies over Occupied Europe had become a dangerous place for the Luftwaffe. Rarely Bf109s or Fw190s took off to engage allied aircraft. German fighters had been committed to the defence of the Reich where bombers pounded the cities day and night. The sky over France had become the hunting ground for the fighter-bomber. Rocket-firing Typhoons of the RAF caused havoc on the Wehrmacht. Low flying Mustangs photographed and attacked barracks, batteries and pillboxes. Mosquitoes roared over, the Germans on the ground are terrified. Trains, barges, even horse-drawn carts were no longer safe from the prying eyes of Allied pilots.

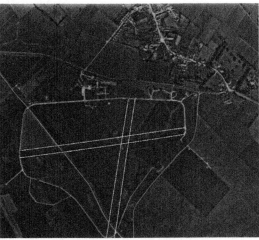

Bottisham airfield during and after the war. The runways have been blown up. The perimeter track and the airfield buildings are still visible. On the left is the village where American service personnel would visit local pubs and drink English beer, for many a strange experience. They also tried to ride bicycles. On 27 April 1944 Lieutenant Jack Cornett took off as one of the P-47 Thunderbolt pilots of the 361ˢᵗ Fighter Group to attack the airfield of Mondésir south of Paris (IWM).

At the same time resistance fighters attacked cars, railroads, bridges, tunnels. Regular radio messages from many groups informed the allies almost daily of army movements. Every time the allies claimed a success, the people regarded the Germans with loathing. The Germans answered with terror. The only thing the enemy could do was to retaliate at the places where they were attacked. It did not matter whether the locals were involved or not. Innocent people were murdered. Corpses of captured resistance fighters and hostages were left hanging from street lanterns or balconies for 24 hours or even longer. Farms and houses were set alight. The Germans no longer differentiated between men, women or children. resistance members.

In the smoky briefing room of Bottisham airfield pilots gathered on 27 of April, soon after dawn, it was not yet 6 o'clock in the morning. The men belonged to 361ˢᵗ Fighter Group. The first members of the Group arrived in Great Britain less than six months ago, on 29 November 1943. They had flown their first mission on 21 January 1944, the last P-47 Group to join the 8ᵗʰ Air Force. The Commander, Colonel Christian Jr. was at Bottisham since the end of February[71]. Like some of his pilots he was a newcomer to the European Theatre of Operations. When the briefing came to an end, he addressed the assembled

---

[71] *Colonel Christian was killed in action on 12 August 1944.*

pilots: 'Hit them and hit them hard!' The Group's mission would take the pilots into France. Their target: the airfield of Mondésir, not far from Etampes, south of Paris, east of Chartres. Eight pilots had been detailed to carry out the mission to be led by Captain Guckeyson[72]. Their aim: To strafe the airfield so heavily to make sure that no enemy aircraft can take off, by destroying as many aircraft as possible and then return safely to base. Their action was one of the many carried out in order to support bombers that had been detailed to attack German targets in France. At 08.36 hours nine P-47s fighters took off from Bottisham. They were a tiny part of a fleet of 357 Lightnings, Mustangs, and Thunderbolts, detailed to protect a bomber force of 596 Liberators and Flying Fortresses.[73]

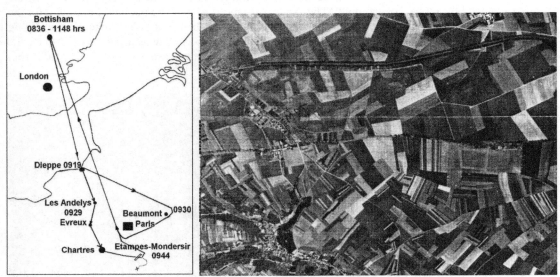

*Etampes-Mondésir airfield, southeast of Paris. 1st Lieutenant Jack Cornett was forced down after attacking it. French patriots helped him to escape. Private pilots use the former military field. Yet, all over the hangars and stone building, we see the scars caused by .50 cal bullets. Cornett barely missed the water tower on the left, when he pulled up after strafing the airfield. The **X** shows where Jack Cornett crash-landed his P-47. (HO/USAFHRC)*

The mission the bombers had to carry out would not take them far away from England. They were to attack 25 targets where the Germans V-1 Flying Bombs were said to be stored and launched from. At about nine o'clock in the morning the eight Thunderbolts of 361st Fighter Group reached the airfield of Etampes-Mondésir, catching the Germans by surprise. A group of four aircraft claimed the first victims, a group of Heinkel bombers parked near the hangars. With screaming engines the P47s immediately climbed, while others attacked from another direction. Their shells caused a great deal of damage and loss of life inside the hangars. The first group of Thunderbolts might have surprised the Germans, but the next four met fierce opposition from the ground defences. As Cole pulled up, he heard a voice on the radio: 'They have got me, I am on fire, I'm going down!!'

He recognised the voice of Jack Cornett, a Rookie, who was on his third mission. 'Get out, get out', said Captain Guckeyson on his radio. But Cornett's voice was heard again: 'I cannot, I am too low, I will try to land.' Immediately Guckeyson told the remaining aircraft to look for Cornett. Leroy Sypher, who flew third position behind Jack, reported having seen a smoking aircraft at 5,000 feet. He believed it was

---

[72] *Colonel Christian, Captains Guckeyson and Keppler, Lieutenants Cole, Feller, Gankler, Armsby, Sypher and Cornett.*
[73] *1st Bomb Division: 11 Bomb Groups, 206 B-17 Flying Fortress bombers. 2nd Bomb Division, 203 B-24 Liberators 3rd Bomb Division, 187 B-17 Flying Fortresses. The fighter cover consists of aircraft from seven Fighter Groups with: P-38 Lightnings, P-51 Mustangs and P-47 Thunderbolts.*

Cornett. Then Cornett spoke again in a hoarse voice, saying: 'I cannot see a thing. Everything is covered in oil. I am going down.' Twice Guckeyson told him to jump[74]. Sadly, contact was lost. In spite of seven other aircraft circling at treetop level, it was impossible to spot the aircraft or its pilot. There was little else to be done but to follow Colonel Christian's orders to return to England. The Thunderbolts climbed and disappeared to the northwest, leaving Etampes-Mondésir smouldering. Near the airfield, Cornett's evasion began. When he arrived back in England after his successful evasion, he told what happened: 'After my aircraft started losing oil, probably because it had been hit by flak, it would not climb higher than 1,000 feet. The plane soon burst into flames, and I decided to attempt a landing. It was a bit rough but I landed in a field, opened the canopy and started running. In the nearby bushes I hid my chute and harness, and started to walk southwards across country at once. It was about 0900 when I started, encountering no one until the afternoon'[75].

2nd Lieutenant Jack Donald Cornet, a young and still inexperienced pilot, was shot down during his second mission. The mission of 361st Fighter Group to the airfield of Etampes-Mondésir. Cornett remembered he was so low that he barely missed the water tower at the airfield. (JC/HO)

After he landed near Etampes-Mondésir Cornett's Thunderbolt may very well have looked like this one. Gendarme Marcel Dussutour and Mayor Lucien Pillias saw the same when they ran to Lt Cornett's P-47, the cockpit open, the pilot gone. This particular a Thunderbolt came down on 23rd June 1944. The pilot was 2nd Lieutenant Walter R. Davis who became a PoW. (USAHRC)

---

[74] *Sworn statement of Captain Guckeyson of 28 April 1944.*

[75] *Strangely enough, Cornett's version is very different from what both German and French eyewitnesses say they have seen. Besides there is a telegram of the Luftwaffe Command LKWO saying that the aircraft made and emergency landing. In this telegram the exact serial number of the aircraft, 42-75219 and the E2-G aircraft code are mentioned.*

Contrary to Cornett's belief, some people had witnessed his descent. Thanks to intensive enquiries by the newspaper 'Le Parisien Libéré' in the Merville area, forty years later, two eyewitnesses were traced. They were the retired Commander of the local Gendarmerie post, Marcel Dussutour and Lucien Pillias, the mayor of Arrancourt, who was in office since 1932. Pillias remembered the event as if it were yesterday. More than eighty years old, and now almost blind he said he would never forget the first day he saw an aircraft forced down: 'I was working in a potato field with one of my farm hands when we both heard shooting from the direction of the nearby airfield. We heard aircraft going down and then climbing back up again. Mondésir was only a small airfield and the military presence was limited. They had a few bombers there and some slow little aircraft. Once or twice, there was a fighter.'

'During March and April, we had seen several American attacks. They used large aircraft with round and flat noses. They were green and with stars on the wings and the sides. They made a very different sound to that of the German aircraft. A few minutes after the shooting began one of these Americans flew over my plot. We saw the pilot, for the cockpit was open. Black smoke came from the front and the engine made a strange sound. It was so low that we felt it was going to crash. We followed it when it disappeared behind the trees. I was sure it had crashed, but it was strange that we did not hear an explosion. We crossed the forest in a few minutes. When we came at the edge of the wood, we saw the pilot. He had a thing on his back, which he took it off and threw into the undergrowth.'

The gendarme and the airman.
Pillias shouted and waved at the pilot. He wanted to help the man before the police or the Germans got him. When Cornett saw the Frenchmen, he ran away and disappeared between the trees. Pillias and his farmhand then looked for the aircraft. After a short walk, they came to a stubble field where they saw the plane in the middle with two people examining the aircraft. Pillias recognised them as two men from Arrancourt. In fact, they were the only two men in the village who sympathized with the Nazis. When they saw their mayor, they took off their caps. Even though Arrancourt had less than fifty inhabitants, Pillias demanded the respect that went with his status as a mayor, in spite of the present government now being the enemy. Pillias recalled: 'They walked around the aircraft and we followed them. I told my man not to say a word and leave the talking to me. The older of the two – they were father and son – said: Bonjour, Monsieur le Maire, isn't it terrible with these aircraft? Did you see there was no pilot in it? Have you seen him, Monsieur le Maire?

Indeed, the aircraft had made a long deep furrow. It was greenish with white stars on its sides. The nose was very dirty, covered with oil that ran all along both sides. For such a big aircraft it was hardly damaged, but the propeller was bent and the belly showed the effects of a wheels-up landing.' Pillias climbed on to the wing and looked into the cockpit. Seeing the pilot's leather gloves on the seat he quickly picked them up and, while the two collaborators watched, secretly slipped the gloves under his jumper. Then the mayor turned to the two men and asked them what exactly they saw. The younger one told Lucien that he saw the pilot run towards Fontenette and that he must go home now and tell the police. Pillias got quite upset and said: 'Do you have any idea what the Maquis will do when they hear it was you who told the Germans where the pilot went? You know how these people are. They know a lot and they have long memories. You remember what they did with that chap in Pithiviers, who informed the Boche about the doctor who had Jews in his house? They shot him, his wife and their two children. Remember that before you see the Germans.' Visibly shocked by this threat the men asked the mayor what else they should do. Pillias told them to go home and forget they were ever here. 'What you did not see, you cannot account for, mes amis.' The two men left in a hurry.

With no Germans around yet, Pillias and his farmhand walked home. After coffee, he phoned the local gendarme, Maréchal de Logis Marcel Dussutour. The gendarme listened to the mayor and replied: 'I will wait for another two hours. Then I call the Germans and go to the aircraft. By that time, the pilot will have had enough time to get away, don't you think?' Round about noon Dussutour called the town commander of Merville, informing him that an aircraft seemed to have crashed in the area some time ago. Some local farmers had just informed him. Of course, he knew nothing about the event, but intended to go there immediately to keep the people away from the aircraft. Knowing that he had satisfied the Germans in Merville of his good intentions Dussutour quietly mounted his bicycle and headed for the scene of the crash.

When he arrived at the site of Cornett's forced landing he saw a small group of people gathered around the Thunderbolt. Dussutour told them to keep their distance, as the aircraft might explode. Next to the aircraft, under the port wing, Dussutour found a leather flying helmet with an oxygen mask attached. A quick glance showed Dussutour that a name has been written inside: '2LT J.D. Cornett.' If the Germans found the helmet, they could identify the pilot! Without hesitation the gendarme put the helmet under his uniform jacket.

Left: a typical briefing at Bottisham. Right: Captain John W Guckeyson led the pilots of 375th Fighter Squadron during the attack against Etampes-Mondésir airfield. Here it shows the names of his crew, Chief Staff Sergeant A. H. Walter and his ground crew. The swastikas on the fuselage show that Guckeyson has shot down two enemy aircraft during earlier missions. One month later on 21 May 1944, he was killed in action when he attacked a German train near Stendhal in Germany.

Lieutenant Eugene Cole was the last one to see Jack Cornett go down. He returned safely to Bottisham in his own P-47 called 'Baby Margene' after his baby daughter back home in the United States. (USAFHRC/EC)

In the meantime, Pillias returned as well, to join Dussutour and they decided to wait for the Germans, at the same time telling each other what to say when the Germans arrive. About half an hour later a German car, accompanied by an army truck arrived. An officer jumped out. He ran to the Frenchmen, shouting: 'Où est l'aviateur?', 'Where is the pilot?', Shuddering his shoulders, Pillias said that he had no idea, since he arrived barely ten minutes ago. Turning to Dussutour the German received an equally nonchalant reply. The Gendarme had already reported the event to their town commander! While outraged Germans surrounded the aircraft a search party tried to find the missing pilot and a Fieseler-Storch communications plane flew over to do an aerial search. The German crew found no trace of the pilot and landed without results of the search. Though the stories of Cornett in the Escape and Evasion report and the one of Dussutour en Pillians differ – maybe because time causes memories to fade – we also tell their story. Once on the ground, Cornett was given some food by a farmer, who came to Jack in the middle of the fields. He was then met by a policeman and another man, we believe they were Dussutour and Pillias. The next day they fed him again and gave him civilian clothes before lodging him.

Maréchal de Logis (Corporal) Dussutour the Gendarme stalled the Germans long enough to allow Cornett to run away and get some distance between him and his P-47 aircraft. Mayor Lucien Pillias, a farmer from Arrancourt, who helped the pilot to get out of his flying clothing and showed him the way to hide before the Germans arrived. He also managed to convince the two collaborators that it would be very unwise to report the pilot to the German authorities. After Cornett was down a Fieseler Storch reconnaissance aircraft searched the area in a vain attempt to find the evading pilot. (HO)

After running away from his aircraft, Cornett had a three hour head start. At about noon he met the first living soul, a Frenchman who, without asking any questions, offered to share his bread and wine. He then left, asking Cornett to hide until he returned. The man came back with a haversack containing a loaf of bread, a few apples, tomatoes and a bottle of wine. 'Bonne chance', he said, shaking Cornett's hand and went on his way. With the aid of the compass in his escape kit Cornett kept on walking southwards until midnight when he found a sheltered spot in a ditch, in which he tried to snatch and hour or two rest. But Cornett hardly slept. The tension of being on the run after his third operational mission, the noises of night creatures, and the fear of being surprised by Germans wore him out. At first light he set off again; seeing a farm he made straight for it, entered the barn, flung himself in the hay and was soon asleep.

A few hours later voices of playing children woke him up. When he came out of the barn Jack was seen by a boy who promptly ran to his mother, screaming! Within moments she entered the barn, nodding her head when Cornett, pointing at himself said 'American pilot, American.'
Signalling him to follow her she took him to the kitchen where she prepared a breakfast for Cornett. While he ate his meal, she kept a look out through the door. Suddenly she ran to Cornett, said something in French at the same time making the Hitler salute and pointing outside! She took Cornett to a small door which led to the farm cellar, where she signed 'silence and hide between baskets and wait', while the door remained locked. He stayed there for the rest of the day, wondering what was happening. In the evening, the woman opened the door again. She was joined by what Cornett guessed to be her husband, a tall French farmer. In his hands he held a suit, which he gave to Jack. It was far too large, so Cornett put it over his uniform – should the Germans catch him, he could always prove that he was a soldier, not a spy.

After midnight Cornett left the house. Again, the woman made the Hitler salute; at the same time spitting on the ground. Many years later this act was still in Jack's memory: how the French hated the enemy. He recalled: 'Until that moment the Germans were opponents, that was all. But now I realized what bastards they must have been to bring so much hatred to kind, simple people's minds.' After two days the Germans gave up and telegrams were sent to the Auswertestelle West at Oberursel[76], to the Commander of the Aircraft Recovery Unit in Nanterre and to Luftwaffe HQ in Paris: 'Date 29 April 1944. Time 1505. From LWKO. Very, very urgent: LLMM No. 290 on 28 April 1944 2015 hrs. To the Evaluation Centre West Oberursel. Copy to the Air-District Command West France Ic VO to Headquarters Air District 4/VII. Report to Commander of the Air Force Recovery unit Paris/Nanterre. Subject: Emergency landing of enemy fighter plane. Date and place 27 April 44 at 1100 hrs. 1 km south of Arrancourt, 8 kms south-east of Mondésir airfield. Identification of the name: Pilot escaped. Type of plane: Thunderbolt P-47 1EF, Marking E2 (Star) G. nr: 275219. Cause of Emergency landing: Probably hit in oil feed. Local Command Mondésir.'

Étampes Mondesir suffered heavy attacks like this one of 23 May 1944. In 1954 only a grass field was left of it.

At Bottisham too, reports were written about Jack Cornett's misfortune: '27 April 1944. Today two missions were flown. These operations brought both victories and losses. In the morning, the Group, led by Colonel Christian, flew mission 316. The pilots flew the following route: Bottisham-Chateau Thierry-Les Andelys-Chartres-Etampes-Mondésir airfield. During the attack against Mondésir airfield three Heinkel 111 bombers were damaged. One was hit by Captain Keppler, two by Captain Guckeyson. Second Lieutenant Jack Donald Cornett of 375th Squadron is missing; it is assumed that he made a belly-landing near the airfield.

In the afternoon, a second mission was flown, No. 317. This time three enemy aircraft were destroyed. The attack was led by Captain George R. Rew. All claims have been made by 375th Squadron pilots. Lieutenants Rames and Crandell claim one Heinkel together, Lieutenant Rawlett claims to have destroyed a Heinkel 111. The third is accounted for by Lieutenant Feller, who shot a Heinkel 111 in flames when he returned to Etampes Mondésir to look for Cornett before he was shot down himself. We had top-cover until just southeast of Vitry François. This was a day of action. For 16 hours more than 3,000 aircraft attacked installations between Pas de Calais and the south-western of Germany. It was the most extensive attack this far.'

Down on the ground Cornett kept on walking the whole night and most of the following day. He went to a village north of Orleans. Around noon he came at the hamlet, a few farms and houses. Cornett stayed on the edge of the forest scanning the area for hours. There were no Germans around; it looked as if the war had forgotten this peaceful village. As the sun was setting Cornett took his courage in both hands,

---

[76] *For information about life at this Interrogation Centre read Raymond Tolliver and Hanns Scharf:*
'The Interrogator.'

boldly walked across the street up to one of the houses. Hoping to meet good people he knocked on the door. The inhabitants let him in, immediately realizing this young man was a stranger. His oversized suit shows there was something wrong while his language proved he is a fugitive. They served him a big bowl of hot soup. While Jack drank the brew, a man came in. After shaking hands with the people in the house, the visitor turned to the pilot. One of the things that amazed the flyers was the French habit of constantly shaking hands with anyone they met. In broken English he asked all kinds of questions. When appearing to be satisfied he put his hand on Cornett's shoulder and said: 'You, OK, I help you.' He was a Mr. Delattre, who spoke English. He was a Parisian who lived at 111 Avenue Émile Zola, and who spent his weekends in the village. He was not a member of Comète. This Delattre took Cornett home to his apartment on the 7th floor in Paris, where he lived with another lieutenant hiding from the Germans. Jack Cornett stays there for a week. On the day of his arrival, Cornett went upstairs to the house of a certain Junefierro Paoli, a former officer of about 50 years old.

The town hall and the main street of Arrancourt today. (HO)

The Boulevard de Sébastopol today and a plaque on nr. 20 commemorating Georges Prevot and Jean Rocher, who were arrested by the Gestapo on 11 August 1944 and died in the camps.(Wikimedia Commons).

Life as a fugitive was very dangerous, especially since Cornett was now in civilian clothes, only having his dog tags to prove his identity. Following several arrests, Cornett was then moved to an attic of this building for a second week. He was then placed for another week with Mr. and Mrs. Joseph Gorjux and their daughter Pierette at Théodore Judlin Square 2 in Paris XV (until May 23). He was then brought back to Delattre for a few days. He then went to Rue Mademoiselle with a teacher who had lived in the USA for two years, and whose husband was also hiding from the Germans. Cornett's guide in Paris each time was a man Cornett remembered as Paoli.

In Paris, Jack Cornett is finally guided and lodged three days with Georges Prevot at 20 Boulevard de Sébastopol. There he received other false documents. In this house were also two Englishmen and a Canadian. After a few days, the whole group of four was then guided to a bicycle shop where they were handed over to a Russian and his sister, who speak impeccable English. According to sources in Comète they were most likely Valentin Yarmonkine and Véra Raffalovich-Yarmonkine[77]. They interrogated the four aviators and then handed them over to Philippe d'Albert-Lake, who turned out to be the most important guide in their evasion. From Paris, Jack Cornett's story becomes identical to the file of Leonard Barnes. Before that, Cornett and one of the two Englishmen were taken to stay with a brunette living northeast of the Champ de Mars. Neither her husband nor her child was present. The 30-year-old woman drove them to the station the next day, where they met Barnes, Hubbard and Willis. He was lodged there one night in an apartment at Rue Vaneau 1bis, in the flat of Virginia d'Albert-Lake. There he met the four other airmen who were to accompany him in the escape to Spain. They were Tom Hubbard, Don Willis, Len Barnes and Ron Emeny. They were about to embark on the last and most dangerous leg of their Journey to the Horizon. Tom Hubbard had been on the road from Eastern Holland since 13th November 1944.

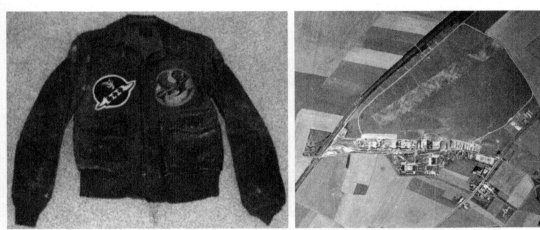

Oddly enough, in 2010 Jack D. Cornett's flying jacket, the one he left behind in France in 1944, was offered for sale on eBay for no less than 21,000 US$ and apparently sold for that price. Etampes in 1954. (eBay/USAFHRC)

Back at Bottisham.
Daily routine returned to Bottisham. Seven Thunderbolts landed and pilots reported for debriefing. They told the Intelligence Officer how they destroyed three Heinkel-111s and completely devastated the buildings at the enemy airfield. Three Thunderbolts had even made a short detour to the airfield of Beaumont-sur-Oise, which they had shot up as well. It was unfortunate that Cornett had not returned. But that's life. Poor Jack, only three missions. He had not even had time to spend his pounds in London. At this same time an extensive German search took place in the Arrancourt area. A Fieseler Storch aircraft flew round and round, its crew scanning the ground trying to find the American. Almost every Frenchman was questioned. But these stupid peasants, they knew nothing, they saw nothing, they heard nothing, they understood nothing!! The American had vanished from the face of the earth and not even pro-German Frenchmen had seen him. In France, arrangements were made to smuggle Jack Cornett out of the country. The photos he carried in his escape kit were used for his phoney French papers. He was questioned once more to establish his identity. On 30 April, the fourth day of his escape, he was in Pithiviers. The next day, while travelling by train between Orléans and Paris, he saw well-camouflaged 88mm guns, feared by aircrews. On 2 May, he arrived in Paris.

---

[77] *They fled after the October Revolution via Yalta in Crimea with the HMS Marlborough on 7 April 1919. The family lived in exile in Paris. They were involved in Comète. In the summer of 1944, Valentin was arrested by the Gestapo. On July 3 1944, they also arrested his sister Vera and her husband André Raffalovich. Vera (1901-1964) survived Buchenwald and Ravensbrück but her husband and brother perished after being taken to the Dora Mittelbau slave labour factories in the Hartz Mountains. André died of typhus on the 2nd December 1944 in Buchenwald concentration camp and Valentin died in Ellrich.*

7. BLIND!

'Semper Paratus'[78]

It is the motto of No. 207 Squadron of the Royal Air Force. For the second time this century, 'Leicester's Own' faced the Germans. Formed in November 1916 as No.7 Squadron, Royal Naval Air Service, it flew Caudrons, Strutters, Short bombers and Handley Pages 0/100 and 0/400 during the First World War. After starting the Second World War with Battles, Ansons and the ill-fated Manchester, it flew the Lancaster. Night after night the four-engine bombers roared over the North Sea to hit German targets wherever possible. Commander in Chief of Bomber Command RAF, Air Chief Marshal Sir Arthur 'Bomber' Harris, decided that one of the important enemy installations to attack was Mailly-le-Camp in France. His reasons were many. Situated south of Chalons-sur-Marne, Mailly was one of the most important armour training bases for the Wehrmacht, housing large elements of the crack 21st Panzer Division.

A Vic-formation of three 207 Squadron Lancasters. This does not necessarily mean that the aircraft in front was the same, as F was the letter given to many aircraft. ND556 is the serial number for one aircraft only Warrant Officer Leslie Harry Lissette, RNZAF. ((IWM/BL)

With the closely guarded 'D-Day' plans a month away, Allied Intelligence felt certain that these troops would be the first to be rushed to the Atlantic coast as soon as their troops landed on the beaches. This made the camp a prime target, to be wiped out at all costs. The forecast of a three-quarter moon in cloudless skies over much of Northern France during the night of 3 May would provide ideal conditions for such a vital operation, giving Harris the incentive to finalize his plans to go ahead on that date. Bomber Command Instructions No.AC15, issued on 3 May 1944 detailed Nos.1 and 5 Groups, and the Pathfinders of No.8 (PFF) Group, to help the main force with two Oboe[79] equipped Mosquitoes while No.100 group supported with six Mosquitoes and three ECM-equipped[80] Halifaxes of No.192 Squadron. They were to fly so-called Special Duty patrols over the target, covering 55 square miles of barracks, workshops, vehicles and tanks, contained in the heavily defended north-west corner.

Wing Commander Cheshire[81], Commanding Officer of No.617 Squadron was in control. He oversaw the Pathfinder Force, marking the target as precisely as he did on previous occasions. This was to ensure

---

[78] *'Always Prepared'*

[79] *Ground-controlled radar for blind bombing. One station indicates the track to follow, the other the bomb release point.*

[80] *ECM: Electronic Counter Measures.*

[81] *Cheshire was rewarded with the Victoria Cross, equivalent to the Congressional Medal of Honour.*

as little damage as possible to the village of Mailly-le-Camp. The Main Force Controller was Wing Commander Deane with Squadron Leader Sparks as his deputy who was to take over if Deane would be out of action. Only when Wing Commander Cheshire was satisfied with the target marking would he order the attack to commence, as soon as possible after their arrival. Timing was of the utmost importance. Harris wanted the attack to start shortly after the Germans were safely home and in bed after a night out. Speed and accuracy were the key words for all in making this not only highly successful but, within half an hour Mailly-le-Camp was to be turned into rubble by Bomber Command giving the Germans a memorable beating without suffering too much loss itself. Sadly however, history proved that even the best-laid plans could go wrong. In this case it resulted in the loss of 255 men, the second worst casualty listed by Bomber Command in a single operation.

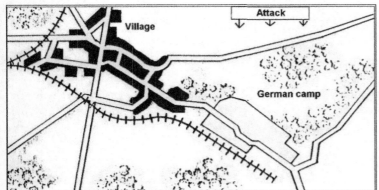

Mailly-le-Camp village and Camp, target for 3 May 1944.

Lancaster EM-F, ND556, No.207 Sqn: W/O Leslie Lissette RNZAF (Pilot, kia); Sgt Nick Stockford RAF (Eng. evd); Flt Sgt John Pittwood (Nav. evd); Sgt Phil King (Wop/AG, evd); Sgt Laurie Wesley (BA pow); Sgt Ron Emeny (MUG, evd); Sgt Ron Ellis (RAG, kia). (HO/BL)

Day dawned brightly on the fateful morning of 3 May 1944 when ground crews of No.207 Squadron prepared the Lancasters for the night operation, timed for a late take-off. All participating air crew reported to the Main Hall for briefing where they saw a large-scale map covering the whole area over which they were to fly including, for the first time, the target for the night. Boldly marked was their route, details of which had already been chartered by the navigators, who now joined their skipper and the rest of the Lancaster crews. All stood up when the Commanding Officer entered the Hall with his Section leaders. They covered the responsibilities of the crews: navigation, signals (radio and radar), engineer (mechanical performance), bombing (attack), gunnery (defence), strategy (tactics and route to avoid enemy interference), meteorology (giving the latest weather forecasts) and the escape officer, who would outline action in the event of a forced landing.

Then all were told to hand in all personal belongings so that in case of an involuntary stay in Occupied Territory nothing helped the enemy in establishing anything else but their names, ranks and service numbers. The Germans were clever. A ticket from the Odeon Cinema, a bill from a tailor, everything was extremely useful for the intelligence people at Auswertestelle West at Oberursel, the reception centre for captured flyers near Frankfurt. German interrogators were shrewd, skilled and tough. Nothing escaped their attention, sometimes it seemed as if they had spies on RAF bases, constantly briefing their masters on events in England as they happened!

Les Lissette, a New Zealander, was well liked by his crew as a friend and a particularly good pilot. His then unofficial fiancée was Florence Dudfield, (Brian Lissette's God Mother)a New Zealand Army Nurse on a Dutch hospital ship Oranje. She was killed in the Erebus disaster in Antarctica in November 1979.
The photos show the crew at the wedding of Laurie & Mary Wesley. Below the crew of ND556 F for Freddie at the wedding of Sergeant Laurie Wesley, who became a PoW but survived the war.
From left to right: John Pittwood, Ron Emeny, Nick Stockford, Laurie & Mary Wesley, Ron Ellis, Les Lissette and Phil King. The crew with their mascot 'Black Peter'. It was returned to Lissette's family. (BL/RE)

Mailly le Camp; a dangerous place.
The crews signed for their escape kits, containing currencies from countries they would fly over, silk escape maps, survival equipment and all kinds of gadgets that helped them stay free if possible. Earlier in the day each of the individual crews selected for the night's 'Op' had been out to the aircraft to thoroughly check if everything was in working order and perfect readiness for the forthcoming flight. One of the Lancasters was relatively new. It was ND556, EM-F for Freddie. It left the factory in January; so far Freddie had flown 190 hours, a short life which, sadly, was not to last much longer. She would be

one of many lost during the coming raid, yet unknown to her crew, Warrant Officer Lissette[82] (pilot) and Flight Sergeant Pittwood (navigator), Sergeants Wesley (bomb aimer), King (wireless operator), Ron 'Curly' Emeny, (mid-upper gunner) and Ron Ellis, who sat in the loneliest place of all, the power-operated rear turret with its four Vickers .303 machine guns.

Top: Ron Emeny with his air gunner's brevet. Centre: Floss Dudfield was a nurse on hospital ships, one being the fast Dutch ocean liner Oranje. Here she is in a nurse's uniform. Right: Les Lissette was happy with his relationship and would have married her after the war. RAF Spilsby. Aircraft at the dispersal points. In the top is an extension to the main runway. (RE/BL/UoK)

---

[82] *A few days before Lissette had been promoted to Warrant Officer, but this promotion had not yet been administrated.*

131

Now all that remained for the crews was to collect their flying kit; clothing and parachutes and board the bus to drive them back to Freddie. Guided by dim blue lights on the otherwise dark airfield, they reached their aircraft, clambered aboard, took up their respective places and waited for the signal to taxi to their allotted take-off position. Meanwhile Warrant Officer Les Lissette and his crew knew little of the great plan in which they were about to play a tiny part; they felt that it was much better to attack a target in France than to go all the way to the Ruhr or Berlin! At around 2230 hours Lissette got the green light; with brakes off, full power and the four mighty Rolls Royce Merlin engines pulling the bomber along the runway. Up came her tail as she picked up flying speed. A few more moments and F for Freddie was airborne. Lissette commenced the long climb to the rendezvous where he joined the other aircraft that were taking part in Operation against the military installations at Mailly.

To protect the bombers and to draw as many enemy night fighters as possible away from the main bomber stream, other RAF aircraft feinted to diversion targets. Eight Mosquitoes of ADGB (Air Defence Great Britain) were to bomb airfields along the Channel coast. Fifteen Mosquitoes of No.2 Group were to bomb airfields at Juvincourt, Amiens, St.Trond, St. Dizier and Rossières. Six Mosquitoes of No. 100 Group were to circle around the target area to intercept approaching German night fighters that had been directed to the Lancasters. At the same time, several Halifaxes and a lone Lysander of No.161 Squadron took advantage of this situation by flying to their drop zones and landing fields in France. Large bombers streamed over France helped mask the work that SOE did to support the French Resistance.

A Junkers Ju88 night fighter with two guns pointing up from the fuselage, crept underneath the Lancaster and shot it down. The 'Schräge Musik' was lethal to the bombers. The continental part of the route from Spilsby to Mailly le Camp and back. Many crosses mark the crashes of too many Lancasters during this attack. W/O Lissette with his nephew Brian, during leave in New Zealand. (BA/HO/BL)

As far as the others were concerned this was not a good night for bombers; the moon gave too much clear visibility, both in the sky and on the ground. Yet, to ensure good results, dispatching this force under these circumstances was considered a calculated risk. The plan entailed a two-fold attack on Mailly. No.5 Group was to attack the south-eastern edge of Mailly while No.1 Group had orders to drop bombs at the north-western part of the area. Mosquitoes were to attack the German Headquarters by surprise. The first aircraft to arrive over the target were the Pathfinders; the clock showed 21:45 hrs French time, when the markers fell on the indicated places. Sporadic anti-aircraft fire was seen, but as telex 794 of Bomber Command said later, this was not the main danger. Much more deadly were the night-fighters. The Luftwaffe reacted promptly and heavy clashes took place. The first Bf-110s attacked when the Lancasters crossed the coast and all crews knew that somewhere in the darkness Focke-Wulfs, Heinkels,

Junkers or Messerschmitts waited for them. While the Pathfinders dropped their markers on the target the first wave of bombers, 140 Lancasters, orbited an area some 15 miles north, anxiously awaiting their orders, unaware of the many problems causing long delays. More and more aircraft were in danger of being sitting ducks for the enemy. Technical problems with the radio sets made it impossible for Wing Commander Deane to contact the waiting Lancasters.

After the raid, an evaluation gave the following explanation: 'The control of this raid in the target area failed to operate according to plan. The initial low-level markers were accurate and were well backed up by Lancaster marker aircraft. The Marker Leader, Wing Commander Leonard Cheshire, ordered the main force to come in and bomb, but the Main Force Controller, Wing Commander L.C. Deane, could not transmit the order to do so to the waiting Lancasters because his VHF radio set was being drowned by an American forces broadcast and his wireless transmitter had been incorrectly tuned. German fighters arrived during the delay and bomber casualties were heavy. The main attack eventually started when the Deputy Controller, Squadron Leader E.N.M. Sparks, took over. During the whole flight to the target everything looked so well. Only a few Lancasters run into trouble. However, once they start to orbit the holding area too much valuable time was lost. Many Lancasters were seen burning in the sky and on the ground. It must have been a stressful wait. Each Lancaster was laden with a 4000 pound 'Cookie' and sixteen 500 pound bombs – a lot of high explosive should a crew have the misfortune to be hit before dropping their bomb load.

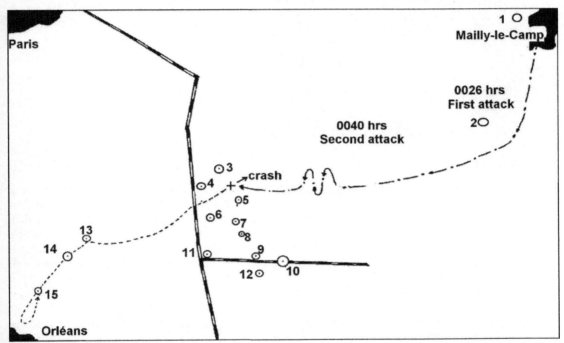

Area in connection to the crash. 1.Mailly-le-Camp, 2.Troyes, 3.Chaintreaux, 4.Dordives, where Lesley was betrayed and captured, 5.Rossières, 6.Ferrières, 7. Grisel-les, 8.La Selle sur le Bied, where Emeny and Pittwood hid in a crypt, 9. Chopilles, hiding place of Emeny and Pittwood, 10. Chuelles from where Pittwood and Emeny went to Paris, 11. Montargis 12. Château-renard, where Dr. Salmon treated Emeny, 13. Beaune la Rolande, hide out Stockford, 14. Boiscommun, 15. Saint Loup, second hiding place of Stockford.

The moment of surprise had been lost; it will be a tough job to bomb and to return to base. When F for Freddie reached the Initial Point, Wesley started to call target-run directions to Lissette. 'Right, right, left, steady, steady, bombs gone, OK let us get the hell out of here.' After the bomb doors closed F for Freddie turned away from the burning target on the ground. All the crew wanted now was a speedy return, a short debriefing, their 'Ops eggs' [83] and rest. But things were to turn out differently. North of Troyes the first attack takes place. On 4 September 1944, Sergeant King reported during his debrief back in England, that after hiding with French patriots and liberated by Allied troops, how the crew had desperately fought off the attacker: 'The Lancaster was flying straight and level at 6,000 feet. I was working on my set when our navigator, F/S Pittwood, called me up on the intercom, and asked me to watch Monica [84]. As soon as I turned my attention to the set I observed an aircraft on the port beam at about 1,000 yards range. I immediately reported this. The enemy aircraft closed in very rapidly, opening fire at about 600 yards.' Both gunners, Ellis in the rear turret and Emeny in the mid-upper, opened fire the moment they saw the night fighter.'

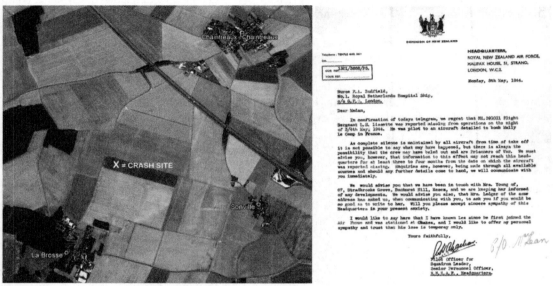

A 2018 picture of the crash site and the letter Ms. Dudfield received after the aircraft was declared missing. (BL)

Directed by his two gunners Lissette dived steeply to port causing the fighter to break off the attack at about 200 yards and pass overhead to starboard. Lissette continued his evasive manoeuvres and then levelled off again. But the German pilot was no amateur. Immediately he attacked again. No less than four times the German came back and four times Lissette managed to evade. It seemed the Luftwaffe pilot was flying circles around the bomber, for all attacks are from the same direction as the first. Each time King picked the German up at 1,000 yards and warned the pilot. During the first, second and fourth attack the gunners were able to sight the night fighter. The third attack came as a surprise and could not be answered by the .303 machine guns of the Lancaster.

The attacker was a Messerschmitt Bf110 of NJG4 [85] with the infamous 'Schräge Musik' guns pointing upwards from its fuselage. This allowed the German pilot to attack the Lancaster in the virtually unprotected belly. After the fourth attack the Messerschmitt disappeared into the darkness. Hopefully, Freddie escaped safely, losing only 3,000 feet altitude in the encounter, which brought her within reach of the feared 88 guns on the ground. Wesley called Lissette as the first shells began to explode suggesting his skipper to climb. 'For God's sake, do something', he shouted when a shell exploded extremely near to the aircraft. Lissette, knowing that the Germans expected him to climb, pushed the controls forward to dive. But almost immediately the Lancaster was hit in the port outer engine. A large streamer of flames

---

[83] *Upon their return from a mission RAF aircrew got a meal with fried eggs as the best part.*
[84] *Monica was a device that has to warn the bombers when a German aircraft approached from behind.*
[85] *NJG4: Nachtjagdgeschwader 4 (4th Night Fighter Squadron) Luftwaffe.*

made the aircraft an even easier target. The entire cover of the dinghy compartment in the starboard wing was shot off by a direct hit. Lissette, feeling that Freddie was doomed, gave the crew the order to abandon aircraft. The crew, however, believed that they still have a chance.

The skipper sacrificed his life.
A Lancaster on three engines would easily be able to fly home. The pilot feathered the propeller, trying the Graviner fire extinguisher to put out the flames. With the port outer engine stopped, the device that spots approaching enemy aircraft, called Monica, was put out of action, so King tried to connect it to the starboard outer engine. While he was busy, the Bf110 attacked again. As the result of a three-second burst cut through the bomber, near the rest bed, fire spread through the bomb bay area. Seeing that he was unable to save the aircraft, Lissette again ordered the crew to jump out. Wesley removed the escape hatch while Sergeant King destroyed the IFF[86]. Then he made his way to the front escape hatch. This turned out to be impossible, as the fire had spread rapidly, sending fierce flames through the fuselage, causing the fire to rage uncontrollably under the compartments of the wireless operator and the navigator.

A crater in the forest marks the crash of Lancaster BQ-H, LL826 of No.550 Squadron at Cheniers.
Local villagers collect the remains of the crew of Lancaster BQ-H at Cheniers (MMMIC).

One of the coffins, covered with flowers. In general, the Germans never allowed local signs of respect and compassion towards killed aircrew, as they considered them criminals. The wreckage of F for Freddie in a French field after the debris had been collected and piled up to be used for the building of new Nazi aircraft. (MMMIC)

Sergeant Emeny, the mid-upper gunner, was also forced to abandon his turret. He moved back through the fuselage struggling to make his way to the rear turret. While the flames poured from the wing root, from the bomb bay door and then raged through the fuselage Emeny did not feel any pain: 'I then saw that the rear turret was on the port beam with the gunner, Sergeant Ellis, still sitting in it. He did not

---

[86] IFF: *Identification Friend or Foe identifies the aircraft as 'friendly.' It had to be destroyed if a plane went down.*

appear to be injured. His parachute was still in its stowage outside the turret. I tried the emergency rotation control by the Elsan toilet but there was no response as the engine that drove the hydraulics had stopped. I started to climb into the rear turret, but Ellis saw me and waved me back. By this time, my clothes were smouldering so I knew I have to jump or die.' When King told Lissette that he could not escape through the rear hatch the skipper ordered him to use the front hatch. At the same time King heard Ellis shouting over the intercom: 'Lads, I've had it!' Unable to help, King went forward with Pittwood. The Lancaster was now at 1,000 feet. Still inside the burning aircraft King pulled his ripcord and with his parachute opening in his arms he rolled out, (Lissette kicked him in his rear end to assist him to escape through the front hatch) following the bomb aimer, flight engineer and navigator. While dangled in his harness King saw another parachute pass by very closely but was unable to recognize it. This was Ron Emeny, severely burned all over his face and hands and screaming with pain.

The German night fighter was still in the area, for, as the crew floated down, they saw the German shooting down another Lancaster. F for Freddie flew on for a few seconds, engulfed in searing flames before a wing fall off, then she dived vertically and crashed with a loud explosion in a field not far from the French villages of La Brosse and Chaintreaux. The Germans later found Lissette and Ellis. Remains of both were buried in the Chaintreaux Cemetery. The next of kin had no idea of the fate of their loved ones. Communications between the Germans and the British via the International Red Cross were slow and sometimes incomplete. When the news of the crash of F-Freddie reached London, Ellis' wife was told that her husband, although missing, had a chance to return home. The news that her husband could be dead was a terrible shock. The next morning a German search party arrived to investigate the site of the crash. The whole area was sealed off. The bodies of the two members of the crew were found in a badly mutilated condition amongst the wreckage.

Gendarmes from the small town of Souppes retrieved the remains and definitely identified W/O Lissette by the identity disc which he wore round his neck. The second body bore no identity disc and was believed by them to be Sgt Stockford, as a pair of gloves with his name in them were found near the corpse. Later Sgt Stockford is one of those who returned to UK and that the other member of the crew who was killed, was Sgt Ellis. The Huns ordered that the remains should be placed in one coffin and they are buried in one grave in the cemetery of Chaintreaux. This stayed unknown in the United Kingdom. Sometime later, Stockford's wife heard that her husband was killed in action while on operations over France. It must have been a terrible blow until he returned home via 'The Comète Line', some months later.

Nicholas John Stockford was born in Steeple Barton in March 1922, to parents George and Elizabeth Stockford, who ran a grocery shop in the village. He attended Chipping Norton County School between 1933 and 1938 and joined the RAF as an engineering apprentice on leaving school aged 16. Between October 1940 and October 1943, he served in South Africa as an engine fitter, returning to England to train for flying duties and was posted to 207 Squadron as a Flight Engineer, with the rank of Sergeant.

And though all aircrew knew that they were in a lethal job, they also hoped and prayed to survive their sorties. It took until two men came home to England and when news was received that Wesley had been found in a German PoW camp all still believed that Stockford was dead. Sergeant Ron Ellis' wife Kathleen did not know the truth until 10 April 1945, when she received a letter from the Casualty Branch of the Air Ministry, telling her: 'According to information received through air force authorities in Paris and supplied by a French gendarme two airmen have been buried at the cemetery of the town of Chaintreaux. Their names were Warrant Officer Lissette and Sergeant Ellis. Both men were part of the same crew as your husband. However, you know now that Sergeant Stockford has since returned to our country. As he had lent parts of his uniform to your husband a most regrettable mistake was made. Now that all survivors of the crash have returned it is certain that the flyer buried next to Lissette was your husband, though as a result of the gendarme's mistake it was assumed that it was the body of Stockford. Now formal steps will be taken to confirm the death of your husband at the shortest possible notice. The Ministry has instructed me to inform you of their feelings of distress.'

F for Freddie was not the only casualty of the raid. In fact, the entire operation was very costly for Bomber Command. Of 346 Lancasters and 14 Mosquitoes of Nos.1 and 5 Groups and 2 Pathfinder Mosquitoes, 42 Lancasters were lost, a staggering 11.6% of the entire force detailed to carry out the attack. About 1,500 tons of bombs had been dropped with great accuracy, hitting no less than 114 barracks buildings, 47 transport sheds and some ammunition buildings in the camp; 102 vehicles, including 37 tanks, were destroyed, 218 German soldiers were killed and 146 injured. Most of the casualties were Panzer NCOs. There were no French casualties through bombing but some people were killed when a Lancaster crashed on their house. The Evaluation Report, made after the raid, told a sad story of failure: 'The night fighter attacks continued over the target and on the return route. Among the aircraft shot down was that of Squadron Leader Sparks, who had stayed over the target to the end. Sparks evaded capture and soon returned to England. The squadrons of 1 Group, which made the second wave of the attack, suffered the most casualties: 28 aircraft out of 173 dispatched. 460 (RAAF) Squadron from Binbrook, lost 5 of 17 Lancasters in the raid.'

These German photographs show the destruction caused by the bombing of Mailly-le-Camp (BA).

The result of the attack of 3rd May 1944. The devastation is huge and the enemy had paid a heavy price in vehicles, men, accommodation and material. Yet the price paid by the RAF is almost as terrible. The next day allied aircraft photographed the terrible devastation from a high altitude. The difference before and after the raid is clearly visual. (MMMIC/IWM).

Though the RAF losses were serious, Mailly-le-Camp was badly hit. However, German losses were less than expected, considering the effort put in by Bomber Command. The Commander of 21st Panzer Division wrote in his report: 'Air raid alarm was sounded about ten minutes before the actual attack; everything went well. The attack itself started with the dropping of 'illumination-bombs' and was followed almost immediately by High Explosive bombs. It went on continuously for 45 minutes. Three attacks from three different directions developed in such a way that between 1000 and 1200 bombs, almost only H.E. covered the area. The calibre was up to 1000 lbs. There was no carpet-bombing, but an attack of bombs in long rows. The concentrations of bombs fell exactly on the main personnel barracks, the ammunition storage bunkers and on an AA battery. According to the Commander of the Orderly troops and after inspections when the raid had finished, most of the losses in personnel were caused by slit trenches caving in.

The concentration of bombs was so intense that apart from direct hits near misses also closed up the trenches. We think that the trenches were too deep (approximately 7 feet) and too heavily covered, so that the men who had been caved in on were unable to extricate themselves. Other losses occurred when the soldiers tried to save equipment and tools during what they thought to be a lull in the attack. This way they were caught in the middle of the next attack. There was little loss of fuel, only 20-30 cubic meters, as fuel had been removed earlier. Losses in vehicles: Because the vehicles had been parked away from camp there was little loss and damage. It paid off to disperse, camouflage and protect them against shrapnel. Preparatory actions: Since there was an increase in enemy reconnaissance flights over the camp, High Command ordered large units to leave the barracks and relocate dispersed over the area. This action proved to be useful.'

When the final count was made, all realized that it had been one of the worst nights for the RAF. No. 1 Group lost 30 aircraft, all Lancasters. Besides these bombers, four Pathfinder Lancasters and two Special Operations aircraft, a Halifax and a Lysander, went down during other operations over Occupied France. A crew member, whose aircraft landed safely but terribly battered after a fight that lasted from the target until past Chartres, remembered: 'After debriefing we felt horrible. Some of us locked ourselves up in the Nissen hut. As for myself, I went to the nearby pub. I do not remember ever having been more drunk than I was on that awful night. It was the first time I ever got drunk, and the last!' The Germans were excited about their achievements in the air over France. They reported to have shot down no less than fifty-seven four-engine aircraft using night fighter planes that performed very well.

Bloody German night fighters…

The Bf110 night fighters of 4th Fighter Division that took off from airfields at Florennes, Coulommiers, Saint-Dizier and Laon, shot down the majority of the RAF aircraft. Yet, single-engine Fw190 ('Wilde Sau' or 'Wild Boar') fighters, who attacked without the aid of radar, relying on searchlights, the moon and the bright exhaust flames of the four engines of the bombers, accounted for many Lancasters, whereas RAF could only claim ten German aircraft, two of which were 'probables'. A trail of crashed aircraft marked the path that the attacking bombers had followed. The whole route from the French coast to the target Mailly-le-Camp and back was dotted with burning wrecks. The final count showed appalling casualties. Of the dispatched aircraft ten abandoned their mission and forty-four crashed. Almost 300 young men have not returned, 270 were buried in France. The raid against Mailly-le-Camp had been extremely costly. Some squadrons had lost half their strength. That sorrowful morning left many empty chairs in RAF messes[87]. Men sat together in silence wondering why the hell so much went wrong. Some were so demoralized that they requested to be taken off flying duty, risking an LMF[88] (Lack of Morale Fibre) stamp on their record. With the morale very low Medical Officers and padres had a busy time. Entire ground crews lost not only their aircraft but also the crew they waved goodbye. For some it was

---

[87] *According to Bill Chorley Bomber Command lost 43 Lancasters. 250 men killed, 18 taken prisoner and 33 evaded.*
[88] *This was the worst that could happen to aircrew. If found LMF one would be removed from the air base, losing rank and being employed far away in a very low and degrading position.*

the second or third time; they never got used to it. Late that night the belongings of the dead and the missing were collected. Lockers were emptied, and rooms cleared.

New men arrived to take their places over the skies of Occupied Europe. Soon new Lancasters were flown in, ready to carry out the next sortie into enemy territory, and after a while names and faces were forgotten. Bomber Command was tough and repeatedly it licked her wounds. Under Sir Arthur Harris or 'Bomber' as his men call him, they stood up and fought the good fight. But now, at Headquarters Bomber Command, High Wycombe, worried staff officers counted losses while one squadron after the other, one station after the other, reported what aircraft and aircrews returned and how many were missing in action. At times, in his nightmares, Ron Emeny relived his jump as if it happened yesterday: 'I bailed and when my chute opened, I found it was only clipped on one side. I could not see from either of my eyes. They had closed up due to the burns I had received. I also found that I had lost all my hair and that my flying clothing was still smouldering. I was completely helpless and the burns were causing a horrific pain. I would not have cared to die, if only it came swiftly.'

The Mémorial de Caen has this wedding dress made by Paulette Tripot from the canopy of a parachute used on the night of 3/4 May 1944 near Mailly-le-Camp during the crash of a Lancaster of No.207 Squadron, shot down by the Germans. Paulette married in this dress on 24 September 1947 in Villemandeur. Ron Emeny was sheltered by Lucien Tripot who had also hidden the parachute until the departure of the German troops from his village on August 23, 1944. Left: Emeny in front of the crypt where he hid in 1944. (LT/RE)

Men on the run.
In France, surviving members of the crew of 'Freddie' were doing their best to stay out of the hands of the Germans. Nick Stockford landed close to the crash site near Chaintreaux. Due to the time between the jumps of Emeny, Pittwood and himself, he landed far away from the others, buried his parachute and started to walk. That night he knocked on the door of a farm whose owner opened it to allow him in and silently pointed at a chair standing by the table. While Stockford waited, the farmer took the telephone and began a long conversation. Unable to understand much of it, Stockford became very anxious at hearing the excited voice say 'Anglaise' several times. Not waiting any longer, he jumped up and ran out of the kitchen, back into the darkness. Following a southerly direction he passed the railroad that runs between Montargis and Nemours. He never knew if the Frenchman was calling the Resistance or if he was betraying him to the Germans. At daybreak he reached the village of Beaune la Rolande. When he knocked on a door again, the scared inhabitant slammed it shut. The same thing happened a few hours later in the village of Boiscommun. The fear of German reprisals had paralysed the terrified local population. It was quite understandable that simple people would not risk their lives and goods for

an unknown airman. For days Stockford roamed the countryside, carefully using the contents of his escape kit. Finally, he reached the forests north of Orleans. Being well aware that he could not go on much longer without help he took one last chance.

Upon entering the village of Saint Loup, he spotted a garage. Casually walking in, he turned to a man who was busy working under the bonnet of a car. Monsieur Durant, the owner, was of a different make. He took Stockford upstairs to a hiding place and then promptly called Father Chenu, the parish priest. Like many clergymen in France, he was a member of the resistance. The priest got in touch with Miss Jublot, the teacher, who was generally known as very anti-German and a member of the resistance. After her school finished and the children were on their way home, Miss Jublot immediately went to Durant's garage to interrogate Nick Stockford. She took notes of his answers and told him to stay put while she asked a young man to stay with the Englishman and watch over him in order to make sure that he did not leave.

On 10 May Miss Jublot returned. Stockford's identity had been confirmed; now they could plan his escape. Miss Jublot had a small room available in the school, below which were the classrooms. When she left, she said: 'Remember: never, never open the shutters.' While Stockford found a hiding place, Pittwood and Emeny tried to survive in enemy territory. They had landed near each other. Pittwood hid his parachute and started looking for Emeny. After a while he found poor Curly sitting against a tree, his face and hands both terribly burned, quite unable to free himself from his parachute.

Pittwood helped his comrade to get out of the harness. The injuries made poor Emeny completely helpless; his eyes had closed, there were large blisters on his face; in reality he was blind. Pittwood did not know what to do. Leaving Emeny would kill him if he were not found in time. If he were found, he would end up in a German PoW camp. On the other hand, German doctors might be able to help him. Pittwood decided that he should not leave his crew mate, but rather try to stay together. It had a dangerous consequence. Taking Emeny with him slowed Pittwood down. But Emeny was determined to try. He led him through the countryside. An escape seemed impossible but there was little else Pittwood could do to make sure that Emeny survived. The whole night the two men struggled on. Emeny's wounds slowed them down so much that it took hours to cover one or two miles. When the first sunrays appeared, they were still near their landing site. They found shelter in a ruined farmhouse where they pushed their parachutes and Mae Wests into the chimney. It was not until much later they heard that a farmer had found the equipment and that one of the parachutes had been used to make a wedding dress! [89] Afraid to stay too long the men decided to move on.

On Emeny's face hard scabs had formed which at times made the young air gunner scream with pain when he accidentally hit a twig. Led by Pittwood Ron reached Ferrières, a small town, not far from the railroad between Montargis and Paris. He was about to collapse; he could go no further. Feeling he was going into shock brought even more screams as the pain became unbearable. Desperate and in agony Emeny said: 'Please, Jack, leave me here', 'Go on. I will just slow you down.' Ron suggested hiding in the forest, giving Pittwood a head start. Once twenty-four hours had passed Emeny would give himself up and try to get medical treatment for his burns. Pittwood was quite determined not to give in and leave his friend behind. Rather than go on he knocked at the first door he saw. A woman opened it and immediately understood the predicament of the two strangers. Helping poor Emeny into her kitchen she prepared warm towels to dab his face. It was the best she could do, except to promise the exhausted, scared and shivering airmen not to say a word about this encounter and wave the two farewell. Pittwood and Emeny walked the whole day until they arrived at La Selle sur le Bied. Ron Emeny, weakened by his pain, was at the end of tether, when Pittwood found a hiding place in a family crypt at the local cemetery.

---

[89] Mrs. Tripot used the dress at her wedding on 24 September 1947. She also used parts of the canopy of the parachute to make a nightgown and other small pieces of clothing. The wedding dress can be seen at the Liberation Museum in Caen, France.

By now, he was also too exhausted to go on. They even discussed a possible surrender to the local police. In the morning, by a stroke of luck, help arrived. Pittwood, heard people digging on the other side of the cemetery wall. He left Emeny and saw an old couple working in a small vegetable plot. Pittwood explained that he was an English flyer who needed help. The couple was caught by surprise, and asked Pittwood to return to the crypt and wait. An hour later a man and a girl entered the cemetery and approached the crypt. Pittwood was told to follow them, while Emeny had to stay in the crypt and wait for the couple to return. The two flyers were reluctant to part. They looked dirty and tired. Biguet, one of the Frenchmen, told Emeny in his best English to trust him. Then he left Emeny to himself.

Helpers found.

He returned an hour later. Both Monsieur et Madame Biguet felt deeply sorry for the helpless air gunner, whose black face was covered with scabs, the pain of which caused non-stop moans. The Biguets were simple, very brave people. They made a very courageous decision. Holding Emeny between them they walked to their house. Mrs. Biguet then ran to the local doctor, explaining that she had two Englishmen in her house, one of them severely burned, virtually blind and barely alive, the other so exhausted he could hardly speak. Doctor Trouveney arrived within ten minutes. He asked Madame Biguet to warn André Bourrabier, a local member of the resistance who, in his turn, went to see his leader, Lucien Tripot. He told Tripot what the doctor said. That evening Tripot visited the Biguets and left with the flyers. Although the doctor, with his inadequate cabinet of instruments, had only been able to give temporary help, Emeny was strong enough to stumble between Jack Pittwood and Lucien Tripot. Together they walked through the fields to Chopilles à Courtemaux, where Tripot's father had a farm. The trip was dangerous, as German patrols were on the road, trigger-happy and scared at the same time. Two hours later they arrived at the farm. Edouard Tripot knew what risks he took for his son.

In the last year the Gestapo had closely watched the farm of Carmignac. Lucien and Luce were close, and consequently Lucien was a suspect as well. Luce Carmignac, member of the local resistance, was not sure if Ron Emeny would survive the ordeal of his burns. He dug a grave at the farm in case the sergeant did not survive his wounds. Carmignac hated the Germans. He always carried his Stengun, dropped by the RAF, hoping to come across a German or, even better, a Milice, an officer of the collaborating police. After the war he remembered: 'It was quite amazing with what ease I killed Germans as well as collaborators. The only problem was that we had to finish them off in the fields rather than in villages as we did not want the people there to suffer the German retaliation.'

The entire Carmignac family was in the resistance. Consequently, they suffered a horrible fate. In June 1943, an airdrop of three tons of weapons and ammunition was made. The Carmignac family handled the reception and then the cargo was delivered and subsequently hidden in the two farms of Carmignac and Mr. Guillemin. But the Gestapo was on the trail of the group and knew that somewhere someone was hiding an arms cache. How they ever found out? Even today rumours are rife. It might have been imprudence of one or more group members or there was a possible denunciation by an unknown villager. A few weeks after Emeny continued his journey south, the Germans closed the trap and they surrounded the Carmignac residence. On July 8, at night, the Carmignacs, all installed on the first floor of their house, heard noises outside. The Germans had surrounded the building and demanded immediate surrender. The Carmignacs, however, opened fire at the Gestapo and the accompanying soldiers. Luce and Roger managed to escape. Roger was wounded but managed to escape as well. The other two men, father and son, defended themselves bravely and killed two Gestapo men, but the large number of enemies made a difficult defence, two against eight. Then father Lucien was mortally wounded. Norbert (the youngest) was killed as well. Seeking refuge, Roger went to the farm of Mr. Gauthier, where he found a hiding place. The doctor feared for Roger's life and in secrecy he was taken to hospital. There he was discovered by the Germans and kept under guard.

The Carmignac family was deeply involved in resistance against the Germans and the Milice, the much hated collaboration police. Father Lucien was leader of the Prosper network in Gatinais. He and his son Norbert were both killed by the Germans on 8 July 1943. Madame Carmignac and her son Roger were both arrested and returned from their deportation barely alive. She survived Ravensbrück, while her son returned from Buchenwald, Dachau and Ravensbrück. Only Luce remained at large with a burning hate for the Germans. A plaque remembers the sacrifice this family suffered for freedom. Their names are also shown of the monument on which Chuelles mourns all their dead from 187- until today. (Tripot/Chuelles).

After recovery, Roger was deported. In the meantime, a search was done in the house. Mrs. Carmignac was handcuffed. But in the house, there was no trace of weapons. The Gestapo took the informant to the scene. The man, embarrassed by the presence of the widow, did not speak but lead the Germans to the arms cache. It was empty as, after learning of the informant, the resistance had relocated everything to the Gauthier farm. Aware of the deaths of Carmignac Senior and Norbert, they had moved all the arms, ammunition and explosive deep into the woods. When the Germans arrived at Gauthier's home he had long gone. However, on his return from work, he was picked up by the Gestapo and also deported. The informant fled to Belgium, where he disappeared. To the chagrin of Luce Carmignac, the traitor was never found. When interviewed by the author he said: 'If I run into that pig, I will kill him with my bare hands.'

Luce never had the chance of fulfilling his wish. After the arrests, the remainder of the Prosper-network dispersed. Fortunately, this blow for the resistance happened long after the flyers had left the area to be handed over to the next chain in the long line to freedom. While the airmen rested in a hiding place, the resistance contacted the allies to make sure they were dealing with real airmen and not with Abwehr infiltrators. Besides, they urgently needed medicine for Emeny, who lapsed into unconsciousness at times. Expecting the gunner to die anyway, the Maquisards first took him to a nearby forest. They sent for a surgeon who lived in a nearby village arranging for him to have a look at this Englishman. Emeny still vividly remembers what happened that night, when in fact a decision was made that saved his life: 'That evening I was taken into the nearby woods and left. After about two hours three men appeared. They were local Maquisards. Carrying an array of weapons and pushing bikes with an extra one for me they had come to pick me up. I was placed in the saddle and with one on each side to support me we cycled a long distance to Châteaurenard. I was taken into the doctor's house and put straight to bed. The doctor immediately started to work on my eyes, getting them fully open so that he could put salve on both eyelids. He told me that I required penicillin or streptomycin. As this was not available in the German occupied countries they would radio London. After the Doctor bandaged me, I was put on the bicycle again and taken to the place where they hoped I would be safely recovering. What I did not know that the resistance had taken precautions in case I would not survive my burns. They dug a grave in a corner of a garden, just in case.

Doctor Salmon whose skill and devotion saved Ron Emeny's life, photographed with some of the pieces of ND556. Thanks to medical supplies dropped by the RAF Emeny survived his burns and a life-threatening blood poisoning. Lucien Tripot too had himself photographed between the remains of P for Peter. (Tripot)

The next stage.
At the same time the men and women of the resistance prepared for the transportation of their British allies. They had to be turned into Frenchmen to enable future movements to Paris. Their uniforms were burned behind the farm. Nothing was to be left that might reveal their true identity. Pittwood was chosen the first to go, Emeny being far too weak. They were not even sure if he would survive this ordeal, let alone travel under such dangerous circumstances. The local doctor, Doctor Salmon, was told about the gravely wounded Englishman. He agreed to tend Emery's wounds. To be prepared for the worst Carmignac and Tripot dug a shallow grave in the garden just in case Ron Emeny would not survive his burns. For a week Doctor Salmon paid daily visits, until he was sure that Emeny was strong enough to stay in the house. The transmitter of the Maquis was used to ask the RAF for medicine. Shortly after they received a cry for help from the resistance the RAF sent a Lysander to a field near Orléans. On board were two secret agents and a consignment of streptomycin and penicillin. A day later a stranger handed the medicine to the doctor and disappeared as secretly as he arrived. Doctor Salmon, who saw Emeny every day, could finally begin his treatment. Whilst Emeny recovered the doctor took him on his rounds in the area. When they came to a German roadblock the doctor told the soldiers that Ron was his nephew who was wounded during an RAF raid on Juvissy. Besides, Emeny's papers proved his identity.

The Germans often expressed their sympathy for the victim of the English 'Terrorflieger.' Emeny felt awful when the people who were his enemies acted so kindly and considerately. They allowed the doctor to pass the roadblock without checking his car. The doctor was quite unscrupulous as it allowed him to bring 'things' to 'people' who needed 'them'! Sometimes he even carried explosives in his doctor's case. While airmen tried to stay out of the hands of the Germans, gravediggers in many towns and villages along the route flown by the bombers carried out their sad duties. Clerks registered the deaths of many young men, as did the clerk of the village of Montigny-le-Guesdier, where Lancaster EE148, UM-S2 of No.626 Squadron from Wickenby has crashed with the loss of all crew members. In beautiful letters, as if to show deep respect for the men who had died, he wrote in the archives: 'No.7, on 4 May 1944 at 01:15 hours J. Waites, 2209456C, airman of British nationality, has died at le Bleine, near Montigny-le-Guesdier.' There is no record about the other members of the crew of this Lancaster, which crashed with secret devices on board, Mandrel and Boozer [90]. They were Pilot Officer Fisher, Flying Officer Larmen and four Sergeants: Crooks, Godfrey, Roper and Hatton.

Ellis and Lissette were buried in a joint grave at Chaintreaux local cemetery. One of the .303 calibre machine guns from the aircraft was placed in front of the grave. After the war, the Imperial War Graves Commission put new head stones at the spot. Local villagers regularly put flowers there. On Ellis' stone it says: In the perfect love of Jesus. He is safe for evermore. Kathleen and Jean. (RE/CWGC)

At Beauchery-Saint-Martin André Jacques, mayor, wrote in the Death Register: 'On 4th May 1944, during the day, we have collected the lifeless bodies of two military aviators of English nationality, and fragments of the bodies of other soldiers, who belonged to the crews of two aircraft that crashed in flames at about one o'clock in the morning. We have put the two bodies and the fragments of bodies in five coffins and subsequently buried them in five graves at the Municipal Cemetery. In coffin No.1 have been put various parts of bodies from the aircraft that has fallen on the house of the widow Lapoix née Simard, Aline, Zoé, Louise. In coffin No.2 have been put various fragments of bodies belonging to the aircraft, which crashed in a meadow, which is the property of Mr. de Boisgelin, situated not far from the Forest of Lunay. In coffin No.3 has been put the body of an aviator, whose identity could not be established. In coffin No.4 has been put the body of an English aviator, Sergeant R.T. Wilson, serial number 1602530, who carried on the left hand a wedding ring of yellow metal with the initials R.T.W.' Sergeant Wilson was mid-upper gunner of Lancaster ND411, PM-J of No.103 Squadron from RAF Elsham Wolds. Wilson and the rest of the crew, Pilot Officer Holden, Flight Sergeant Gay and Sergeants McCallum, Moore, Hockford and Sykes all died in the crash.

He continued: 'In coffin No.5 we put the body of an aviator, having a wedding ring on the right hand, made of plastic, who was identified as Haes or Haet.' The man identified as Heas or Haet, might very well have been Sgt K.N. Read, the bomb aimer of Lancaster JB405, PH-M of No.12 Squadron from RAF Wickenby. Eight were killed when their aircraft crashed: Pilot Officer Carter, Warrant Officer Close RAAF, Flying Officer Ward and Sergeants Long, Hayhurst, Simpson, Johnson and Read. Pittwood had a safe yet very eventful journey to freedom and returned to England within a few weeks. We will read about that journey in detail as he was helped by another organisation than Comète. At the same time Emeny was recovering while confined to his safe house. Therefore, he had no idea that Jack had informed his relatives that their son was still alive. For three more weeks Emeny stayed in Châteaurenard. Slowly his wounds healed. Only scars showed the horrible ordeal the Englishman had gone through. His eyelids were open now, making Ron Emeny thrilled to be able to see once more.

---

[90] *There is no record of the other six members of this Lancaster crew. When the plane crashed, it had two secret devices, on board, Mandrel and Boozer, both devices to jam enemy radio and radar transmissions. Aircraft of No.100 Group were especially equipped for this purpose.*

Lucien Tripot, Maquisard, dressed with a French helmet, a German camouflage cape and a German machine-gun. Luce Carmignac, Maquisard, burning with hate and ready to kill any German he comes across. In his hand a British Sten gun. For Ron Emeny he remained a friend for life. Emeny slowly recovered from his burns. As his health improved, he was allowed to leave the farm in the evening and enjoy the fresh air. Yet it took a while before his hands and face have healed enough to prepare him from the train journey to Paris, where he was to wait for the signal that his time for departure to the Pyrenees had come. (Tripot/Carmignac/Emeny)

To Paris and to a prison camp.

Then, one day, the time had come for Curly to leave his friends and go on his way. Emeny and Tripot took bicycles and went to the small railway station of Chuelles. The Germans did not guard it and it seemed relatively easy to buy a ticket to Paris. Tripot accompanied him as far as Montargis. Here he handed his guest to another member of the resistance, a man whom Emeny only knew as Avignon. He took Curly to Paris. Emeny was escorted to Boulevard Sebastopol, where Genevieve Rocher lived. She ran one of the Paris safe houses where allied soldiers waited for their turn to travel south. She had good reasons to detest the Germans. The Gestapo had arrested both her father and brother. After terrible torture, the two men were executed. Yet she was a cheerful friendly woman, who fed her guests and tried to make them feel at home during the short spell in her house[91]. After a few days Emeny was moved again. He arrived at another house, that of Philippe and Virginia d'Albert-Lake, the linchpins of Comète in Paris. Here he met the men with whom he would continue his journey to the horizon with, Hubbard, Willis, Barnes and Cornett. While the children learned and played, and Pittwood and Emeny continued their escape to Paris, Nick Stockford stayed above the school until early June. He heard of the invasion when one day Miss Jublot came running upstairs with the wonderful news that the allies had landed.

That night Father Chenu, Miss Jublot and Sergeant Stockford celebrated the great event, in silence, for the allies were still far away. A few days after D-Day more news came! Stockford was to prepare for his departure. A man was said to come shortly and made himself known by saying: 'Saint Loup, I have 27 pupils.' This was the code to prove that the man was a genuine member of the resistance. Unfortunately, however, plans like this did not always go as expected. The guide could not find the village of Saint Loup and wandered through Orléans, where a part of that town had the same name. Unable to find the address he went to Montargis, where another quarter with the name Saint Loup was situated. At the same time Miss Jublot got increasingly anxious about the safety of Stockford and the members of the resistance who knew of him. Had they been betrayed? Was the Gestapo near to arrest Stockford? Had the Germans arrested the guide? And if they had, would he tell them of his mission?

---

[91] *Rumours said that Mrs. Rocher was a double agent. Ron Emeny never succeeded in tracing her after the war. She vanished from the face of the earth. When Emeny made inquiries, someone came to him and hissed: 'She was a communist'. When the Author researched in France, the authorities told him that the Gestapo has arrested her and her husband in 1944 and deported to Germany. Supposedly, they returned after the war in 1945 and died later.*

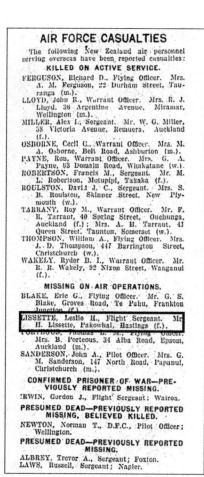

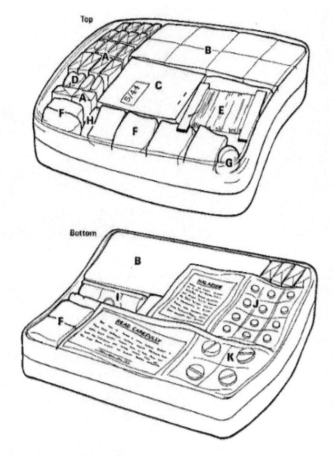

Left: The public announcement of RNZAF casualties must have been a great shock to people who recognised the names of friends or family members. Right: Allied escape boxes and pouches contained the following items: Horlicks tablets. Chocolate. Milk (tube). Benzadrine (against fatigue). Halazone tablets (water purifier). Matches. Adhesive tape. Chewing gum. A water bottle. Compass. The Purse held the following: Maps. Compass. File (hacksaw). Foreign currency. Issued separately from the above were the Aids to Escape (Gadgets): Compass; there were seven types: Round, Stud, Swinger, Fly-Button, Pencil Clip, Tunic Button, and Pipe. Some air crew had special flying boots (and knife). Here we see the Halex Ltd Escape Kit with: A. Malted Milk Tablets; B. Toffees; C. Matches; D. Chewing Gum; E. Fishing Line; F. Boiled Sweets; G. Compass; H. Needles & thread; I. Razor & soap; J. Water Purifying Tablets Halazone; K. Benzedrine; A water bottle in bottom.

The poor teacher travelled to Orléans to find the guide. She rode through the countryside, looking for clues. With Miss Jublot away, officially recuperating from an illness, the guide arrived in the right Saint Loup, exhausted and totally frustrated. To make the confusion complete, a substitute teacher, who knew nothing of the Miss Jublot's activities, had taken her class. When the guide said the words 'Saint Loup. I have 27 pupils', the replacement looked at him and said: 'Well, I have 32.' The guide understood that this teacher was not the person he wanted to talk to, so he left in a hurry. Upstairs Stockford had seen and heard enough to know that something was terribly wrong. But since he was told not to show himself, he remained upstairs. With great disappointment he saw his rescuer leave, turn, look back to the school and disappear.' When Miss Jublot returned that night Stockford could only tell her how close he had been to starting a further escape on his own. Father Chenu managed to restore contact and a few days later Mr. De Saint Paul, as the guide was called, returned to the school. Nick Stockford survived thanks to the sacrifice of W/O Lissette.'

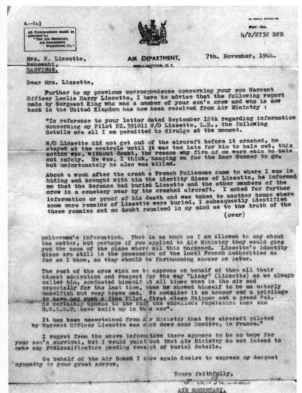

On the left: a letter from the Air Department dated 7th November 1944. On the right: the Graves Registration Report Form.

GRAVES REGISTRATION REPORT FORM

COUNTRY FRANCE — REPORT NO: - — SCHEDULE NO: 1.
PLACE OF BURIAL: CHAINTREAUX COMMUNAL CEMETERY (Seine et Marne)
Land belongs to
The following are buried here:-
Certified complete and correct
Signature ... Date 22 AUG 1956

R.G.	No. & Rank	Inits. Name & Honours	Unit	D/D	For Wks. use
Joint Gr.	5376.2 Sgt. (A.G.)	R. ELLIS	207 Sqdn. R.A.F.	4.5.44	C H
	391011 W/O (Pilot)	L.H. LISSETTE	RNZ 207 Sqdn. R.N.Z.A.F.	4.5.44	C H

On 7th November 1944 Lissette's mother who lived in Pakowhai in the North island received a letter from the Air Department in Wellington, confirming that her son had been killed in action, while trying to save the lives of his crew members. Top right is the Graves Registration Report. (BL)

He wrote: 'On the night of 3rd May 1944 we took off aboard Lancaster EM-F ND556 of 207 Squadron, at 2205. The target was a massive German military camp situated near the village of Mailly-le-Camp that consisted of 20,000 troops and a Panzer Division of tanks. I do not know what went wrong, but the Germans were waiting for us. ND556 was attacked by German night fighters, evading one but falling to a second, the dinghy hatch was blown off, the bomb bay was hit and a fire started. The stricken Lancaster crashed at Chaintreaux in Seine-et-Marne; the pilot Warrant Officer Leslie Lissette RNZAF remained at the controls. His remains are in the grave in Chaintreaux with his rear gunner Sergeant Ronald Ellis, who lived in Duns Tew. The bomb aimer bailed out first and I followed him. I landed in a wood some miles north of Ferrieres. I freed my parachute from the tree in which it had become entangled and buried it, together with my Mae West, in the undergrowth. I set out at once, walking south by my compass, and continued across the fields for about three hours, when I hid in a wood until dawn. I removed my brevet and service chevrons and threw away my loose silver. I could see that I was near a small village, and later that morning (4th May) I moved towards it. About midday, as I was hiding in a hedge, two girls walked by and though they saw me, they did not stop.'

'Half an hour later, an old man came straight towards where I was hiding and said he was the father of the two girls who had seen me and reported my presence. He told me that I had reached Fontenay. When he heard that I intended to make my way south, he warned me against going through Montargis, which, he said, was full of Germans. At 14:00 I set out in what I thought was a south-westerly direction, so as to make a detour round Montargis I crossed the railway and the main road and finally reached a stream, which I followed, thinking it was flowing in the direction I wanted to go. After scrambling through thick undergrowth in my efforts to follow the course of the stream. I came out on a secondary road leading to a bridge across a stream. I crossed the bridge and then realised I was hopelessly lost. Seeing a man working in a wood yard, I beckoned to him and asked him where I was. He told me I was on the outskirts of the village of Nargis. I made my way towards the town and then hid in woods for the night. I set out again early next morning (5th May) for Chateau-Landon. Before I reached the town, I decided to seek help at a farm. There were several people working in the fields, but they took no notice of me. I finally managed to attract the attentions of an old man, to whom I declared myself. He took me back to the house and gave me some wine to drink. People at once crowded round and offered me food, which I refused as I was not hungry.'

'They were just discussing the question of providing civilian clothes for me, when a woman came running up and told me I must leave at once, as the farmer had informed the authorities of my presence. I ran down the hill, through some woods and across a stream, finally crawling into the undergrowth on the far side, from where I was able to keep a good lookout for anyone searching for me. About 15:00 a man saw me and came towards me.' 'By this time, I was extremely hungry, as the only food I had eaten since jumping out was some Horlicks tablets from my escape box. The man promised to return in an hours' time with some food. He returned shortly afterwards, however, without the food, which he said he would not give me until I had written in his notebook that he had helped me. I was feeling desperate by this time, so I did as he asked me. The man then disappeared for several hours, and it was not until 19:00 he returned with a loaf of bread and some cold potatoes. he was extremely nervous and asked me to leave at once. I continued on my way towards Chateau-Landon and reached the outskirts that evening. I passed several people, but they took no notice of me. I entered a small coppice and rested there for a while. Shortly after several youths passed close by my hiding place whistling 'Tipperary'. I realised they were looking for me and beckoned to them. They told me they were members of the Maquis, though I did not believe them as they had no arms. I told them I wanted to get to Beaumont, whereupon they led me out of the town and left me on the road to Mondeville.'

'That night I lay up in a wood just outside the town. The next morning (6th May) I walked through Mondeville and reached the outskirts of Beaumont. I stayed near the town all day, hoping to contact someone who could help me, but saw no one. Early next morning I walked through Beaune-Le-Rolande and continued along the road. I was feeling very weak by this time, so I entered a field and slept for some hours. At 17:00 I set out again and walked through Boiscommun which was very deserted. Beyond the town I saw an old man working in the fields and asked him the way to Vitry. He pointed to the road I should take and I continued along it. I passed several people, who completely ignored me, though I heard one man mutter 'les Boches' as I passed. A little further on I came to a clearing in the woods beside the side of the road. I saw a water trough standing in the clearing and went straight towards it, as I was feeling extremely thirsty. As I was drinking, I saw three people standing in front of a house watching me. I went up to them and asked for something to eat. After they had given me some food, I declared myself to them and was immediately invited inside. The owner of the house said that his son was away at the moment, but when he returned, he would be able to put me in touch with an organisation. His son returned shortly afterwards and said he would be able to help me. I spent the night in the garage attached to the house, and the next day the son went to see a member of an organisation. That evening (8th May) I was visited by a young woman, and from this point my journey was arranged for me [92].' On the night of 14/15 July 1944 he arrived at Whitchurch Airport near Bristol on a civil airliner from Lisbon. His papers were made out for a John White, a civilian escapee from Vittel internment camp in France. He revealed his true identity to the security guard.

A letter from France to Mrs Stockford:

'21st December 1947. Dear Madame. We have been grievously saddened, my sister and I by your letter telling us of the death of your dear Nick because he to us had been profoundly sympathetic. We assume that his sudden death is due to heart trouble, the airman's illness. Will you accept, for yourself and for his family our sincerest condolences? He had promised us to visit us again, with his wife and his children in order to thank us. His plane had been brought down in the neighbourhood of Nemours and he had entered a house, where he realized that someone was telephoning to betray him to the German Gestapo

---

[92] *All evading men knew that they were never to tell anything about their experiences with the resistance movement.*

Alas, many people feared the terrible pain inflicted by the Germans to those hiding allied airmen. Then he had fled from there and after crossing Beaune la Rolande and Boiscommun, two small neighbouring towns where no one spoke to him on account of his uniform, they took him for a German. Soon, hunger and thirst made him stop in an isolated house at the edge of the large forest of Orleans.'

Shortly after he came home, Nick Stockford died of a lung disease, which he contracted in France. (BL)

There he made contact and Mr. Durand hid him during several days his motorcar garage. On Monday morning his sons came to inform me of his presence because I was the head of the local resistance and I went to see our schoolteacher Mlle. Jublot, who later became Captain Jublot, after school hours went to make sure of his identity talked to him for a long time in the garage and saw me again at 11pm that night. Wednesday, 10th May she went again on her bicycle to look for him. They returned on foot and dined at my house. Mlle. Jublot concealed him in her room where he remained hidden until Friday, 2nd June absolutely forbidden to open the shutters because the classroom was below, and the children's playground was in front of the room. During this time neither the children nor the neighbours suspected anything. For four weeks my sister took something for him to eat and drink to the school at midday and each evening after dark, he came to eat at my house with Mlle. Jublot. during this time, my sister washed his linen. Dramatic moment, an agent of the S.S. coming from Loudres to fetch him away arrived at Orleans with the password 'St. Loup I have 27 pupils'. After having searched in a suburb of Orleans, then in another place near Montargis, he arrived in the third St. Loup. That day Mlle. Jublot had taken one of her pupils to sit for an examination at Montgrais. The agent spoke to the other teacher who replied, 'no sir, I have 32 of them'. He understood then that this was not the person he was seeking and demanded her absolute silence. Through the shutters Nicholas had seen him but he did not dare to speak to him. The agent came again the next day and told Mlle. Jublot that he would be moving her prisoner.

She went to buy him a shirt of white silk and a pair of trousers and the next day at noon in broad daylight he left St. Loup on foot to return to Boiscummun where he found the S.S. Agent and both of them made for Paris. There, that is all we know, but Mlle. Jublot, Mow Mme Leveau, mother of two small children and living at 77, Boulevard Alexandre Martin, Orleans (Loiret) will be able to give you other details of his stay in St. Loup during these for weeks. The letter you wrote to her came to my house and I have re-directed it to her. We hope that she has received it and that she will reply to it herself. In July 1944 we still had hidden two other English soldiers, one of who came again to see us in the uniform of an Air Force Officer, he was there about 1 year. That was about one year ago. And it is for having saved these 3 English soldiers that I have received a diploma from the British Government signed by Air Chief Marshal Tedder. We also saved three American airmen and received a diploma signed by General Eisenhower. Above all, from May to August 1944 we had to accommodate 4 Officers of the Head Quarters Staff of the Resistance Movement who used to keep in touch with the W.O. de Loudres by a transmitter placed in our house where there was already hidden ammunition received by parachute. By the Grace of God, we had the good fortune never to be denounced to the German enemy. We people are coming to be overlooked in France in an endeavour by the Soviet Russia to establish here the Communist Regime, but the Government and the majority of the population are opposing it. We wish you a Happy Christmas and are pleased to send you our very best wishes. Signed: Abbe A. Chenu. Catholic Priest Certified teacher at the University at Paris. Decorated by the insigne of the Free French Forces, diplomas of the Governments of England and America, recommended for the Liberation Medal. I visited Oxford in 1911 and today I am 71 years old.'

This scroll commemorates
Warrant Officer
L. H. Lissette
Royal New Zealand Air Force
held in honour as one who
served King and Country in
the world war of 1939-1945
and gave his life to save
mankind from tyranny. May
his sacrifice help to bring
the peace and freedom for
which he died.

CHAINTREAUX COMMUNAL CEMETERY
(Index No. Fr. 1387)

Chaintreaux is a village and commune 25 miles (40 kilometres) south-south-east of Melun, and 8 miles (12 kilometres) south-east of Nemours.
The most practical way of visiting the cemetery, which lies on the eastern side of the village on the road leading to Ramauville, is by taxi from Nemours. The joint grave of 2 airmen, 1 from the United Kingdom and 1 from New Zealand, is some 18 yards south-east of the monument in the centre of the cemetery.

ELLIS, Sgt. (Air Gnr.) RONALD, 537642. R.A.F. 207 Sqdn. 4th May, 1944. Age 25. Husband of Kathleen Ellis, of Duns Tew, Oxfordshire. Joint grave.

LISSETTE, Wt. Offr. (Pilot) LESLIE HARRY, 391011. R.N.Z.A.F. 207 (R.A.F.) Sqdn. 4th May, 1944. Age 26. Son of Harry and Nellie Georgina Lissette, of Napier, Hawke's Bay, New Zealand. Joint grave.

Memorial Scroll sent to parents of L.H. Lissette. The headstones of Sgt Ellis and W/O Lissette. A page about the graves at Chaintreaux. (BL)

The letter from the Air Council to Mrs. Lissette read:

'Further to my previous correspondence concerning your son Warrant Officer Leslie Harry Lissette, I have to advise that the following report made by Sergeant King who was a member of your son's crew and who is now back in the United Kingdom, has now been received from Air Ministry. In reference to your letter dated September 12th regarding information the pilot NZ.391011 W/O Lissette, L.H., the following details are all I am permitted to divulge at the moment. W/O Lissette did not get out of the aircraft before it crashed, he stayed at the controls until it was too late for him to jump out. This action was without doubt, the reason why five of us were able to jump out safely. He was, I think, hanging on for the rear gunner to go, but unfortunately, he too was killed. About a week after the crash a French policeman came to where I was in hiding and brought with him the identity discs of Lissette, he informed me that the Germans had buried Lissette and the other members of the crew in a cemetery near by the crashed aircraft. I asked for further information or proof of his death and was taken to another house where some more remains of Lissette were buried. I subsequently identified these remains and I have no doubt in my mind as to the truth of the policemen's information. That is as much as I am allowed to say about the matter, but perhaps if you applied to Air Ministry they would give you the name of the place where all this happened.'

'Lissette's identity discs are still in the possession of the local French authorities as far as I know, so they should be forthcoming sooner or later. The rest of the crew wish me to express on behalf of them all their utmost admiration and respect for the way 'Lizzy' (Lissette) as we always called him, conducted himself at all times when in the air and especially for the last time, when he showed himself to be an utterly unselfish but very brave man. We consider it an honour and a privilege to have had such a fine

Pilot, first class skipper and a grand pal. He certainly upheld to the [end] the excellent reputation that the RNZAF had built up in this war.' The formal letter to the family said: 'It has been ascertained from Air Ministry that the aircraft piloted by Warrant Officer Lissette was shot down near Dordrive in France.' I regret from the above information that there appears to be no hope for your son's survival, but I would point out that Air Ministry do not intend to make any reclassification pending receipt of burial details. On behalf of the Air Board, I once again desire to express my deepest sympathy in your great sorrow. Yours faithfully (signed) Pilot officer (for) Air Secretary [93].'

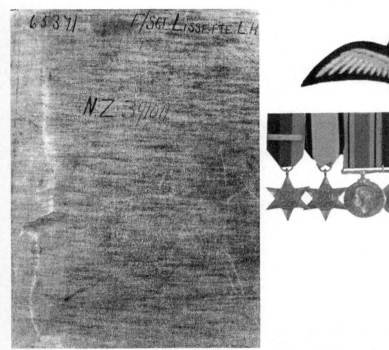

W/O Lissette's logbook, his pilot wing and his medals. In the logbook we read all his flights from the first on as a passenger to the one but last. Often the fatal sortie was written in the logbook by one of the clerks. From left to right: Air Crew Europe Star with Bomber Command Clasp, Aircrew Europe Star, Defence Medal, War Medal 1939-1945, NZ War Medal, and the Memorial Cross.

---

[93] *Original letter held by the Lissette family in Hastings, N.Z.*

8. LANCASTER AIRCREW AFTERMATH.

Life in Stalag Luft 1 [94].

Very little is known about the tail gunner Sergeant Ron Ellis RAF who died in the aircraft either prior or as it crashed - Sergeant Ron Ellis, the twenty-six-year-old rear gunner, was a boy apprentice engine fitter before the war. He turned to gunnery before heavy bombers needed flight engineers, a job which would have been more suitable for him. From Doncaster, he was married to Kathleen. They had a daughter, named Jean. In the next chapter we will read about the other members of the crew and how they tried to evade capture.

We also know little about the rest of the crew of Barnes. Flying Officer Geisler, the navigator, had been captured soon after his parachute landing and ended up prison camp Stalag Luft 1 near Stralsund at the Baltic Coast. The same happened to Sergeant Gregg, the bomb aimer, who also went there. Stalag Luft 1 was situated near Barth, Western Pomerania, Germany, as a camp for captured Allied airmen. Stalag Luft I had been opened in October 1942 as a British camp. By January 1944 the Germans detained 507 American Air Force officers there. The strength of the camp grew rapidly from this date, until April 1944 when the Red Cross reported 3,463 inmates. New compounds were opened and quickly filled. Nearly 6000 PoWs were crowded into the camp in September 1944, and at the time of the liberation of the camp housed almost 9,200 prisoners. After the Russians occupied the camp 7,717 Americans and 1,427 Britons were returned to military control. By then were five times more American than British prisoners.

The arrival of PoWs at the railway station of Barth, to be marched to Stalag Luft 1. (BuA)

Early in 1944 the camp consisted of two compounds designated as South & West compounds, containing a total of seven barracks, in which American and British officers and enlisted men were housed. A new compound was opened at the end of February 1944 and was assigned to the American officers who were rapidly increasing in number. This compound became North 1. and the opening of North 2 compound on 9 September 1944 and North 3 compound on 9 December 1944 completed the camp as it remained until 15 May 1945.

---

[94] *Stalag Luft I: An Official Account of the PoW Camp for Air Force Personnel 1940-1945 (An Official History) 2018.*

When Colonel Hubert Zemke arrived the command of the Americans was turned over to his command. Because the advance of the Russians indicated an early liberation Colonel Zemke changed the organisation to an inter-Allied wing; nominating Group Captain C.T. Weir as chief of staff of the organisation called Provisional Wing X. Group commanders were retained and continued to be responsible for the administration, security, discipline and welfare of their own groups, but more emphasis was directed toward staff operations in the event of liberation.

Top: Like all PoWs Geisler and Gregg marched from the station of Barth through the Dam Tor to Stalag Luft I The gate of Barth still stands. Rumour has it that Barth was never bombed because of the vicinity of the camp. (BuA/HO)

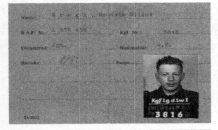

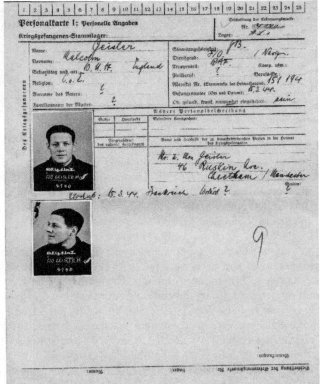

Radio Letters From Local Prisoners

RADIO letters from local prisoners of war were received yesterday from a German source. They were sent by: Sgt. Gregg (1576438) of 8, Richmond-road, West Bridgford:

"Dear Mother,—Don't worry. Fit and well and in good company. Tell Comforts Fund to send parcel. Write as often as you can and let Hazel have my address. I can only write a few letters a month, so spread the news. Pipe tobacco preferred. My fate is assured now, so you no need to worry any more Love.—Malcolm."

After their arrival both prisoners were processed. Gregg's number was 3816, and his billet was hut 8/12. He was allowed to write to his family, which was duly published in the local paper. Geisler must have arrived later, for number was 4140. (BA/HO/PG)

For this work, the following staff was appointed and served until the entire camp was evacuated. The German personnel changed frequently during the existence of the camp. The officers with their positions, as from the moment Geisler and Gregg arrived, were: Oberst Sherer, September 1943 to April 1945 and Oberst Warnstadt from January to April 1945. Following the Normandy invasion, the ardent Nazis tried to discuss the Nazi policy with the senior officers and to sway them to the German viewpoint of the war against the Russians. The allied prisoners did not enter into any discussions. Prior to April 1944, treatment was considered fairly good. Following a meeting of the Protecting Powers that month however, the German attitude towards PoWs became more severe. After Oberst Warnstadt became commandant conditions, became even worse. Instructions to the guards on the use of firearms were liberalised, and on 18 March 1945, and American officer was killed and a British officer was wounded, during an air raid warning that was not heard by 95% of the men in the same area. The defective system and the shoot to kill order were responsible for this incident. Both Oberst Warnstadt and Oberst Scherer were inclined to inflict mass punishment, restricting an entire barrack for one person's infraction of a rule, and several protests to the Protecting Power had to be made about these occurrences. However, little satisfaction was gained from these protests, and mass punishments continued to be the general policy.

Sergeant Plowman in better days: Showing a fish he just caught and riding his bicycle in his flying gear. (GEP)

Stalag 357 Fallingbostel

After being captured Sergeant Plowman, was taken to Camp 357 Fallingbostel, also known as Kopernikus. There were two camps there: Stalag XIB and Stalag XID were two prisoner-of-war camps (Stammlager) located just to the east of the town of Fallingbostel in Lower Saxony, in north-western Germany. In September 1944 Stalag 357 was moved from Thorn in Poland to the site of the former XI-D, with construction being carried out by Italian prisoners from XIB.

This new camp was used to house mostly British and Commonwealth PoWs. In November 1944 British paratroopers who had been captured at Arnhem arrived at Stalag 357. Led by their formidable RSM John C. Lord of 3rd Battalion, Parachute Regiment, they set about raising the standards of the camp. Lord insisted on proper military discipline with regular exercise and parades. At that time 17,000 PoWs; mostly British, but also Russian, Polish, Yugoslav, French and American prisoners were crammed into the camp causing severe overcrowding. Each hut contained 400 men, though it had bunks for only 150. By February 1945, the PoWs of XI-B and 357 were suffering from lack of food and medical supplies exacerbated by the influx of several hundred American PoWs captured in the Battle of the Bulge and Operation Nordwind. These newer arrivals found themselves accommodated in tents. In early April 1945 Sergeant Pilot James 'Dixie' Deans RAF, the camp leader of 357, was told by the Commandant Oberst Hermann Ostmann that 12,000 British PoWs were being evacuated from the camp in the face of the Allied advance. Regimental Sergeant Major Lord had also been selected to leave, but hid under the floor of a hut for five days in order to avoid it.

Top left: Prisoners entering Fallingbostel as 357 was also known. Top right: South Compound 357. Centre left: The gate of Stalag 357 Fallingbostel. Centre right: The caption on the back of the print read: 'The dividing up of swede peelings, mostly rotten, from the German mess. Each represented a hut of 80 prisoners and waits in front of the cardboard box into which his and his mates' share is put.' Bottom left: Arrival of the British Hussars at the camp. Bottom right: RSM Lord with moustache after the liberation. Even Montgomery came to see the PoWs shortly after their liberation. (IWM/ PRA/BuA)

The men then marched from the camp in columns of 2,000. After 10 days they arrived at Gresse, east of the Elbe. There they were issued with Red Cross parcels, but were also strafed by British Typhoon fighter-bombers, mistaking them for German troops. Sixty PoWs were killed and many wounded. Sergeant Deans confronted Oberst Ostmann and bluntly gave him a choice: to be captured by Russians or by the British. Ostmann provided Deans with a pass and a German guard and Sergeant Deans headed west to contact the advancing British troops. On 1 May, Deans and his guard were sheltering in a house east of Lauenberg when they heard over the radio the news of the death of Adolf Hitler. The next morning the house was overrun by troops of the British 6th Airborne. Deans was taken to the commander of VIII Corps and explained the situation. He was given a captured Mercedes car and drove back to Gresse. Two days later the column marched back across the British lines.

Meanwhile, the camps at Fallingbostel had been liberated on 16 April 1945 by British troops from B Squadron 11th Hussars and the Reconnaissance Troop of the 8th Hussars. They were met at the main gate of Stalag 357 by a guard of Airborne troops, impeccably attired and led by RSM Lord.

The aftermath of the survivors of F for Freddie
With the crash of EM-F ND556, and the gallant sacrifice of RNZAF 391011 Warrant Officer Leslie Harry Lissette, we will also see who these men really were, ordinary British boys, some of them a member of regular air force, others member of the RAF Volunteer Reserve. Their skipper, as the pilot was often called, was a Kiwi, a New Zealander. First, they had spent a long time training before being declared combat ready. Then it would be a matter of sheer luck if they would make it to the end of their operational tour. It was only shortly before they arrived at Spilsby that they would team up as a crew, a band of brothers [95]. As we read in the previous chapter the training from nothing to a qualified Lancaster pilot was long and expensive. Yet the chance of survival from bomber crews was small.

Top: The famous photo of a Lancaster over Mailly, lit up by explosions and flares. (IWM)

Leslie Lissette was born in Hastings, New Zealand on the 24th August 1917. His parents were from Pakowhai near Hastings on the North Island. Leslie attended Pakowhai Primary School and received his secondary education at Hastings High School. His sports were rugby, cricket, tennis and shooting. At the time of applying for service in aircrew in June 1939 he was employed as a teamster by the Hawkes

---

[95] *On the eve of the battle of Agincourt on Saint Crispin's Day, Henry V urged his men, vastly outnumbered by the French, to recall how the English had previously inflicted great defeats upon the French. The speech has been famously portrayed by Laurence Olivier to raise British spirits during the War, and by Kenneth Branagh in the 1989 film Henry V, and it made famous the phrase 'band of brothers'. The play was written ± 1600, and several later writers have used parts of it in their own texts.*

Bay River Board, and on being accepted was enlisted on the 24th October 1939 at Royal New Zealand Air Force Station Ohakea, where he was employed on ground duties [96]. He was posted on the 28th October 1941 to Royal New Zealand Air Force Station Nelson for similar duties. He trained as a pilot in his own time with permission of his Commanding Officer. On the 6th April 1942 he re-mustered as a pilot under training and was posted to the Initial Training Flying, Rotorua; thence on the 12th June 1942 to No.2 Elementary Flying Training School New Plymouth, for his basic flying training. On the 2nd October 1942 he embarked for Canada to continue his training under the Empire Air Training Scheme. Shortly after his arrival in Canada, Warrant Officer Lissette was posted on the 7th November 1942 to No.3 Service flying Training School, Calgary, Alberta. While here, on the 5th March 1943 he was awarded his flying badge and promoted to the rank of Sergeant. Meanwhile, on the 15th March 1943 he had proceeded to No.1'Y'Depot, Halifax, Nova Scotia, to await embarkation for the final part of his training in the United Kingdom.

Lissette arrived at No.11 Personnel Reception Centre Bournemouth on 5th April 1943. He was promoted to Flight Sergeant on 1st May 1943 and was posted on 15th June to No.20 (Pilots) Advanced Flying Unit, at Kidlington and later at Weston on the Green, both in Oxfordshire. Late in June 1943 he attended an instrument flying course at No.1515 Beam Approach Training Flight, Swanton Morley, Norfolk. On 26th August 1943 he went to No.28 Operational Training Unit at Wymeswold, Leicestershire for crewing up and completion of his training on Wellington bombers. During February and March 1944, he converted to Stirling bomber aircraft at No.1661 Conversion Unit, Winthorpe, Nottinghamshire. He proceeded on 10th April 1944 to No.5 Lancaster Finishing School, Syerston, Nottinghamshire, for the final conversion to Lancaster heavy bombers.

After coming home both Stockford and Gregg received the Caterpillar Club Certificate and the pin as a reward for saving his life with an Irvin parachute. Right is the letter from the Company. (PB/PG)

On 24th April 1944 he was posted to No.207 Squadron at RAF Spilsby, Lincolnshire and commenced operational flying. With this squadron and as the captain of a Lancaster he took part in four operational flights comprising attacks on Schweinfurt in Germany and Clermont Ferrand, Tours and the final one to Mailly-Le-Camp in France. 1st May 1944 he was promoted to Warrant Officer. Three days after his promotion and before all administration of this promotion had been finished, his life came to a sad end. In fact, it had been a little over two years when the end came for Lissette. His posting with No.207 Squadron had only been for ten days. After he and his crew failed to return to Spilsby or elsewhere in the UK, from this operation during the night of the 3/4th May 1944, all members of the crew including Warrant Officer Lissette were classified as missing. Later, it was learned that five of the crew had managed to make a parachute descent and on their return to England they stated that Warrant Officer

---

[96] *It is extremely sad to discovered that a career that started on 24th October 1939 lasted until 4 May 1944 killing Lissette after four operation sorties in less than ten days!*

Lissette had stayed at the controls until it was too late for him to bail out, this action being, without doubt, in order to give the others, the opportunity to bale safely. Then same informant stated that a French policeman had come to where he was in hiding bringing with him Warrant Officer Lissette's identity discs.

The policeman stated that the Germans had buried Warrant Officer Lissette and the other member of the crew who had not escaped in a cemetery near the crashed aircraft. In consequence of this information Warrant Officer Lissette was reclassified as missing believed killed in action. In due course his death was officially presumed to have occurred on the 4th May 1944 as the result of air operations. Subsequent investigations established that, Warrant Officer Lissette had been buried in the cemetery at Chaintreaux, France. At the time of his death, he had accumulated 477 hours as pilot. His service record showed how long the training to become a qualified pilot had been and how short a man's career could be.

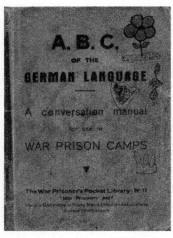 

Left: While in custody the PoWs could study German from a booklet provided by the YMCA. During World War II, YMCA was involved in supporting PoWs as well as the interned Japanese Americans. It set up War Prisoners Aid to support prisoners of war by providing sports equipment, art materials, radios, gramophones, eating utensils, musical instruments, and other items. When the war was finally over Lissette's Mother received his mascot Black Peter. Mrs. Lissette later added the RNZAF pilot wings, the stripes and the New Zealand shoulder flash to the mascot. (PG/BL)

Pittwood's story.
May 3rd 1944. Left base at 10:30 hrs for attack on Camp Mailly, crossed English coast at Beachy Head at 11:05 hrs expecting to cross back home two hours later, crossed enemy coast at 11:15 hrs arrived over target at Midnight, a/c goes up in front of us on Bombing run, flak started to come close just as Wes closed the bomb doors and Liz put the aircraft into weave at 12:10. Port outer engine set on fire by flak order to feather given, but at first fire refused to douse and Liz gave orders to put on chutes but Nick managed to put out fire and we set off for home and just as we turned onto course, fighters came in and at 12:40 we abandoned the aircraft

May 4th 1944. I landed lightly in a ploughed field surrounded on three sides by woods and by a road for the fourth. I had not seen any other chutes on the way down and was surprised to see Curly come over to me and ask what his face looked like and what I intended to do and I told him to get rid of his chute harness and May West as we were going to make a run for it, we made for the woods and someone called to us French or German? We do not know and we did not stop to ask. Jerry must have known we were around as searchlights were being played across the ground once in the woods we decided to move south and get as far away from the aircraft as possible so guided by the stars we started our first trek towards freedom. The woods were thick and I got covered in scratches but they gave first class cover and lasted for several miles we eventually came to a clearing and found ourselves alongside a railway, it was as light as day and I kept praying that the clouds would cover the moon but no such luck. A train was in sight heading north so we lay low at the edge of the wood our hearts beating like thunder and every snap of twig sounded like an explosion as soon as the train had passed, we crossed the rails. We were on a swampy plain and our only way for the next few miles was along the main road so we disguised our uniform as much as possible, burying Curly's outer suit in a well and once again started walking. It was now three o'clock and we were beginning to feel a little more settled and away from the first hue and cry and Jerry would not start a proper search until morning so we decided to get as far as possible before five o'clock and then find a hiding place for the day. We walked on through a small village, every dog barking and scaring us to death and then we approached a town and from notices we found out that it was Ferriers. We skirted the town, later to find out that it was a German garrison town, so lucky we did, and found us by a river to the S.E. of the town and we purified some water and ate a little chocolate and some Horlicks tablets and lay under the hedge to sleep remaining there all day. We were going to carry one walking the following evening but as Curly was in pain we did not get very far and decided to try a farm for help. At first the farmer did not like the idea but after a short while decided we could stay in the barn as long as we did not stay more than one day. He gave us some wine and some bread and what was most welcome, something to bathe Curly's face. We stayed in the barn that night and the following day but got little sleep as one of us had to be on watch and Curly was too ill and was best asleep.

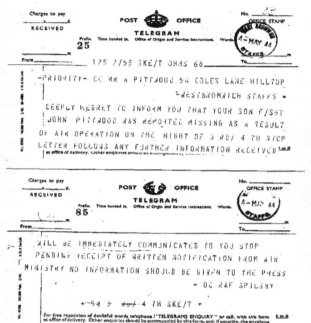

Left: The telegram father Pittwood received after his son went missing during the raid against Mailly. After the war his son John Jr. visited the crypt where he and Emeny rested. (Pittwood)

May 6th 1944. We decided to move just after midnight and as it was obvious Curly's face wanted treating, we decided to find a doctor, and went back to the main road towards Ferriers and called at a big house on the out-skirts of the town where they gave us more wine and some bread and jam, by this time we were beginning to feel hungry as our last meal had been supper on the 3rd and all we had eaten was a few odds and ends. The old lady informed us that Ferriers was a garrison town and that the doctor would probably hand us over, but 17 kilometres down the road was La Selle de Bain where there was one who would help us, so off we went to La Selle. We had to travel along the road and it was beginning to get light and we were still in uniform, we passed several Frenchmen going to work but no one stopped us. On approaching La Selle we met a woodman who gave us a drink of cognac and told us to go on a little further and call at another house and after being passed through several houses at each of which we had either wine or cognac we were eventually taken into the village, by this time the whole village knew we were there and we became the object of a crowd of sightseers. The doctor told us to wait in the cemetery

---

[97] *One of the questions he asked was 'What is the name of the pub you drink in at home?' Pittwood replied that it was a Greets Green, West Bromwich and that it was called Bowens. He was later told that it was wrong and that it was the Cross Inn but the locals called it Bowens after the landlord. This was one way the resistance checked their identities (JNP).*

where a schoolteacher the first English speaking person we had met, asked us a few questions and then took us to a barn. The doctor dressed Curly's face and after taking our identity discs told us that we should be taken to the Maquis that evening. The villagers brought us plenty of food and drink and we really ended our hunger. It was about 10 p.m. that night the schoolteacher and another Frenchman returned and gave us revolvers and a cloak and we were taken to the schoolhouse, where we had our first French coffee (our first warm drink) and explained to us that we had about 18 kilometres to go and were taken to a farm. We were taken into a back room where we met a French boy on the run from the Gestapo. We were given a meal and for the first time for four days we properly slept.

May 7th 1944. After a French breakfast of coffee and rolls we were given civilian clothes. Our uniforms etc. were buried and another farmer, who was presumably the local boss came to see us and Dr. Salmon came to see Curly.

May 8th and 9th 1944. Doctor came to see Curly and decided that his daily visits to the farm may arouse suspicion so he has taken to the doctor's house. Sebastian, my guide later and Georges two students both able to speak English came to interrogate me and told me I should be leaving in two days for Paris and be ready to leave on the Friday.

May 10th 1944. Uneventful.

May 11th 1944 (Thursday) Georges came for me on a motorbike and told me that we were not going direct to Paris as the train was controlled, i.e., passengers checked, but were going by bus to Sens from Montorgy and going to Paris the following day. We went by motor bike to a house in Montorgy where I was given an identity card and ration cards and after dinner went to the bus station and here came into contact with German troops for the first time and I can't say I felt happy they were waiting for the same bus as we were and I can't say how relieved I was to get off that bus at Sens. Of all my experiences I think that ride was the worst. As we walked through Sens, I seemed to think that every German soldier must recognise me and it was not for quite a few days that I began to cease being afraid. We stayed the night in Sens in the house of a schoolteacher.

May 12th 1944 (Rita's birthday). Went by train to Paris, Gare l'Est and by tube to Gare de Lion (Lyon). The tube is always full of German soldiers and here I made my first boob. I knocked down a German's rifle and picking it up I said 'sorry' but luckily, he did not catch on. We then went to Langy, where I was to stay until May 26th. Sebastian took me to a house where I met the local resistance chief another schoolteacher and I was then taken to the next village where I met Sergeant John Pearce, a rear gunner also shot down at Mailly. It was grand to talk to an Englishman. I was then taken to 13 Rue de la Paix, Langy, Seine et Marne where I met Marguerite and Bert Cane, Madame Rheti and two girls. Monsieur and Madame Boutte were also there and we had a good talk Bert translating everything. I was given new clothes and a bath and was shown my bedroom it was next to the nursery and had a big French window looking into the woods and my instructions were to go into the woods that in any emergency.

May 13th 1944. My first visit to Paris. Met Georges, saw Notre Dame and Les Invalides for the first time. German horse drawn traffic which reminded me of films of the Civil war. The Americans bombed Orly. Sebastian told me that Curly's face was healing quickly and he was returning to the farm at La Choppibles.

May 14th 1944. Went to Damper to see Sergeant Pearce, spent morning rowing on the Marne and chopping wood for the bakery, this exercise was very welcome. Went for a drink with John and the Captain, bar was full of Luftwaffe personnel but Captain did not worry.

May 15th 1944. Went to cinema with Marguerite and Madame Rheti.

May 16th 1944. Squadron Leader Sparks, controller at Mailly came to Damper. Went for a drink with Hank, shot down from a Thunderbolt, staying in Langy. Cafe Foche is becoming quite allied. John and Sparks came to No.13 also Madame Boutte and a Frenchman who had been in prison with Bert. Chief came to see me and introduced the Gendarme as a member of the underground. This was the first time he knew I was in the house or that the Canes were patriots. Neither did they know who he was.

May 17th 1944. Attended a conference of local FFI at the schoolhouse. Was informed that at a minutes notice an army of 10,000 all armed could be used in Paris, Seine et Marne area. This little army was a credit to any country. The chief and his wife, Bert and Sebastian and two more boys, students and two girls also probably students. They discussed supply dropping what arms and ammo were needed, distribution of weapons and technical points of new weapons. The girls talking like experienced armourers. First indication that final preparations were being made for the invasion.

May 18th to 22nd 1944. Remained at No.13 saw John each night.

May 23rd 1944. Rosie came to see us and gave us the gen about the second front and told us they were trying to arrange an aircraft or boat to pick us up.

May 24th 1944. Agent disappears after landing from London. Plans altered; we will go to Spain.

May 25th 1944. John, Sparks and I went to Paris and waited in a park near Gare de l'Est for Rosie. Jack and I were taken to Georges and to another sightseeing tour and introduced to the Officer of the Paris Gendarmerie, the men who later led the barricades battles.

May 26th 1944. Met at Petain School. 7 Yanks, 6 English given new identity cards, railway tickets, permits to travel, we were to catch the 19:30 train from Paris to Toulouse and from there by local to Pau where we were to wait in open ground near station until we were picked up. This was to be the worst journey I have ever had. We split into two and made our way to the station luckily by this time we had begun to disregard the Germans. After leaving Petain School we walked across Paris to Gare de l'Est working in groups of two or three, with two guides about 100 yards ahead of us. Arriving at the station we found our train was in and was fairly packed and once again we began to feel uncomfortable, we were expecting to be on the train anything from twenty four to forty eight hours and on the train were 13 people who could not talk French and we just had to hope that no one would try to make conversation.

We stayed in the corridors and although we kept in two's and three's I felt that it must be obvious that we were a party and the way we whispered to one another must have seemed suspicious. There were many German soldiers, sailors and Luftwaffe on the platform, the rear of our train was a troop train and the train opposite was going to the West Coast and was mainly troops they would walk up and down the platform yelling at the porters and pushing out of their way any Frenchmen who happened to be in the way and Frenchmen after looking around would spit at them after they had passed, eventually at about 8 p.m. we left Paris and about an hour later reached Juvissy, which had a month ago been attacked by the RAF and boy you would have to see it to believe it.'

'I had seen Villeneuve St. George, La Chappel where 20 of 23 bridges had been knocked down. Juvissy beat the lot it was not craters or broken tracks and smashed trains. It was one great tumult just like a garden after it had been dug over. It was four hours before we before we left Juvissy we were moved part way by electric train, part way by steam and in the middle, they borrowed the engine to shunt a goods wagon across. The French people seemed used to this they just got out of the train and strolled around until the controller told them we were moving. We took the opportunity of eating. Eventually we moved and so John and I lay in the corridor and slept. It was just after waking that I had one of my greatest heartbeats a Gendarme came over to me and asked me something in French all I caught was 'La or Se' and luckily, I knew this meant there or their so I just pointed and said 'la' and luckily I was right.

We arrived in Toulouse at 7 a.m. on Saturday night and had to change trains to our final destination Pau and on the Toulouse station we had what I think was our greatest and last real scare we followed our guide on to the electric train and just as it was about to go out, he found it was the wrong train and we all got out, and tore up the platform and for about a quarter of an hour we ran around trying to find our train. When we eventually got on the train, we found that it was only going as far as Tarbes. At Tarbes, a porter asked to see our tickets and started talking to us, but luckily he was friendly and locked us in a room until our train came in the morning.'

'From Tarbes we could see the Pyrenees clearly and looked rather high to climb. We arrived at Pau and waited for our contacts as instructed and for the first time the whole 13, lucky 13 for us, were together we must have looked a sight as we had only eaten a boiled egg and two sandwiches in the last 48 hours and we were unshaven and hadn't had a wash, we were dressed in old clothes. At the end of two hours no contact had turned up so the guides went out to see what had happened and it was another three hours before they came back and we went with different people. I went with Rosie and stayed in a hotel.

May 27th 1944. We all met again and went to a farm about 4 miles out of town and stayed in a disused house. We got to know each other Sparks, Johnny, Ginger and myself all from the Mailly raid, a Rhodesian and a Typhoon pilot, who had crash landed only a few days ago, Junior and Canack and Bill Lewis who had bailed out about the same time as us. This was all the RAF. I met Hank Dillinger who had been in France 15 months and twice ran out by the Gestapo called Dillie for his hunted look, Rebel a southerner knocked down in his first flight from a Mustang, Lucky and Harry from Fortresses and Slim from a Liberator all thought it had been planned that there would be no waiting in Pau. I think these few days together did us a lot of good it gave us some rest and enabled us to get to know each other. We were here four days and spent the time telling our experiences, playing cards and preparing as well as possible for our climb. We washed our clothes and several changed shoes to get the best fit. Our food was brought up from the farm although rough, we ate well. We cleared the house out and lay on straw and apart from complaints of mice running around we slept well. There were plenty of cherries to be picked and we drank our first mountain water. Rosie and a Frenchman came to see us and brought us some Lucky Strike cigarettes and Cognac and cube sugar.

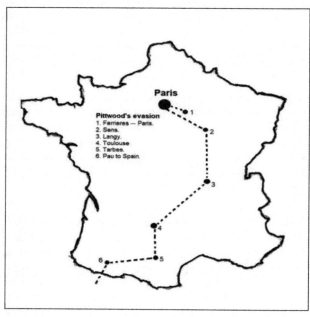

After the war Pittwood described his successful evasion and escape to Spain. He remembered several towns, though some spelling errors made it a bit difficult to find all the locations where he was.
The plan was to fly him out in a Lysander, but this was not possible. He mentions the following stages on his road to freedom; 1. From Fere to Paris, 2. Sens, 3. Langy, 4. Toulouse, 5. Tarbes, 6. Pau and into Spain.
He also mentioned names of other allies he met. Some of the names are: Sergeant John Pearce, Squadron Leader Sparks, a US airman he only knew as Hank, seven other unknown Americans, six Englishmen, a Rhodesian, a Typhoon pilot, and several men with names like Bill Lewis, Canack, Lucky, Junior, Hank Dillinger, Harry and a Yank called 'Rebel'.
Their names are not on the list that Comète compiled, so we believe they were helped by other evasion groups than Comète. (HO)

May 28th to May 30th no entries. (HO)

May 31st 1944. We left the farm in small parties for Pau where we were to catch a bus to Lassenex where a taxi would take us to the point where we were to start our climb, when they said 'taxi' we thought they had gone mad, even in Paris a taxi was a museum piece but somehow, they had one waiting for us. We boarded the bus at Pau; I have never seen a bus so crowded. Conductors complain that a bus is crowded when 5 or 6 people are standing, but this was a thirty two seater single decker bus and in-side there were about 45 people with 20/30 on top. Behind was a pig cart which some passengers had hitched on and people rode on that. The bus was driven by cokes and every time it hit a bump, we left red hot coke on the road. The conductor knew who we were and he was to open the rear door when we arrived at a given place, by the time when we left, I think everyone knew who we were and there were 'bonne voyage' as we left. Six of us got into the taxi and went about 15 miles to the foot of the Pyrenees and then it went back for the others. We had food for two days, 2 boiled eggs each, about a pound of bread each, a pound of chocolate between us and a little meat and cheese. We ate a boiled egg between two and a little bread and a drink of cognac. It was now ten o'clock and we were to move on as soon as it got dark about midnight and the first night should take us past the German first frontier posts and then our danger would be patrols of dogs and men and then right on the frontier the last posts.

Our party consisted of a guide, a Frenchman called Charles who had been told to go over with us as his time was up in Paris, seven Englishmen, and six Yanks. We left at midnight and for about six miles followed the road and then we took to the fields we had to cover twenty miles the first night but it wasn't bad going and we reached our shelter about 5 o'clock in the morning, it was a cowshed, we were just past the frontier posts but the shed was in full view of them and we were not allowed outside at all. If everything had gone well, we should have ten hours the following night and then four hours the evening after, but the mountains which had for weeks been clear became cloud covered and it started to pour with rain, the darkness came and we all cut ourselves sticks and started again. Before us we had our first ridge too, but the tracks had become marl and instead of 4 or 5 miles an hour we were doing 200/400 yards an hour. We were soon covered in mud and drenched. The top of the ridge brought us no respite as the decent was even worse, we slipped time and time again but keeping together prevented anyone from sliding down the hill.

At three o'clock we came to a hut and as we had no chance of reaching the next shelter had to pack in and stay there for the day. I was glad of the rest and Dillie, his 15 months captivity with little exercise had left him weak, he was practically out. We had very little food and the guide went to see if he could get any, he was unsuccessful at first but later he managed to get a can of soup which was warm and very welcomed, we ate a little bread with it and this left us with two eggs a little meat paste and about a pound of bread but we still had some sugar and cognac and luckily, we decided to keep this as long as we could. We were extremely uncomfortable here and so as soon as it began to get dusk we started to move again. Charles who had done a lot of mountaineering helped Dillie along. The rain had stopped but we were still in the musty wet bottom of the clouds and the climbing got steeper but we knew that once over this lot we should not be long before getting back to Blighty.

We came to an almost vertical bank of clay and it seemed impossible to climb it but the guide got up and tied a rope to a tree and we were soon moving ahead again, we found a few cherries and had plenty of water. We rested the next day at a goat man's hut and the following night reached what should have been our shelter the second night. Several times we heard dogs but never saw anything of a patrol. The fifth night was fairly level going but owing to the mist it was very slow and we moved in crocodile fashion, we stumbled quite a few times and each time I think I managed to put my head on nettles, we crossed several streams but now we were so wet that we just waded through them, then we came to a river and alongside a farm and two or three houses. From out of the bushes the guide swung a kind of bridge rather flimsy but it got us across the river. We reached a hut and stayed there, we now had one more ridge to cross. We chopped up the last egg with some meat paste and ate it.

June 1st to June 5th no entries, possibly due to the gruelling crossing of the mountains. (HO)

June 6th 1944. We started out just after midnight the going was rough as it was grass, fairly steep and slippery and perhaps because it was the end it seemed to go on forever. We crossed the first boundary at 4.15 a.m. We were now in no-man's land and at 6.10 a.m. We crossed into Spain. We were now descending, but the mist was freezing on our clothes, although it was June there was snow. We found a little hut, lit a fire and dried a little and then pushed off towards the nearest village. Hank, Junior, Lucky and I went ahead and were going fine; even the sun was beginning to shine and then from behind the hedges came two soldiers with guns. We thought they were Jerries, but they turned out to be Spaniards. They lit us a big fire and we waited for the rest and were then taken to Isabh where we were taken to jail. They promised us a meal and about two hours later came in with a great bowl of potatoes and a spoon each but it was more than welcome.'

June 7th 1944. We were taken by bus to Pamplona and handed over to the consul and then to the Spanish Air Force. Afterwards we were sent to the British Embassy in Madrid, I shall never forget the journey on account of beggars asking for food or money. I have never seen so many poor people, that is Fascism everything for the few. We were given money and stayed in a hotel. Food awful everything floating in olive oil, showed chef how to make Cherry pie. We went to a bullfight and nearly caused a riot because we refused to give the Fascist salute. Spaniards not very friendly. After a time, we were sent to Gibraltar and eventually got a plane home.'

A letter to a Mother.
When Jack Pittwood was safely in England, he wrote a long letter to Lissette's Mother. The author received the letter via Brian Lissette and believes that the reader should experience the high regard this crew had for their 'Skipper'.

Being written in wartime the letter was opened and read by a censor: '6/11/44 Dear Mrs. Lissette, first of all I must introduce myself. I am Les's navigator and I was with him on the night of 3rd/4th May. I am afraid I cannot give you any good news or any hope of Les's safety. Les gave his life for us. I did not write before as I was not quite certain what had happened to 'Lizzie', as he was known to us all over here, but now more of the crew have come home and there is no longer any doubt. His death was a hard blow to us. We have lost a grand pilot, a grand captain but an even greater friend. He died as he lived, for his crew. We were set on fire by flak and fighter, and Les gave the order to jump out.'

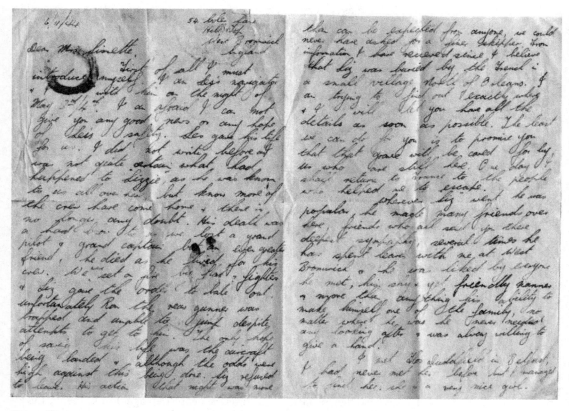

'Ron, the rear gunner, was unfortunately trapped and unable to jump despite attempts to get to him out. The only hope of saving his life was the aircraft being landed and although the odds were high against this being done Lizzie refused to leave. His action that night was more than can be expected from anyone, we could never have asked for a finer skipper. From information I have received since I believe that he was buried by the French in a small village north of Orleans. I am trying to find out exactly where and I will let you have all the details as soon as possible. The least we can do for you is to promise you that that grave will be cared for by us who are still here.'

'One day I shall return to the people who helped me to escape. Wherever Lizzie went he was popular, he made many friends over here, friends who all send you their deepest sympathy. Several times he has spent leave with me at West Bromwich and he was liked by everyone he met. His shy yet friendly manner and more than anything, his ability to make himself one of the family, no matter where he was, he never needed any looking after and was always willing to give a hand. I met Miss Dudfield in Belfast. I had never met her before, but I managed to find her. She is a genuinely nice girl. There are three of the old crew safely back here. Phil King, wireless operator, Curly Emeny, mid gunner and myself. Nick, the engineer, escaped with us, but died of pleurisy in this country.'

'Of Laurie, our bomb aimer, we have not heard of since we bailed out. I have written to Mrs. Young [98] and have had a letter from her. Mother and all at home send there [their] deepest sympathy. Dad is the same as Mr. Lissette, a Lincolnshire person and I was born in Scunthorpe Lincs. My kindest regards and deepest sympathy to you'.

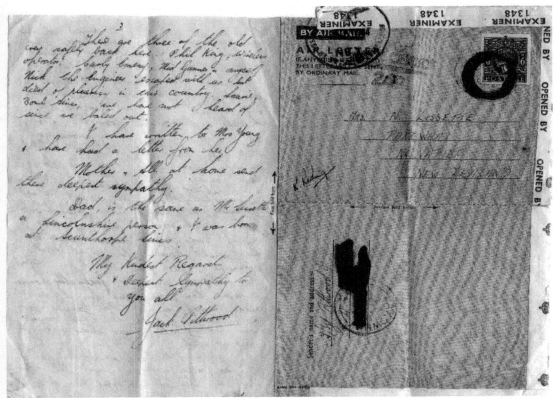

Two pages John Pittwood's letter to Mrs. N. Lissette in Pakowhai near Napier on the North Island[99]. (BL)

---

[98] *(Hilbre Young was an English relative of Lissette's mother's family and was his contact in England).*
[99] *It is interesting to see the censor deleted Pittwood's home address on the envelope and left all the things he said untouched.*

Pittwood's notes from take-off in England until his return to Gibraltar

Pittwood used these notes to help him remember facts and names during his interrogation.

03 May	10:30 Left base for Mailly.
03 May	11:05 Over Beachy Head.
03 May	11:15 Crossing enemy coast.
04 May	00:10 Attacked by night fighter and weaving.
04 May	00:40 Abandoned aircraft. Landed.
04 May	03:00 Left landing area.
04 May	04:30 Arriving in Ferriers and turned back.
04 May	05:00 Rest and drink.
05 May	Stayed hidden all day, Emeny very sick.
06 May	00:05 To Ferriers, meeting old lady, who warned to move on.
06 May	09:00 Cemetery La Selle sur le Bied.
06 May	10:00 Met teacher and other man, taken to house, meal and sleep.
07 May	08:00 Civilian clothes, uniforms buried, met doctor Salmon.
08 May	Visit doctor to see Curly.
09 May	Interrogated by Resistance and/or MI6. 'In 2 days to Paris'.
10 May	Nothing.
11 May	Farewell to Emeny. By bus to Montorgy and Sens.
12 May	By train to Paris Gare de l'Est to Gare de Lion and to Langy.
13 May	Sightseeing Paris (Notre Dame, Les Invalides) Americans bomb Orly.
14 May	To Damper, met Sergeant Pearce.
15 May	To Cinema with Mme Rheti and Marguerite.
16 May	Met Sqn Ldr Sparks and USAF pilot 'Hank'.
17 May	FFI meeting.
18/22 May	At No.13 Rue de la Paix in Langy.
23 May	Met 'Rosie' to discuss pickup by aircraft.
24 May	Informed of journey to Spain.
25 May	To Paris with John and Sparks and to new safehouse.
26 May	Met 7 Americans and 6 Britons, prepare to leave.
26 May	19:30 Walking to Gare de l'Est, 13 fugitives.
26 May	20:00 Train leaves Paris to Juvissy night trip
27 May	07:00 Arrival Toulouse, change train to Pau via Tarbes.
27/31 May	Group is taken to safe house for 4 days.
31 May	Bus from Pau to Lassenex. (?) [100]
01 June	00:15 Left on foot.
01 June	05:00 Hiding in cow shed then continue to walk.
02 June	03:00 Walk in the mountains all day arrive at hut.
03 June	After climb rest in goat shed.
04 June	Walking in the mist all day.
05 June	Cross the river stayed in hut.
06 June	00:00 Crossed a border.
06 June	04:15 Crossing no-men's land.
06 June	06:10 Arrived in Spain.
07 June	Bus to Pamplona, handed over to British Consul and to Zaragozo air base. From there to British Embassy Madrid.
23 June	Departure Gibraltar, 24 June arrival Bristol.

---

[100] *Dates are correct, hours are estimates by Pittwood. Some names of villages are not traceable on the map of France. We also believe that Pittwood and the others did not travel via the Comète Line, but probably via another line.*

A concentration camp inmate.

The Germans had a horrifying experience in store for Laurie Wesley. When the allied air forces took control of the skies over Europe in the summer of 1944, Adolf Hitler ordered the immediate execution of allied flyers accused of committing certain acts. Their bombing of German town was considered a crime by the man who agreed in the devastation of Warsaw, Rotterdam, Coventry, Hull and London, to name a few towns that suffered from the Luftwaffe's 'strategic attacks. Another activity punishable by death was the attempt to evade capture and escape to neutral countries. The most common act was to be captured by the Gestapo or Secret Police in civilian clothing, often without their dog tags and being unable to prove that they were soldiers rather than spies. Of course, the Germans knew that these airmen had been shot down over Germany or the occupied countries, like France, Belgium and the Netherlands. However once through treason they were turned over to the Gestapo and Secret Police by traitors within the Dutch, Belgian and French Resistance, there was little chance of being treated according to the Geneva or The Hague Conventions while attempting to reach England along escape routes such as the Comète and the Pat Line. A notable traitor was Jacques Desoubrie, who was responsible for betraying a significant number of allied airmen to the German authorities. These captured airmen were given the name Terrorflieger (terror flyers), and were not given a trial. The German Foreign Office however, expressed concern about shooting prisoners of war (PoWs) and suggested that enemy airmen suspected of such offenses not be given the legal status of PoWs. Following this advice, the Gestapo and Security Police informed these captured allied airmen that they were criminals and spies. Using this justification, 168 allied airmen from Great Britain, United States, Australia, Canada, New Zealand and Jamaica were taken by train in overcrowded cattle boxcars from Fresnes Prison outside Paris, to Buchenwald concentration camp. Laurie Wesley was one of them.

Buchenwald, who cares about the Geneva Convention!

After five days in the boxcars, they arrived at Buchenwald on 20 Aug 1944. Nationalities of the 168 airmen: 82 American, 48 British, 26 Canadian, 9 Australian, 2 New Zealander, 1 Jamaican.

During his debriefing he reported on the frightening experiences, when he talked about his 3½ months in the hands of the Gestapo and the SS: 'Gestapo Headquarters Paris, Fresnes Prison Paris; Buchenwald Concentration Camp, near Weimar. Dates of imprisonment: 4th July to 19th October 1944. Prison No: 78399. Reasons and circumstances surrounding imprisonment. As a member of an RAF air crew, I was shot down over France on the night of 3rd/4th May 1944. For several weeks I was successful in evading capture and in fact did not know for certain that I had been betrayed and was in enemy hands until on 4th July 1944, dressed in civilian clothing, I was driven from a third-rate Paris hotel to Gestapo HQ [101]. Later that day, after interrogation I was taken to Fresnes Prison where other British and American aircrew members were in captivity among hundreds of 'political' prisoners of all European nationalities. After a period of solitary confinement, I shared a cell with two (sometimes three) other captives. On 15th August 1944, the whole prison was evacuated in the face of the Allied advance across France and the next five days were spent in appalling conditions travelling by cattle truck train (90 in the truck in which I travelled) to 'Konzentrationslager Buchenwald' where we arrived on 20th August [102].'

'I need hardly elaborate on the appalling conditions which pertained in this infamous camp, presided over by the SS where, together with thousands of other prisoners including some 168 of us British and American Air Force personnel, I was incarcerated for two months. We were shaved from top to bottom and our clothes and shoes were taken away from us. There was no accommodation and we were treated as vermin. Health was naturally affected by the totally inadequate diet and by the atrocious conditions under which we lived. For the first two or three weeks I and my colleagues had to sleep in the open with no clothing excepting what we wore, and there was precious little of that. Later we were accommodated

---

[101] *The Germans would threaten aircrew caught in civilian clothes with execution for espionage unless they told them who had given the clothes and who had helped them evaded capture.*

[102] *Between 20 August and 19 October 1944, 168 allied airmen were held prisoner at Buchenwald concentration camp. 166 airmen survived Buchenwald, while two died of sickness at the camp. 82 were American, 48 British, 26 Canadian, 9 Australian, 2 New Zealander and 1 Jamaican.*

in a hut which houses literally hundreds of men in all stages of misery and suffering due to malnutrition and lack of medical care and attention. One of our number in fact died during to these circumstances. Eventually our appeals that we should be treated as prisoners of war under the Geneva Convention resulted in the appearance of two Luftwaffe Officers who interrogated us in batches and finally after the lapse of several more days, and were escorted by Luftwaffe guards, were taken under fairly reasonable conditions, although again by cattle truck train, to Stalag Luft 3 at Sagan in upper Silesia.'

S/L Lamason, a Lancaster pilot from New Zealand, was ASO in Buchenwald. Thanks to Luftwaffe LtCol Hannes Trautloft the allied prisoners were rescued from certain execution and taken to Stalag Luft 3 Sagan. Camp Kommandant Hermann Pister was captured when the Americans liberated Buchenwald. His trial began on 11 April 1947. He was found guilty and sentenced to die by hanging. He died on 28 September 1948 of a heart attack in Landsberg Prison. Wesley made the march from Sagan to the West. He died in the nineties. (Wesley/IWM)

It took some research to find out who was the Luftwaffe officer responsible for the transfer of the prisoners from Buchenwald to Stalag Luft III Sagan. The two Luftwaffe officers who went to Buchenwald were Inspector of the Day Fighters, Colonel Hannes Trautloft and his adjutant. Trautloft were about to leave the camp when captured American airman Bernard Scharf called out to him in fluent German from behind a fence. The SS guards tried to intervene, but Trautloft pointed out that he out-ranked them and made them stand back. Scharf explained that he was one of more than 160 Allied airmen imprisoned at the camp and begged Trautloft to rescue him and the other airmen. Disturbed by the event, Trautloft returned to Berlin and began the process to have the airmen transferred out of Buchenwald. The inmates all are sure that they owe their lives to Trautloft, who was not a Nazi!

In early 1945 Trautloft joined other high-ranking pilots in the 'Fighter Pilots Revolt', protesting the squandering of the precious Luftwaffe fighters and pilots in useless high-loss operations like Operation Bodenplatte. Following this revolt, he was relieved of his position and sent to command the 4 Flieger-Schule Division (4th Pilot School Division) in Strassburg. He spent the remainder of the war there and ended the war as an Oberst. After the war he joined the new Bundesluftwaffe on 1 October 1957 with the rank of Brigadegeneral. He served throughout the 1960s as deputy Inspector General of the Bundesluftwaffe, and retired in 1970 as a Lieutenant-General. He was an active member of many veteran organizations including the Gemeinschaft der Jagdflieger until his death on 11 January 1995 at Bad Wiessee.

'Leaving Buchenwald on 19th October we arrived at Sagan on 21st October.' Wesley, with prisoner number 8122, could finally write a card to his wife: 'Prison Camp 28.10.44. 'My dearest Mary, if this card reaches you before the letter I sent you a few days ago; I will probably repeat what I already wrote. I am OK and there is nothing I need. I have sufficient warm clothing for the winter and a good stock of cigarettes. Please do not worry about me, but tell me everything about yourself, for I am anxious to hear how you and the baby are. I hope to have more news around Christmas. I have just finished a card to dad and mum. Please give them my regards and I repeat: Do not worry about me. With all my love and many kisses, my darling, Forever, your loving Laurie.'

When Russian troops closed in on Sagan, Sergeant Wesley and thousands of other prisoners were forced to make the long march to the West. At the end of April, the torment came to an end when American troops liberated the prisoners. Sergeant Laurie Wesley, looking shabby in worn out pieces of uniform and with a moustache, had his picture taken by his liberators. The Americans did everything possible to get the prisoners home. He arrived in England on 6 May 1945. For the first time in a year, he saw his child. In 1964 the Foreign Office asked Wesley to write a statement about his experiences in the dreaded German concentration camp.

He wrote: 'From the moment I was under control of the Luftwaffe, until liberation on 27th May 1945, I was treated as an ordinary PoW (# 8122). I have no disability as a result of treatment received. I am attaching a newspaper cutting taken from the Daily Telegraph dated 11th September 1945, in which the penultimate paragraph refers to the airmen I have mentioned above. Also attached is one of the number tags with which I was issued at Buchenwald for sewing to coat or jacket for identification purposes. (Please return these two items in due course together with birth certificate). L.Wesley, 2nd Sept 1964. RAF No 1581817'. The experiences in Germany left a deep impression on Laurie Wesley. Well aware that he was involved in a war and the risks he ran, he nevertheless expected to be treated the same way as German prisoners were treated by the Allies. Needless to say, that Laurie and Mary Wesley never again visited Germany.

Sergeant Stockford's experiences.
After he successfully returned to the United Kingdom Stockford was duly interrogated and declared: My flight and experiences are the same as those of Flt/Sergeant Pittwood up to the time that I bailed out. The bomb aimer bailed out first and I followed him. I landed in a wood some miles North of Ferrieres. I freed my parachute from the tree in which it had become entangled and buried it, together with my Mae West, in the undergrowth. I set out at once, walking south by my compass, and continued across the fields for about three hours, when I hid in a wood until dawn. While I was resting here, I removed my brevet and service chevrons and threw away my loose silver. I could see that I was near a small village, and later that morning (4 May) I moved towards it. About mid-day, as I was hiding by a hedge, two girls passed by, and though they saw me, they did not stop. Half an hour later, an old man came straight towards where I was hiding and said that he was the father of the two who had seen me and reported my presence to him. He told, me that I had reached Fontenay. When he heard that I intended making way south, he warned me against going through Montargis which he said, was full of Germans.'

'At 1400 hrs I set out in what I thought was a south westerly direction, so as to make a detour round Montargis. I crossed the railway and the main road and finally reached a stream, which I followed, thinking. it was flowing in the direction in which I wanted to go. After scrambling through some thick undergrowth in my effort to follow the course of the stream, I came out on to a secondary road leading to a bridge across the stream. I crossed the bridge and then realised that I was hopelessly lost. Seeing a man working a wood yard, I beckoned to him and asked him where I was. He told me that I was on the outskirts of Nargis. I made my way towards the town and then hid in some weeds for the night. I set out again early next morning (5 May) for Chateau-Landon. Before I reached the town, I decided to seek help at a farm. There were several people working in the fields, but they took no notice of me. I finally managed to attract the attention of old man, to whom I declared myself. He took me to the back of the house and gave me some wine to drink. People at once came crowd around and offered me food, which I refused as I was not hungry.'

'They were discussing the question of providing civilian clothing me, when a woman came running up and told me that I must leave a once, as the farmer had informed the authorities of my presence. I ran down the hill, through some woods and across a stream, finally crawling into the undergrowth on the far side, from where was able to keep a good lookout for anyone searching for me. About 1500 hrs a man saw me and came towards me. By this time, I was feeling extremely hungry, as the only food, I had eaten since baling out was some Horlicks tablets from my escape box. The man promised to return in, an hour's time with some food. He returned shortly afterwards, however, without the food which said he would not give no food until I had written in his notebook that he had helped me, I was feeling desperate by this time, so I did as he asked me. The man then disappeared for several hours, and it was not 1900 hrs that he returned with a loaf of bread and some cold potatoes. He was very nervous and asked me to leave at once. I continued on my way towards Chateau-Landon and reached the outskirts that evening. I passed several people, but they took notice of me. I entered a small coppice and rested there for a while. Shortly afterwards several youths passed closed by my hiding place whistling 'Tipperary'. I realised that they were looking for me and beckoned to them. They told me that they were members of the Maquis, though I did not believe them as they had no arms. I told them that I want to get to Beaumont whereupon they led me out of the town and left me on the road to Mondreville. That night I laid up in a wood just outside the town. The next morning (6 May) I walked through Mondreville reached the outskirts of Beaumont. I stayed near the town all day hoping to contact someone who could help me, but saw no one.'

'That evening, I walked through Egry and reached outskirts of Beaune-La-Rolande. I spent half the night a wood and then hid in a haystack near a farm. Early next morning, I walked through Beaune-La-Rolande and continued along the road. I was feeling very weak by this time I entered a field and slept for some hours. At 1700 hrs I set again and walked through Boiscommun, which was very deserted. Beyond the town I saw an old man working in the fields and ask the way to Vim. He pointed to the road I should take and I continued along it. I passed several people, who completely ignored. me, though I heard one man mutter something about Les Boches as I passed. A little further on I came to a clearing in the woods by side of the road, I saw a water trough standing in the clearing went straight towards it, as I was feeling extremely thirsty was drinking, when I saw three people standing in front of a small house watching me. I went up to them and asked for something to eat.

After they had given me some food, I declared myself to them and was immediately invited inside. The owner of the house said that his son was away at the moment, but when he returned, he would be able to put me in touch with an organisation. His son returned shortly afterward and that he would be able to help me. I spent the night in the garage attached to the house and the next day the son went to see a member of an organisation. That evening (8 May) I was visited by a young woman, and from this point my journey was arranged for me.'

As usual no information was shared with anyone about the identity of his helpers, the towns and villages he passed through or stayed and the means of transportation used to get him to Spain. He returned home via the Comète escape route over the Pyrenees and into Portugal, arriving back in England on 15th June 1944.

On 8th August 1944 he married Joyce Jones, of Heythrop, at Chipping Norton Methodist Church, living at 30, Spring Street, Chipping Norton. He tragically died suddenly from pleurisy at RAF Longtown near Carlisle on 18th September 1944 aged 22. He is remembered on Chipping Norton's town and church memorial on the Heythrop war memorial. He lies buried in Heythrop Saint Nicholas Churchyard. His death shocked all who knew him and three years later his French helpers found out and contacted his widow.

One of them was Abbe Chenu, the priest, who had been such a great help in the evasion of Nick. He wrote on 21th December 1947: 'Dear Madame, we have been grievously saddened, my sister and I, by your letter telling us of the death of your dear Nick because he had been profoundly sympathetic to us. We assume that his sudden death is due to heart trouble, the airman's illness. Will you accept for yourself and for his family our sincere condolences? He had promised us to visit us again, with his wife and his children in order to thank us. His plane had been brought down near Nemours and he had entered a house, where he realised that someone was telephoning to betray him to the German Gestapo (Alas, many people feared the terrible pain inflicted by the Germans to those hiding allied airman).'

'Then he had fled from there and after crossing Beaune la Rolande and Boiscommun, two small neighbouring towns where no-one spoke to him on account of his uniform, as they took him for a German. Soon, hunger and thirst made him stop in an isolated house at the edge of the large forest of Orleans. There he made contact with us and Mr. Durand hid him in his motorcar garage during several days. On Monday morning his sons came to inform me of his presence because I was the head of the local resistance and I went to see our schoolteacher Mlle. Jublot, later Captain Jublot. I went after school hours to make sure of his identity and talked to him for a long time in the garage. He saw me again at 11pm that night. Wednesday, 10th May again went to look for him on her bicycle. They returned on foot and dined at my house. Mlle. Jublot concealed him in her room where he remained hidden until Friday, 2nd June.'

On 8th August 1944 Nick Stockford married Joyce Jones from Churchill, at the small Chipping Norton Methodist Church. Left to right we see George Stockford, possibly Nick's Mother, Jack Pittwood, and Nick Stockford, his bride Joyce, Gay Stockford, Fred Jones and seated Edith Jones. Nick tragically suddenly died at Longtown from pleurisy on 18 September 1944[103]. (Paul Burbidge)

'He was absolutely forbidden to open the shutters, because the classroom was below and the children's playground was in front of the room. During this time neither the children nor the neighbours suspected anything. For four weeks my sister took something for him to eat and drink to the school at midday. Each evening after dark he came to eat at my house with Mlle. Jublot. During this time, my sister washed his linen. A dramatic moment occurred when an agent of the resistance coming from Loudres arrived with the password 'St. Loup I have 27 pupils' to take him away to Orleans.'

'After having searched in a suburb of Orleans, called Saint Loup like our village, and then in another community near Montargis, he arrived in the third St. Loup, our village. That day Mlle. Jublot had taken one of her pupils to sit for an examination at Montargis. The agent spoke to the other teacher who replied: 'no sir, I have 32 of them'. He understood then that this was not the person he was seeking and demanded her absolute silence. Nicholas had seen him through the shutters, but he did not dare to speak to him. The agent came again the next day and told Mlle. Jublot that he would be moving her prisoner. She went

---

[103] During an Act of Remembrance and a live broadcast on You Tube of 8th November 2020 in St Mary's Church, Chipping Norton, the crew of W/O Leslie Lisette and especially Nick Stockford were remembered. (https://youtu.be/RLg9XZpWT0Q)

to buy him a shirt of white silk and a pair of trousers and the next day at noon in broad daylight he left St. Loup on foot to return to Boiscummun where he found the resistance agent and both of them made for Paris.'

'There, that is all we know, but Mlle. Duplot, now Madame Leveau, mother of two small children and living at 77 Boulevard Alexandre Martin, Orleans will be able to give you other details of his stay in St. Loup during these for weeks. The letter you wrote to her came to my house and I have re-directed it to her. We hope that she has received it and that she will reply to it herself. In July, 1944 we still had hidden two other English soldiers, one of who came again to see us in the uniform of an air force officer, he was there about 1 year. That was about one year ago. For having saved these three English soldiers I received a diploma from the British Government signed by Air Chief Marshal Tedder.

We also saved three American airmen and received a diploma signed by General Eisenhower. Above all, from May to August 1944 we had to accommodate four officers of the headquarters staff of the resistance movement who used to keep in touch with the War Office in London by a transmitter placed in our house, where there was already hidden ammunition that we had received by parachute. By the Grace of God, we had the good fortune never to be denounced to the enemy. We people are coming to be overlooked in France in an endeavour by Soviet Russia to establish a communist regime here, but the Government and the majority of the population are opposing it. We wish you a Happy Christmas and we are pleased to send you our very best wishes. Abbe A. Chenu, Priest[104].'

The last crew member to bail out was Phil King, the wireless operator.
Sergeant Philip Norman King, wireless operator was the last person to bail out of EM-F ND556. He too wrote a report about his experiences, giving a lot of information about his evasion: 'At 0130 hrs, on 4 May, I came down a few yards from a barn to which I immediately went to hide my chute and Mae West. Having done this, I took out my compass and started out in a westerly direction. Soon I was on the main road from Dordives to Chateaudun Laundon. I kept walking until 0500 hrs. When I laid down by the side of a small river. After thinking it over I decided I could be seen too easily so I moved over to a grain stack nearby, falling asleep. I was awakened, by a very old Frenchman with a pitchfork, who immediately began jabbering in French. When I had finally indicated to him that I was English and showing him my identity discs, he took me to a nearby farm. On 13 May two chaps came in a small van, taking me to a small house in the village of Souppes, where I spent the night. Next day I was taken to a farm near Dordives, which also had on it a French worker, who had escaped after being conscripted as a forced labourer. I left the farm about 15 July to help the French operate the dropped radio and also to help them in parachute operations.'

'While helping the French I met a chap who will remain anonymous because he had been dropped from England. He took me to Chambon and from there to Saint Loupe de Vignes. At the place I was staying in Saint Loupe I was introduced to Major Fenwick, who was in charge of a detachment of the SAS Brigade. I had been with them but a week in the forest when word came that the German commander at Orleans had asked for three divisions to clear the forest (Foret d'Orleans) of Maquis and British which were believed to be there. While in the forest I met Pilot officer O'Neill (RAAF), Staff Sergeant Frank Hives (USAAF), and Flying Officer Vidler. 'I went to Ladon with Vidler and stayed for two days at a house where Vidler had stayed before. A Gestapo scare sent us back to the forest and I arrived there on 5th August, to find Major Fenwick getting ready to clear his unit out. We spent the night in camp and at 1530 hrs. Sunday, 6th August, we heard sounds of firing coming from a water hole 200 yards from the camp. It developed that 600 Germans with mortar and light artillery had entered the camp from the NE and West. At the advice of one of Major Fenwick's sergeants we headed South on our own toward Nancrey-sur-Rimarde.'

---

[104] *During the occupation of France many priests as well as the higher hierarchy were sympathetic to the Petain government in fear of communist rule and unrest as experienced before the occupation.*

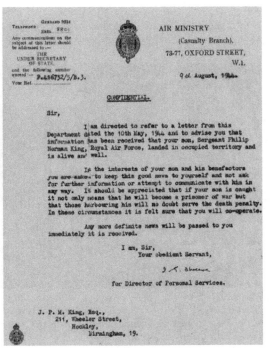

Phil King as a young airman in the flying clothing one would wear in the open cockpit of Tiger Moth. Phil King in 1944. It must have been a great relief for King's next of kin when a letter of the Air Ministry arrived with the news that Sergeant Philip Norman King was alive and well. King's father was warned however, not to mention anything to anyone as it might endanger the life of his son and that of all the brave French who risked their lives to help Philip. (Phil King Jr.)

'We spent the night in a small wood, and as we were setting out again in the morning, we encountered a lad who said Major Fenwick was in a little wood nearby and wanted us to follow, six SAS men remaining with us. A half an hour had hardly pass when we heard gun and mortar fire from Chamon. A few minutes later the same lad who had taken us to the Major earlier in the day rushed in to say that the Major had been killed and his jeep wrecked. We struck out immediately on our own for the house in which we had been helped Saint Loupe. Our helper allowed us to remain three or four days, sending us to Courcelles, where we were directed to a farm 2 kms NE of the town. Here spent but one night, pushing on to Escrennes. The following night we went to Grigneville, finding on our arrival there three of Major Fenwick's men, troopers Curran, Philips and Hunt. The next night as spent at Cahantillo le-Ri, as were the next few days, from Monday 14th to Sunday 20th August.'

'On Saturday afternoon Lieutenant Williams from the XII Corps came by, and on Sunday we joined a lieutenant whose name I do not remember from the XII Corps, thus coming into Allied hands.' (Sergeant King, interview 21st Aug 1944).

More on Major Ian Fenwick from Para Assault Airborne Data:

He was born in September 1910 in Malmesbury, Wiltshire, the son of Captain Charles Harry Fenwick of the 60th Rifles. Ian was an excellent sportsman and played for Winchester College's 1st XI in 1929. Ian went to Pembroke College and then to art college in Berlin. He was busy as an artist during the 1930s. His drawings appeared in many magazines, including Punch, Men Only, and London Opinion. His own books, and other which he illustrated, included: Pick-Me-Up, Songs of a Sub-man, The Bed Book, Weepings and Wailings, I'm Telling You When and Where to Winter Sport, Start Early, Car Canny and Enter Trubshaw (a posthumous collection of Ian's drawings). Ian was commissioned as a Second Lieutenant in the Leicestershire Yeomanry on 20 February 1937, after reaching the rank of Lance Corporal whilst serving with the Cadets of the Winchester College Contingent, Junior Division Officer Training Corps. With the re-organisation of the Army in early 1940 the Leicestershire Yeomanry became an artillery regiment. Consequently, Second Lieutenant Fenwick was transferred to the Royal Artillery on 15 February 1940. He was then transferred from the Royal Artillery to the King's Royal Rifle Corps on 30 June 1940 and then seconded to 'a specialist appointment' at Coleshill with the rank of Captain.

After training, he was posted to Somerset as Intelligence Officer where his charismatic leadership established the country's second largest number of Auxiliary Units, trained in insurgency in the event of German invasion, building up to 300 men in 44 patrols working out of 50 secret Operational Bases.

Fenwick behind the wheel of a jeep with four Vickers-K guns mounted in pairs in France. The SAS adopted the Vickers K-guns for their hit and run tactics in their jeeps. The SAS found them superior to the .303 in water-cooled Vickers or the Bren gun as it was used by the other British troops. In the field with three members of his SAS troops in France, 1944.

Ian then served in the Middle East, the North African desert campaign right through to Tunisia and then took part in the invasion of Sicily/Italy. He probably served with the 2nd Battalion, the King's Royal Rifle Corps. Upon returning to the United Kingdom, in 1943, he volunteered for airborne forces and was transferred to The Army Air Corps, The Parachute Regiment, on 1 September 1943. He qualified as a parachutist at RAF Ringway on course number 87, 13 to 25 October 1943. Upon completion he was posted to the Depot & School Airborne Forces at Hardwick Hall, Near Chesterfield. His instructor's comments: Average performer, height 6 foot, 3 inches affects speed of exit, good nerve control, fine spirit. Ian then joined the Special Air Service in February 1944, while serving as a Captain. A few months later, as commander of 'D' Squadron, 1st SAS, in Operation Gain, and holding the rank of Major, he parachuted into France on the night of 16/17 June 1944, with some 60 men in the vicinity of Orleans, together with a number of Jeeps. This was just shortly after the Normandy landing, but well over a hundred miles behind enemy lines. Their job was to disrupt enemy communications, they proceeded to do just that, blowing up railway lines and, working with the French Resistance, derailing many trains. After another successful night attack on a train carrying troops and ammunition Ian reported that, 'We are happy in our work.' By the end of Operation Gain, 16 railway lines had been put out of action and two locomotives and 46 trucks destroyed.

However, on 7 August, 1944, their operating base was surrounded by some 600 German soldiers as a result of intelligence they had gathered from a double agent. The base party was successful in breaking out, while Ian was out on an operational patrol at the time, but returned to assist in the withdrawal.

But there is more to the story than that. A fuller account suggests that Ian had been informed (wrongly) that his soldiers had been killed, and that as he was headed to join up with another group under the command of Captain Jock Riding, his jeep was seen by a German spotter plane, which radioed his whereabout to the SS troops on the ground. The Germans set up an ambush for him near Chambon. An elderly French woman, it is said, stopped his jeep and warned him of the ambush. Ian, perhaps still enraged by the news of his men's fate, is supposed to have said, 'Thank you, Madame, but I intend to attack them', and proceeded to do just that, with all guns blazing. They nearly succeeded, but Ian, who was driving, was shot through the forehead. Of the others in the jeep, Lance-Corporal Albert Menginou of the French Resistance was also killed, and Corporals Duffy and Dunkley were captured. Dunkley was executed by the Germans the next day; Duffy escaped. Major Ian Fenwick was killed in action on 7 August 1944, aged 33. and is buried at the cemetery at Chambon-La-Foret Cemetery, France, Plot D, Grave 1.

Major Fenwick was a very good cartoonist. He enjoyed to make cartoons about life in his unit.On the left the soldier in the middle says: 'Reckon we looks likes f.....ng Christmas trees in this kit'.

On the right one the sergeant says to the officer 'Well, try this one on, Sir', mocking the inexperience of many of the young officers who joined the SAS.

Major Ian Fenwick in his No. 1 uniform and his grave at Chambon-La-Foret, France, Plot D, Grave 1.

King's notes when he was debriefed in England:
Phil King later recorded all the hiding places where he had been:
1. First taken by old farmer to farm of M. Mois Bretanue.
2. Farm at Dordive was called La Carabinieri and was owned by Mme. Sonya, married to, but later separated from a collaborator named Petit.
3. Spent the night in priest's house at Saint Loupe de Vignes after being taken there by André a parachutist dropped from England.
4. Stayed in Ladon with Dr. Prudence Huoy.
5. Agrippa was the code name of the White Russian who had been dropped from England whom we met at the two houses outside the forest.
6. The Priest at Saint Loupe sent us to the Priest at Courcelles.
7. The farm 2km NE of Courcelles was called 'Mona Lisa' and was owned by M. Legrand.
8. At Escrennes we stayed with M. Grossier, a local wine merchant.
9. At Grigneville we stayed with Marie-Jeanne Beauballet.
10. At Chantillon-le-Roi we stayed with Yvonne Bruneau.
11. 4-13 May 1944 Mr. and Mrs Bretanue, farm near main road Dordive to Chateau-Landon.
12. 14 May-15 July 1944 - Mme Sonya (unreadable) at Dordive.
13. July 44 and again in August 44 – (unreadable).

A letter to Mrs. Lissette from Sgt King.

Flight Sergeant King also wrote a letter to Mrs Lissette in New Zealand: 1580576 F/S KING, P.N., Sgts. Mess, RAF Bishops Court, County Down, N-Ireland. 3.9.45. He wrote:

'Dear Mrs. Lissette, Thanks very much for your welcome air letter which I received a couple of days ago. Sorry you did not receive the first letter I wrote to you; I should have written you again, but was waiting for a reply from you. However, it could not be helped. First, I will try and answer your questions for you, then perhaps you will feel a bit better. The trip on which Les lost his life was our fourth bombing trip, we had done one trip over Germany and the others were over France. It was a brilliant moonlight night on the 3-4 of May and there were pretty well all German night fighters about as well as searchlights and an anti-aircraft guns. We were flying in a Lancaster bomber with about six tons of H.E. bombs on board, our target was a place called Mailly near Rheims France.'

'We got to the target OK and dropped the bombs, but when we were about 40 minutes out of the target area our aircraft was attacked by two German fighters, we fought them off successfully for about ten minutes but during one of our evasive manoeuvres one of our engines was set on fire by a direct hit from flak, the wing was on fire and the aircraft was filled with smoke. However, Les did not lose his head and continued to control the aircraft as if nothing was the matter. We managed to put out the fire on the wing but only having three engines, our speed was cut down and the aircraft could not be manoeuvred so much as before. Our rear gun turret was next put out of action, then another fighter came in, and hit us with incendiary cannon shells. The aircraft caught fire in the bomb bay and spread very rapidly to the rest of the kite. There was nothing we could about it, so Les gave us the order, to bail out, four of the crew got out very easily, but the rear gunner, Ron Ellis was sprawled out across his guns and could not get out. I told Les this as I went forward to get out myself, and, told him to get out himself. However, he ordered me to jump and the last thing I saw of him was fighting the controls to keep the aircraft on an even keel.'

'No, Mrs. Lissette, Les was not frightened, he was in my estimation cool and courageous and I am proud that I flew with such a grand skipper and pal. (There's very little space left so I will continue on another air letter, which I hope you receive the same time as this). Continuing where I left off in my other letter. After the aircraft crashed two bodies were found, one was that of Les and the other of Ron Ellis. Les's identity discs were found and I saw them in the possession of a French policeman. He said that he intended to send them to you after the war, so I gave him your address. I was taken to a cemetery at Chaintreaux Seine et Marne, and shown two graves, one of which was Les's and the other Ron's. Both graves were covered with flowers and had red, white and blue ribbons in the shape of a V on them. The local French people tended the graves every day and fresh flowers were put on them. Part of Les was buried by a Frenchman in a garden and I asked to see the remains, from what I saw I positively identified Les. It was a piece of his arm with his battle dress still attached, and on the battle dress was his New Zealand flash and his three stripes and crown. There was also something else I identified but I do not wish to tell you that. But believe me Mrs. Lissette I could not have made any mistake in my identification, so I hope I have answered some of your questions.

Les or 'Lizzy' as we used to call him was a grand fellow, he was older than the rest of us and used to look after us like a father. We had some good times together and he was liked and admired by all our folks whom he met at some time or other. My wife was particularly upset when, I told her of his death, and even now I find her with tears in her eyes when she thinks back on the days before that dreadful night. We all owe our lives to your son Mrs. Lissette and you can perhaps find comfort in the thought that he did his duty to his King, country and to you. I speak for all of us when I say that he will always be honoured in our memories as a brave and very courageous man. Well, I must come to a close once more, but I shall be writing to you again very soon and if I get any more information from France, I shall let you have it immediately. My wife joins with me in wishing you and Mr. Lissette all the very best of luck and hope that you are both in the best of health. So, until next time. Cheerio and God Bless, very sincerely, (Signed) Phil King.'

After he landed Phil King hid and found a hiding place in a barn, described by him as 'a few yards from the place where I came down.' Right: Phil and son some twenty years after the war. (PK)

The last indirect victim of the crew, Lissette's girlfriend.

When the war was over Lissette's girlfriend Florence Dudfield ended her posting as a nurse on the Dutch hospital ship Oranje and returned home. Oranje sailed back to the Netherlands and its home port of Amsterdam, to be refurbished as the luxury cruise liner she was before the war.

It was the end of a short, yet very fascinating history. Almost a year after the festive launch, on September 4, 1939, the ship had embarked on its maiden voyage as a passenger ship. However, World War II had started. While the ship was working on the first voyage, the scheduled services on the Netherlands East Indies were immediately discontinued. The danger to mines in the North Sea was too great. The Oranje was forced to change course. The ship was taken to Sydney where, at the expense of the Australian Navy, it was converted into a floating hospital to return wounded Allied soldiers from the front home safely. The ship sailed up and down between North Africa, the Middle East, Australia and New Zealand.

During the war the ship was under Australian command, but it retained its Dutch crew and also continued to sail under the Dutch flag. After the capitulation of Japan and the subsequent Indonesian Independence Struggle, an initial migration flow from the Dutch East Indies and later Indonesia to the Netherlands started. Between 1945 and 1965, an estimated 300,000 people who wished to leave the new Indonesian Republic, or were forced to do so, made the crossing to the new 'homeland' they had often never seen before. For several thousands of them, the Oranje was the ship with which this change of course took place. Sadly, passenger travel by ship had become impractical and expensive with the overwhelming interest in flying. In 1964 the ship was sold to the Italian cruise shipping company Lauro and subsequently got the name Angelina Lauro. The shipping company used the ship for cruise travel in the Caribbean. In 1979, a fire broke out on the Angelina Lauro near the U.S. Virgin Islands. The passengers could be rescued, but the ship itself was a total loss after the days of furious fire. An attempt was still made to tow the shipwreck away. During this voyage, however, the ship flooded and on 24 September 1979 it sank in the South Pacific.

Left: Sergeant Phil & Mavis King and their family at their wedding. Sadly, Philip King died on 18 March 1981. Right: Florence Dudfield in her uniform as a nurse on board the MV Oranje. (PK jnr/BL)

The Dutch ocean liner Oranje became a hospital ship until she finally returned to Amsterdam in 1946. (NDSM)

Left: Shattered remains of Air New Zealand 901 after it hit Mount Erebus on Ross Island, killing all 237 passengers and 20 crew. Right: The New Zealand Mount Erebus memorial at Waikumete.

A few months later disaster struck for nurse Dudfield, who had since retired to New Zealand and who was living a happy life with her husband. She was the godmother of Brian Lissette and married Robert Tremaine and lived in Taupo, until she got involved in a horrible event that many New Zealanders still remember. Her death on 28 November 1979 deserves to be mentioned. She and her husband Robert were passengers on board Air New Zealand Flight 901, during a then popular sight-seeing flight to Antarctica. During this flight the aircraft hit Mount Erebus on Ross Island, Antarctica, killing all 237 passengers and 20 crew. Scheduled Air New Zealand Antarctic sightseeing flight had been operating between 1977 and 1979. This flight was scheduled to take off from Auckland airport in the morning and spend a few hours flying over the Antarctic continent, before returning to Auckland at night via Christchurch. The initial investigation caused an uproar of anger as the committee concluded that the accident was caused by pilot error. Public outcry led to the establishment of a Royal Commission of Inquiry into the crash. The accident was New Zealand's deadliest peacetime disaster, as well as the deadliest in the history of Air New Zealand. Sadly, the body of 'Floss' Trermaine-Dudfield was never found and identified. The crash and the subsequent handling of this disaster still is an open wound in the hearts and minds of many New Zealanders.

Len Barnes after his return.

In Kent Online of Tuesday March 10, 2020, appeared an interview with Len Barnes' daughter, written by Gerry Warren, saying: 'Kent family of RAF pilot Len Barnes tell of great escape during Second World War that brought everlasting French connection. RAF bomber pilot Len Barnes owed his life to the family who hid him from the Germans after his Lancaster was shot down over occupied France. Now 70 years later, his daughter has told of the unique bond of friendship that still exists between the two families. As the last to leave the stricken aircraft of 630 Squadron where two of his crew already lay dead, Len's only chance was to parachute to safety. Pilot Len Barnes owed his life to the family who hid him from the Germans. What followed was an extraordinary story of heroism as the 24-year-old airman found refuge from the Germans through the bravery of French farmers and freedom fighters. They hid him for six weeks and helped him escape down through the Pyrenees and eventually back to Britain where, remarkably, he took to the skies again.

After the war, Len – who became a printer – moved to Chestfield with his wife Merville, known as Merv. But 23 years later, his saviours – the Coigné family – found a jar he had buried containing some of his belongings, including his RAF pin brooch and his home address. With the help of a French television company, they tracked him down and it led to an emotional reunion in 1963 in Fere-en-Tardenois near Reims, where he had hidden in a barn. Len died 25 years ago (1988), but the bond between the families is as strong as ever. Now Len's three daughters, Amanda Burrows from Herne Bay, Angela Barnes from Canterbury and Glynis Spencer from Whitstable, have led a 15-strong family visit to Fere-en-Tardenois. There they were given a huge civic reception and a welcome from the mayor. It is not the first time they have returned to the scene of Len's remarkable survival, but it was made all the more poignant by being the 70th anniversary.

It is also the place where Len's two fellow airmen are buried. So close have the families become that Amanda, 50, even named her daughter Madeleine after Madame Coigné, the farmer's wife. While she and her husband Leon have now passed on, they still treasure their friendship with Len's descendants. Amanda, of Glen Avenue, Beltinge, said: 'The bond that exists between us is unbreakable. I know my dad would be so proud and pleased that the friendship he found in 1944 continues between us today. He was eternally grateful to those who hid and cared for him. The Coignés took immense risk in hiding my dad and could have paid for it with their lives. Without them we would not be here today. The welcome we received was amazing and we were treated like royalty. It was very emotional on both sides and they really feel like our French family.'

D-Day news for Ken Walker.

In Saint Barthélemy Walker heard the news of the landings in Normandy. A few weeks later the first signs of a German retreat were visible in the area. Moving along the French roads on horse drawn carts, old buses and other means of transportation German soldiers tried their best to keep ahead of the allied armies. The local resistance kept a low profile and did not encounter the enemy. Yet here and there shots were fired at the German columns. Fortunately there was no pointless bloodshed as in some other places, like Ouradour-sur-Glane. Then, one day, in mid-August, a strange silence spread over the area. Saint Barthélemy had become 'no man's land.' The next afternoon the first American reconnaissance patrol entered the village. Young cheerful men, driving fast jeeps and bristling arms took positions. The locals welcomed them with great enthusiasm. The Americans had arrived.

When the 7th Armoured Division under Major-General Lindsay McDonald Sylvester (left) had established their Headquarters in la Ferté Gaucher Ken Walker reported himself as returned for further service. When the Americans knew he was a genuine soldier, they did all they could to help him.

Now it was safe for Walker to come out of hiding. In his civilian clothes he reported to the men of the reconnaissance unit. The Americans were in a hurry, so they told Ken Walker to wait for the armoured troops that follow them. On 27 August soldiers of 7th US Armoured Division of Major-General Lindsay McDonald Sylvester arrived. Walker asked the soldiers to see their commander. He was driven to the Headquarters at la Ferté Gaucher. At first the Americans were so amazed to see this young man who claimed to be a hiding English airman, that they interrogated him thoroughly. When they were completely satisfied that Walker was a genuine airman and not a German spy, they did all they could to help. First, they threw a big party; four days later Walker was able to leave. The Americans gave him a jeep, a driver, rations and an American uniform. Walker left his brave French hosts and went to Paris. He was given a room in the Hotel Maurice in the posh Rue de Rivoli. His parents were informed that their son was alive and well. On 10 September Ken Walker returned home. After a brief leave, he was posted to No.195 Squadron, where he continued to fly operations, contrary to most aircrew who had been in a similar situation. One of his last flights was a food drop over starving Occupied Western Holland in April 1945.

9. THE LAST TO LEAVE.

The five evaders still on the move in Paris.

We pick up the story and return to the days before the Invasion. On 30 April Willis and Hubbard were in Paris. It was a wonderful summer. The Germans in field grey showed life was different. Day and night allied aircraft could be heard. Often, during attacks against targets in and around the French capital, aircraft were shot down and soon more aviators arrived in the resistance hideouts. In spite of the constant danger of treason and infiltration, a Belgian resistance member called Jacques Bolle, regularly travelled from Brussels to Paris, escorting nervous young men. At the Gare du Nord Madeleine Boutreloupt was one of the courageous girls, waiting to guide very nervous young men to one of the safe houses. Those who did not know her, even many of her friends, regarded her as one of the many Parisians who tried to survive as best as they can. Only a few knew how she risked her life almost every day.

These amazing photographs were made in Paris near the Trocadero and the Eiffel Tower in 1944. From time to time evading air crew were allowed escorted walks in Paris.

We see three allied airmen with a French escort stroll along the boulevard. They cross the path of a German naval officer and are about walk by German soldiers one of them carrying his rifle. The German naval officer does not notice them. Even surrounded by armed Germans no one seems to worry about the danger of these walks. Guides of Comète had to have very strong nerves.

Top: The German naval officer is almost surrounded by four young men, who stroll past him, but as we think with their hearts beating.

Bottom: Seven Germans, at least three of them carrying a rifle, stand around the four men, who manage to behave as if nothing is abnormal... (d'A-L)

The responsible resistance official in Paris was tall Philippe d'Albert-Lake. With his American wife Virginia, they controlled the whole operation virtually under the noses of the Germans. Even before the USA had been dragged into the war, Virginia travelled by rail or on her bicycle to help young Britons, Canadians, Czechs, Americans, New Zealanders, Australians and Poles. Strangely enough she had not been interned when America entered the war. Now she was an indispensable member of Comète.

At the end of May 1944, no less than twenty airmen waited for the day of their departure for the Pyrenees. In early June Philippe informs Hubbard, Willis, Barnes, Cornett and Emeny that their day of departure is near. On 4 June, the moment comes. In the evening, a man appears at the house. He will lead the fugitives to Austerlitz railway station. The procedure is simple. The entire five have to do is follow him at a safe distance, never losing sight of each other. The five escapees will travel to Bordeaux by night train. As the train stops only once or twice there is little chance of German or French identity checks in the train. The only risks are checkpoints inside the station. Pierre Camus, as their guide is called, will travel with them to the South and then hand them to Max Roger, who had done many shipments of young rabbits, kittens or books as the men are called to conceal their true identity. Walking casually but with a beating heart the men follow their guide. Paris is almost as busy as in peacetime. But for the leader it still was dangerous enough to be very careful.

The Paris Metro was a relative safe way to take arriving evaders from one safe house to the other. The crowds using it made it more difficult to check all the passengers, though the entries and exits were often blocked by the Germans for ID-checks. Philippe and Virginia 'd Albert-Lake are the responsible leaders of Comète in Paris. They ensured the safest possible stay as well as the last part of the journey to the Spanish border. Virginia was an American citizen by birth. Her husband Philippe d'Albert was a Frenchman, who adopted his wife's maiden name Lake as his second name. (MdP/d'Albert-Lake)

If the guide spotted German soldiers carrying rifles or German naval officers on leave in Paris, the men waited until the Germans disappears. In their pockets they had forged ID-cards, naming them Jean-Louis Ménard, painter or Antoine Duval, clerk. They had forged Ausweise, documents permitting them to travel by train. Philippe d'Albert-Lake was 'Paul Etchevery from Caboure in the Basque country.' As an official of the French railways, he travelled by train. Pierre Camus' papers identified him as Robert Lienard, a controller of the French railways. For young Pierre it was the second time he escorted airmen. The first time he travelled under supervision of an old fox, Marcel Roger, known in Comète as Max. Marcel was a confidant of 'Franco', Jean-François Nothomb and 'Aunt Go' de Greef, the Mother of Comète. As the trip took many hours, maybe the whole night, it was decided to take the men to a park near the station. There they sat on benches, pretending to sleep in the afternoon sun. In fact, they waited for it to be dark enough to board without too much risk. At Austerlitz station the men joined the queue of waiting passengers, showed their ID to the gendarmes and the German guards. Pierre told the five to spread over five compartments. This gave the others a chance to escape if one of them was recognized and arrested. Pierre had already bought their tickets and nothing seemed to endanger their departure.

It often happened that the lines had been sabotaged or that trains had to hide until preying fighters of the allied air forces had disappeared. Sometimes railways had been blocked to ensure the safe passage of troop trains and military supplies. Sharing the carriage with peasants, German soldiers and travelling salesmen the five pretended to be sleeping. Willis held a Vichy newspaper in his hands and read it while some French passengers gave him a dirty look. This was the moment he had waited for; he was on his way home! The journey from Paris to Bordeaux was uneventful. During the long trip, the men made mental notes of German military installations they passed. At Orléans they saw railway cars with tanks and artillery. Hubbard still carried the envelope with information about American bombings, given to him by the Brussels resistance. And he carried his Browning pistol under his shirt.

After eight hours the train entered the station of Bordeaux. The longest part of the journey had been successful. Now came the dangerous part, entering the border zone. Pierre walked ahead, casually as if he was on his own. The five followed him to the other platform where the stop train to Bayonne waited. This train was relatively safe, as it did not connect with the lines into Spain. The express train drove to Hendaye, the French-Spanish border station where Hitler once met dictator Franco of Spain. The train and the platforms were under constant surveillance of the Gestapo, Feldgendarmerie or SD. No one knew that trouble lay ahead. Pierre remembered how problems began after they boarded the train to Bayonne: 'We were less than ten miles from Bayonne when one of the airmen ran into troubles. He shared the carriage with a couple of Germans who had been drinking quite a lot. First, they started talking to him. When they got no answer, they got annoyed with what they thought was one of these French peasants showing contempt. They began to push and pull and called the airman names. The poor chap did not know what to do. I could not help since I was at the other end with the American major Willis. It would not be long before we would have a crisis on our hands.

Emeny also remembered the incident, as he was the victim. He was nervous due to a bizarre mistake of Willis, who was supporting himself by holding one of the straps above his head. Unaware of it he proudly displayed his air force issue watch on his wrist. Emeny wanted to warn Willis, but there was no way to get closer or draw his attention. When, about ten minutes later, drunken Germans began to bother Curly, the frightened gunner could think of only one thing: 'I had got to get away from these Jerries.'

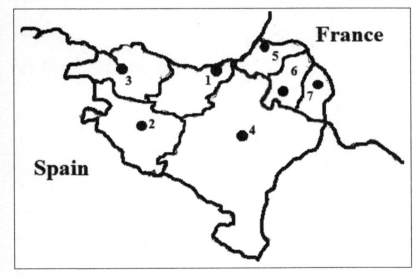

The Basque country was cut in two by Spain and France.

The Spanish regions were:
1. Gipuzkoa (San Sebastian),
2. Araba (Vitoria-Gasteiz),
3. Biskaia, (Bilbao) and
4. Naffaroa. (Pamplona).
   The French regions were:
5. Lapurdi (Bayonne),
6. Nafurroa Beherea (St Jean Pied de Port),
7. Zuberoa (Mauléon-Licharre).

The French regions are all in one single département, eg. province.

When the train slowed down, about five miles from Boucau, with Bayonne in sight, Emeny opened the door, jumped off the train and ran like hell, leaving the Germans standing absolutely amazed[105]. Pierre Camus and Don Willis watched helplessly; the others had not even noticed what happened.

There was little else for Pierre to do but to wait until they arrived at Boucau, where Max waited with bicycles, brought by a local baker, Martin Garat of Larressore, who kept them for use by Comète. Gravely worried about Emeny's future the group left the train and walked to the exit. The group passed the

---

[105] Barnes would later say it was Cornett, who jumped from the train in panic.

German checkpoint without any problems and met Max as agreed in front of the station. Pierre briefly told him what has happened. Max signalled the four to follow him to their safe house. At the same time Pierre Camus tried to find Emeny, hoping to re-join the group as soon as he found Curly.

Roger and the four started to ride off to Anglet. Camus with his excellent papers decided to follow the railway track to 'inspect' the state of the rails and the signal poles, at the same time hoping to find Emeny hiding somewhere along the line: 'I cycled along the track, all the way to Saint Vincent de Tyrosse, asking every railway worker if he have seen a man walking by. No one could help. On my way back I met a few men who told me they have seen a youngster hiding further back, so again I rode along the line. In vain. The pilot has disappeared. This caused a serious problem, as we were not sure what had happened. He could have been captured; he could have talked. They did not speak much French and if they did, they had horrible accents, especially the Americans. Late in the afternoon I returned and went to see Max to tell him that one of our packages was missing.' Max decides to give it one last try. Together with Pierre he made a second trip along the line. No sign of Emeny. Deeply worried the two men returned to the safe house.

One of Virginia's forged permits. The Germans allowed her to leave Paris for one month due to ill health. The paper was signed by an SS officer, very impressive. To ensure free access to all the destinations of the French railways, Philippe and his people carried forged French Railways ID Cards. As Paul Etchevery, Philip worked as a Group Chief (d'Albert-Lake). Much feared were the Feldgendarmen, the German Military Police. Because of the plate and chain on their chest they were known as Kettenhünde (Chain dogs). (dA-L/BuA)

All this time Sergeant Ron Emeny wandered south to the town of Bayonne. A sudden confrontation with the Germans and the possible discovery of his real identity had been the reason for his impromptu leap. Now he had caused a bigger problem. He had no money, no contacts and did not speak the language. He decided to follow the railway line to the south. For several hours Emeny walked south. Then another strange incident occurred, one that might very well have caused his arrest. While he walked by, an elderly Frenchman, who was working in the garden of his cottage, approached him. Looking at Emeny he said: 'Soldat Anglais?' 'Oui, aviateur [106],' replied Emeny. The Frenchman told him that he had fought at the front in France together with the British, during the Great War. He also said that he easily recognized the Englishman, because of his walk, which looked more like a military march. Then the Frenchman pulled Emeny's beret over his eyes, gave him a packet of French cigarettes, and put his hands in his pockets to demonstrate a few steps. Patting Curly on the back he pointed down the road and said: 'Bonne chance, mon ami!' So Emeny walked on, much relieved but still very worried about his future here in the border area. He was so close to the border, yet there seemed little chance of getting across unchallenged.

---

[106] *English soldier? Yes, aviator.*

In the foothills of the Pyrenees.
At about 7 o'clock in the evening Max and Pierre returned to Bayonne. The passage of the others could not be put in danger any longer. A decision had to be made. Hide them until they were sure the 'escaped escapee' had been arrested? Lay low until danger had passed, or continue with one man less? Suddenly Pierre said to Max: 'Look, there he is!!' Indeed, they recognized Emeny as the man who was aimlessly walking on the other side of the street. They managed to attract Emeny's attention and 'rescued' him without much notice; to his intense relief they finally arrived at the house of Marthe Mendihara, whose inn was used as the last resting place before the escapees set off for a crossing of the border. Emeny's comrades were upset, but when Curly explained his reasons, assuring them he had not been in touch with anyone, they accepted his apologies. In the meantime, Marthe prepared a meal. In the Auberge, as the inn was known, many strangers had come and gone. Friendly gendarmes told Marthe when to expect Germans or their own patrols. Shortly before the German arrived people were seen to leave and disperse into the woods near-by until all was quiet again. Often small groups arrived at the back of the inn, disappearing up to the first floor, where, in a hidden room, there awaited a warm meal and a soft bed. In the meantime soldiers off duty drank beer singing their loud German songs. Gendarmes took a small Izarra, the local potent alcohol so very much appreciated by the Basques themselves. The Germans did not understand the strange language the local people spoke, and even the gendarmes, who often came from other parts of France, had no idea what these people are talking about in their presence. For many centuries, the Basque country had been split in two by the border between France and Spain.

The countryside is extraordinary beautiful. Thin layers of fog cover the hills in the morning. In the north, near Biarritz, the waves of the Bay of Biscay roll over the beaches, now covered by pillboxes and bunkers. These areas are off limits to all but military, even the locals and the fishermen can only work when escorted by German vessels and with German soldiers on board. In the hills many small villages have very strange names like Herboure, Olhette, Lehenbiseaye, Souraïde and Ainhoa, all in a landscape laced with little rivers like the Nivelle, the Sare and the Bidassoa, the river that forms part of the border with now Fascist Spain.

The people flatly refused to communicate with the foreign soldiers who had invaded their land, completely ignoring their presence whilst talking loudly to each other in their strange language! The men wore their black berets and sometimes watched the youngsters playing 'pelote[107]' against the high wall in the village square. They earned their living working in the fields and raising cattle. Some men made beautiful furniture, while others produced the Izarra, which made Germans talk after a few too many! At night, the men earned an extra centime or two; the 'contrabandistas', as they were called, cross the border along the many paths that lead into the hills. The French customs officers could never catch them – even the dog patrols of the German Feldgendarmerie were useless.

On the other side of the border were Spanish soldiers and policemen, who turned a blind eye for a small share in the business. Cattle, tobacco, alcohol, wheat, passed relatively freely from east to west and back. At night, when the moon disappeared behind the clouds, the Basque mountains belonged to the Aguerres, the Etchevestes, the Etchegoyens and the Goicoecheas. They were the men who took fugitives to safety. Many passed through Marthe's café. She was always kind to the Germans and smiled when they sat in her inn. But inside she hated the Boche. No German had ever known that above their heads enemy soldiers slept and waited for the moment to vanish into the hills. Many years later Marthe remembered the last five soldiers she helped the night before they crossed: 'Usually the pilots spent the night upstairs in the cafe. After they had slept and felt strong enough Max would come and take them to a forest near Larressore. We always waited for the Gendarmes to tell us when the German patrols had left. The Gendarmes themselves patrolled somewhere else, so that they never ran into the escapees.
Sometimes the fleeing men stayed in the forest for the remainder of the day. They were not supposed to show themselves and had to wait until the 'passeur' came to collect them.

---

[107] *Pelote is a similar game as played in Mexico. Two men with a 'basket' tied to their hand, swing a ball against a wall as hard as possible. The idea is to catch the opponent's ball and throw it back.*

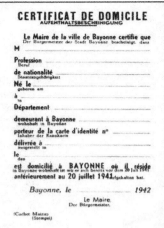

Forged documents; the key to a successful evasion. (dA-L)

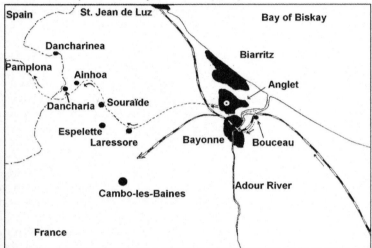

Pierre Camus was made a Technical Controller. Of course, Monsieur Robert Lienard only had access to the 2nd Class, whereas Mr. Etchevery had the right to choose his own class. Each year these ID cards have to be renewed, as can be seen by the stamp '1944.' The last part of the journey was the most dangerous one; After leaving the train from Paris at Bayonne or Boucau, the evaders had to cycle via Laressore, Souraïde and Ainhoa to Dancheria, where they had to cross the border on foot. Not until they had passed the 10 miles border zone of Spain could they report to the authorities and be interned. If captured earlier they were often handed to the Germans. (dA-L/HO)

There were several routes across. In the north a man called Florentino Goicoechea, a giant, very brave and scared of nothing, ran the route. His route lead from Cibourne into Spain. There were different trails for different 'passeurs'. There were men like Jean Elissondo, Pierre Etchegoyen, and the brothers Jean-Baptiste and Pierre Aguerre. Michel Etcheveste took the last five pilots to Spain. He guided them across the border through the hills and then walked them to a farm called 'Igna Bideco Borda.' It belonged to the in-laws of one of the Aguerres. Via this 'Larressore Line' they 'passed' 197 pilots. One night a German patrol saw a group of six pilots with Pierre Aguerre. They shot Pierre through his hand, but in spite of the blood and the pain he went on. Unfortunately two pilots lost contact and were never seen or heard of again. Some said the Germans executed them, others claimed they died of exhaustion. Marthe remembered the anxiety: 'I do not know, but we never saw them again. The other four stayed with Pierre arriving safely in Spain without any further troubles.' Hubbard, Willis, Barnes, Cornett and Emeny followed the same route into Spain. Once at Marthe's inn they disappeared into the back room of the house, spending the night sleeping on the first floor. At three in the morning Marthe woke them up to serve them a good breakfast. At five they left and walked to Larressore. Accompanied by the guide they quietly cycled through Espelette and Souraïde.

Left: The railway station of Boucau, last stop before the crossing of the mountains. Right: Max Roger (left) and 'Auntie' Go de Greef, casually looking at the photographer while they rest at one of the small lanes of the Basque hills, with two airmen they are taking to the spot where the walk across the Pyrenees will begin. (MdB/AC)

The last leg of their journey lay ahead of them. In the distance the first sunlight shone through the trees on the hilltops they were to cross to get into Spain. In Souraïde Michel Etcheveste prepared for another illegal crossing. It was 5 of June, a day like any other. Michel had made this crossing so many times. He had driven cows, goats, and even prize bulls across the frontier. Numerous times he carried tobacco; always making a good price for it. He could not remember how often he led terrified fugitives into Spain. Frightened Jews, fearing for their lives, close to freedom, soldiers, resistance fighters from as far away as Holland and Belgium. Indeed, the Basque guides had fetched a good deal of money, but with the deadly risk of arrest and possible execution in mind, Etcheveste believed that he was entitled to be paid. Without any hurry he collected what he needed for his long march: bread, some cheese and a bottle of Izarra. Late in the afternoon he left his village and walked to the forest where he arranged to meet his customers.

The five waited all day, nervously sitting down deep in the forest. All they could do was to sit and wait. Etcheveste easily found the five who, for the last hours have eagerly spent their time waiting inside a farm barn in the forest. Emeny was uncomfortable inside the old building, which was: 'Very primitive; animals wandered in and out all the time. We stayed in a loft used for containing animal fodder with fleas, thousands of fleas. The guide pointed to our shoes and gave us 'Espadrilles', the Spanish rope-shoes. We were told to take our shoes off and put these things on. Then we left.' Not speaking anything but Basque and colloquial French and Spanish, Etcheveste pointed ahead, walked away firmly indicating that they must follow at a safe distance. Then he noticed that the tallest of the five carried something under his coat, Etcheveste stopped, turned to the Texan, pointed at the package, wanted the know what the stranger is carrying. But to no avail. Hubbard refused to part from his parcel, containing the reports, photographs and sketches of the American attacks against Brussels with other sheets of invaluable information for allied intelligence.

Garat from Larressore, was responsible for recovering the bikes. He brought them from the 'Pont du Diable' back to Bayonne to Henri Claverie, a mechanic at the rue Tour de Sault. Henri was responsible for maintaining them, so that they could be used again by the next batch of evaders from Dax station to

Anglet-Sutar and Larressore. The role of the bakery community, particularly the millers in the flour mill Ustaritz has not yet been researched. In fact, the messages that arrived at the Larre inn were well hidden in the breads delivered by 16-year-old Christiane Saldias. As nearly every village had its own bakers in those days, they were an important hub around which village life revolved. Someone at the flour millers at Ustaritz was active on Comète's behalf and, this way messages for the various networks would arrive with the flour, baked into the bread for distribution far and wide. It is not yet clear who originated the messages.

Martin Garat, the Laressore baker was responsible for the recovery of all the used bicycles. His bakery was the next stage in the long march to the border, an exhausting undertaking through hill, forests and bare mountains.

Now that the fugitives were forced to walk through the shrubs, they soon began to feel the strain of the physical challenge. Michel Etcheveste shrugged his shoulders and moved on. He worked alone, so, apart from the five men, there was no one who could betray him anyway. Etcheveste had a simple, yet effective philosophy: 'If one man does the job, no second man can cause a problem.' At first, Michel had difficulties explaining what he expected the five to do. But then, to his surprise, one of them, a short man, spoke Spanish. It was Don Willis, who knew the language from the days before the war when he smuggled liquor into the United States from Mexico. 'The Little Silent Man', as Etcheveste remembers Willis years later, translated to the others what the guide said: 'Do not speak, keep your distance, but also make sure you always see me. If I stand still, you stand still. If I lie down, you do the same. Only move when I tell you. Do not smoke. Beware of the Gendarmes. I will deal with them. If I spot Germans, we turn back, wherever we are. They patrol in couples and always have a dog. They are scared, so they will shoot immediately. Walk on, do not rest. It will be a long march, so we will have to keep going all night. The darkness is our only friend. When the sun rises, we must hide. We will not stop until I tell you we have crossed the border. We have to be at least one hour away from the border, for if the carabinieros catch us within their patrol zone, they will hand us over to the Germans. They have a deal with them and get money for you. Should we be captured I must leave you, for you will be prisoners, I will be dead!'

The five nodded, knowing what was at stake. Their future was in the hands of this small guy with the black beret. Michel ordered the men to destroy their French identity papers and bury them. At sunset, the men followed a trail between the hedges around the small fields. They slowly moved south, closer and closer to the border area, where the Wehrmacht and the French Gendarmerie patrolled day and night. At first, the march seemed easy, but as it got darker, the men became exhausted. The trail went down and up and down again: from Souraïde to Ainhoa, where the border was. Etcheveste went with ease. The five airmen, however, found it difficult to follow. They were not used to these marches; it was not an airman's job! Michel was forced to leave the track and walk through the undergrowth wearing the five men out.

Nothing is easy in the mountains.

The distance of five miles between Souraïde and Ainhoa took almost three hours. And, from Ainhoa to Dancheria, where the French border post was, it was another two miles. At about 0130 hours on 4 June, the group arrived at the bank of the small river, which ran east of Dancheria to form a natural border between Spain and France. In the darkness, the voices of Spanish border policemen could be heard, presumably at Dancharinea, on the Spanish side of the border. Etcheveste took off his shoes and put them under his coat. Then, rolling up his trousers, he gestured that the five must do the same. Slowly he

The café of Marthe Mendihara in the Sutar quarter of Anglet, was the last safe house before they crossed the border. Here they got a hot meal, a good day's sleep and food to take with them on the last leg of their evasion. On the ground floor German policemen and soldiers drank their wine and beer, while on the first floor allied aircrew rested before they started on the long march into Spain. She always smiled at the Germans, but she hated them deeply (HO/MM/HO).

Four brave Basques who risked their lives to help the evaders cross the mountains into neutral Spain: Left to right we see Michel Etcheveste, Pierre Elghora, Jean Elizondo and Marthe Mendiara. (EVA).

put his feet in the icy water, and, followed by his companions, crossed the river. When they reached the other side of the river, Etcheveste lead the men into the darkness of the trees. 'España', he whispered. The men had now left Occupied France and were in fascist, neutral Spain. The small 'passeur' did not allow them a rest. At daybreak, they had to be deep in Spain to be safe from the Guardia Civil and the Carabineiros. Etcheveste waited until they had all reached the side of the road from Dancharinea to Elizondo, where the road to Pamplona began. Cornett could hardly walk anymore, Emeny felt pain all over his body and even tough Don Willis was wilting under the strain.

Etcheveste decided that it had been enough for now. In a small wood, he allowed the men some rest, opened his haversack and gave the fugitives bread and cheese. Then he passed the bottle with Izarra. Coughing the men drank the potent alcohol that fired their bodies into action again. Then Michel stood up and briskly motioned to follow again. Hubbard, with enormous blisters on his feet, was hardly able to last longer. Cornett had to drag himself from tree to tree. Barnes had not spoken for hours while Ron

Emeny sometimes wished that the German soldiers would come, arrest them and put him in a wonderful cell with a place to sleep for hours. As dawn slowly appeared in the east, they reached an old dilapidated sheep pen. Etcheveste told them to stay there, not to leave the sheep pen under any circumstances, and just wait for him to return. He did not say where he was going or why, he simply left them behind in the midst of rotting hay and stinking sheep droppings.

Drinking water from little brooks, desperately looking for something to eat, they decided that they could not go on much longer. The five languished for the whole of 6 June. Etcheveste had left his haversack so they could share the bread, the cheese and a little Izarra, providing some slight lift in their flagging spirits. Then one after the other fell asleep. In the early evening, Michel Etcheveste came as he went, suddenly and without a sound, waking the men up and urging them to follow him at once. Again, they walked for hours, deeper and deeper into Spain. None of them had any idea where they were going. The sun showed they were still heading west and slightly north. At sunset they were still on the move. Again, they walked all night. Then, when it was still dark, two figures appeared from the shadows. Michel seemed to know them for he talked with the two men in his unintelligible patois. Turning to his five escapees he shook hands with them. Without further ado, he picked up his haversack and walked away, back to France. They never saw him again. Then something happened that aroused Willis' suspicions. Until now, he had not shown that his command of Spanish was almost fluent. Len Barnes turned to one of the children in the kitchen asking in English where they were. The children, failing to understand, asked their mother what the stranger said. She replied: 'I do not know what he said, but do not speak with them and do not tell them where they are.'

Left: The Basque country, a beautiful area. However, without an experienced guide the journey across the border was a lethal trap. Right: Michel Etcheveste, with his black Basque beret. He took the men from Laressore into Spain and ensured their safe passage (HO/Echeveste).

Willis was sure now that something was very wrong and nonchalantly told his friends that there was a chance that they were being 'sold out' to the authorities. Being that close to freedom, none of them wanted to be sent back to France again! Promptly they decided to take their destiny into their own hands and left as quickly as they could. In spite of the woman's protests, they left the farm and headed to the west. Without a compass or a map, not knowing their whereabouts the men followed the track, which disappeared behind the hill. There was nowhere to hide, keeping the road to Elizondo down in the valley in sight they walked for hours while the sun rose. In the early morning, the group saw a man, a shepherd, sitting on a large rock with some bread and a skin of wine. The man greeted the escapers and even shared his food with them, motioning the men to follow him. After a few miles, they rested and Willis told the others to wait. With some French francs from his escape kit, he wanted to try to buy some food from a nearby farm; at the house he met the occupants who, though puzzled, immediately understood that this dirty, unshaven man was a fugitive from France. They told Willis to go the police. Don declined. All he wanted was food and he was willing to pay good money for it. The farmer sold Donald some raw potatoes, a bottle filled with well water and a loaf of bread. The farmer's son told him that he was only a few miles from Pamplona, so Willis left the farm to re-join his friends. Within an hour they saw Pamplona in the valley. Again, Willis volunteered to go in first. While the others waited on the hillside he tried to get in touch with the British or American consul in San Sebastian. Following the two new guides, the fugitives headed for what seemed to be a small village below in the valley. No word was spoken, yet the five runaways felt there was something wrong. At times, the two Spaniards whispered to each other while they looked at the five. Willis tried to communicate with them, but they only shook their heads. The five men pondered what to do next. With the glow of the lights of some town in the west, they decided to press on to the village. Don Willis explained to the guides what their aim was. The two men told the escapers not to worry, as freedom was near. Then they took them to a farmhouse. The farmer's wife welcomed them, and led them to her kitchen where she gave them bread, onions and milk. The men had walked some 60 miles since they left Anglet. But now it was over.

All they could do now was stay together and wait for things to happen. It was worth trying. Don entered Pamplona and luckily soon found the post office. Inside he told the operator that he wanted to make a phone call to the American consulate in San Sebastian. When the connection was made Willis told the consulate of the arrival of five escapees from France. However, while Willis spoke to the consul the operator called the Guardia Civil and informed the police about the stranger and the call he was making. Within minutes four uniformed men with funny-looking black leather hats arrived. They were soldiers of the hated Guardia Civil. When Willis left the building he was quickly arrested. A few minutes later they escorted him to Police Headquarters. At the police station Willis could do little else than tell the officers who he was, where he came from and that his friends were waiting for his return. Soon a group of soldiers and policemen took Willis to the place where the others were. When they arrived at the scene all four were sound asleep. Len Barnes was the first to wake up. To his horror he saw how some fifty soldiers surrounded their hideout while others came closer, their weapons ready to fire.

There was no escape. Surrounded by the Spaniards the five men were taken into Pamplona. The reception at the police station was cordial and friendly. One of the Guardias left the room and when he returned the reason for this kindness was evident! Blazoned over the front page of a Spanish newspaper was the news all people in Occupied Europe had been waiting for: '6 de junio; Desembarco aliado en Normandía!!!'(6th June; Allied landing in Normandy!!!)

While the men struggled through the mountains allied soldiers finally arrived on the Continent. Since yesterday Spain knew that it would be wrong to commit itself to Germany. The five evaders did not know that since early 1943 an agreement had been concluded between the Spanish and British governments, allowing British embassy staff to visit escapees to check if they really were fellow Allies. From that moment on the Spanish authorities would no longer hand over arrested refugees to the Germans, but assist in a speedy transport home!

The Americans stayed in Madrid until 25 June, when the United States military attaché, Colonel Frederick Sharp, told them that they would be taken to Gibraltar. They were made temporary members of the staff of the American military mission under Colonel H. Forster. In Gibraltar Willis suddenly heard a voice crying out loud: 'Hva i helvete gjør du her Yank [108]? When he turned around, he saw a Norwegian naval flier in the black uniform he remembered so well. He had met one of the Norwegians with whom he flew in 1940. They had said farewell when Willis returned from Canada so the United Kingdom after his encounter with the Canadian Court. Three years ago, it had been and now they met at the Rock. The Norwegian was now a pilot with BOAC and flew passenger aircraft between Bristol and Lisbon and Gibraltar.

---

[108] *What the hell are you doing here, Yank?*

THOMAS H. HUBBARD
LIEUT. COLONEL, RAF

It is with deepest
appreciation and many
thanks for your courage
and good work that I
wish you good health
and good luck always.
(signature)
105 CRESTWOOD DRIVE.
FORT WORTH, TEXAS.

LEONARD A. BARNES
PILOT OFFICER RAF

THANKS CHUM

122 UPPER NORTH ST,
POPLAR,
LONDON E.14.

MAJ DONALD K. Willis
Gyn Mills Holt Ftd. Paul
I wish you good luck
and Happiness may.
I thank you for your
help.

2nd Lt JD Cornett
821 Mitchell st.
Klamath Falls
OREGON
With my deepest
apreciation

1393167 Sgt. EMENY. R. RAF.

30 MANTON ROAD.
ABBEY WOOD
LONDON S.E.2.

Thanks for everything
only heartfelt thanks
only.

All five wrote thank you messages in a notebook of Pierre Elhorga. It was not until forty years later that these notes were seen again. Obviously, they were aware of the risks taken by their escorts. (PE/EVA).

The 100 Franc note, signed by Michel Etcheveste, Pierre Elghora, Jean Elizondo Tom Hubbard, Len Barnes, Ron Emeny, Jack Cornett and Don Willis. In Gibraltar Don Willis was kitted out and received a new uniform, including his coveted RAF wing. He met a Norwegian officer with whom he was in Norway in 1940. One of the first things Willis did while waiting in Gibraltar was to treat himself with a nice black cigar (PW).

Same event, different memories. Ron Emeny's story.

Long after the war, during the days when he was very much involved in the Royal Air Forces Escaping Society, Ron Emeny wrote down his recollections of the last part of the evasion: the final leg through the mountains into neutral Spain. It differs somewhat from both the Escape and Evasions reports as well as from the recollections of the others: 'On 4 June 1944, the last five evaders to cross the Pyrenees via the Comète Escape Line began the final leg of their journey close to the mountains. USAAF airmen Lt Colonel Thomas Hubbard, Major Donald Willis and Second Lieutenant Jack Cornett were already acquainted with RAF Pilot Officer Len Barnes and Sergeant Ron Emeny from Paris.

They had travelled down to Bayonne 'separately' with their guides in the usual Comète style and had cycled through the hills to the Café Larre run by Martha Mendiara arriving just before nightfall. Hubbard was a P47 Thunderbolt pilot with the nickname 'Speed'. This character stamped him, as despite the risks involved, he had refused to surrender his Colt 45 pistol to Comète and still carried the weapon. Cornett flew the same make of aircraft whilst Willis, also a fighter pilot, had come down in a Lockheed Lighting. Len Barnes and Ron Emeny were aircrew on separate RAF Lancasters. Both men had experienced tricky journeys to reach the Café Larre. Barnes the pilot was the only survivor of his crew to still be at large, whilst Emeny a gunner had also ridden his luck to reach this point.

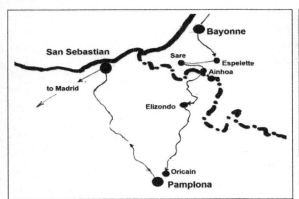 

Once they five men had reached Pamplona, they were far enough from the Spanish/French border not to be handed to the members of the Guardia Civil. (HO/EVA)

The evaders had recorded their thanks in the notebook of Comète guide operator Pierre Elhorga. In the early morning of 4th June, the five evaders left on bicycles with their guides, travelling to a wood where they hid for the rest of the day to wait for a Basque guide to collect them for the journey to the Spanish border. This area near the frontier was extremely dangerous and often frequented by German patrols, so the guides using remote back lanes and tracks. As darkness approached, a short and stocky man brought them bread, cheese and milk. He only spoke Spanish, but Donald Willis was able to understand and translate the guide's instructions to the others. His knowledge of the language had come from working around the Mexican border. The journey became a relentless slog with the airmen struggling to cope with the pace and testing route which the guide was taking in order to avoid detection by German patrols. For the evaders, weeks and months on the run, sometimes with inadequate food had already begun to tell. Rest breaks meant more time in the danger area and the airmen sometimes had to beg for the group to stop.

After five hours of walking, they arrived at a river (a tributary of the Nivelle) forming the border between France and Spain. The guide stepped into the icy water, with the evaders struggling to keep up and retain their balance on the slippery rocks. Once out of the river, the party struggled on with another guide until 4:00 in the morning. It was essential to clear the immediate area as Spanish patrols were operational and the danger of arrest, imprisonment and being handed over to the Germans was a real threat. Eventually the party was forced to stop as the evaders were unable to continue. After a stop and drink they struggled on, arriving just after sunrise at an old sheep shed where the guide left them for the day, with instructions to rest and he would return at dusk that night. Without food or drink, the airmen fell asleep exhausted.

The guide returned as promised and they left. Hubbard had developed badly blistered feet and was soon in agony with every step. Fortunately, Willis administered a last injection of morphine from his escape kit and they were able to continue. Just as the airmen reached a point where they were unable to carry on, two men came into view and waved them forward to follow. A few minutes later they reached an isolated farm where they were able to rest for the night in a barn. The following morning, events took a more sinister turn. Willis overheard the agitated farmer telling his daughter not to speak to the airmen, or tell them exactly where they were. This was immediately relayed to the others and Barnes made the decision despite the physical state of the group to leave immediately. He quickly led the way out followed by the others and they later learned that one of the men who had led them to the house had been to the police. They were to have been arrested and returned to the Germans in France for a reward of a sack of grain for each airman. The evaders had no map or knowledge of their current whereabouts. Willis had never surrendered his compass, so the group decided to move in a southerly direction. They soon arrived at a road, which they tracked seeking cover when necessary so as not to risk attention.

After walking for another two days with no food and only water from troughs and streams the evaders decided they must finally ask for help. Many stories of journeys via the Larressore or Souraide routes over the Pyrenees show long periods without food or water, huge distances walked and minimal shelter being taken in rough stone sheep sheds or barns. They were dangerous times over inhospitable terrain. Despite most of these men being young, it is difficult to imagine how they kept going. Willis and the other evaders passed through the foothills near Oricain and spotted an isolated farm. They had to take a chance and make themselves known. The plan was to get food in exchange for French money, with Willis the only Spanish speaker doing the talking. They approached the farm and he knocked the door. The farmer, startled by the five scruffy men in front of him, would not feed them and directed the party towards Pamplona, a town lying a few miles below. He recommended they go to the police. In the early afternoon of the 8 June, the men arrived in the town. No one had challenged them and they reached a park before collapsing with exhaustion. This was hardly surprising, as they have travelled around 100 km over the 5 days.

The final gamble.
The last throw of the dice was to somehow try and contact the nearest British or American Consulate before they were finally arrested and imprisoned by the Spanish. Willis would try to reach the town Post Office, convince the clerk that a telephone call to the Consulate was imperative and persuade them to let him use the phone. He managed to locate the Post Office and Willis succeeded in convincing the suspicious employee to allow him to make the call. The British Consulate in San Sebastian took the details but advised that they would be arrested immediately as the Police were sure to be notified. Leaving the Post Office, Willis noticed a Spanish Police Officer and two of his men ahead. It was over, and he knew it. The Policemen instantly spotted him and he told them where the other evaders were. Len Barnes remembered opening his eyes in the sun and staring at a gun barrel pointing at him.

What happened next did not follow the pattern experienced by many evaders picked up in Spain. A picture of dirty jails or camps before eventual release and transfer to the British authorities in Gibraltar would have been a likely scenario, but instead the evaders were taken to clean themselves up, then escorted to a restaurant and given food. The next day, they rested between three good meals and a spa, before being taken by bus to San Sebastian and from there on a short train journey to Irun where stayed in a hotel for a week. Amazingly in Irun, they ended up only a few kilometres from the border with France and 30km from the Café Larre, where their epic journey began. After a week's stay in a hotel and with fresh clothes from an English family, the group were ready to move. Willis, Hubbard and Cornett were collected by a representative from their Consulate in Madrid and then put on a train to Gibraltar. Hubbard and Willis flew to England on 28 June 1944 and Cornett followed on two days later. Barnes and Emeny spent one night in Saragossa, five days in Alhama and two days in Madrid, before arriving at Gibraltar on 23 June. They were flown from Gibraltar on 24 June arriving at Whitechurch on June 25 where they were debriefed the same day. The last journey from Bayonne into Spain via the

Comète Escape Line had passed like many before; with exhaustion, lack of food, cold, inhospitable terrain and fear of capture testing the strength and spirit of the evaders. Events did take a more variant turn for the final five men whilst they were in Spanish custody and the days spent in Gibraltar must have mirrored the experiences of many previous evaders who had reached safety.

A decision had already been made to abandon the Comète route to Spain due to the planned destruction of the French railway network before D-Day. Instead, agents were ordered by London to create holding camps in remote areas and collect rescued airmen until they could be liberated by the advancing Allied armies. Evaders were to be assembled in camps in the Belgian Ardennes and around Châteaudun in France. This was also a political decision to try and prevent the death or incarceration of helpers and lodgers, and where possible avoid the key assembly point cities of Brussels and Paris where so many enemy infiltrations had already occurred.

Escapers and evaders still ran the risk of being collected in by the police and taken to the concentration camp at Maranda de Ebro, near Vitoria. Those unfortunate to end up there spent months of boredom and deprivation, waiting and hoping for their name to appear on the list of men to be released after British diplomatic pressure.

Comète agents were later brought under the umbrella of the new Marathon Network which covered the camps. The spider in the Spanish MI.9 web was Michael Creswell, a member of the British embassy in Madrid. Together with two leading officials of MI.9, Airey Neave and Donald Darling, he was part of a magic trio, constantly striving to help escapees. With the names Saturday, Sunday and Monday they were responsible for assistance and quick transit of returning airmen. Creswell often drove them in his CD car. After a brief stay in Pamplona our five were taken away in a coach. The farewell was very friendly. Escorted by Guardia Civil soldiers they made the short trip to the station, from where travelled to San Sebastian. After they arrived their guards invited them for a meal of wine, cheese, bread and fruit; after the meal they took them to Irun, where their guards simply commandeered rooms in Hotel Norte in the town centre. Irun still showed the damage Civil War that raged through the country not so long ago. In the hotel lobby they met escapers who had arrived from other places in Spain. They even met Germans who spent a brief leave in Irun, with whom they were strictly forbidden to have any contact, as some of the Germans were Abwehr agents who were here to obtain information that helped them collect intelligence about evasion organisations in Occupied Territory. Rumours said that they had even attempted to hijack airmen and return them to Occupied France! An English lady, who lived in town, paid daily visits, the consul arranged for new clothing. Until recently every immigrant had been transported to Miranda de Ebro, a mosquito-infested camp where people were incarcerated without much hope of a speedy release. But now the British government had rented a spa hotel in Alhama de Aragon, where every member of the forces could rest.

The Spanish change sides...

The Spanish authorities had even allowed the British government to collect people from the places of their arrest and drive them to Alma de Aragon in a car with CD-plates. A similar deal was struck with the Embassy of the United States. As long as both governments paid for food and lodging of their people, the Spanish government was quite happy to be very co-operative once the soldiers had safely passed the border area with France. Realizing that the gigantic power of the allies could cause dire problems for Spain in the event of a German defeat, the previous attitudes of the Franco regime, which had caused so many problems while Germany, appeared invincible, changed completely.

The Bidassoa River had a very strong current that caused some people to drown while crossing. Michael Creswell was the contact between MI9 and Comète. He gave money and support as much as he could. In Biarritz he met the crew of a C47, which landed to pick up US personnel still in the south of France. Here a wartime photograph and one at a later age. He was part of the trio Saturday (Airey Neave), Sunday (Donald Darling) and Monday. (AC/MC/HO/ IWM)

From the moment they interned escapees the authorities now immediately notified by the American and British embassies. As the five did not know how long they would stay together Willis asked them to sign a 100 Franc note, which he kept all through his evasion. His companions added their signature and even some of the Spaniards, one of them called Juan Gomez, the owner of a bar the five regularly visited, did the same. Then the day came when Willis, Hubbard and Cornett were collected by a member of their Embassy and left for Madrid. On 22 June Barnes and Emeny were told that they would proceed to Madrid the next day. Len Barnes and Ron Emeny left too. First, they travelled to Zaragoza where they spent the night at an air base. They met others with whom they were taken to Alhama de Aragon for a period of rest and recuperation.

Darling's main role was in the reception, supervision and interrogation of escaping allied personnel who arrived in Gibraltar as well as organising the infiltration of agents into Spain. In other words, he and his sidekick Brian Morrison were basically in charge of all MI 9 activity on the Rock. After two days a lorry drove them, with fifteen other allied soldiers via Seville to La Linea, where they crossed into Gibraltar. When they walked through British customs, Emeny said to one of the men on duty: 'It smells here.' The reply was: 'You are right. But it did not smell before you arrived.' Soon after their arrival both Len Barnes and Ron Emeny met Donald Darling of MI.9 who first interrogated them and had them kitted out with new uniforms. On 25 June 1944, Pilot Officer Len Barnes and Sergeant Ron Emeny took off from Gibraltar in a Dakota of the Dutch KLM airlines and that same night landed at Lulsgate Bottom near Bristol. Still under guard they were taken by train to London where they stayed in the Grand Hotel near Marylebone Station. In London they were again interrogated and debriefed by Airey Neave. After a brief leave both men returned to duty. They got no permission to fly over occupied territory.

Three men were responsible for checking the new arrivals' identities: Donald Darling (top left), Michael Creswell (top centre) and Airey Neave. (left bottom). The interrogations started at the Madrid Melodia Hotel.

The small town on the road from Zaragoza to Madrid looked like a holiday paradise. Barnes and Emeny enjoyed the swimming pool and roamed through town. They met the owner of the local ice-cream parlour with whom they spent many enjoyable evenings. One morning Barnes and Emeny said farewell to their friends and Spanish hosts and boarded a bus to Madrid. In the capital they stayed at the Melodia Hotel. The embassy gave Barnes and Emeny each 5 Pounds, which they spent in 24 hours in the British-American Club. According to Emeny it was the place of their first interrogation by the British. They were met by Donald Darling, who was officially the civilian assistant to the Governor on intelligence matters, but who actually worked under Colonel John Codrington, the head of station for SIS - the Secret Intelligence Service which covered MI 6 an MI 9.

Home to England.
The flight to England was rather dangerous as German Condors and Ju-88s regularly patrolled, looking for aircraft. They showed no mercy, for several civilian airliners had been shot down, one of them a KLM DC3, carrying the British actor Leslie Howard. In Lisbon Dutch aircraft from England sometimes parked next to former KLM aircraft that had been requisitioned by the Germans in 1940 and now flew for Lufthansa. On 28 June Hubbard and Willis arrived in England, followed by Jack Cornett two days later. Before the five survivors were allowed to go to home and contact family and friends, American intelligence officers debriefed them. Then the Americans returned to the USA while the Britons re-joined the RAF after a brief spell of leave. Don Willis decided to stay in England. His fiancée Patricia did not know that he had arrived. On 1st July, the phone rang in a hospital in northern England. A voice asked the operator to connect him with nurse Giles. When Patricia answered she heard a familiar voice, saying: 'Hi Pat, it is me. I thought you 'd like to know that I am home.' Don Willis' Journey to the Horizon had come to an end...

After their return to Britain the escaped airmen had to go through a long series of interviews, debriefings and interrogations. Wisely, they all stopped their accounts at the moment they were found by the resistance. In all Escape and Evasion Reports we read the same final sentence: 'From that moment on my journey was arranged by others. The next thing was a period of leave and in case of the Britons, of reunions with their loved ones. American escapers were often sent home or like their British comrades got a job that would make it impossible for them to fly across the North Sea and the ETO, the European Theatre of War.

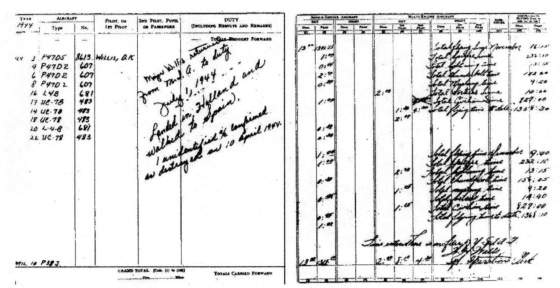

After Willis returned to England the following amendment was written in his flying logbook: 'Major Willis returned from MIA to duty on July 1, 1944. He landed in Holland, walked to Spain. 1 unidentified a/c confirmed destroyed on 10 April 1944.' On 3rd July he resumed flying when he took off in a Thunderbolt P47D, nr. 8613. (PW)

At about the same time as the five who evaded capture together, Sergeant Walker also returned home. He was debriefed and told the people of the Intelligence services what he could. For obvious reasons he did not talk much about the personal circumstances of his life with the Theveniault family. However, he was able to give a good idea of the time spent as a farmhand. There was a report and there were some pictures. He had himself interviewed by a newspaper. At the same time Barnes and Walker reconnected while they were safely home again. As a good skipper Barnes also wrote to the families who had heard that their sons has been killed or were locked up in a German camp. It was difficult and both Barnes and Walker tried whatever they could within the limitations of secrecy and lack of information. We should remember that at the same time war was still raging in continental Europe and in spite of the allied advances in the East and the West, Germany still fought a hard battle and there were still thousands of prisoners waiting for their freedom. In the next chapter we return to the activities of the Comète Line and the infiltrations by the Germans and their helpers.

10. DISASTERS AND SALVATION.

A blow by the Germans.

For the members of the resistance the war was not over yet, nor were the dangers they had to face. In spite of the successful invasion, the liberation of Europe laid in the far future. One of the many exceptionally brave women involved in operations for the Comète Line was Virginia Roush-d'Albert-Lake, about whom we wrote in an earlier chapter. Born in Dayton in 1910, Ohio she was raised in Saint Petersburg in Florida. Teacher Virginia Roush met Frenchman Philippe d'Albert-Lake in 1935 and married him in 1937. They settled in Paris. In 1943 she and Philippe began to work for the Comète escape line extending from Brussels to Gibraltar, which had been founded in 1940 by Belgian Andrée de Jongh in order to organise the evacuation of downed Allied airmen. The couple hid 66 airmen in their Paris apartment and home in Nesles on the northern outskirts of the French capital. Philippe eventually headed the Paris area of the Comète before being forced to go to London via Spain after his wife's arrest in June 1944. As mentioned earlier Virginia and her American airman Alfred Wickman were arrested by a German patrol as they were accompanying a group of eleven airmen by bicycle to a hidden camp for downed aviators at Freteval not far from Châteaudun.

In July 1944, the Gestapo arrested Virginia 'd Albert-Lake while she escorted pilots to a safe place. Philippe was able to escape to England. From London he informed his in-laws about the dreadful situation.

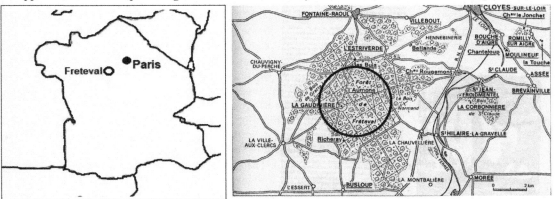

The Forest of Freteval, SW of Paris with the area where the evaders were waiting their liberators.

As it was considered safer to hide downed airmen in France rather than moving them around while the Allies were advancing several holding camps were built inside forests in France. The new organisation was called Marathon. MI9, the British intelligence organisation, created the operation to gather downed airmen into isolated forest camps where they would await their rescue by allied military forces advancing after the Normandy Invasion of June 6, 1944. The Comèt Line operated the forest camps with financial and logistical help from MI9. The most important of the forest camps, code named Sherwood, was in the Fréteval forest of France and sheltered 152 British and American airmen between May and August 1944. The airmen were liberated by MI9 executive Airey Neave and a small allied force on August 14, 1944. Other forest camps in France and the Ardennes forest in Belgium held another 150 or more airmen who were liberated by Neave and the Comet Line with the advance of the allied armies. Yet still aircrew were coming down; still Philippe and Virginia d'Albert-Lake risked their lives to save these men. Sadly, Marathon almost got off to a disastrous start. A man who called himself Pierre Boulain had been helpful to de Blommaert and his colleague Ancia. They scheduled a meeting with him on May 7 in Paris with the plan of giving him 500,000 francs (about 2,500 British pounds in 1944 currency) to help in the operation. However, Michelle Dumon learned that Boulain was actually a German agent whom we now know his real name was Jacques Desoubrie. She alerted de Blommaert and Ancia, exposed Desoubrie as a German agent, and all three avoided capture by the Germans, although Michelle had to flee to England. Living in Cancaval, near Saint Malo in France. Philippe remembered those days after the Invasion: 'On D-Day, June 6th 1944, we had 16 airmen and no more means of transportation. MI9 had asked us to form a new organisation under the name Marathon.

People gathering in the 'Marathon' kitchen. De Blommaert welcoming the British liberating troops. (EVA)

Its aim was to find safe places all over France, where large numbers of escapees could stay to wait until the allied armies could come and liberate them. For this they sent a Belgian Baronet to us. His name was Jean de Blommaert. He was very brave and had come from Spain. Not far from Châteaudun, in the forest of Frèteval, we had established a camp, where soldiers waited for the allies. In the morning of 7th June Virginia and I left Paris. Eleven airmen guided by three girls, Anne-Marie, Michelle and Any. Virginia and I, with one of the Americans went on our bicycles. The others were to take the train to Châteaudun. In Dourdan, ±18 miles south of Paris, we would re-join. Our plan was to form small groups of two or three airmen with one of us. It was a difficult journey; the weather was horrible. The next day we decided to enlarge the groups, to make up for the time we have lost. Virginia, the American and I went ahead to prepare the people at Châteaudun for the arrival of the others. Once we had arrived, Virginia returned to collect the group and take them to the camp. Jean, one of my best men, waited outside town and had to bring them in on a farm cart. That is how the first group arrived. When Virginia came with the second lot, everything went wrong. Virginia arrived the evening before with an American flyer and spent the night at the farm of the Merets. The group consisted of a dozen Britons and Americans who were to be transported the next day. The next day they collected a group of 7 or 8 airmen near Fontenay-sur-Conie. The idea was to escort the entire group to the relative safety of the forest of Fréteval. Virginia walked in front of the group with an American, the others were following in a covered cart. Little was Virginia to know that this fateful day would be the beginning of a ghastly road through prisons and concentration camps. Nothing would have gone wrong if it had not been for three German policemen asking the way. It did not take long for them to realize that Virginia and the man were foreigners and that something strange was going on in the cart.'

Arrested at last.

Virginia never forgot what happened next: 'I still always believe that the Germans knew what we were doing. A few days before we arrived with the first group, they have been seen patrolling the area. Normally they never left the main roads, but now they also searched the country lanes. When I came through a bend in the road a large black car caught up with us and stopped. Men got out; it was obvious that they were Gestapo. The American was their first victim. He did not speak any French, while the German was fluent. The American was immediately arrested. Then they wanted to see my papers. When it showed that I was an American citizen the German got very suspicious. They took my purse and found a large number of Francs. I told them that I was running away and trying to reach Spain because I have private problems. I hoped they would not connect me with escape work. But the German was a professional. He put me and the American into the car. Thank God, Jean had seen everything from a distance. Immediately he and the other Americans managed to escape; the Germans did not even see them run.'

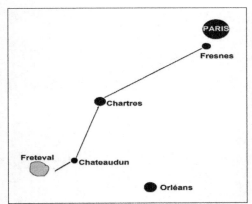 

Virginia and one American were arrested before entering the Forest of Freteval. They were first taken to the police station at Châteaudun, followed by a journey to Chartres (above), temporarily ending in Fresnes.

Fresnes Prison, in the southern suburbs of Paris in the Val-de-Marne department of France.

First the Germans took Virginia and the pilot to the police station of Châteaudun. There they were searched and interrogated. The Germans overlooked a piece of paper in Virginia's purse, containing addresses. Virginia managed to eat it before the Germans took her away. So ended a rescue that has started so very promising...

Jean de Blommaert had the hard task to break the dreadful news to Philippe, who was waiting for the group at the Forest of Belandre. Immediately after Virginia's arrest Philippe returned to Paris, joined by Pierre Camus. As it was quite possible that his wife would not be able to endure the Gestapo interrogation techniques, he wanted to make sure that the house at Rue Vienneau was empty when the Germans arrived.

Immediately after the house was 'clean', Philippe and Pierre fled south, following the same route so many airmen did before. Florentino, the trusted Basque, took them across the border. In July Philippe arrived in London, having no idea of the fate of his wife. He sent a telegram to the USA, informing Virginia's parents of what had happened. After her arrest Virginia was incarcerated in Chartres prison. Then, after a week, the Germans took her to the prison of Fresnes, the most infamous place in France. Virginia had no idea that one of her fellow-inmates was sergeant Wesley, one of the crew of Ron Emeny's Lancaster. When the allies closed in on Paris the Germans put the prisoners under SS-guard and transported them to Germany. After being held in Fresnes and Romainville she was taken to Ravensbrück camp in Germany on 15 August 1944, ten days before the liberation of Paris.

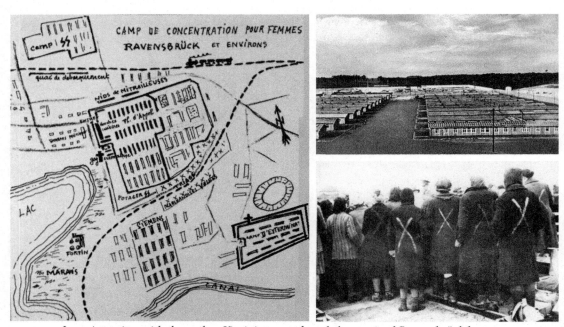

In an interview with the author Virginia remembered she survived Ravensbrück because she refused to give up.

A long and frightful time.

Although movement of airmen across the Franco-Spanish border had mostly ceased with the D-Day invasion of France on 6th June 1944, the Basque guide Florentino Goikoetxea continued to cross the border to deliver messages to British authorities in San Sebastian in Spain. Returning from a mission on July 26, he was shot four times by German border guards although he managed to hide the documents he was carrying. He was then taken to a hospital in Bayonne. The local resistance forces and the de Greefs decided to rescue him. On July 27, Elvire visited him the hospital and told him a rescue would be attempted. Later that day two German-speaking Bayonne policemen working with the resistance showed up at the hospital in an ambulance driven by Fernand. They pretended to be Gestapo agents, and demanded to take Florentino (as he was universally known) with them. They put him in the ambulance and drove away. He remained in hiding until the Nazis abandoned the Basque country a month later. It is amazing that some 150 men, British, Americans, Canadians, South Africans, Belgians, New Zealanders and even Russians were safely ferried to the forest of Freteval without being found by the Germans. Bread was supplied daily by a boulangerie in nearby Fontaine Raoul. Cigarettes were a problem and were important for morale purposes so raiding parties were arranged to steal them from stores in Cloyes and Chartres. Remarkably store owners were later paid by 'anonymous donations'. There were even weekly visits by a barber from Cloyes. The camp was so well organized they even had a radio set up on June 14. The receiver was kept in the camp but the transmitter was mobile so as to avoid detection. Forest paths were given the names of London thoroughfares including Hyde Park Corner which was a point where most of the paths crossed. Here there was a tree used as a notice board, bearing lots of personal messages received on the radio set. The code that was of most interest was 'La Tour Eiffel penche a droite' (The Eiffel Tower leans to the right). This meant a parachute drop of supplies of food, clothes, medicines and money was coming that night. After a drop, the men would go out and brush the grass back up so there was no obvious sign of activity overnight in the area. Camp member William Brayley is quoted from his diary as saying, 'It was unbelievable that with all the German patrols scouring the area it was possible for 150 men to gather in the forest, operating a radio to London and spend hours playing golf[109].'

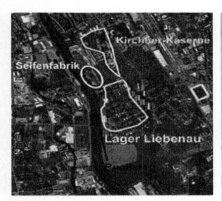

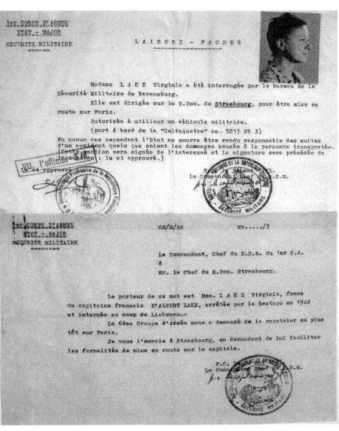

When French troops liberated Liebenau, they interrogated Virginia. Declared a genuine patriot she got military transport to get home. The French document says:' Mrs. Lake, Virginia was interrogated by the Military Security Bureau Ravensburg[110]. She has been directed to the office in Strasbourg to be sent on her way to Paris. She is permitted to use military vehicles. The State is not responsible for accidents that might happen to the person concerned. The second document says that Virginia was arrested by the Gestapo in 1944 and that the 6th Army Group asks to repatriate her as soon as possible. It was the end of a horrible time in the hands of the Germans. (BA/Pd'A-L).

Ravensbrück was a German concentration camp exclusively for women. Located in northern Germany, 90 km (56 miles) north of Berlin at a site near the village of Ravensbrück the camp held about 132,000 women. More than 80 percent were political prisoners. Many slave labour prisoners were employed by Siemens & Halske. Among the thousands executed at Ravensbrück were four members of the British World War II organisation Special Operations Executive (SOE): Denise Bloch, Cecily Lefort, Lilian Rolfe and Violette Szabo. From Ravensbrück Virginia went to Torgau munitions factory at a camp near Buchenwald and then to a camp at an airstrip near Königsberg Neumark. There she experienced a false dawn of liberation on 2 February 1945 when the prisoners believed that they were about to be freed by the Soviet army, only to be ordered by the German SS to begin a death march back to Ravensbrück. Next stop for Virginia was Ravensbrück concentration camp where she stayed until April 1945. She was barely alive when she was taken to Liebenau Camp near Lake Boden, a camp for so-called Prominent

---

[109] Extract from PO-Life.
[110] They probably mean 'Ravensbrück'.

Prisoners. One of her best friends there was a niece of the French leader and future president Charles de Gaulle, Genevieve. She had already been arrested in July 1943 and spent a long time in Fresnes Prison. Having been deported to Ravensbrück in February 1944, she could tell Virginia what to do and what not to do. SOE agents who survived were Yvonne Baseden and Eileen Nearne, who was a prisoner in 1944 before being transferred to another work camp and escaping. English woman Mary Lindell and American Virginia d'Albert-Lake, both leaders of escape and evasion lines in France, survived.

Thanks in part to the unstinting efforts of her mother and the United States State Department, she was sent to Liebenau internment camp for enemy nationals on February 28, more dead than alive. The camp was finally liberated on April 21. At the moment of her liberation, her weight had fallen to 34 kilos. Virginia d'Albert-Lake was freed by the French army on April 21, 1945 and on May 27 she was back in Paris. The couple re-united and in 1946 had their only child, Patrick. She never wanted to speak about her experiences after her arrest; she only spoke up in court when collaborating French were tried. Then they left Paris and that was it. It speaks for the tenacity and mental strength that she and Philippe were able to rebuild their lives once the war was over.

Still shaken by her arrest, she is photographed by the Gestapo Virginia like a common criminal. They cut her hair and take her to Chartres prison. She then is transferred to the most feared place of Frances, Fresnes prison. Only a few days before the Allies freed Paris she was taken to the concentration camp at Ravensbrück. At the end of April, she is barely alive. The Germans transfer her to Liebenau, to a camp for Prominent Prisoners. (dA-L)

Scary last months.

The continuous attempts by prisoners to escape captivity and reach Switzerland, Sweden or any other place where they were no longer under German control, became a heavy burden to the Germans, who had to dedicate more and more men and resources in keeping the behind barbed wires of recapture them. Hitler, who already mistrusted the Luftwaffe and the Wehrmacht now put the responsibility with Heinrich Himmler, the SS and the Gestapo. He went into a rage after the escape of Officers from Stalag Luft III, later known as the Great Escape. The day after the mass escape from Stalag Luft III, Hitler initially gave personal orders that every recaptured officer was to be shot. Reichsmarschall Hermann Göring, head of the Luftwaffe, Reichsführer-SS Heinrich Himmler, chief of state security, and Field Marshal Wilhelm Keitel, head of the German High Command, who had ultimate control over prisoners of war, argued about the responsibility for the escape. Göring pointed out to Hitler that a massacre might bring about reprisals to German pilots in Allied hands. Hitler agreed, but insisted more than half were to be shot, eventually ordering Himmler to execute more than half of the escapees. Himmler fixed the total at 50. Keitel gave orders that the murdered officers were to be cremated and their ashes returned to the POW camp as a deterrent to further escapes. Himmler set up the logistics for actually killing the men, and passed it down through his subordinates in the Gestapo [111]. The general orders were that recaptured officers would be turned over to the Criminal Police, and fifty would be handed to the Gestapo to be killed. As the prisoners were recaptured, they were interrogated for any useful information and taken out by motor

---

[111] *Wikipedia*

car, usually in small parties of two at a time, on the pretext of returning them to their prison camp. Their Gestapo escorts would stop them in the country and invite the officers to relieve themselves. The prisoners were then shot at close range from behind by pistol or machine pistol fire. The bodies were then left for retrieval, after which they were cremated and returned to Stalag Luft III. British Military Intelligence was soon made aware of the extraordinary events even during conditions of wartime by letters home and as a result of communications from protecting power Switzerland, which as a neutral party regularly reported on conditions in prisoner camps to both sides.

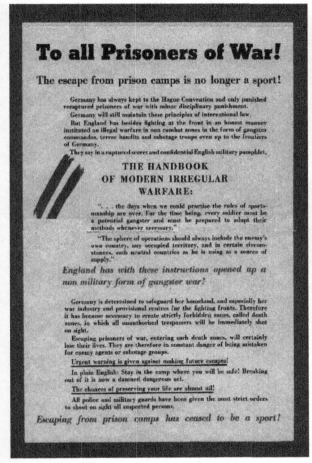

Left: After the escape of officers from Sagan Stalag Luft III Hitler ordered the death of fifty of the recaptured prisoners.
Top: Field Marshall Keitel signs the surrender for Marshal Zhukow and the Allies in Berlin on 8 May 1945. Finally, he was made responsible for murdering recaptured POW's. It was part of his death sentence in Nuremberg.

On 19th July 1944, an order was issued by Hitler calling for the preparations to be made for moving of all Prisoners of War to the rear. This instruction prolonged the war for hundreds of thousands of allied soldiers and airmen, forcing them into misery, starvation and, in some cases, death. Notices posted in all Allied Prisoner of War camps on 23 July 1944 that 'The escape from prison camps is no longer a sport' in the wake of the Stalag Luft III escape, as well as the suspicious deaths of fifty officers during their recapture, led the British government to suspect a war crime had occurred. This may have been one of the reasons why airmen were told to surrender if they fell into the hands of the Wehrmacht or Luftwaffe and to try to evade the Nazi organisations or the SS if at all possible. Further they were told that escaping from a camp was no longer a duty and that it would be wiser to await the liberation by the Western Allies or the Soviets. We do not think the Allies expected the prisoners to be forced to long marches during the winter of 1945. The Judge Advocate General originally placed the blame on Field Marshal Keitel, feeling publication of the notices linked him to the notice to shoot the prisoners.

The Great Escape: Murdered by the Gestapo between 290344 and 120444.

Brettell, E.G.	Flt Lt	GBR	No.133	Sqn RAF	290344	Danzig
Marcinkus, R.	Flt Lt	LTU	No.1	Sqn RAF	290344	Danzig
Bull, L.G.	Sqn Ldr	GBR	No.109	Sqn RAF	290344	Brüx
Kierath, R.V.	Flt Lt	AUS	No.450	Sqn RAAF	290344	Brüx
Mondschein, J.T.	Flg Off	POL	No.304	Sqn PAF	290344	Brüx
Bushell, R.J.	Sqn Ldr	GBR	No.92	Sqn RAF	290344	Saarbrücken
Catanach, J.	Sqn Ldr	AUS	No.455	Sqn RAAF	290344	Kiel
Christensen, A.G.	Plt Off	NZL	No.26	Sqn RAF	290344	Kiel
Espelid, H.	Lt	NOR	No.331	Sqn RNoAF	290344	Kiel
Fuglesang, N.J.	Lt	NOR	No.332	Sqn RNoAF	290344	Kiel
Gouws, J.S.	Lt	SA	No.40	Sqn SAAF	290344	München
Kidder, G.A.	Flg Off	CAN	No.156	Sqn RAF	290344	Mörisch Ostrau
Kirby-Green, T.G.	Sqn Ldr	GBR	No.40	Sqn RAF	290344	Mörisch Ostrau
Picard, H.A.	Flt Lt	BEL	No.350	Sqn RBAF	290344	Danzig
Scheidhauer, B.W.M.	Lt	FRA	No.131	Sqn RAF	290344	Saarbrücken
Stevens, R.J.	Lt	SAF	No.12	Sqn SAAF	290344	München
Walenn, G.W.	Flt Lt	GBR	No.25	OTU RAF	290344	Danzig
Williams, J.E.A.	Sqn Ldr	AUS	No.450	Sqn RAAF	290344	Brüx
Hall, C.P.	Flt Lt	GBR	No.1	PRU RAF	300344	Liegnitz
Skanzikas, S.	Plt Off	GRC	No.336	Sqn RGAF	300344	unknown
Wernham, J.C.	Flt Lt	CAN	No.405	Sqn RCAF	300344	unknown
Birkland, H.J.	Flg Off	CAN	No.72	Sqn RAF	310344	Liegnitz
Evans, B.H.	Flt Lt	GBR	No.49	Sqn RAF	310344	Liegnitz
Humphreys, E.S.	Flt Lt	GBR	No.107	Sqn RAF	310344	Liegnitz
Kolanowski, W.A.	Flg Off	POL	No.301	Sqn PAF	310344	Liegnitz
Langford, P.W.	Flt Lt	CAN	No.16	OTU RAF	310344	Liegnitz
McGill, G.E.	Flt Lt	CAN	No.103	Sqn RAF	310344	Liegnitz
Leigh, T.	Flt Lt	AUS	No.76	Sqn RAF	310344	Görlitz
Casey, M.J.	Flt Lt	GBR	No.57	Sqn RAF	310344	Görlitz
Cross, I.E.K.P.	Sqn Ldr	GBR	No.103	Sqn RAF	310344	Görlitz
Hake, A.H.	Flt Lt	AUS	No.72	Sqn RAF	310344	Görlitz
Pohe, J.	Flg Off	NZL	No.51	Sqn RAF	310344	Görlitz
Wiley, G.W.	Flt Lt	CAN	No.112	Sqn RAF	310344	Görlitz
Stewart, R.C.	Flg Off	GBR	No.77	Sqn RAF	310344	Liegnitz
Stower, J.G.	Flg Off	GBR	No.142	Sqn RAF	310344	Liegnitz
Swain, C.D.	Flt Lt	GBR	No.105	Sqn RAF	310344	Liegnitz
Valenta, A.	Flt Lt	CZ	No.311	Sqn CzFAF	310344	Liegnitz
Cochran, D.H.	Flg Off	GBR	No.10	OTU RAF	310344	Natzweiler
Kiewnarski, A.	Flt Lt	POL	No.305	Sqn PAF	310344	Unknown
Pawluk, K.	Flg Off	POL	No.305	Sqn PAF	310344	Unknown
Tobolski, P.	Flg Off	POL	No.301	Sqn PAF	020444	Breslau
McGarr, C.A.	Lt	SAF	No.2	Sqn SAAF	060444	Breslau
Grisman, W. J	Flt Lt	GBR	No.109	Sqn RAF	060444	Breslau
Gunn, A.D.M.	Flt Lt	GBR	No.1	PRU RAF	060444	Breslau
Hayter, A.R.	Flt Lt	GBR	No.148	Sqn RAF	060444	Breslau
Milford, H.J.	Flt Lt	GBR	No.226	Sqn RAF	060444	Breslau
Street, D.O.	Flg Off	GBR	No.207	Sqn RAF	060444	Breslau
Williams, J.F.	Flt Lt	GBR	No.107	Sqn RAF	060444	Breslau
Kroll, S.Z.	Flg Off	POL	No.64	Sqn RAF	120444	Breslau
Long, J.L.R.	Flt Lt	GBR	No.9	Sqn RAF	120444	Breslau

11. EPILOGUE.

A new life in peace time.

For the five evaders the return to England and the USA was the greatest joy for their families other loved ones. The home coming of Tom Hubbard was in the local newspaper. It wrote in capital headlines: 'Speed' Hubbard, lost for 7 months, comes home. 'Speed' Hubbard is back home. For sheer drama, a great part of which cannot be revealed for military reasons, the homecoming of the 31-year-old Thunderbolt fighter pilot, who was listed as missing in action in the European Theatre for more than seven months, might almost be compared to a return from the dead. Minus the moustache he has worn for some time and quite a few pounds lighter, Lt. Col. Thomas H. Hubbard was reticent about his adventures when interviewed at the home of his mother, Mrs. Fay Hubbard at 108 Crestwood Drive.

Left: Mrs. Faye Hubbard was reunited with son Tom, after he had been missing in action for 7 months. Home on leave he was given 30 days to enjoy his regained freedom. He still has not had time to grow his Clark Gable moustache. Right: Colonel James Goodwin Hall (right) demonstrates with his hand a close shave he had as he and Colonel Thomas H. 'Speed' Hubbard, one of the Thunderbolt pilots of the 8th Air Force, got together at the Fort Worth Club. Sitting at left is an unidentified man wearing a military uniform. Colonel Hall will soon become a civilian again. Colonel Hubbard is now assigned to the Army Air Forces Training Command. (AAFTC) Headquarters in Fort Worth, Texas. (USAFHRC)

'I went out on Nov. 13 and had a long trip. I was missing from my base in England and returned to it on June 29,' was the only explanation Hubbard could give of the lengthy absence which will undoubtedly make extremely good reading when the war is over and the full story can be told. Listed as officially missing in action over Holland as of the November date no word was received concerning him until early in July when his mother's steadfast faith that he would return was rewarded with a cablegram that he was well and safe. A Distinguished Flying Cross and Purple Heart were awarded Hubbard shortly before he left England for a 30-day leave at home. The awards were made under the date of November 13 but the contents of the citation are confidential. With the medals he already had, Hubbard's decorations will considerably more than fill his lapel, if and when he returns to 'civvies'. He had the Silver Star, awarded for gallantry in action at Guadalcanal, and the Air Medal with an oak leaf cluster. He has almost literally fought the way around the world in the war which began for him a few hours after the first shots were fired at Pearl Harbor, when the Japs attacked Clark Field, outside Manilla (Philippines), in their second assault against American territory. Hubbard, who had landed in the Philippines in November of 1941, was ordered to Australia before the islands fell. He saw action in New Caledonia and Guadalcanal before going to an English air base.

'The nickname of Speed, earned in his schooldays here because of his slow drawl and deliberate manner of picking his words, has clung to him in the air force where it has been lengthened to 'Colonel Speed.' I'm ready for surprises where Tom is concerned,' Mrs. Hubbard said Sunday of the fact that his arrival home Saturday night was preceded two hours sooner by a telegram. She had known he had a leave due but not the exact time it was to be granted. Hubbard said he had no plans for his first visit here since 1942, other than 'to watch the bright lights burn.'

Left: Hubbard had to wait until 25 May 1945 before his love Nelly Rosiers from Belgium. arrived in Texas. The description of the left picture reads: 'Lt Col Thomas H. Hubbard of Fort Worth, Texas, with Belgium bride, on Army transport that docked here today. Col. Hubbard, 33, a P-47 pilot, was shot down over Belgium over a year ago. His 23 year old bride is a daughter of the family that befriended him and hid him from Nazis until Belgium was liberated. Mrs. Hubbard is wearing a plaid double-breasted coat and her hair cloth 'top knot' hat. Colonel Hubbard is dressed in his military uniform with insignia and theatre ribbons and stars for his battles and service.
Right: They hold a D Ring of parachute held by Hubbard when he was found by a group of young Dutch boys after being shot down. The handle was later sent to the United States. In October 45 Len and Merville were married and after he returned to England, he completed the remaining 26 operations with the squadron. The war over he returned to his job as a printer for Glyn Mills & Co bank having been with No.630 Squadron as the adjutant until the squadron disbanded. (UTAL/Barnes

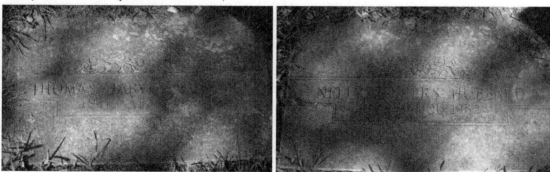

The graves of Tom and Nelly Hubbard at Greenwood Memorial Park and Mausoleum in Fort Worth. (HO)

'That is a novelty to him after England's blackouts. He is going to try to make a short trip by plane to California to see relatives there if transport can be arranged. Then he will return to his English base. Hubbard while here will not occupy the bachelor wing his mother started to add to her home while he was still listed as missing in action. It is not finished yet. But to her surprise he showed no surprise when shown the addition. A friend in England had passed on a clipping in which the project was described; 'Star-Telegram Photo Published Star-Tel Morn. Aug. 7, 1945.' Mrs. Hubbard is standing in the doorway of her home. She is wearing an eyelet shirtwaist dress with a woven belt and lots of and a military pin.

She is wearing clip-on earrings and has a dark handkerchief in her breast pocket. Lieutenant Colonel Hubbard is standing next to his mother in an at ease position. He is dressed in his military uniform with his tie tucked into the front of his shirt and insignia on the breast and collars. Inside the house near the door is a piano.'

When the war was over the five escapees lost touch. Tom Hubbard, Jack Cornett and Don Willis stayed in the USAF. Hubbard retired in his birthplace Dallas/Fort Worth. He died in 1983, and was buried at the Greenwood Memorial Park and Mausoleum in Fort Worth, Texas. His wife Nelly, born in 1921 and deceased in 1987, rests at his side. Len Barnes ended his career as an adjutant until his Squadron was dissolved and returned to civilian life, as did Ron Emeny. After the war, Barnes as well as Emeny returned to France to see their hosts when in the sixties lost connections were rewired and from that time both Len Barnes and Ron Emeny and their wife became close friends of the Tripots, the Carmignacs and the Coignés. Len Barnes returned to Fère-en-Tardenois to meet Léon and Mimi Coigné and their daughter Christiane. They visited all their helpers and during the decades of peace, they regularly spend time with the Coignés, Tripots and Carmignacs. A long and deep friendship developed which continued until one after the other died. At the same time Curly Emeny joined the group of volunteers at East Kirkby airfield, where they built a museum and maintained Lancaster with the name 'Just Jane'. Though it could not fly, all four engines allowed regular ground runs and brought great thrills for visitors. Emeny also arranged for a separate room commemorating and honouring the men and women of the escape lines. Jack Cornett rose to the rank of Colonel in the USAF and later retired in Oregon.

After Pilot Officer Barnes came home from Gibraltar, he completed the remaining twenty-six operations with his squadron. In October 1945 Len and Merville were married. After demobilisation Len returned to his job as a printer for Glyn Mills & Co bank having been with No. 630 as the adjutant until the squadron disbanded.

Willis in command.
Don Willis also stayed in the United States Air Force. After VE-Day he first commanded a Thunderbolt Squadron. Then he became the Commanding Officer of Hörsching Air Base in Occupied Austria and Fürstenfeldbruck Air Base near Munich, Germany. In January 1947, he took Patricia to Mexico where they married. Then they returned to the United States. Willis became a test pilot doing the first JATO (Jet Assisted Take-Off) trials. In the late 1950s, zero-length launch many experimental programs for launching fighter aircraft were carried out by the United States Air Force using high-thrust, short-burn duration booster designs of similar appearance and function. The USAF used a modified Republic F-84, designated EF-84G, which used the MGM-1 Matador cruise missile's. Aerojet General-designed solid fuel booster of two second thrust duration. Shortly before his retirement was due, Willis left the USAF. First, he and Patricia started a chicken farm while living in Indiana. Then they moved to Florida and Donald took up his pre-war job as a Quartermaster and went back to sea. First, he sailed on a barge line from New Orleans to Tampa. During the war in Vietnam, he was a quartermaster on a ship doing regular voyages from the West Coast of the United States to South Vietnam. However, on a trip to Tokyo he showed the first symptoms of the disease that was to kill him later.

Like many seasoned war pilots Willis was also put in command, and hardly able to fly. After the war he was in charge of airbases like Hörsching near Linz in Austria.

His last command was Fürstenfeldbruck near München .His new bride Patricia went with him. He wears his RAF wing and Eagle badge on his USAF uniform. (PW)

He returned to the USA as a test pilot, doing Jet Assisted Take Off (JATO) flights with F-80 Shooting Star fighters of the USAF. (PW)

He returned to America by plane and was admitted to a Naval Hospital. Medical examinations confirmed that the time would come that he would no longer be able to take care of himself: Don Willis had Alzheimer's disease. The man who had beaten the odds in Finland, Norway, Britain and Europe had finally been defeated. Patricia first nursed him at home. On 27th April 1977 Donald Kenyon Willis died. A funeral service was held at the local Episcopal Church after which he was cremated. At Donald's request, his ashes were strewn over the Gulf of Mexico. His obituary in the Ocala Star-Banner of 28 April 1977 did not mention his daring escape from Occupied Europe. It only said: 'Donald Kenyon Willis, 65, of 1105 NE 6th Street, died Wednesday, April 27, 1977, in the Medic-Home Health Center, Ocala. A native of Marion, Ind., he came here From English, Indiana, 21 years ago; was a retired Lieutenant Colonel with the US Air Force and a member of Grace Episcopal Church of Ocala. Survivors include his wife Mrs. Patricia Willis of Ocala; two daughters, Miss Linda Willis and Mrs. Donna Williams, both of Ocala; a son, Stewart Willis of England; a brother, Clinton Willis of South Bend and two sisters, Mrs. Betty Reidy and Mrs. Virginia Marais, both of South Africa.' For many years the last evasion across the Pyrenees before D-Day remained unknown. It was a coincident that connected a crash in Oud-Gastel in April 1944 with the evasion of five men in June that year. It also led to Pat Willis' return to Europe and the author's flight to Ocala Florida, where a treasure grove of information awaited me.

TO WHOM IT MIGHT CONCERN.

Declaration.

I hereby certify that I have known major Donald K. WILLIS of the United States Air Force when he did voluntary service in the Finnish Air Force in 1939-40 and later, last year in Norway with the Norwegian Air Force.

To my knowledge he has during these periods not given any declaration of allegiance th the national authorities of the said countries, except in cases what was needed to assure his reliability for the periods of campaigns.

OSLO, January 10th, 1951.

W HANSTEEN
Lt.General.

Lieutenant-General Hansteen, Royal Norwegian Air Force, who knew Willis from the war in Norway, confirmed his service in the air forces of Finland and Norway. Patricia and Don with daughter Donna, not long before Don died. (PW)

Pat Willis comes to Europe.
In 1980 I did some research about a mystery forced landing near Oud-Gastel in April 1944, when a P-38 came down and the pilot disappeared without a trace. Curious to find out what happened I went on a quest for facts. Covering events in nine countries [112], the story of The Journey to the Horizon, presented me with such a vast collection of fascinating data, that in order to a truthful documentary I decided to visit and meet as many as possible of the people and places that still existed after more than half a century. I also invited Patricia Willis, asking her to accompany me in part of this endeavour. After much hesitation, she agreed and on the 7 March 1985, she flew from the USA to Amsterdam airport. Her visit became a

---

[112] *Finland, Norway, Great Britain, Canada, United States, Netherlands, Belgium, France and Spain.*

confrontation with a past she knew very little about. Yet it was a great experience for all who got together again and remembered the past. Allow me to tell you this story as well.

Two days later Patricia and I drove to Oud-Gastel to see the site where Donald's P-38 Lightning came down. She walked in the meadow where Donald landed his aircraft. In the background was the old church. Apart from a barn that had been constructed nearby, nothing seemed to have changed since that day in April 1944. Patricia was visibly moved and said: 'It feels so strange to stand here. Imagine this aircraft, Donald and the people. Now it is so quiet, with nothing to see to remind us of that awful event.'

Left: Patricia in front of the house of Kuppens at the Meierstraat in Oud-Gastel, where 'guest' Willis stayed. Right: Mrs. Kuppens listening to Pat telling about her war-time life with Willis. (HO)

Young Jef Kuppens' and his grave at the cemetery Pandu at Bandung in Indonesia. Jef was a sergeant when he killed on 1 February 1947 at Moeara Batoen in the former Dutch East Indies. Patricia stands at the spot where her husband's aircraft came to a halt in April 1944. (Kuppens /HO)

Together we walked to the village, following Willis' footsteps, almost forty years later. Patricia saw the church and the house where Donald was confronted with the German soldier. We entered a bank where she wanted to change some money. While we waited in the queue an old man, overhearing she was the wife of the pilot, as he simply calls Willis, could not stop talking. He was one of the eyewitnesses. He recalled seeing the aircraft circling overhead. He ran towards while it lay on the ground. He did not speak any English, but his handshake and the look in his eyes said more than a thousand words.

At three in the afternoon, we arrived at the small house of Marinus Kuppens in the Meir Street. When we entered the living room Patricia met, for the first time, the woman who sheltered Donald and gave him money, a coat and sandwiches. All the children of Mr. and Mrs. Kuppens were present. All dressed at the Sunday best. Patricia walked to the old lady. The first meeting was very emotional. Two women embraced and kissed each other. Patricia cried while old 'Mamma' Kuppens hugged Patricia and said in Dutch: 'It does not matter; I am so happy to meet you at last. He was such a nice boy. I am so please he survived and thank you for coming to see me.' Patricia was told that Mr. Kuppens had since died and that Jef, one of the sons involved in Donald's escape, has lost his life in 1947, fighting as a soldier in the Dutch East Indies. Patricia says that Donald died as well. The gathered Kuppens family was silent. Mrs. Kuppens happily accepted a framed photo of Don Willis, showing him in his flying clothing, next to his Spitfire. There was coffee and cake, and there was silence.

When Patricia expressed her admiration for Mamma Kuppens' act of resistance, the old lady replies: 'I was not in the resistance, that was too dangerous. I was only helping the poor boy.' With pride she showed the certificate her husband received after the war. It bore the signature of General Ike Eisenhower and honoured Mr. Kuppens and his family for their bravery. She also showed a picture of the grave of Jef, far away in Indonesia. Mother Kuppens had never been able to visit the grave. All she had was a bit of earth from the plot where he was buried. After an emotional but happy afternoon I took Patricia home.

Our next destination was Mons in Belgium. Patricia was to meet Yvonne Bienfait, who, as 'Monique', sheltered Willis and Hubbard in her apartment in Brussels. The emotion of the previous day repeated itself. Two nurses, both linked by the common experience, war. There was happiness and there were tears. 'You saved his life', said Patricia. 'Il était un camarade, He was a comrade', replied Yvonne, while she told how Don walked around the table, determined to return for 'I have to get back to Pat, I have to.' Yvonne then heard how Donald's life ended. As a nurse she understood what Patricia went through. When we drove back to Holland Pat did not say much. 'It closed so many gaps, there were so many things he never talked about. But it has helped me to thank them on Donald's behalf. Isn't that wonderful?' After another week in Holland Patricia Willis returned home with fond memories and new friends.

After the war Emeny was promoted to a Warrant Officer. He paid a visit to the Tripots and had pictures taken with Father and Mother Tripot, the dog and his lifetime friend Lucien. (RE)

Walker returns to his helpers.

At the end of the war Ken Walker had been posted to No.195 Squadron at Wratting Common. During the days when the RAF dropped food for the starving Dutch in Operation Manna, he made one of his final flights over Occupied Territory. Like many allied soldiers Ken Walker also returned to the French patriots who had so bravely taken care of him during the Occupation. Not having been in touch since the Liberation he was relieved to see that everyone was well. He received a warm welcome, very French, with meals and wines, more meals and more wines. Now they could freely speak without fear for the Germans or French collaborators. Since Ken had been with the Theveniaults a warm friendship had grown which lasted until the end.

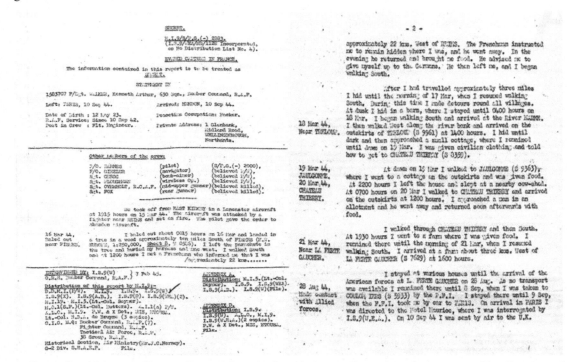

In September 1944 more became known about Walkers hiding in France. He kept a copy of his Escape and Evasion Report.

When he returned the Theveniault family presented him with a lot of photographs that had been made during the time he was hiding at the farm as a hand. Little shows in these images the deadly risk the French farmers took to save an allied airman or soldier from captivity

NORTHAMPTONSHIRE EVENING
TELEGRAPH, Mon., Sept. 11, 1944 **5**

"THE FRENCH WERE WONDERFUL"

Missing Wellingborough Airman Safe

After completing only a few bombing missions, Sgt. Kenneth Walker, R.A.F., younger son of Mr. A. H. Walker and the late Mrs. Walker, of 1, Glen Bank, Midland-road, Wellingborough, was reported missing in March. Five months elapsed, with no hint as to whether he was alive or not, and things began to appear for the worst.

But this week-end came the joyful news that he was safe and well, and hoped to be home shortly—thanks to the Allied liberating armies in France. Sergt. Walker's experiences make a dramatic story: When his plane, in which he flew as flight mechanic, was shot down over Occupied France in March he hid from the Germans with the assistance of the French people. Now the sweeping advances made by the Americans have liberated the district in which he sought refuge.

In a letter revealing these facts to his family, he says: "I'll bet you will have the surprise of your life when you receive this; I have plenty more to tell you when I arrive home again. I have had so many invitations for dinner since the liberation that it is impossible to accept them all. The French people have been wonderful to me, and after the liberation I was really overwhelmed by the handshakes and kisses of the population—and I think you will find that I am a little fatter now than the last time I saw you—there aren't many of the Huns around here now—the good old Yankees and the Resistance Movement have seen to that!"

Aged 21, Sgt. Walker joined up in September, 1942, and was previously employed by The Piturite Co., High-street, Wellingborough.

He told the Northamptonshire Evening Telegraph about the bravery of his hosts and shared some of the photos with the newspaper such as these, made of all the members of the Theveniault family in the apple orchard and behind the farm.

215

Mr. and Mrs. Terlet and their dog lived in a large apartment building in the Rue de Seganne in La Ferte Gauchez.

Arthur Pierrot/Ken Walker among his friends. Who would believe the lethal danger of being caught and arrested? Some of these photos were given to Walker when he returned to France after the war, others were made during his reunion with the Theveniaults and the Terlets. Clockwise they show Kenneth second from right with the entire family of Mr. and Mrs. Theveniault. Bottom right: Ken Walker returned to the RAF and was posted to No.195 Squadron at Wratting Common His last operational sortie was quite different from the ones he had flown during the war. He went to Holland to drop badly needed food for the Dutch during Operation Manna. Here he stands second from left before his food drop flight on 29 April 1945.

The Journey to the Horizon as a family holiday.

In July we travelled south to reconstruct the route the five took to reach final freedom. On our way to Gibraltar, we intended to visit people and places relating to the Journey to the Horizon. On 10th July we arrived at Arrancourt. It was hidden in a valley, southwest of Etampes. The village had only 78 inhabitants. The first villagers we met took us to the Mayor, Lucien Pillias. He lived on a farm with his wife and son. We were amazed to hear that he had held the position of mayor since 1932 and had recently celebrated his golden anniversary. The town hall was only a small building behind the farm. It had just one room and was open on Monday mornings and Thursday afternoons only! In the afternoon Pillias took us to the place where Jack Cornett came down. It was an empty field, only the stubble of the corn showed that some time ago the harvest had been brought in. After walking across the field, we decided to drive to nearby Mondésir airfield. The airfield had been demilitarized many years ago and was now used by private planes and gliders. Yet, the old hangars still showed the signs of the battle, with bullet holes clearly visible in the walls of corrugated iron. In a report made after the attack by the Thunderbolts of 375th Fighter Squadron these hangars were mentioned as having been strafed. An old Noratlas transport plane of the French Air Force, on display at the entrance, was a reminder of its former occupants on this large grass field. From here German anti-aircraft guns hit Cornett's aircraft, forcing him down. The single concrete runway, constructed after the war, was in a bad state and was no longer used by aircraft. In the afternoon Marcel Dussutour, the former Gendarme, joined Lucien Pillias. The three of us followed the route Cornett had taken after he came down. We walked through the forest to a brook. Crossing the small footbridge we entered the valley until we came to fishponds, where Cornett was last seen before he disappeared. We spent a few more days on the meadow beside the town hall, enjoying the hospitality of the old Mayor, and his delicious wines.

From Arrancourt we drove to Chalette-sur-Loing. We met Lucien Tripot, who saved Emeny after his Lancaster was shot down. Tripot had not changed since 1944. When he opened the door, we recognized him immediately. After a warm welcome he took us to the house of Luce Carmignac in Ferrières-en-Gatinais. To our great surprise Carmignac had organized a big party to welcome us. He told us that he had an even bigger surprise; upon entering the house we met two of the men about whom this book had been written, Leonard A. Barnes and Ronald T. Emeny. Both spent a short holiday with the Carmignacs before travelling to Barnes' wartime hosts, Léon and Mimi Coigné in Fère-en-Tardenois. That afternoon Tripot, Barnes, Emeny and I drove to several places that were connected with the crash of F for Freddie, Emeny's Lancaster. We saw the spot where the burning aircraft crashed. We visited the small cemetery of Chaintreaux where Emeny's two comrades rest. We went to Chopilles to see the room where Emeny recovered from his burns and where Tripot dug a grave, just in case! Emeny took us to La Selle sur le Bied to show us the tomb where Pittwood and he spent the night, exhausted and close to giving up, until Monsieur and Madame Biguet, found them. Afterwards we drove to Chuelles. The station was deserted and no longer used, but the old stationmaster still lived there.

During the party at the house of Lucien Tripot we heard how Len Barnes and the villagers that helped him, managed to reconnect, as Len Barnes' daughter Amanda told many years later; 'It was some twenty three years to the day (i.e. 15/03/1967) that ND530 was shot down Len received a letter, which showed a French postmark and as Len did not know anybody in France, this intrigued him. He could not have prepared himself for what he was about to discover. The family with whom he had stayed at Fere-en-Tardenois, the Coigné family, had dug up a jam jar in the garden and tried to make contact with Len. However not known to them, two weeks after returning to England the family home in Upper North St. Poplar had been bombed out and the Barnes family had moved. Undeterred the Coignés found 'their Englishman' through a French programme called 'Rendezvous des Souvenirs.' This letter was for an invitation for my parents to go to France and for Len to be reunited with the Coigné family. While waiting in a small French restaurant in the town of Fere-en-Tardenois my father kept saying to my Mum. 'They've got the wrong bloke Merv. I don't recognise any of it!!' But of course, he had only ever seen it in darkness, just going out on one occasion to the barbers.

Since 1945 Ron and Jessie Emeny often visited the graves of Skipper W/O Lissette and Sgt Ellis at Chaintreaux.

His fears were dispelled as he walked down the long track towards La Cabane, accompanied by Marina Gray, a French television presenter. The curtains twitched and then Leon and Mimi appeared. There are no words to describe the emotions felt that day!! Just imagine it and then multiply it tenfold!! After the television crews had disappeared Len and the Coignés began the rekindling of the already strong bond between them. Len was taken to the crash site and spoke to eyewitnesses of the crash. They told of how they could hear the plane struggling and the flames reaching double the length of the body of the aircraft. And then the explosion. This explained how Len had been blown clear, to fall through the air. At this point one villager shot into her house and took a knife to a cushion. As she ripped off the cover, she handed the contents to my father: his pilot seat! Indeed, the villagers had used what they could, making sure that anything that would be helpful to the Germans had disappeared!' One such person was the village grave digger who used the propeller blades to sharpen his lawn mower. He was adamant that he had buried the pilot and it turned out that one of the crew had been wrongly identified as Pilot Officer Len Barnes.

It transpired that the three crewmembers who had been captured identified Jim Overholt's body as that of my father by virtue of his boots. Len wore a particular type of flying boot that could be cut down to look like civilian shoes should the need arise. He was the only member of the crew to wear them. However, it was later discovered that Jim had been to the stores that morning and had been issued with an identical pair of boots. Both Jim Overholt and Thomas 'Freddy' Fox are buried in the village cemetery at St Gilles. They are cared for beautifully by the villagers even sixty years on. The bond that exists between our two families is unbreakable and my own daughter is named after Madame Coigné. We took our son and daughter to Fere-en-Tardenois for a holiday last year. Although my father died in 1988, I know he would be so proud that the friendship started over sixty years ago continues. And through this research I have made contact with Sergeant Malcolm Gregg's son. And so, a new friendship begins.'

Reunion at the Tripot residence. Left to right: the author, Len Barnes, Jessie Emeny, Merville Barnes, Ron Emeny and Lucien Tripot. Standing Mrs. Tripot with next to her Mrs. Carmignac. Three men reunited: Luce Carmignac, Ron Emeny and Lucien Tripot. (HO)

We continued our quest to Bayonne, visiting Boucau but were quite unable to find the old station as it had been demolished many years ago to make room for a new building. At the town hall we were presented with an old photograph showing the old station in its neo-romantic glory. In Bayonne, we visited Yvonne and Robert Lapeyre, former members of Comète. They took us for a drive into the Basque country. Many places still looked as over forty years ago. The Lapeyres took us to the small house where Marthe Mendihara lived. She was a grey lady now, but still with dark eyes that the many escapees who stayed with her during the Occupation told us about. She still laughed when she remembered the foolish Boches, who had no idea what went on over their heads.

Then we drove to Larressore. Yvonne asked at the post office if Michel Etcheveste still lived here. The lady did not hesitate a moment; she knew the address and pointed us where to go. Ten minutes later we stood in front of a house and a middle-aged woman approached us curiously. 'Yes, I am Madame Etcheveste. My husband is not home. Ah, Monsieur is from Holland. Why has he come? To speak to Michel. About pilots? Yes, Michel had something to do with pilots when the Germans were here. Why don't you come in and have a cup of coffee?' In the kitchen she made a phone call and a long conversation in Basque follows. The only word I think I understood sounded like 'Hollanda.' Then she told us that Michel would see us tomorrow.

The next morning at ten we arrived at the house called Armora. An elderly gentleman with a Basque beret on his head welcomed us. There was coffee, cake and Izarra. I told him why I had driven the long road from Holland to Larressore: to talk about his memories of allied pilots. 'Ah, Monsieur, I had to, that is all.' I laid a number of photos on the table. All of them showed young men. Airmen, actors, even Dutch football players. Would Monsieur Etcheveste recognize any of these photographs? 'Ah, look, the little one. He spoke Spanish. And there, the tall American. Did monsieur know he carried a parcel? Later I found out that he had a pistol. Some of them had one, you know. Very dangerous and very stupid. I told the little one that the Germans would shoot us if they found the parcel. The little one said: 'Well, make sure we don't meet any. And there is the one who could hardly walk.' Michel Etcheveste had picked out Willis, Hubbard and Emeny. He does not recognize the other two, Barnes and Cornett. He remembered they were five, for they were the last soldiers that took across. 'How much was he paid? Ah, Monsieur it is such a long time ago. I do not remember.' We agreed that I returned on our way back from Gibraltar.

Amazingly people immediately recognized photographs of the fugitives. In all case the five airmen were immediately lifted from a collection of many different photographs, like here in Bayonne, the last stop before the crossing of the mountains. (HO)

He would then take me across the border into Spain, as in the old days. From Larressore we drove to Souraïde. From the hill we saw Ainhoa and the French border post near the river. The next day we crossed the border and drove through Dancharinea, following the road to Pamplona. A visit to the Police Headquarters brought little or nothing. We did not get any further than a sergeant at the door, who only spokes Spanish and who was unwilling to call someone else! On our way south we came through Alhama de Aragon. Again no one was able or willing to help. An officer of the Guardia Civil, asked about the spa hotel, wanted to see my passport first, only because I asked him a question. As ordinary people did not talk to him, why should he speak to a stranger? Some of the hotels could be the one we look for, but when we asked about stories of allied airmen there was a stony silence, no offer to help. 'Who wants the talk about the days of that man Franco? Only fools and fascists, Senor!'

The road to Gibraltar via Madrid and Seville, though beautiful was long. It failed to bring any new information for problems between the British and Spanish governments caused the Spaniards to seal off the Rock for tourists. Unfortunately, a Dutchman, who claims to be researching a story that they never heard of about a time they are not keen to remember, fails to impress the Spanish border guards. After a few useless days on the Spanish side of the border we decided to travel back, in the meantime enjoying the countryside. Four weeks later we returned to Larressore as agreed with Michel Etcheveste. I presumed he had spoken to friends and they had agreed that he should help. He took us into the hills and told me to leave the car and follow him on foot, while my wife and children were told to return to Larressore and come back in five hours, as Michel suggested. The two of us followed a path that led into the forest. Michel said: 'Let us go', this is the path I always took when I crossed with my merchandise.' I asked him what the merchandise was. 'Everything, tobacco, sugar, many other things.'

The path went upwards and sometimes I could not see where it was. But Michel did not seem to have any problems finding his way. As in 1944 we made a detour to avoid Dancharia and Dancharinea where the border posts are. On our right, in the valley we saw the French tricolour at the customs office. A little further to the west was the Spanish office with its red-yellow-red flag. After about two hours Michel said: 'On est là', 'We are there.' We stood in front of a small river. This was the Bidassoa, the same river the five travellers crossed during a night in June 1944. A dilapidated wooden bridge connected the French with the Spanish side. It was built by a Spanish shopkeeper to assist his French customers, who came to buy cheap alcohol. The authorities did not seem to mind, for, as we passed the shop, a Spanish policeman watched French people carrying bags with bottles and did not interfere. Fifteen minutes later, when most of the customers had left, a gendarmerie car stopped on the French side. A Gendarme got out, crossed the bridge and returned after five minutes, carrying two large paper bags. Smuggling has always been part of life in the Basque country. Two hours later we were back where we started. My illegal crossing was not as very dangerous as it was in 1944. Then followed a long journey north, from the border to the north east, between Paris and Nancy.

Once having crossed the Bidassoa the traveller has arrived in Spain. This does not mean the route to Pamplona gets any easier (HO)

Our next destination was Mailly-le-Camp. The Officer in Command of the Camp, Colonel Babron, received us with great hospitality. As he knew the reason for my visit, cleared and kindly prepared by the French military attaché in The Hague, he told one of his officers to do a thorough search in the archives of his establishment. Interesting information had been found. He gave me four photographs; the originals are framed on the wall of his office. They were taken by the Germans the day after the attack, showing the tremendous destruction caused by the Lancasters. Few buildings remained undamaged. Unfortunately, there was little other information. When the Germans withdrew from Mailly they burned their archives and all the buildings.

The following afternoon we arrived at Fère-en-Tardenois, where we met Léon Coigné and his wife. We drove down the lane that led to their house 'La Cabane'. There was the same house where Barnes stayed after he failed to return from Stuttgart. The Coignés were very hospitable people. They told us to park our camping trailer in their garden. We would be part of the family for the days to come.

We did little that evening, as Léon wanted us to try his wine and the champagne he recently bought. Mimi was busy in the kitchen, preparing a delicious meal. Léon took our little son Mark outside and asked him which chicken he liked best. When the little boy pointed at one, Léon grabbed the poor animal and killed it. 'Only the best food for my friends', he said. Little Mark was devastated; he felt responsible for the murder of the chicken and refused to eat it. Instead, he settled for sausages; my wife asked Léon not to mention the pigs.

Léon, Mimi and Christine Coigné at their house 'La Cabane in 1982. (HO)

Léon Coigné preparing supper in the garden of his house in Fere-en-Tardenois. When the Germans searched in Fere-en-Tardenois, Léon used a new hiding place for Len behind the house of the Lesguilliers.

Behind the house was a hole covered with logs, earth and plants looking like a part of the garden. They never discovered the trapdoor to Barnes' hiding place. (HO)

The next morning after breakfast Léon showed me a box, filled with maps, cards, photographs, equipment he took from German soldiers after they surrendered. I wondered how many people in France had so many firearms at home. That morning Léon and I drove through the countryside. Léon insisted on taking two spades. We first went to Saint Gilles to see the graves of two of Pilot Officer Len Barnes' crew members. Then we visited the spot where P for Peter crashed. The site of that crash was still very visible. In the corner of a field was a subsidence. Little corn grew there as the ground was still contaminated by aviation fuel, according to Léon. He got the spades out of the car and said: 'Five minutes, and we will find parts of the Lancaster, believe me.' He was right, for soon we found the first bits and pieces. A few .30 calibre cartridges, pieces of fuel pipe, a large piece of aluminium, still vaguely showing the dark green camouflage paint.

Within an hour we had collected a big box full of pieces. Léon and I decided that after photographing them, they were to go to Len Barnes. At the Lesguillier villa Léon showed me the hiding place at the far end of the garden where Jacks and Barnes hid until the Germans gave up their search for the escapees. The present owner knew little about the history of the house. He had no idea of secret passages and hiding places. He was thrilled when Léon revealed a secret trapdoor under the large kitchen sink. It was the first time the man saw it. It led to a small hiding place. 'We kept our explosives here', said Coigné with a smile. 'Don 't worry there is nothing left.' Five days later we left the Coignés and returned to the Netherlands. It had been very worthwhile.

More debris of Barnes' Lancaster found by the author and returned to Len Barnes. The author went to Whitstable in Kent and interviewed Len Barnes at length about his experiences as a pilot and a fugitive in Occupied France.

Len Barnes remembers.

The next visit was with Len Barnes. We travelled to Whitstable in Kent, bringing a small gift for Ken: parts of his Lancaster, found during a superficial dig in the field where his aircraft came down. As for Len Barnes, when the war was over, he married his darling Merville and returned to his civilian occupation. He decided to tell his story on a number of cassette tapes. Which he kept in his house without the idea to ever used them. These tapes were recently found by one of his daughters. It was not until after he met Hans Onderwater in France and at his home, and when he was handed bits and pieces that had been found at the crash site. During a whole afternoon Ken remembered and told his story

This did not fundamentally change the story. Len made a few interesting observations about the crossing of the mountains which were not mentioned in the E7E Reports of the five, but can be revealed here and now: When the five escapees were handed over to a young about 18 years old Basque guide by their French guide, they were led to an isolated farm, where they spent the night in the hayloft and were given food. This is where they learnt that the D-Day landings were beginning. That day they felt a bit freer and wandered a bit on the hillside, reminiscing and learning of each other's experiences. They found a cave, but decided not to explore it and they picked blackberries. Then they returned to the hayloft to await the guide's return. They were then taken to another farm at night. Len remembers hearing the name Jose and a seeing man leaning out of the window and these two men led them onwards through a night of teeming rain and they had to take shelter for a while in a sheep pen.

Suffice it to say that Len took an immediate dislike to these two men, though he could not say exactly why. Hubbard's feet were very blistered and he was in some distress. Eventually they arrived at another farmhouse where the farmer spoke in Basque and the mother in Spanish. They had no idea where they were, though they thought they might be near San Sebastian. The farmer and his wife had two children, who spoke both languages, a girl of about 15 and a boy of about 12. The two guides left and the escapees spent another night on an isolated farm. In the morning the mother gave them breakfast of soured goat's milk and a black type of bread and the farmer left to work in the fields as Len presumed. One of the group asked one of the children where they were but the mother interjected and said they were not to be told.

Don Willis spoke Spanish and understood what was whispered. When Willis told the others what was being said, Len began to have doubts about these people. Len later said, 'It seemed strange to me that we were in a neutral country. We were not going to run away. Why should we not know where we were? It was then that he got Don Willis to ask the kid which way was San Sebastian and he could see no harm in this and duly pointed in that direction. Later on, we asked him which way was Madrid and after giving us three different directions where we were positioned, with the small piece of map we had which

Willis had kept the map and had folded into a matchbox; I was able to get a rough fix on where we were. I informed them that we could not be far from Pamplona. That town was about 50 miles I think away from Bayonne. So, we had walked 50 miles! This seemed rather strange to me because the border came round and we were as near to the border as we were on the first night of crossing it. I decided that I was not going to stay there any longer and I informed the colonel that I was going to move on. I said ,' You are senior rank to me. I do not know whether you have got jurisdiction over me or not but whatever you say, I am going. I am not going to get b... caught after all this.' The colonel thought for a while and said, 'Give us a couple of hours rest'. I said ,'Right but at 12 o'clock (noon) I will be moving on. At twelve o'clock I got up and, on my way out, I lifted a couple of pairs of raffia shoes. There was a big pile of them up in the loft. They all took a couple of pairs each and we left the farmhouse. But in the meantime, I think the woman must have realised there was something wrong, because she sent the girl off to get the guides back. It was a very long road from the farmhouse and we could hear the guides calling us back.'

What made Len Barnes so suspicious? Len said that things did not add up and why were they so careful not to let on where they were, when they were in a neutral country? Subsequently Len found out that these guides were young and were going to hand us over to the Spanish Carabinieros or the Germans and they would have got a sack of corn each, for each one of us. The French side had done their work perfectly but with the Spanish Basques it was different. Life was very difficult for them. Willis later referred to Len as 'The impetuous Englishman who wanted to keep on the move!'

A new life for Virginia and Philippe d' Albert-Lake.

It would not be until 27 May 1945 when Philippe could hold her in his arms again. She was emaciated, dirty and the sufferings of the camp have made her look a lot older. But her spirit was unbroken. After the war, Philippe and Virginia rebuilt their lives. They opened a small antiques business in the village of Cancaval in Brittany. Both received many decorations from allied governments. Virginia and Genevieve both were awarded the French Légion d' Honneur. During Easter 1983 another journey took us to France. This time we had been invited to meet Philippe and Virginia d'Albert-Lake. Our idea was to research the last part of the escape, from Paris to the Spanish border.

Top: Virginia d'Albert-Lake in 1946 and 1947. Centre: Hans Onderwater, Virginia and Philippe at their house in Brittany, and Virginia with the Legion d'Honneur.

We arrived in Cancaval, Brittany, where the couple had a beautiful house, overlooking the river Rance. In the evening they showed us an amazing collection of information. Photographs of every individual escaper, stacks of unused ID-cards, both French and Belgian, forged rubber stamps of SD, Wehrmacht, Organisation Todt, the French railways and numerous French municipalities. Philippe kept copies of letters, informing him about the safe arrival of 'five books', 'three shirts' or 'nine rabbits.' Who would believe that the items in these books, shirts or rabbits, were men who flew in Lancasters, Mosquitoes, Thunderbolts or Flying Fortresses?

I said it was dangerous to keep so much vital and sensitive information. Philippe said: 'These Germans would never have found it.' Virginia showed us copies of the correspondence of her parents in the United States with the International Red Cross in Switzerland after Virginia's arrest by the Gestapo. She told me how shocked she was when Philippe told her, on the day of her safe return in Paris, that her mother had died without ever knowing her child had survived. She remembered Willis, smart, calm and calculated. She spoke about Hubbard, slow, kind, dominant, always a Colonel. Then there was this Englishman Barnes, quiet, appreciative and obedient. Philippe told about Emeny and Cornett, both so young, very eager to return, but sometimes emotional and careless.

Philippe and Virginia allowed me to take everything with me that I felt I might I need for my book. 'It will give you a good reason to come back and see us again', said Philippe when we say goodbye the next day. Weeks of reading, copying and sorting followed to get an idea of the work Comète did. It was truly amazing. We said goodbye, never meeting again. Virginia died at her family home in Cancaval, Brittany on September 20, 1997. Her husband Philippe died on 10 February 2000.

Upon arriving home there was a letter bearing a US stamp in the mailbox. I opened the letter: 'Dear Mr. Onderwater, my name is Jack Donald Cornett. I have been informed you wish to contact me about my escape from France. I will be delighted to help.' In the letters that followed he described the mission, the fears and the excitement. He also said that he kept in the background much of the time. 'There was a colonel and there was a major and they knew what to do. I was a 2nd Lieutenant and my job was to keep quiet and do what I was told. I was a rooky and knew my place. I think that is the reason why I was home so soon…' Then suddenly no more replies came to my letters. It was not until many years later that I found out that Cornett had died in 1986.

Left: Lucien Tripot, shortly before he died. His face shows the same smile that can be also be seen on wartime pictures; that of a simple farmer, who apparently had no clue. Headstone on the grave of Jack Cornett at Willamette National Cemetery in Portland.

In the paper La Republique du Centre an interview with Lucien was published: 'Lucien Tripot, in his twenties, helped escapees to cross into the free zone, aviators and young people fleeing the compulsory labour service. 'We were not heroes. We did our duty. When Lucien Tripot tells his story, that of a young man who joined the resistance during the Second World War, he is more than modest. 'We were aware that it was dangerous. I lost a lot of friends. But it had to be done.' When a professor at the Montargis conservatory, discovered his history and decided to illustrate it with a show mixing music and texts, the resident of La Boisserie was amazed. 'I do not like honours very much. I had medals but I do not want to see them. You know, many of us entered the resistance, 'insists the old gentleman, staring at you with his little blue eyes.'

'His story, however, deserves to be told. Lucien Tripot was born July 16, 1923 in Montcorbon. His parents had a big farm near Courtenay. He joined the resistance in 1941. 'I started by helping French war escapees. They were taken to Saint-Florent-sur-Cher, on the border of the free zone', says Lucien. In one year, nearly sixty escapees passed through his parents' farm. When the Arbeitseinsatz (Compulsory Labour Service) was established by the Germans, he came to the aid of boys who wanted to hide. The young man took care of many aviators who failed in the region.

With others, he was busy to recover them. He took care of finding a cache for them, getting them false papers, taking care of their needs. They had to go through the free zone. With certain people whom he helped, he remained very close. As with British air gunner Ron Emeny. To recognise all his courageous actions during the 1939-1945 war, he was received at Buckingham Palace in London, with other resistance fighters, after the conflict. 'We had played the Marseillaise. There was Queen Elizabeth, recalls the man who said, simply, to have been a small link in a large network. Lucien Tripot was never arrested. 'I escaped four, five times,' he recalled when he was 89 years old.

In 1984 Len Barnes and his wife Merville were invited to Buckingham Palace to meet the Queen and receive an MBE for his sterling work for the RAF Escaping Society. He always proudly showed his RAFES badge. The two couples Emeny and Barnes during another visit to France. Len in his garden, harvesting the 'sweetest strawberries of the neighbourhood'.(HO/AB)

Return to Chaintreaux

In 2015 Brian Lissette decided he wanted to see the area where his uncle died so heroically in 1944. He and his wife Jean travelled their Journey to the Horizon, to Chaintreaux in France. The Weekend Sun in Tauranga, New Zealand of Thursday 24 December 2015 gave a report of the pilgrimage: 'Retired Policeman's work finally complete' it said, and last week Brian Lissette visited the grave of his Uncle, Warrant Officer Leslie Harry Lissette, in the small French commune Chaintreaux, some seventy years after the skipper's death on the night of May 3, 1944. At the cemetery Jean Lissette stepped back and let husband Brian walk in on his own. 'It was so peaceful and quiet in there. I stood at the foot of his grave and I said, 'I am here, I have finally done it.' The simple marble headstone tells anyone who is interested that 391011 Warrant Officer L.H. Lissette lies here; that he was a pilot, Royal New Zealand Air Force, who died May 4, 1944, age 26. Although the raid began on the night of May 3, Brian's uncle sacrificed his life in the early hours of May 4. Nothing of his exploits, his bravery; his sacrifice. But the French do not need reminding. They are deeds etched in folklore for all time. Brian whispered a few words to his Uncle, congratulating him on what he had done.

'I know I had a huge lump in my throat and I found it very hard holding back the tears.' Brian and Jean also visited a patch of ground in a paddock just beyond the perimeter of Chaintreaux. It is hallowed ground; exactly where an aeroplane and a New Zealand pilot died May 4, 1944. Brian may as well still be standing at the crash site as he haltingly unfarmed, ungrazed, and tells the story. 'That was the moment for me.' Since that day in 1944 the ground has gone unmowed, gives up chunks of metal. A piece of that metal from EM-F sitting on the Lissette's drinking table in Otumoetai. Brian holds it, fondles it, and ponders. 'I must find out what part of the plane it is. They are good people; they are very kind people. And very grateful.'

On May 8 Brian and Jean assembled with 300 others outside the Mayor's office in Chaintreaux. It is VE Day, Victory in Europe Day, 'la fête de la victoire, le jour de la liberation'. France stops to celebrate freedom and an end of Nazi oppression. Church bells ring, the tricolour is hoisted, La Marseillaise is sung with full voice across the land, and the schoolchildren of Chaintreux are reminded of Leslie Harry Lissette. 'It is very humbling,' said Brian. Two river stones from the Pakowhai, New Zealand home of W/O Lissette were cemented onto the grave, and a Brian was decorated with the Medallion of Chaintreaux. So out of difficult dark days seven decades ago came gratitude, respect, and goodwill. Then they all wandered back to a marquee for what they call a glass of friendship,' says Brian. 'There were many speeches, like the one by Pierre Boyer, retired honorary mayor of Chaintreaux, who as a schoolboy in 1944 heard the night fighters shooting and then heard ND556 crash. A letter from the Chief of the RNZAF, Air Vice Marshall Yeardley to the mayor of Chaintreaux was presented by the New Zealand Defence Attaché in Paris, Captain Shaun Fogarty RNZN, as was a letter from the mayor of Hastings, New Zealand to the mayor of Chaintreaux.

Brian spoke on behalf of his family. But on VE Day in Chaintreux a 'glass' of friendship can 'runneth over'. Many glasses were taken, and darkness had fallen when everyone left the tent. The town is now considering a Lissette memorial at the crash site. And a former Policeman's work is done. 'I am satisfied.' In Brian's mind sincere thanks and gratitude must be passed to all citizens and children of Chaintreaux and surrounding areas for the kind and respectful manner in they were made most welcome in their community. The words 'thank you' are not enough to express their feelings and gratitude to these lovely people. Special thanks also must go to their 'French Controller' a Chaintreaux teacher Maria Sanna for arranging this. Brian went to this community to thank the people for paying tribute at his uncle's grave, for maintaining the grave for so many years, and was told that it was the French people's task to thank New Zealand as a country for sending troops to Europe to give them their freedom back.

Left: Brian Lissette next to the grave of Warrant Officer Lissette and Sergeant Ellis. Centre: Brian at the crash site with John Pittwood Jr. Right: Marcel Goubard, Brian Lissette John Pittwood in front of the crypt in 2015. (BL)

Left: the grave of Sgt Plowman, wireless operator/air gunner in the crew of Len Barnes at Cust-West Eyreton Cemetery Waimakariri New Zealand. Right: When the parents of Overholt died, they had the name of their son added to the headstone at Princeton Cemetery in Blandford-Blenheim in Ontario, Canada.

The last relatives found; Plowman and Overholt.
It was not until we found out through the help of Len Barnes' three daughters. It turned out that Plowman had emigrated to New Zealand after the war and died there on 23 November 2010. Research in New Zealand fairly quickly established that he had a daughter who lived in the Christchurch area. She was very keen to help us and supplied us with the information she was able to give. We also found out that the parents of Sergeant Overholt, the Canadian air gunner, had the name of their son written on the headstone of their grave at Princeton Cemetery in Blandford-Blenheim in Oxford, Ontario, Canada. It read 'their dearly beloved son Sergeant James Henry Overholt RCAF, killed in action, March 16, 1944, age 20…' During an act of Remembrance Act of Remembrance - live broadcast on You Tube om 8th November 2020 at St. Mary's Church Chipping the crew was remembered.

Jean Ellis, daughter of Sergeant Ron Ellis.
He is the Rear Gunner buried next to W/O Lissette, his skipper, in Chaintreaux. His daughter wrote: 'I live in a small town called Brackley in Northamptonshire, it is halfway between Northampton and Oxford. You probably had a job to trace me because growing up I was called by my stepfather's name of Jefford. I have been married three times, my first husband was killed in an accident at the age of 26, leaving me with three children. I later remarried and had one other son, so have 3 sons and a daughter. My father Ronald lived in Doncaster by the way and worked for the railway. She told us she never knew her father as he died a few months before she was born. It was one of the dreadful tragedies that would happen to families at war.

Ron Ellis under the wing of what looks like a Wellington, in RAF great coat, with his wife Kathleen, in the group of new RAF airmen. The graves of Lissette and Ellis and his daughter at his grave in Chaintreaux.

In searching for a descendant of Ron Ellis, none of the air crew descendants had any information regarding the Ellis family that could help us. Mrs. Pittwood, wife of navigator Jack Pittwood, used to write to Mrs Ellis after the war, but lost contact with her. We ascertained that Mrs. Ellis married John Jefford and resided in Northants. Brian Lissette had an English cousin write to the occupants of the Northants address: no reply. Brian then wrote to the council in Northants: no reply. He wrote to the newspaper in Northants: no reply. A friend who has an Ancestry.com account located Ron Ellis on a family tree; all he ascertained was Ronald Ellis and Kathleen Cooper married in 1939 in Doncaster, Yorkshire, and his Mother was Hilda Pretoria Ellis. Brian emailed the owner of that family tree: no reply. Ron 'Curly' Emeny once told us that Ron Ellis and Kathleen had a daughter also named Kathleen, which put us off completely, and it was not until Brian Lissette closely read the inscription on Ron Ellis's head stone, the penny slowly dropped when Lissette read 'Kathleen and Jean' at the base of the head stone. That posed a question – was Jean a daughter or sister?? It was not until Brian joined some Bomber Command pages on Facebook, and posted a query about Ron Ellis that Jean Ellis contacted him. She wrote her son Kevin had seen one of Brian's Facebook postings and subsequently notified her. Jean Ellis had used the surname of her stepfather Jefford for many years. It also became known that the Jeffords had been invited by Brian Lissette's grandmother to emigrate to New Zealand as there was a shortage of mechanics. But he turned that offer down. And so ended the quest for people and was in possible after more than 75 years to re-united the families of both Lancaster crews described in this book.

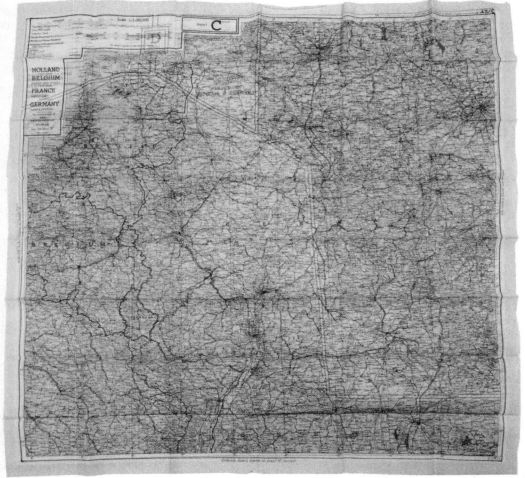

An escape map for North Western Europe, part of the equipment of aircrew operating over this area. (HO)

12. APPENDICES:

These appendices have been compiled to give the reader background information about events, situations, facts and figures in this book. It deals with backgrounds of the wars in Scandinavia, the American volunteers in the RAF, official instructions in case of captivity, the life in PoW camps, the organisations of the Comète evasion line, copies of several Escape & Evasion Reports, backgrounds of the five evaders. There is more information about the targets of the days our evaders went down over Occupied Europe and it talks about the aftermath of the war and the institutes that should be able to supply a genuine researcher with information. We hope that these 26 chapters A to Z, will help the reader and maybe encourage him or her to do research about an event of local or personal interest.

A. Eagle Squadrons; Yanks in the RAF.

Before the United States' entry into the Second World War, many Americans volunteered for service in the RAF and RCAF. The Battle of Britain raged from May through October 1940. Most Americans followed the battle in the news and knew that in time the United States would be involved in the war. In the early beginning of the war, many Americans travelled to Canada and after training and successful completion became members of the Royal Canadian Air Force. They then sailed from Canada to Great Britain to join RAF Squadrons. Some became pilots; others flew as air gunners or navigators. The stories of the RAF pilots flying their Hurricanes and Spitfires inspired many to look into joining the RAF. Because of the Battle of Britain, the RAF was short on pilots so a call went out for pilots to replace the

RAF's depleted ranks. Of the thousands that volunteered, 244 American pilots were to fly for the Eagle Squadrons: Nos.71, 121 and 133 Squadrons of RAF Command.

It was the RAF's policy to appoint Englishmen as squadron and flight commanders and 16 of these British pilots served with the Eagle Squadrons. From the time the first Eagle Squadron was formed in September 1940 until all three squadrons were disbanded and incorporated into the USAAF in September 1942, they destroyed 73½ German planes while 77 Americans and 5 Britons were killed. An organisation called the Knight Committee was responsible for recruiting nearly 90% of the Eagle Squadron members. The basic requirements for those interested in joining the Eagles were a high school diploma, between 20 and 31 years of age, eyesight that was 20/40 correctable to 20/20, and 300 hours of certified flying time. These requirements were somewhat less strict than those required for service in the USAAF, which is the reason some of the pilots joined the RAF or the RCAF in the first place.

RAF Eagle Squadrons[113]. No.71: September 1940, No.121: May 1941, No.133: July 1941. Eagle Squadron badge that was on right sleeve top. (IWM)

Members of No.121 Eagle Squadron, a Spitfire and their Commanding Officer. Front kneeling left/right: Jim Taylor, Seldon Edner, Gunner Halsey, Leon Blanding, Ernest Beatie, James Happel, Don Smith, Don Young and Hugh Brown (IO RAF). Standing left to right: Sqn Ldr William RAF (XO), Sqn Ldr Hugh Kennard RAF (CO), Denys Laing RAF (MO), Gene Fetrow, Frank Boyles, Aubrey Stanhope. On the wing left/right: Bill Kelly, Cadman Padgett, Fred Vance. On the Spitfire left to right: Barry Mahon, Jim Daley, John Slater, Roy Evans, Philip Fox. (via Dr. Laing).

Most Eagle Squadron pilots did not have a college education or prior military experience. The reason most of the pilots volunteered was quite simply for adventure. Leo Nome wrote: 'I think that all of us, with few exceptions were simply adventurers and romanticists, and perhaps idealists.' Robert Patterson[114] noted: 'I joined the RAF not primarily for patriotic reasons. We all knew a war was coming. I used this as a quick way for some flying excitement.' Strickland observed: 'We were all motivated by the thought of high adventure, the excitement of combat flying, and a desire to help the British.' Red McClain wrote: 'Some could not take the long routine in the US. services to become military pilots when they were already experienced aviators.'

Once in England the new recruits were sent to an operational training unit (OTU) for two to four weeks, where they learned to fly Miles Master trainers, Hurricanes and Spitfires before they are posted. After OTU some of the men went straight to one of the Eagle Squadrons while others first served with other

---

[113] *The Eagle stood for the American eagle and was worn on the left arm of the RAF uniform.*
[114] *Patterson was shot down over Holland and made an unsuccessful attempt to evade capture. He was arrested in Amsterdam.*

RAF squadrons before being transferred to an Eagle squadron. Having arrived at his squadron, the new Eagle pilot had to become proficient in formation flying and knowledgeable of the current tactics. The formation most commonly used was the line astern formation where the squadron's planes flew in three lines of four, with each section spaced 200 to 300 yards apart. Each line of four, or flight, was referred to as white, red, or blue flight. Also used was the line abreast formation with the planes again divided in flights of four with the middle flight out in front of the other two. In the area of tactics, the pilots were instructed to get in close, fire in short bursts, use height for advantage, turn to face an attack, maintain high cover, and hit hard quickly and get out.

Top left: Barry Mahon, Bill Kelly and Jim Daley on the dispersal truck. Right Pilot Officer Don Young with Eagle badge (Laing)Left: When the first American Eagles returned to the USA they were hailed as heroes, rather than as mercenaries or soldiers of fortune. They were invited to the Pentagon; the caption says: 'Shown at the Pentagon Building, Arlington, VA., are four former members of the R.A.F. Eagle Squadrons who are credited with shooting down a total of twenty-one planes and damaging fifteen others. Left/right: Major Carroll W. McColphin, Buffalo, Captain Sam A. Mauriello, Astoria, Queens, Major William J. Dailey jnr, Amarillo, Tex., and Captain Reade Tilly, Clearwater, Fla.' They proudly display the RAF wing on their right and the USAAF wing on their left breast. The times had indeed changed. (NYHT)

As soon as they had been declared operational, the squadrons took part in a variety of missions. Convoy escort patrols were common, long, and very monotonous. Usually, a convoy escort was done by 2 planes flying circuits around the ships at an altitude as low as 100 feet. Given poor weather, fog and haze it was not uncommon for planes to crash into the sea. Rhubarbs were two plane low-level ground attack missions. McColpin said: 'Of all the missions, the rhubarb was the most fun. Flying a few feet off the ground, you shot up railroads, troops, tanks, ships, or anything else of military value.' A hit to a Hurricane or Spitfire's glycol system however meant a jump over enemy territory. A Circus was a combined bomber and fighter mission designed to draw out the Luftwaffe. Ramrods were bomber escort missions. The bombers were generally Blenheims, Bostons or later B17s. A Balboa had the fighters serving as decoys while bombers hit a nearby target. Among the German-occupied targets over which the pilots flew were Ostend, Belgium, and Dunkirk, Lille, Abbeville, St Omer, Calais, Boulogne, Dieppe and Cherbourg, France. A fighter sweep was referred to as a Rodeo. Those squadrons based at the bases like North Weald and Biggin Hill usually flew sweeps as part of a three squadron wing while those based at smaller bases such as Martlesham Heath flew solo sweeps or top cover for the wing in their sector.

When informed of the Japanese attack on Pearl Harbour most of the Eagle Squadron pilots wanted to immediately join the Air Corps. Nos.71 and 121 Squadrons sent representatives to the American Embassy in London and offered their services to the US the following day. No. 71 squadron then decided they wanted to go to Singapore to fight the Japanese and a proposal was put to Fighter Command but turned down. It would take some time however for the USAAF to organize and ship to England the elements necessary to support air operations.

HQ 8th Air Force opened on 18 June 1942 in London with Major General Carl Spaatz in command. On 26 June 1942 air echelons of the 31st Fighter Group (307th, 308th and 309th Fighter Squadrons) were established at Atcham and High Ercall, England. These were the first combat personnel of the VIII Fighter Command to reach the UK. These squadrons were equipped with Spit Vs and flew their first mission on 17 August 1942. The first US air operation over Europe was on 4 July 1942 with the 15th Bombardment Squadron (Light) flying 6 Bostons belonging to No.226 Squadron RAF. Negotiations regarding transfer to the USAAF between the Eagle Squadrons, USAAF and the RAF had to resolve a number of issues. Determining what rank, they would assume in the USAAF had to be negotiated with most pilots given a rank equivalent to their RAF rank. None of the Eagle Squadron pilots had served in the USAAF and did not have US pilot's wings. It was decided to give them US pilots' wings upon their transfer.

General Spaatz wanted to spread the experience of the Eagles amongst various new US fighter squadrons but the three Eagle Squadrons wanted to stay together as units. The RAF wanted some compensation for losing three front line squadrons that they had heavily invested in. Compensation to the RAF had to be negotiated. An agreement had to be reached between the English and the Americans to supply the squadrons with aircraft after they transferred to the USAAF. The US did not have any suitable aircraft in 1942. Part of the agreement called for the new squadrons to be equipped with Spitfire VBs. Although transfers between the Eagle Squadrons were common, they were not under the same type of unified command structure that they would later find themselves under as members of the Fourth Fighter Group. In fact, the only operation that all three squadrons participated at the same time was the Dieppe raid of 19 August. On 29 September 1942, the Eagle Squadrons became to 4th Fighter Group USAAF as 334th (71), 335th (121) and 336th (133) Fighter Squadron.

B. Escape and Evasion, a duty at all times.

There is a significant difference between escaping and evading. An escaper is one who has managed to escape from 'secure enemy custody', whether it be a prison, PoW camp, prison train, or from guards on the ground. Once free, he then has to turn to the tactics of evasion. WW2 escapers tended to be mainly Army personnel. An Evader has not been captured and has, with luck, managed to retain some of his kit and equipment – his task is to remain undetected, outwit the enemy and stay free from capture in order to return to his unit. WW2 evaders tended to be mainly aircrew or members of Special Forces. A sound understanding of survival skills is a prerequisite for successful evasion; knowledge of both is needed to complement each other. The escaper has a different set of rules from the evader, starting from the time when he is captured. It reads clear and simple: with the United States in a war over Germany and the occupied countries it would be obvious that American aviators ended up in German hands. For this reason, Major-General Spaatz had a document circulated among aircrew stating what was expected of them if captured:

RESTRICTED.

Instructions for officers and men of the Eight Air Force in the event of capture. AG 8 AF No. 1 21 July 1942. This document must not be taken into a plane. The information contained in this document is not to be communicated, directly or indirectly, to anyone not in the armed forces of the United States. CO's are to see that a copy of this publication is issued to every member of the 8th Air Force whose duties might take him over enemy territory. Inevitably, some members of the 8th AF will be captured by the enemy. This document contains information and instructions for guidance. It should be preserved and read from time to time so that its contents will not be forgotten'.

I. General instructions: Any officer or enlisted man who becomes a prisoner of war remains in the military service of the United States. He is to escape when practicable, to perform other military duties when ordered and to obey his American military superior in the prison camp. No parole is to be given to the enemy except with permission of the senior American officer or non-commissioned officer and then only for periods of several hours' duration and for special purposes. No broadcasts are to be made from prison camps for any purpose. Prisoners of war have many rights. These are fully stated in the Geneva Convention of 1929, which the United States and all the great powers except Japan have signed and ratified. According to its terms, a copy of the treaty should be available in every prison camp. Insist on this being done. Study it and insist on your rights. There is a neutral Protecting Power to whom all serious complaints can be addressed by the senior American officer or non-commissioned officer through the Camp Commandant.

II. – What information can be given to the enemy: A prisoner must give name, rank, serial Number. This is required by the Geneva Convention of 1929. No further information of any kind should be given.

III. – What the enemy will try to find out from you: The American Air Force is a new factor in the war, so the enemy will try desperately to ascertain its strength and capabilities. They will want to know:
- The number, strength and location of your squadron or unit.
- The location of other squadrons and of airdromes.
- The length of time you have been in England and the way you travelled from America.
- The training you have received.
- The size of the American Air Force.
- The types of aircraft used with their performances and armament.
- The signals and radio equipment used.
- The tactics used by the American Air Force.
- Anything and everything about AA defences and Air Defence organisation.
- Anything and everything about the Ground Forces of the American Army.
- Any facts about the RAF or its co-operation with the American Air Force.
- Anything about conditions in Great Britain and in America: food supply, politics, moral among civilians and the armed forces, production of war supplies, etc.

IV. – How the enemy will try to learn these things from you:
There are three sources through which the enemy can obtain information from you. They are:
1. Your aircraft and its equipment.
2. Your papers either official such as maps and documents, or personal letters and diaries.
3. Your talk. The enemy cannot add to the information provided by your plane or papers, but he can do a lot to make you talk. The first Americans captured must expect the most rigorous interrogation and must be prepared for all the tricks that the Germans have used. Among the methods, which the enemy has employed to get people to talk, and which have been reported by prisoners of war who actually experienced them, are the following:
   a) Direct interrogation, sometimes for long periods in the hope of wearing you down and sometimes renewed long after capture.
   b) Indirect interrogation through casual conversations about flying and the war in general -shop talk - in the hope of having you reveal something.
   c) He will try to impress you with his great knowledge about yourself, your plane and the American Air Force in the hope you will think he knows everything and therefore there is no harm in talking freely. He may suggest that others have told everything so your silence is no longer necessary.
   d) He will appeal to your vanity by letting you show how much you know.
   e) He will try to arouse you to angry protest by ridiculing the war efforts of the United States.

f) He will flatter you with special attentions, inviting you to parties with German airmen of great prominence. A spirit of good sportsmanship will prevail and liquor will flow.

g) He will reveal all sorts of German facts and secrets to you in the hope that you will feel like a heel if you do not tell him something.

h) He may try to intimidate you with threats.

i) On first arriving at a prison camp, a Red Cross official, really an enemy officer, may give you a blank to fill out which will ask you to supply you squadron number and location. He may say your capture will not be reported or your mail transmitted if you refuse to fill out the blanks.

j) Enemy officials may dress in Allied uniforms to engage PoWs in conversation.

k) Hospital nurses or attendants may try to gather information by being very sympathetic.

l) Microphones will certainly be used as they are a favourite German device and may be expected in every room at every stage of your imprisonment.

m) In addition to the above much-used methods, the enemy will resort to many other tricks to extract information from you.

V. – How you can defeat the enemy?

1. Destroy, if possible, your aircraft, maps, etc., by fire if brought down. You have instructions how to handle this. Do not forget to follow them.

2. Do not carry and do not allow anyone else to carry any unauthorized papers, official or private, on a flight. An envelope, a bill or the stub of a movie ticket may give away the location of your squadron. In writing letters after becoming a prisoner, do not address them in such a way as to reveal the location of your squadron or any other unit. Use the official APO or write c/o War Department.

3. Tell your Name, Rank and Serial Number. If you answer other questions, you are helping the enemy. Say 'I cannot answer', 'I do not know', or following the advice the enemy gives his own airmen: 'Would you answer that question if you were me?' By sticking to these, you win,

4. Do not talk shop with the enemy. He is not anxious to talk with fellow flyers. He wants knowledge, which will help him in the war. Do not try to deceive him with lies. He is an expert interrogator and among your lies, he will find some truths. Outwit him by saying nothing.

5. Do not be impressed with his knowledge, which may have come from papers or markings in your plane. It may partly be a guess or he may want you to confirm something. No facts are harmless. They may be used to persuade the next prisoner that all is known and he may as well talk.

6. Do not try to prove to the enemy how big you are by telling him what you know. He will only think you are small, and you will be satisfied with yourself afterwards if you have told only your name, rank and number.

7. It is good to be patriotic, but you can best prove your patriotism by keeping silent and not by telling how much the United States is doing.

8. The enemy will not treat you nicely and offer you drinks because he likes you. Remember he treats any likely prospect that way. He is after information to use against us. Among the 'good sports' will be one or several interrogation officers waiting to seize on any chance remark you may let slip. It is not good sportsmanship but a stupid mistake to go on parties with the enemy.

9. Never believe what you are told from enemy sources. Even if he gives you correct information, it is reasonably safe for him to do so, while any fact you reveal may cost your friends their lives.

10. Threats are bluff. The enemy will not dare to carry out threats; he knows reprisals follow.

11. In order to have your capture promptly reported and your mail delivered you only tell Name, Rank and Number.

12. Remember the person to whom you are talking may be an enemy. The only friend you can be sure of is the man you knew before capture.

13. Tell no enemy person anything except your name, rank and number.

14. Because you cannot find a microphone do not think there is not one. We know that there is and that the enemy, who has had years of experience in eavesdropping, is listening. If you have plans to discuss with friends do your talking outdoors and even there be careful.

15. You can defeat every effort of the enemy by keeping silent.

VI. – What else you can do to defeat the enemy.

1. You can plan to escape. Opportunities will be offered. Even attempts, which fail, are worthwhile as they have an appreciable nuisance value and the information collected will make later attempts successful. If you succeed in escaping and arriving in friendly territory do not discuss your experiences with anyone, in military service or out, until you are interviewed by proper military authorities. And never, under any circumstances, mention the name of any person who may have helped you to escape.
2. You can damage enemy morale by spreading proper ideas and correcting misinformation among the prison guards and such civilians, as you may be able to reach. You can, if you are an enlisted man and go out of camp on working parties, do as little work as possible and you may be able to do real damage. You can keep your eyes and ears open at all times. We want information. Help us get it.

C. Another successful evasion.

While writing the Dutch version of this book the author found that on 13 November 1943, the day when Tom Hubbard started his long journey to Gibraltar, another attempt by allied airmen was made to evade capture by the Germans. It is the story of Victor Ferrari. Though he travelled via a different 'Line', he also depended entirely on strangers to reach the free world. His story also begins over the troubled skies of Holland. It is the story of B-24 Liberator 42-7483 of 392nd Bomb Group. The crew of 42-7483 consists of a crew of ten: Pilot Isaac Marx, co-pilot Jim Chenet, navigator Victor Ferrari[115], bombardier Eddie Roberts, radio operator Nick Mandell[116] and gunners Pose, Sanna, Wright, Fletcher and Stewart.

On the way to Bremen one of the engines was hit and the propeller had to be feathered. Flying on three engines the B-24 could keep up with the other aircraft and remain within the safety of the formation. The crew knew that the Germans would mercilessly attack any straggler. Navigator Ferrari, sitting at his navigator's desk remembered many years later: 'Shortly after we dropped our bombs and turned for the home leg, our second engine was hit. Immediately we lost contact with the rest of the formation. This was suicide for we all knew that we would be prime targets for the Germans now. Soon one after the other had a go at us and I remember that at one moment no less than nine or ten aircraft were virtually waiting for their turn to fire at us. Though the attacks continued all the time these aircraft did not shoot us down. A twin-engine Bf110 or 210 attacking us from the back and firing little rockets or exploding grenades at us caused our mortal wound. One of these really put us out of action. There was no internal contact as the hit have severed all intercom lines. This lack of communication caused another problem. When Marx gave orders to jump only the co-pilot knew what have been said and bailed with Marx. During one of the attacks, I happened to look up into the pilot's compartment and noticed that Marx' legs have disappeared and followed a few second later. Therefore, the bombardier and I worked our ways to the bomb bays and bailed out. Unfortunately, the four gunners stayed in the back of the aircraft, not knowing what have happened in front.' At that moment, the Liberator of Lt. Marx was over Overijssel Province in Holland, in the same area where Lt. Marks' B-17 and two P47s of 355th Fighter Group have crashed. A German fighter has crashed as well. In the area between the border of Holland and Germany and the Zuiderzee no less than 6 aircraft have fallen: two B24s, a B-17, two P47s and a Messerschmitt 109. The further story of Marks' crew is unbelievable.

With four air gunners and no one at the controls the aircraft started a shallow dive and crashed into a canal in Western Overijssel. The impacts threw the gunners to the front of the aircraft and one of them got stuck. He threatened to drown, so the three others, after overcoming the shock of the impact, managed to pull him clear. Soon the Germans arrived and took them prisoner. The wounded gunner was admitted to a hospital. The pilot, co-pilot and flight engineer were captured only a few hours later. This meant that only three of a crew of ten were still free: Ferrari, Mandell and Roberts. November is a cold month in Holland. Sergeant Roberts landed near Ferrari and hit the ground with great force. Ferrari saw that his friend did not get up. A small canal separated them, so Ferrari slid into the ice-cold water and waded to Roberts. A few moments later Eddie opened his eyes and complained about terrible pains. He had obviously broken his shoulder and needed medical attention.

---

[115] *Ferrari successfully evaded capture and is on the 1943 escape list of Comète.*
[116] *He too appears on the 1943 escape list of Comète.*

Standing left to right: Ferrari, Chenet, Roberts, Marx. Kneeling left to right: Stewart, Mandell, Pose, Sanna, Fletcher, Wright. This photo was made in late 1943 at Smokey Hill AFB Topeka, Kansas, USA. Their B-24 looked very much like 42-7470 of the same Group, which crashed a few days earlier.

At the same moment, the first Dutchman arrived. He gestured to the two Americans that they are to follow him in a hurry, for the Germans are all over, searching and collecting the landed crew. Ferrari and Roberts followed the unknown Dutchman. The man gave both Americans a bicycle, but as it showed clearly that none of them have ever ridden a bike, they threw them from the bridge into the water. Then he pointed to the men and to the water. Ferrari understood that the only way to hide was to stay under the bridge in the cold water and hope for the best. For over five hours they waited, almost unconscious from the freezing cold and shivering all over their bodies. When darkness fell the two men were totally exhausted and are ready to give up. The pain was killing Roberts who needed immediate medical attention. Ferrari and Roberts left their hideout and slowly walked in the direction of a house. They decided to ask for help and surrender to the Germans.

While they were on their way, Henk Eikelboom, the man who helped them that afternoon, approached them again. He gestured to the two airmen that they must follow him at a safe distance. He still was not satisfied they are real Americans, as he did not have a chance to check their identity. Often German infiltrators tried to pose as allied aircrew, trying to uncover the escape line and capturing many people. Without saying anything Henk Eikelboom led them to a house. In the kitchen they got bread, dry clothing and warm milk. Then they were taken to a haystack and told to stay there. Henk stayed with them; someone had mentioned to the Germans that two airmen have been seen with a young Dutchman leading them. If they got Henk, he would not survive the ordeal. Besides, as long as the Americans have not been declared genuine it clearly was his job to guard them. After three days the men were told to come out. Two people, a man and a woman were waiting for them in the kitchen. Now Ferrari and Roberts were in the hands of Henk and Mimi van den Hurk, both members of the resistance. The following day, after an interrogation have satisfied the resistance of the true identity of the two Americans, the Van den Hurks took them to the town of Meppel. Now properly dressed in civilian clothes they look like everyday Dutchmen. Yet, there was a great danger. None of them understands nor speaks a single word of Dutch. They do not yet have 'genuine' forged papers and, above all they clearly look like the healthy young men who are supposed to be in Germany, contributing to the German war effort in a factory.

At 2000 hrs. they arrive at a house. Victor Ferrari got very worried, for there were a lot of Germans about in the street. However, knowing that it was unwise to ask questions under these circumstances he decided to wait and see what would happen. With the curfew in Holland, it was extremely dangerous to be out in the open in the evening. The Germans and their collaborators were the only ones who could move freely after dark. They looked for victims in this country. Anything suspicious would be enough for these people to arrest you and take you to the Police or, worse, to Gestapo Headquarters. So, Ferrari and Roberts could do little else but follow. Their new friends led them to the attic where they were to stay until the people who lived in the house, but who were now staying away from them met them. At five o'clock the next morning Victor Ferrari woke up to the sound of marching boots and singing voices.

Though of poor quality this is an interesting picture of Lieutenant Mark's Liberator on the bottom of a canal in Holland. Only the tail section with the 'circle D' emerges from the ice-cold water. (Ferrari)

After he have scratched the ice from the window, he saw endless columns of German soldiers marching by. Ferrari walked downstairs and met his hostess in the kitchen. He asked what she thought of these Germans singing and marching but she did not speak any English. A little later her husband arrived and explained to Ferrari that the Germans have a basic training ground near Meppel and that these recruits were marching to their daily training out of town. He also told the American that he was a clergyman and often have to receive visitors. Therefore, the two Americans need not worry, because at the vicarage there was always a lot of coming and going. Besides the Germans would not expect the Underground to hide Americans so close to the German barracks.

Ferrari and Roberts had arrived in the house of Reverend Van Nooten. The family consisted of five, father, mother and three children, the youngest child five years old. Ferrari was amazed that such a family have the courage to take the deadly risk of hiding allied soldiers. The two stayed in Van Nooten's house for one month. In mid-December, a young woman came. She was Joke Folmer, who worked as a courier for the resistance. She took the two Americans south, to the city of Maastricht, where they were handed over to a policeman, Eduard van der Noorda. Many years later Van der Noorda, retired and now living in The Hague, vividly remembered the two men: 'I met Ferrari in the dark evening, at the entrance of the Maastricht station. He stood next to a young woman, who have brought me aircrew before. It was not until after the war that I knew her name. We always met in the dark, very briefly and without much talking. It was for our own safety not to know names, for the Germans used any means to extract them from you. In the Maastricht Police I was a member of the technical branch. One of the departments was 'Identifications'.

So, it was relatively easy to turn the Americans into good Dutchmen, with photographs, fingerprints and a past that could not be checked because 'their home town have been bombed by the allies and all the ID cards in the town archives have been lost.' We knew exactly what towns were safe for these purposes. One of my contacts was a man called Tony Gielen. He did brilliant work during the war. Vic Ferrari stayed with me for two weeks Then we prepared him for his crossing into Belgium. The Belgian part of our Line was controlled by Piet Souren, a Dutchman who has his house in Belgium and could safely cross the border.'

Left to right clockwise:
Co-pilot Lt.Victor Ferrari, Radio Operator
Sgt Nick Mandell,Gunner Mario Sanna,
Bombardier Omar Ed Roberts (on a photo
for his phoney French ID-card.
Right: Ferrari's evasion route.

Victor Ferrari as a senior USAF officer and
president of the USAA Federal Savings Bank
and his grave at Fort Sam Houston National
Cemetery San Antonio, Texas. (via Ferrari)

'After two weeks preparations were made to get the two Americans across the border into Belgium. Ferrari and Roberts were taken to a place near a German checkpoint. Ferrari continued: 'The Dutch underground workers told us to stay put. Sometime during the night a red light would be flashed from a window. At that moment we were to enter the back yard of a house, occupied by German soldiers, climb over a fence and run to the river Maas, where members of the resistance would be waiting for us. We hid in the brush from about 1800 until 0200 hours the next morning, at which time we saw the light and did what we have been told to do. We knew that there would be some girls entertaining the Germans. As promised people of the underground waited for us at the bank of the river. Germans, in Belgium, guarded the bridge across. We were told to join a group of four people. They would do the singing as we passed over the bridge and pretend to be inebriated. It all went well and with amazing ease we walked into Belgium.'

'Next day we both entrained and rode to Brussels. We were in Brussels for a day and a half. That night they planned to place us on the train to Paris. We were given falsified ID-cards, establishing us as Belgians working at the Paris airfield. We were on our way back from a short vacation 'at home'. The train was to have left Brussels at 1800 hrs, but because of allied bombing raids the train did not leave until 2300 hrs. This created a really dangerous situation for us because the Gestapo and the Belgian gendarmes were constantly checking on information and Identification Cards. Besides, we did not speak a single word of Dutch or Flemish. They had taught us to say a few words in French while we were hiding in Brussels. We memorised all the answers to the obvious questions we would be asked. Everything went according to plan. We left the train at the border, passed the checkpoint on foot and answered the questions we have been prepared for. We were not required to answer any additional questions. We got back into the train and went to Paris. It all sounds so easy now, but we were extremely nervous and very scared. In Brussels we have been given directions to a small hotel, where we were to go to and wait. Unfortunately, the Germans have raided the hotel a day or two earlier. We were now told to walk around from 11.00 till 1900 hrs while our guide tried to make some connections for a place for us to stay. I saw our guide at about 1700 hrs; he was very despondent because he had no success in making new contacts. He was worried about our safety because at curfew time, which started at 2000 hrs, all people on the streets would be searched and required to have some kind of special document.'

'At 1800 hrs he came to us and said we would be boarding a train to leave the city and would stay at a farmhouse a short distance out of Paris. We stayed at the farm for two weeks and then returned to Paris. A Catholic priest who led us to a building that appeared to be a public building picked us up. We went down a trap door, which, it seemed to me, was about 30-60 feet below ground. Here, there were other American and British airmen. It was a very difficult period and I, fortunately or unfortunately, contracted an infection throughout various parts of my body. When it was time to leave, a member of the French underground made it plain that, if we could not walk for 35 hours, they would leave us behind. I told the guide that I might need some assistance. She took me up to the ground floor the next morning at 0500 hrs, where they have a doctor and a medical nurse. I was told it was impossible for me to accompany the group so they were going to take me to the apartment of the nurse until I recovered. I tried to resist, but they made it clear that I would not be leaving with the group. I was taken to the apartment, which was surrounded by German military families who were in Paris. With the Eastern Front in mind Paris was extremely popular among German military personnel and those who have relatives in Wehrmacht or Luftwaffe tried to arrange to be as much as possible with the French. I was put under the care of a doctor and stayed there for three days until I felt I was ready to travel.'

'It was on the second day in the apartment we learned that the group that left Paris had been picked up by the Gestapo or the Abwehr in Southern France. They were hidden in some barns in a valley when actually they should have been on top of a mountain. Because of snow and fatigue, they were not able to keep on schedule. Therefore, they exposed themselves by being in the valley and were picked up by the enemy. Mandell, one of my crewmates, was able to escape but poor Eddie Roberts was taken prisoner. After two weeks I also made the trip to Southern France. We stayed in Toulouse for two weeks just before going over the Pyrenees. It was at the base of the Pyrenees that I met Nick Mandell again. We started our long trip through the Pyrenees, but the snow was so deep that it was impossible to pass. We remained in the foothills for a two more weeks and finally undertook the journey over the highest peak in the Pyrenees. We could not follow any of the lower passes because the Germans were guarding those areas. It was a very difficult trip with many of the participants wanting to give up. Some of them were very weak because, at that time, we have no food for three days. In going over the Pyrenees, we have entered the town of Bosost. There we were taken prisoner by the Spanish soldiers, who were very sympathetic to the Germans. You should remember that basically Hitler and Franco were one of a kind. Fortunately, we met some members of the Spanish Communist Party who notified the American Embassy of our presence. Otherwise I believe we would have been turned over to the Germans as have been done in the past. There were Germans in civilian clothing throughout the area. The communists identified these people and told us to be careful in conversation with these Germans. They also told that Germans hijacked people into France while the Spanish border guards looked the other way.'

'After having been in Bosost for two weeks we walked to a town called Lerida. A Dutch boy and I were put in jail in that town. Some Spanish police picked us up while we were attending mass. They thought the Dutch boy, during the service, acted in a manner that made him a communist suspect. As I was with him, I was also guilty. We spent three days in the jail until American Embassy personnel were able to gain us both a release. In about a month we were able to make our way to Gibraltar. From the Rock we were flown to England for an intelligence debriefing and then I was sent home'.

D. Comète.

The successful escape of the last five airmen was, above all, thanks to the Comète Organization. The story of this escape organisation, set up by a young woman, running from Brussels to the Spanish border, is absolutely incredible in its sheer simplicity, yet amazing in its audacity and courage. The birth of

Comète occurred in August 1941 when three people arrived at the British consulate, Bilbao, Spain. One of them was an attractive young Belgian woman, Andrée de Jongh. With help of her father and some friends she was able to set up hideouts from Brussels to the South-western part of the Pyrenees.

In 'Saturday at MI.9', Airey Neave described his first meeting with this young woman: 'It opened with a crumbled passport photograph of a laughing young woman. It was a compelling, feminine face, with her hair brushed back over the forehead. She had fine eyes and a determined mouth. Even in this faded, inadequate photograph, there was no doubt about her personal charisma. They had come from Brussels and crossed the Pyrenees on foot with a Basque guide. She gave her name as Andreé de Jongh, aged twenty-five, living with her parents at 73, Avenue Emile Verhaeren in the Schaarbeek district of Brussels. Her father was a teacher and she have been helping soldiers and airmen since 1940.

Léone having been forced to leave Belgium; her father took over control there while she continued to maintain the line through France to the Pyrenees. Her question to the British consul was straightforwardly and simple: 'Are the British interested in receiving escaped soldiers and, what are they willing to do to help?' When the consuls asked her if she realised the financial consequences of help by His Majesty's government, Dédée told him that the price to bring the men to the Spanish border was 6000 Belgian francs, while Basque guides asked 1400 pesetas to take the men across the border. The consul got in touch with the British embassy in Madrid.

Members of Comète: Left to right: Tante Go de Greef' 80th birthday. Dédée shortly before her arrest. Micheline Dumont and Baron De Nothomb, and Florentino, who was a veteran of the Spanish civil war and smuggler wanted by authorities on both sides of the frontier. He was also the leader of the Pyrenees Comète guides who made most of the trips with airmen. He was a hero to every airman who met him. (AC)

On 17th October Dédeé, as Renée was affectionately known, met Michael Creswell, who was MI9's man in Madrid, who called himself Monday. Michael Creswell, an outspoken, earthy man, with a warm humanity, was deeply impressed by the courage and the honesty of Dédeé. Her proposal was that MI.9 would pay for the transportation of the escapees, as well as for the guides. Dédeé insisted that MI.9 should be paid back when the war was over. From that moment on MI.9 knew her as 'Postman.' Insisting on her independence from MI.9 Dédée de Jongh and her group organised a constant flow of escapees who arrived in Spain at regular intervals. At the French side of the Pyrenees is a small town called Anglet. In this town was the house of Mrs. Elvire de Greef. Known as Tante Go, after her deceased pet dog GoGo she worked closely with Dédeé from the earliest beginnings of the war. After she failed to escape to England, she rented a villa in Anglet, where she lived with her husband Fernand and her son and daughter. Neave described her: 'She was involved in numerous black market operations to obtain the best possible food, and by these activities lulled suspicion of her real work.

Tante Go knew all the local smugglers and undercover agents in the bistros in Bayonne and Saint Jean de Luz and on more than one occasion she blackmailed German officers by threatening to reveal their possession of black market goods and thus she escaped arrest. Her husband worked as an interpreter at the German Kommandantur in Anglet. Having access to official documents, blank identity cards and passes for the border zone, he was valuable to the organisation. In fact, these two women were the last link between freedom and captivity for many airmen. Airey Neavy estimates that 337 airmen and soldiers of all the Allies passed through their hands before they arrived in Spain. Renée and her people wanted Comète to be entirely independent from MI.9. She wanted MI.9 to help; she would not allow MI.9 to take over. 'Monday' convinced Renée that it was of the greatest importance to give priority to Allied aircrew. She agreed; the fastest transport was that of an RAF crew, back to England a week after they have been shot down.'

The Germans used any available trick to crush Comète. The most important members in the Basque area, one of them the Basque guide Florentino Goicoechea, managed to stay out of German hands. Airey Neave spoke about Florentino with great respect, as a great powerful man of the mountains. His features majestic and wild. Speaking no word of Spanish or French, only Basque. In the war he could carry a man on his shoulders across the torrent of the river Bidassoa, which forms the frontier at Irun. He was indifferent to fatigue or danger. Without him, Dédée and the Comète escape line which followed her could never have rescued so many airmen. Sadly enough, many were betrayed, captured and tortured. Amazingly nobody spoke a word. The Germans overran the house where the De Jongh family lived and one of the daughters was arrested; she died as a result of the German interrogation. De Jongh and his daughter Renée disappeared in Paris. MI9 paid for their apartment.

In Brussels Baron Jean Greindl reorganised the Line. When Paris became too dangerous for the De Jonghs, they were told to escape to Spain. Their own escape ended in horror. On 14 January 1943 Florentino, Renée and three airmen prepared for crossing the border. The weather, however, was so terrible that Florentino decides to wait one day. Somehow the Gestapo knew, for on 15 January they attacked the farm in Urrunge where the five were waiting. One of the airmen talked, Renée's identity was revealed and before she knew it, she was taken to Gestapo Headquarters in Brussels. No less than ± 100 Comète members were also arrested. Elvire Morelle, a close friend of Renée, and Baron Greindl, were caught on 7 February. Eight months later the first Comète-members stood in front of a firing squad. Soon the surviving members found out why the Line have been destroyed: a tall, blond man called Jean Masson, who have acted as a guide so many times, was a Gestapo double agent. Masson, his real name was Jacques Dessoubrie, have escorted several aircrews. Nobody suspected him of being a traitor. In fact, it was not until he stood trial after the war that the immense damage, he caused in Comète was revealed.

In spite of this temporary defeat Comète did not give up. Baron De Nothomb, 23 years old, took command as 'Franco'. He too was arrested, as was Aunt Go. For some odd reason, however, the Germans released her. She knew so much about the black market activities of the German officers that they bought her silence with a quick release. The surviving members of Comète continued their work until the Allies landed in Normandy. From that day all downed aircrew or evading soldiers were told to stay where they came down. Many of them were concentrated in large encampments deep in the French countryside. 'Comète' became 'Marathon'. The majority of the former members returned to their daily jobs. The war was over, there was no reason to do anything else but to assist in the reconstruction of their countries.

After the war Comète formed an Amicale. Each year they gather, remembering their fallen comrades and enjoying the company of their former 'visitors' from the allied air forces. The Amicale still exists to stay in touch with RAFES and AFEES until no evader, escaper or helper dwells among us. In 2018 researchers came to the following count: 287 Allies crossed the Pyrenees into Spain, 11 Army (6 Scotsmen, 4 British, 1 Russian), 275 French airmen and 1 marine, 108 Americans, 105 Britons, 31 RCAF airmen, Americans who enlisted before the USA entered the war, 10 Poles, 3 New Zealanders, 2 Australians, 1 Belgian, 1 Byelorussian, 1 Frenchman, 1 Norwegian, 1 South American, 1 Ukrainia, 76 civilians crossed the Pyrenees: 57 Belgians, 12 French, 3 Dutchmen, 2 Britons, 1 Canadian and 1 American woman. Some of those civilians joined the Belgian Forces in Great Britain, some to join the Belgian government in exile in London, still others attempting to reach the Belgian Congo. The French people were mostly secret agents returning from a mission, or airmen or even burned agents wanted by the enemy and attempting to re-join their country's Free French Forces in London. The numbers above thus represent a total of 367 persons who, thanks to Comète, managed to reach the United Kingdom via the Pyrenees. The figures include the four children of De Greef and Morelle, taken to safety in Spain. At least 237 airmen and others we arrested during their evasion. At least 44 airmen were handed over to other evasion lines. At least 249 airmen were kept in camps of Operation Marathon in France and Belgium. At least 3 airmen were killed during their evasion. Jim Burch drowned with Count Antoine d'Ursel during the night of 23/24 December 1943 while crossing the Bidassoa. Their bodies were found in Biriatou par the Germans, but to date the location of their burial is still unknown. Gerald Sorensen was killed with Roger Abeels, by a German grenade, on 3rd September 1944, during the fights for Enghien. They are buried together at the Ganshoren cemetery. Robert Garrett was shot on 7th September 1944, at Queue-du-Bois by a member of a SS unit in retreat. Buried at Queue-du-Bois. More than 155 members of Comète died in their commitment to the cause of freedom. More than 1000 persons were thus helped by Comète at one stage or another of their evasion.

Returning from a mission to Spain shortly after D-Day, he was intercepted by a German patrol, gravely wounded by machine gun fire and captured. His escape from a prison hospital was arranged by Tante Go, complete with a fake German officer and ambulance crew and false papers authorizing the movement of the prisoner to another location. On the right photo we see Len Barnes, Florentino, Ron Emeny and Mrs. Lapeyre, who ran the Comète line from Bayonne.

Escaped airmen arrived in Gibraltar they would be flowing in BOAC aircraft to Whitchurch airport near Bristol. There were flights from Lisbon and Stockholm as well. The flights were not without danger as Flight 777 found out in 1943.
This aircraft was shot down over the Bay of Biscay by a Junkers Ju88. All on board died, one of them the actor Leslie Howard. This famous photo shows a Douglas DC-3 of BOAC in front of the Rock, illuminated by searchlights. (IWM)

A Spanish First Day Cover signed by Yvonne Lapeyre, Lucienne Dassie, Ron Emeny Len Barnes. The cover was one of 871, taken from RAF Marham to San Sebastian by the MV Southern Ferries, carried to Bayonne, taken across the Pyrenees to Gibraltar and flown back to the UK. Florentino died in 1980.(AC/RE)

E. Security checks in and Escape and Evasion Organisation.

In order to check if escapees and evaders were genuine, the resistance used lists with questions that could only be answered by an airman. If necessary, these questions would be asked repeatedly at various hiding places. If for any reason there was serious doubt if the unknown guest were a genuine fugitive or not, it would not be long before he would be taken to a secluded place. Then a single shot in the back of the head would be the least painful way to end his life. Some of these lists are still available in collections of former members of resistance groups, like this questionnaire, that was used to interrogate RAF aircrew. The list was copied literally, including errors in spelling etc.:

TO READ CAREFULLY BEFORE ANSWERING QUESTIONS !
The questions and interrogations are strictly secret. Only you are allowed to see them, so take very good care and see to it that the envelope was still closed when you received it. If it is opened, write it in your answer. Show neither questions nor answers to anybody, not even to your host or the person who brings you to them. Put your answer again in a closed envelope.

Write your name and address in block letters but write the other particulars in your own handwriting.

Name: Address in England:
Next of kin: Born at: on:
Rank and trade in the aircraft: RAF number:
Type of aircraft and number: Target and time of departure:
Names of crew and other survivors:
How do you call the leave form?
How many parts are there on the leave form?
What do you write on the back of a leave form?
How do you call the charge form?
What means Duff Gen?
Who was or is Pilot Officer Prune?
What means to go in for a Burton?
What means to hit the deck?
What is meant by Ditch?
What means: ITW, AFU, PFF, AD, WAAF, ATS, RNVR?
Describe a glider pilot's badge.
What badge wears a so-called Pathfinder of the RAF?
Who is Squadron Leader 'X'?
What is a Chieffy?
What is a Groupy?
Are officers in the RAF allowed to have WAAFs for house servant?
Who are the wingless wonders?
What station is nearest to Grosvenor Hotel London?
Did you ever see Waltzing Matilda?
What kind of people would like to see a maple leaf?

Put your answer in a closed envelope and give it to the person who has given it to you. Keep mum.

Sometimes resistance groups used shorter questionnaires to determine an airman's identity. The questions on these forms were different, one asked special questions for RAF personnel, while the second one was typical for USAAF servicemen. It had everything to do with the differences in both air forces. Whereas British, New Zealand, Australian, or South African troops knew everything about cricket, football, (field) hockey, rugby, pub life etc, Americans would know about baseball, American football, (ice)hockey and other American activities. Canadians could be expected to know them all.

For RAF: QUESTION	(ANSWER)
What is Tee Emm?	(RAF magazine)
What is a Belly Ache?	(Someone who complaints a lot)
What is a Prang?	(A forced landing)
What is Prune's rank?	(Pilot Officer)
What is a Stooge?	(Black sheep or trainee pilot)
What is an AC Plonk ?	(Lowest RAF rank)
What do you keep your fingers?	(Well out...)
What is a gong?	(Medal)
What is a Groupy?	(RAF Group Captain)

For USAAF: QUESTION	(ANSWER)
What is New York's Baseball Team?	(Yankees)
What is the Can?	(Toilet)
Who's Lou Gehrig?	(New York Yankees player)
Who played him in the movie?	(Gary Cooper)
Who uses 'Little Joe'?	(Gambler)
Who is Ma Perkins?	(Labour Secretary USA)
What is a Whimpy?	(figure from 'Funnies')
Who is Dizzy Dean?	(Baseball player)
Who said: 'Ask the man who owns one?	(Packard)
Fill in: If better (--) are build, (--) will build them.	(cars, Ford)
Fill in: The (--) who came to (--)	(man, dinner)
What is the Snorter Club?	(Club of pilots who crossed the Atlantic)
The difference between a pilot's and flight surgeon's wings?	(Gold and silver)
Who is Tail-End-Charley ?	(The last aircraft)
What is 'A Pregnant Cow'?	(B-24 Liberator)
What is a 'Clay Pigeon'?	(Pilot of C47)
What is a 'Pea Shooter'?	(P26A Fighter)
What is a 'Flying Prostitute'?	(B26 Medium Bomber)
What means PX?	(Post Exchange)
What is 'Tin Fishing'?	(Submarine hunting)
What is a 'Hangar Queen'?	(A/C with continuous maintenance problems)
What is a Monkey Suit?	(Flying Overall)
What are geets?	(Money)
What are Pinks?	(Officers uniform)

We would like to quote the late Sir Basil Embry, himself an escaper in 1940 and a man of great bravery. In his foreword to Paul Brickhill's book 'Escape or Die', Sir Basil said: 'The fact that so many RAF prisoners of war managed to escape in World War II and that so many shot-down airmen successfully evaded the enemy was due partly to escape training and partly to the efforts of thousands of civilian men, women and even children. Many of these civilians, living under a regime of terror in their own countries, helped our men with a most remarkable cold-blooded courage. Often, they risked much more than the escaping or evading airman. If the airman were caught, he would become a prisoner of war, but the civilians who helped him faced sudden death and torture.

F. List of successful transport of evaders, compiled by Comète[117].

1941

Australia:	H.E.Birk.	1	
Canada:	J.Lives, A.D.Day.	2	
UK:	L.A.Warburton H.B.Carroll, J.L.Newton, J.W.Hutton, G.T.Cox,	5	
Poland:	S.Tomicki, M.Kowalski.	2	
Scotland:	J.Cromar, B.Conville, A.G.Cowan.	3	13

1942

Australia:	R.Pearce, E.T.Heap, J.Collins, I.H.Davies, S.H.May, J.P.Haydon, G.Silva	7	
Belgium:	L.O.Prevot.	1	
Canada:	H.E.de Mone, J.B.Angers, J.H.Watons, J.A.MacLean, E.G.Price, A.E.Fay, S.P.Smith, W.H.Ledford, R.Windsor, L.E.K.Ropf, P.G.R.Freberg, R.van der.Bok,	12	
UK:	T.J.Sim, N.J.Hogan, J.McCairns, L.W.Carr, R.M.Horsley, S.E.King, L.H.Baveystock, P.Wright, B.W.Naylor, B.F.Goldsmith, B.F.Evans, W.J.Norfolk, J.T.Pack, R.Brown, E.Bradshaw, T.J.Broom, R.Frost, A.J.Whicher, J.T.Bennett, J.H.J.Dix, W.McLean, W.S.O.Randle, L.C.Pipkin, J.E.Cope, J.A.Winterbottom, J.B.Black, G.H.Mellor, A.A.Beber, H.J.Spiller, A.W.Beard, W.Palmer, E.A.Costello-Bowen, C.C.Fox, R.J.Fuller, O.Ramsden, H.S.Coombe-Tennant, N.Fairfax, D.R.Geldridge, W.Brazill, W.R.Murphy, J.E.Rainsford, R.E.Barckley,	43	
Ireland:	M.J.Joyce.	1	
Poland:	W.Czekalski, M.Zawodny, E.Siadecki, K.Rowicki, A.Wasiak, T.J.Frankowski.	6	
Russia:	P.K.Pinchouko.	1	
Scotland:	W.MacFarlane, A.Mills, J.M.L.Goldie, A.S.Barkwright.	4	
Ukraine:	A.Estadnik.	1	
USA:	D.C.Mounts, W.R.Orndorff, F.D.Hartin.	3	
Wales:	W.R.Griffiths, J.L.Griffiths.	2	81

1943

Australia:	R.G.T.Kellow, N.Parker.	2	
Belgium:	J.Clark.	1	
Canada:	J.B.Chaster, T.R.Wilby, W.Cook, B.H.Marion, R.de Pape, C.H.Witheridge, D.J.Webb, W.L.Canter, G.C.Crowther, J.P.O'Leary, J.L.Kennedy, R.S.Clements, G.I.Brownhill.	13	
UK:	A.A.Mellor, J.H.Curry, F.Wallinton, J.R.Whitley, W.S.Munns, R.J.A.Mc Leod, K.L.Rabson, D.C.Foster, C.W.Passy, G.H.Ward, K.J.Bolton, J.E.Grout, R.W.Laws, F.X.Harkins, T.A.H.Slack, A.F.Kellett, H.A.Penny, M.A.J.Pierre, H.T.Street, R.LH.Dench, G.F.Lorne, K.Garvey, R.P.Mantle, E.J.C.Johnson, W.I.Lashbrook, P.B.Smith, H.T.Hudson, G.E.Amadgett, R.C.Morley, T.Hesselden, V.W.Davies, D.Chornsey, R.W.Cornelius, F.N.Lawrence.	34	
France:	J.H.Schloesing, M.Cesar.	2	
Holland:	P.Laming.	1	
Ireland:	A.Martin, R.Clarke, E.Kinsella.	3	
New Zld:	D.A.Sibbald, R.A.Hodge, L.G.Donaldson.	3	
Norway:	J.K.B.Ræder.	1	
Poland:	A.J.Wczerzwinski, B.Malinowski.	2	
Russia:	V.Inikrasow.	1	
Scotland:	H.Reid, M.Strange, W.Todd, J.Harkins, J.Melliott.	5	

---

[117] *The names are not necessarily in order of escape.*

USA:	C.E.Cole, J.E.Williams, J.R.McKee, J.W.Spence, L.A.Funk, J.White, G.Watt, R.E.Walls, S.Devers, I.L.Fegette, W.A.Whitman, D.Coehn, W.P.Maher, E.E.Mc Taggart, G.T.Schowalter, A.L.Robertson, J.E.Wemheuer, B.M.Galleani, T.J.E.Hunt, C.A.Bennett, K.F.Fahncke, J.J.Walters, R.F.Claytor, J.F.Buice, M.F.Leszar, W.F.Crowe, M.Hager, B.A.Koenig, R.T.Conroy, J.H.P.Sarnow, J.T.Clary, J.D.McElroy, P.Shipe, J.Allen, R.D.Muir, W.Aguiar, A.T.Diminno, T.C.Shaver, L.F.Douthett, L.G.Judy, R.W.Metlen, W.Brinn, H.T.Sheets, D.A.Fry, M.G.Minnich, W.R.Hartigan, R.D.Smith, F.C.Cowherd, W.H.Booth, D.O.Mills, J.L.Connell, R.J.Nutting, D.G.Wright, L.E.Frazer, J.W.Burgin, T.E.Combs, J.L.Berry, H.C.Johnson, W.B.Whitlow, C.N.Smith, L.E.McDonald, H.Pope, E.F.Kevil, L.A.Stanford, C.L.Spicer, G.P.Gineikis, J.J.Majorca, T.B.Wiggin, J.F.Burch, H.E.Norris, J.K.Justice, W.L.House, R.Z.Grimes, T.B.Applewhite, A.J.Horning, J.T.Ashcraft,	76	
Wales:	M.A.T.Davies, J.A.M.David, W.F.Catley.	3	147

1944

Australia:	N.J.Matich, L.C.Morrison.	2	
Canada:	D.K.MacGillivray.	1	
UK:	C.J.Billows, I.Covington, F.T.Williams, W.Meddy, A.Ph.Pepper, F.D.Hill.	6	
Scotland:	W.A.Jacks.	1	
USA:	A.G.Lindsay, G.L.Hinote, R.G.Gilchrist, S.A.Lukonies, P.Gregory, B.T.Martin, R.L.G.Wilson, A.Brewer, R.Nield, C.R.Leslie, R.Mattson, A.Teitel, W.Wolff, S.Krawczynski, H.J.D.Zwonkowski, J.Dalinski, F.Wernersbach, P.Macconnell, R.E.Sheehan, N.Campbell, R.Reeves, J.D.Miller, M.D.Sheppard, T.H.Hubbard, D.K.Willis, J.D.Cornett.	26	
UK:	L.A.Barnes, R.T.Emeny.	2	38

Evaders across the Pyrenees total[118]: **279**

The Basque mountains were extremely difficult to cross. Staying away from dwellings or farms, the escapers had to endure the hardships of fleeing under the constant pressure of being captured by Germans or Spanish border guards.

This is American airman Robert Grimes who successfully evaded capture in 1943.

---

[118] *Many airmen mentioned in this list appear in the book as having met or crossed the path of our evaders.*

G. Escape and Evasion Reports.

Almost immediately after they reach friendly forces or own territory, all returned soldiers were interrogated by their Intelligence Agencies. They were to tell everything about their experiences during their combat mission, the reasons for their baling out, their experiences while alone in enemy territory, their observations, while on the ground. The reason was to get the latest news about life in Occupied Europe. However, the returned are never asked to give details about the resistance. Therefore, their reports end at the stage where the resistance finds them and begins to arrange for the evasion. The reports are also used to brief other soldiers on escape and evasion techniques. During my research the British government still held a ban over their reports. However, with the US having copies of MI.9 reports, both these and Escape and Evasion (US) Reports can be obtained at the United States Air Force Historical Research Center, Maxwell Air Force Base, Montgomery.

1. Lieutenant Colonel Thomas H. Hubbard

HQ European Theatre of Operations. P/W and X Department MIS.
E&E Report No. 802 Evasion in Holland, Belgium and France.
Target Escorting B-17's from Bremen.
Thomas H. Hubbard, Lieutenant Colonel, 0-380248.
MIA: 13 Nov 43 (22 missions) Arrived UK: 28 Jun 44 Group HQ, 355th FG.

We were escorting B-17's returning from raid on Bremen. Over Holland my engine dropped forward in the frame. The aircraft was out of balance, and the gas and oil lines broke. I got away from the bombers and bailed out at 25,000 feet, remembering that I wanted to delay my jump, but because I was blacking out, I pulled the ripcord above 20,000 feet. I came to at 10,000 feet. I was too groggy to notice much, but I looked for towns or camps. People were running toward my chute as I came down. I landed about 50 feet from a farmhouse, and three young Dutchmen rushed up. They were friendly and said this was Holland. A crowd have collected by now, took me to a farmhouse and gave me some hot milk. One of the Dutchmen spoke some English, and when I asked him for some clothes, he told me not to worry about that yet but to go into the woods and hide until dark, when I could get help at any farmhouse in the neighbourhood. I ran alone to a field about one km from the farmhouse and hid in the tall grass of a drainage ditch.

The Germans arrived very soon after that and got my chute, because the Dutchmen to whom I have given it have not taken it away yet. The people in the fields directed the Germans away from my hiding place. I was in the ditch from noon until after dark. I went back to the original farmhouse then and met again one of the young Dutchmen who have befriended me from the first. He was hiding from the Germans to avoid a labour camp and took me to a prepared hiding place. I slept there three nights while the Germans searched the area systematically, and then my friend moved me to a house from where my journey was arranged. Appendix to E and E Report No. 802. Statement of information covering the period from 13 Nov 43 to 18 Jun 44.

a) In early December, the evader saw a large airfield 1 km E of Venlo. It was one of the largest and best in the area. There was a dummy field a few km N of the large field. The dummy field have lights and a presentable runway. It has been bombed several times, but not the main field which was well camouflaged. There was a monastery near the large main field.

b) Philips factory at Eindhoven was being repaired, ready to be back in operation. (Dec 1943).

c) Belgian source stated that there was an important target at Neerpelt: three bridges over a canal ± 1 km from Neerpelt toward Hamont: one railroad bridge and two road bridges. Heavy troop movements and supplies were carried over the RR bridge.

d) A large German H.q. on Rue Van der Kindere in Brussels was pointed out to the evader.

e) German troops in Belgium were not front line troops, according to evader.

f) Belgians said Germans were buying property in Belgium to live there after the war.

g) The food situation in Belgium was acute. The only good food obtainable seemed to be in the black market. There seemed to be much tuberculosis.

h) AA fire over Brussels is heavy and accurate (March 1944).

Remarks:

1. AIDS BOX: I had little need for the aids box. I used the Benzedrine tablets when crossing the Pyrenees. All items were satisfactory.
2. I do suggest the addition of a small toothbrush to the first aid box.
3. PURSE: I carried a red purse and turned the contents over to helpers.
4. PHOTOGRAPHS: I have five passport photographs and used two.
5. LECTURES: I heard evasion lectures by Group intelligence officers. The lectures were helpful.
6. SUGGESTION: From my experience I suggest evaders always do as they are told by helpers and that they force themselves to be patient.

2. Leonard A. Barnes, Pilot Officer

MI.9/S/P.G. (-) 2000. The information contained in this report is to be treated as SECRET.
Statement by Pilot Officer Leonard Alfred Barnes, 630 Squadron, Bomber Command RAF.

Left: Gibraltar 24 Jun 44	Arrived: Whitchurch 25 Jun 44
Date of Birth: 22 Feb 20	Peacetime Profession: Printer
R.A.F Service: 17 Jun 40	Private address: 122 Upper North Street
O.T.U.: No. 17 (Silverstone)	Poplar, LONDON
C.U: No.1654 (Wigsley)	Post in crew: Pilot

Other Members of the Crew:

F/O. Griesler (navigator)	(Believed P/W)
Sgt. Gregg (bomb aimer)	(Believed P/W)
Sgt. Plowman (wireless op.)	(Believed P/W)
Sgt. Walker (engineer)	(Believed P/W)
Sgt. Overshot (m-u gunner)	(Killed)
Sgt. Fox (rear gunner)	(Killed)

We took off from East Kirkby in a Lancaster aircraft at 1830 hrs on 15 March 44 to bomb Stuttgart. We bombed the target successfully, but on the return journey we were attacked by a night fighter just west of Rheims. The oxygen supply system and the hydraulics were damaged, while two gunners and the navigator were wounded. I found it difficult to take evasive action, as the rudder control was also damaged, and at the second attack I gave the order to prepare to abandon aircraft. I dived down to 12,000 ft. when the fighter came in a third attack. At the fourth attack both the starboard engines were hit, and I gave the order to abandon aircraft. I could get no reply from either of the gunners and was the fifth to jump out at 0130 hrs (16 Mar). I landed in a field about 4 miles NE of Dravegny. I buried my parachute, Mae West, harness and the tops of my flying boots, and started to walk South West by my compass. A mile further on I saw a parachute hanging from a tree. I dragged it clear and buried it, but I forgot to look for the name on the chute. A short while later I reached Dravegny and walked through the town. I found some water and drank it, but I did not stop to fill my bottle, as a dog started to bark and I thought I have better get away at once.

I continued across the field to Cohan (T0376), which I reached about 0530 hrs (16 Mar). In the distance I saw a farmer leading his horses towards a farm. I waited until he had gone into the house, when I entered a barn and hid under the hay. At 1030 hrs, when I thought there was no one about, I came out of my hiding place and took out my maps. I was looking at them when a man appeared and, as he had seen me, I declared myself to him and asked for help. He brought me food and drink and allowed me to bath my eye, which I have hurt as I bailed out. Two more men appeared and showed me my position on the map. I returned to the barn, and at 1500 hrs a young girl, who could speak English, came to see me. She questioned me closely and examined my kit. She left shortly afterwards, saying that she would send a friend to see me that evening. That evening a man came for me, and from this point my journey was arranged for me.

3. Donald K. Willis, Major

Headquarters European Theatre of Operations. P/W and X Department MIS. E&E Report No.800. Evasion in Holland, Belgium and France.
Target: Bombing Mission (P-38) Aerodrome in Germany. Donald K. Willis, Major 0-885159.
MIA: 10 Apr 44 (86 missions) Arrived in UK: 28 Jun 44. Headquarters 67 Fighter Wing.

I crash-landed on the coast of Holland near the Walcheren Islands after one engine have been hit by flak. I put the P-38 down between a football field where a game was in progress and a dike. A wing struck one of the dikes and smashed the aircraft. Spectators and players were running from the football field when I got out of the plane. At least 500 people were milling about the crash and along the dikes. I ran to the path where the people have left their bicycles and took one, grabbing with it a long red coat to throw over my flying jacket and green trousers. The coat had ten guilders and a watch in the pocket. I got in among some cyclists on the path at the top of the dike and pedalled toward the German soldiers who were running from a nearby gun post. The soldiers were busy for the first few minutes trying to keep people away from the plane though several climbed on the dikes and searched the countryside with field glasses. I pedalled beside a woman who kept watching me out of the corner of her eye but never spoke.

When we rode into a small village the woman turned down a side street. I parked the bicycle by a stone bench and sat there trying to think out my next move. A carload of German soldiers drove into the village and stopped in front of the church. They got out, lined up in two ranks, and were sent into the fields with dogs to search. I walked around the town waiting for them to get some distance away before following the route taken by one of the parties. After they searched a barn, I crawled in thinking it was the safest place to hide at the moment. A woman who owned the barn saw me and she hurried out to tell me I not to stay there. I have little trouble understanding her because I speak Norwegian, which is somewhat similar to Dutch. She promised me not to tell that I had been there unless the Germans came back. I crawled down a drainage ditch to a field of high grass and hid for the rest of the day. I then was approached by a man who gestured me to follow him, which I did. He took me to his house where I met the rest of his family. They gave me some food, hot milk and some money. I stayed there until late at night. When it was dark, the man warned me that he was going to take me somewhere else. I was given a coat. We then walked away from the village I checked my compass and we walked cross-country in a SW direction. It was not easy walking because of the many dikes and fences.

The man pointed to the south and then left me to myself. At midnight I stopped to rest at a barbed wire entanglement and was just missed by three German soldiers walking along a footpath. I thought they were a searching party and I did not move until I discovered they were the relief for a small gun post that I have nearly stumbled into. I went towards a group of buildings to see if I could find a place to sleep. A young boy and girl hailed me as I started to crawl into a haystack, and after some difficulty I convinced them that I was an American airman. I waited at the haystack while the boy took the girl home. He returned with food and said he would walk with me. He knew the country well and by 0800 hours we have reached Roosendaal. My friend turned back then after giving me excellent directions. There were some German strong points to be avoided but I was shown how to get around these. I was helped by traffic signs put up by the Germans. I found the road to Antwerp and followed it, keeping to a safe distance in the fields.

Around noon I reached Esschen. I passed many people but so far have not spoken to anyone. At the edge of Esschen I saw Germans on duty at a control post and stopped an old woman to ask her how I could pass this barrier. She mentioned that I should go around the control. I went into a wood for the afternoon and hid where I could watch the people working in the fields. When they finished work, I followed some of them along a small road into the town. There was either no control post here or the workers going to their homes in the evening were not checked.

I found the Railroad on the other side of Esschen and walked parallel to it until dark, when I made my bed in a straw stack. I walked steadily all the next day, avoiding towns and speaking to no one. Twice I ran into German officers hunting in the fields but each time I hid before they could see me. I arrived at

Antwerp in the afternoon and tried to get around it before dark but I picked the wrong direction and ran into water. In retracing my steps, I walked into a German AA battery and the soldier on sentry duty motioned me away. At dark I crawled into a haystack but I could not sleep because of the cold. Before daylight I went up to a farmhouse and got the farmer out of bed, but he would not open the door. Finally, he said to come back in the daytime. I waited for him to get up because there were no telephone wires to the house and I did not see how he could notify anyone of my presence. He gave me some food and asked no questions. I went into Antwerp that morning, having decided to ask someone how to get through town. I stopped at a store where a man was loafing in the doorway, and after I started talking, he asked if I was an American and took me inside. He gave me 230 Francs and, after assuring that he liked Americans, told me I could ride a streetcar to the southern end of Antwerp for one Franc and without too much risk. He gave me good directions for doing this and when I have got outside of the town, I stopped at a roadside cafe to get some beer. There was a sign advertising 'Bock' beer, so I put down a Franc note and said, 'Bock'.

The few people in the cafe paid no attention to me, but the Belgian who gave me the beer guessed my identity. I was taken into a back room and given some eggs and bread, but not a word was spoken to me. Just as I was leaving the Belgian brushed off some straw that was clinging to my back and smiled while doing it. I started to Brussels, following the RR line, but got on the wrong tracks. Because I have more confidence now and felt some desperation about getting help, I went into a small railway station and tried to buy a ticket to Brussels. There was only a porter in the station and he explained that I was following about the only RR in Belgium that did not go to Brussels. He wanted to know if I have parachuted and said he knew an English speaking person. He went to see this person who said I would be helped, but while I was eating someone came in and said the police have been informed. I ran out the back door and got away from the place without seeing any activity.

I arrived at Boom about mid-afternoon. The RR and road bridge were controlled by sentries and many people were being checked as they crossed. I was afraid, because only those people recognized by the guards did not have to show papers. Not having found a way to cross by dark I found a haystack to sleep in that night. The next morning, I watched some labourers carrying poles across the bridge. After they have done this several times, I saw the guards were not paying any attention to them. My opportunity came when two women stopped to talk to the guards and while their attention was diverted, I went up to one of the labour groups and hitched onto the pole they were carrying. The men looked at me but said nothing. I walked to the woods where the men were sticking the poles and found that their work was directed by a German soldier with a rifle. At first, I thought he was a guard, but he was paying too little attention to the workers. I was not sure how I could get away without arousing the German's curiosity and was pretending to work when a peddler arrived with an ice-cream cart.

I crowded with the workers, put down a 5 Franc note and walked off while the German was arguing with someone and have his back to me. In the afternoon I stopped at a small cafe to buy a glass of beer and was followed out by a man who waited until we were alone before asking if I was not an American. When I admitted it and asked what he was going to do about it he said he would like to help. From there my journey was arranged. During my evasion while I was living in a large Belgian city, I watched an American raid on a nearby target. I saw a B-17 catch fire and leave formation. Soon after that several parachutes opened above the city and one floated down into the section of town where I was. I have a good view of it and watched this parachutist land in a walled-in garden of a house. Just as he touched the ground a German motorcyclist stopped in front of the house and ran around to climb over the garden wall at the back. When the German returned to the front door, the American burst through the front door of the house, hopped on the German's motorcycle and tore off down the street blowing his horn as loud as he could and cheered on by the Belgian people.

Unfortunately, although I saw the start of his evasion, I never learned how he made out, nor did I find out who he was. Comment: 'This brilliant evasion was made possible by a split-second appraisal of the situation and immediate action It is a commonplace of evasion that if a man can elude search parties for the first hour or two, he is well on his way out. Comment: Major Willis' intelligent application of unorthodox briefing is well worth study.

Appendix E&E Report 800.

AIDS BOX: I rationed the Horlick's tablets and chocolate bar to cover a period of four days. I also used the matches, adhesive tape, chewing gum and compass.

PURSE: I carried a purse containing 2000 French Francs.

I gave this money to helpers and used the maps of France, Holland and Spain.

PHOTOGRAPHS: I have three escape photographs and used them.

LECTURES: I have been lectured on evasion at Debden; information given was very valuable.

4. Jack D. Cornett, 2nd Lieutenant.

Headquarters European Theatre of Operations. P/W and X Department MIS. E&E Report No.819. Evasion in France. Target: Strafing on Fighter Sweep. Jack D. Cornett 2nd Lt, 0-816632 MIA: 28 APR 44. 375 Ftr Sq., 361 Ftr Group (3 missions). Arrived in UK: 30 Jun 44

I strafed an airfield in France and in doing so must have been hit by flak, for my plane began to leak oil and would not climb higher than 1000 feet. The plane soon burst into flames, and I bailed out. I landed in a field, hid my chute and flying equipment in a clump of bushes, and walked southwards across country at once. It was about 0900 hrs when I started, and I encountered no one until the afternoon. Then a man working in the fields came over to me as I walked by and made motions for me to hide. I obeyed him, and he returned with food and wine for me. He talked to me but I could not understand him; and so, after he have brought me more food, I took off again.

I walked until midnight and then lay down to sleep in a field. When I awoke the next morning I felt ill, and so I entered the first barn that I found and went to sleep. At 0900 hrs a child found me. He ran for his mother who, when she discovered my identity, brought me food at once and then hid me in a root-cellar because there were Germans in the neighbourhood. That night the family brought civilian clothes to my hiding place; and early the next morning I hurried off into a wood. I walked through the wood all day and at nightfall came to the edge of a village. There I reconnoitred a house, which I finally approached. When I declared myself to the people there and asked for food, they took me inside and told me to wait. In a few minutes they brought in a man who could speak English and who assured me that I was in safe hands. From there my journey was arranged.

Appendix to E & E Report No 819. Statement of Information from 28 Apr 44 to 20 Jun 44.

a) On the roads and in the fields around Pithiveirs many German troops were seen engaged in training exercises (Observation 30 Apr 44).

b) Along the eastern side of the Paris-Orleans railway line from the outskirts of Paris to a point 20 miles S of the city there are many 5-inch field guns in revetment with net camouflage (Observ. 1 May 44)

c) RAF bombing of the Orleans railway yard was an excellent job. The station and yards were thoroughly demolished (Observation 27 May 44)

1. AIDS BOX: I used the peanut bars, Halazone tablets, matches, chewing gum, compass, and sewing kit. The water bottle was useless.

2. PURSE: I have a red purse and used the 2000 Francs to pay my guide.

3. PHOTOGRAPHS: I have 6 photographs, which were used for French papers.

4. LECTURES: I heard lectures on evasion given by S-2 officers at Fort Myers, Florida, and at my Base in UK. They were of value to me.

5. John Pittwood, Flight Sergeant.

MI.9/S/P.G.(-)1988. The information contained in this report is to be treated as SECRET.
Statement by 1219454 F/Sgt. Pittwood, John. 207 Squadron, Bomber Command, RAF

Left: GIBRALTAR 23 Jun 44   Arrived UK: 24 Jun 44

Date of Birth: 07 Oct 23   Peacetime Profession: School

RAF Service: Since Jan 42   Private Address: 59 Coles Lane

OTU: 28 (Wymeswold) Hilltop, West Bromwich Conversion Unit: 1661 (Winthorpe)

Post in crew: Navigator

Other Members of the Crew:
W/O. Lissette, L.H.RNZAF (pilot)   (no information)
Sgt. Ellis, R. (rear gunner)   (no information)
Sgt. Emeny, R. (m.u. gunner)   (in SPAIN)
Sgt. Wesley L. (bomb aimer)   (bailed out)
Sgt. King, P.N. (wireless operator)   (bailed out)
Sgt. Stockford, N. (engineer)   (bailed out)

I was navigator of a Lancaster aircraft, which left Spilsby on 3 May, 44 at about 2220 hrs to bomb Mailly-le-Camp (NW Europe 1:250,000, sheet 8, T3813). On leaving the target we were intercepted by fighters, and the port out motor was put out of action. We were able to continue, but just south of Paris we were attacked again. The aircraft caught fire, and we were ordered to jump out at 0040 hrs. I came down in a ploughed field in the neighbourhood of Rossieres (France 1:250,000, Sheet 16, X3371). My mid upper gunner, Sgt. Emeny, joined me within five minutes. We pushed our parachutes, Mae Wests and harness into a hedge and started to walk South. We crossed a railway and a road and when we reached a wood, we took off our badges of rank and then we continued South. At daybreak we found ourselves East of a small town. As Emeny was rather severely burnt, we decided to approach a farm. At about 0500 hrs we knocked on the door of one, which we later discovered was very near Griselles (X3454). The farmer hid us in a loft and gave us some oil for Emeny's face. We stayed all day (4 May) in the loft. Early on 5 May Emeny became worse and we decided that we should have to try to find a doctor. We approached the farmer, who told us that a doctor nearby was not a collaborator. We therefore went to him, and from this point we were put into touch with an organisation, which helped us.

6. Ronald T. Emeny, Sergeant.
MI.9/S/P.G.(-)2001. The information contained in this report is to be treated as SECRET.
Statement by 1383167 Sgt. Emeny, Ronald Thomas, 207 Squadron, Bomber Command, RAF.

Left: Gibraltar 24 Jun 44   Arrived: Whitchurch, 25 Jun 44
Date of Birth: 06 Sep 23   Peacetime Profession: Mechanic
RAF Service: Since 23 Jul 41   Private Address: 30 Manton Road
O.T.U.: No. 28 Wymeswold   Abbey Wood, London S.E.2
Conv. Unit: No.1661Wynthorpe.   Post in crew: Mid-upper gunner.

Other Members of the Crew:
W/O. Lissette (pilot)   (no information)
F/Sgt. Pittwood (navigator)   (S/P.G.(-)1988)
Sgt. Ellis (rear gunner)   (no information)
Sgt. Wesley (bomb aimer)   (bailed out)
Sgt. King (Wireless operator)   (bailed out) and
Sgt. Stockford (engineer)   (bailed out).

My flight and experiences are the same as those of F/Sgt. Pittwood (S/P.G.(-)1988) up to the time we received help from an organisation.

Post-war career of Ron Emeny:
January 1945 No.3 AGS Castle Kennedy. March 1945 Manby 68AG(1) course EAAS.
March 1946 46 MU Lossiemouth, HMS Fulmar. April 1946 207 Squadron Stradishall.
1947 met WAAF Telephonist Jessie Owen; April 1948: married Jessie Owen.
February 1949 207 move to Mildenhall. May 1950 No.4 Radio School, Swanton Morley.
March 1951 CXX Squadron, Kinloss. April 1952 To Aldergrove with CXX Squadron.
March 1953 Joint Anti-Submarine Flight, HMS Sea Eagle, Londonderry.
January 1954 1 ANS Hullavington. May 1954 2 ANS Thorney Island.
March 1957 1 ANS Topcliffe: awarded AFM. October 1958 236 OCU Gaydon, AEO V Force.
March 1959 18 Squadron Finningley. November 1963 32 MU St Athans: V Force Test Flight.
December 1964 Beverley Conversion Course: Air Engineer.
1965 Left the Service not wishing a ground posting to Northwood.

H. Service records of Donald Kenyon Willis.

Born: 07 August 1911 at Marion, Westfork, Marion County, Indiana, United States of America.

Occupation: Owner of Furniture Factory.

Service Record Finland and Norway:

18 Feb 1940 : Entered Finland at Tornioon.
20 Feb 1940 : Volunteer-Corporal/Pilot with 2nd Air Regiment Finnish Air Force.
22 Apr 1940 : Fled Finland to Norway.
28 Apr 1940 : Entered Norway at Kirkenes.
28 Apr 1940 : Reported to 14th Infantry Regiment 'Sörland' at Mosjöen.
05 May 1940 : Reported at Flatoya/Bergen Naval Air Station as Volunteer Quartermaster,
07 May 1940 : Flying with FA2 (2.Flyafdeling) as co-pilot and air gunner on Heinkel He-115s.
08 Jun 1940 : Ordered to evade capture with aircraft and fly to Shetland Islands, Great Britain.
08 Jun 1940 : Landed at Sollum Voe, Shetland Islands with Heinkel He-115 of NNAF.
09 Jun 1940 : Arrived at MAEE RAF Helensburgh.
?? July 1940 : Departed for Canada with Norwegian military on board MV Iris.
20 Aug 1941 : Convicted to nine months imprisonment for bigamy.

Service record Great Britain:

25 Aug 1941 : Granted a commission as a Pilot Officer serial number 105136 on probation in the GD Branch of the Royal Air Force (Volunteer Reserve) for the duration of hostilities
25 Aug 1941 : No.3 Reception Centre, supy
29 Aug 1941 : No.50 Group (Pool), supy, flying training No.8 Elementary Flying Training School.
29 Aug 1941 : No.53 Operational Training Unit.
05 Nov 1941 : Married Martha Catherina McNicol at Holy Trinity Church, Saint Andrews, Fyfe, while living at Brae House, Helensburgh, Dunbartonshire, Scotland.
31 Mar 1942 : No.61 Operational Flying Unit, flying.
02 Jun 1942 : No.121 Eagle Squadron Royal Air Force, flying.
19 Aug 1942 : Posted to RAF Rochford, Southend, supy, posted overseas, flying.
25 Aug 1942 : Conformed in appointment and promoted to Flying Officer (War substantive.)
23 Sept 1942 : Relinquished commission on appointment to a commission in the USAAC.

Service record United States Army Air Corps, US Army Air Force, US Air Force.

23 Sep 1942 : Granted commission as a 1st Lieutenant/Flying (temporary) in the US Army Air Corps, serial number 0885159 for the duration of hostilities.
29 Sep 1942 : Posted to 355th (Pursuit) Squadron, 4th Fighter Group, Station 358, Debden.
xx xxx 1943 : Posted to HQ 67th Fighter Wing as Tactics Evaluation Officer, Walcott Hall.
10 Apr 1944 : Force-landed at Oud-Gastel, Netherlands after Droop Snoot mission against Gütersloh.
12 Apr 1944 : Start of evasion south via Antwerp and Brussels to Paris.
4/6 Jun 1944 : Passage of Pyrenees from Laressore to Pamplona.
06 Jun 1944 : News of D-Day while in Pamplona.
23 Jun 1944 : Departure to Madrid.
25 Jun 1944 : Entry into Gibraltar.
01 Jul 1944 : Return to Duty in Britain.
xx Jun 1945 : Officer Commanding Hörsching Air Base, Austria
xx xxx 1947 : Married Patricia Giles in Mexico.
xx xxx 1947 : Officer Commanding Fürstenfeldbruck Air Base, Bavaria Germany
xx xxx 1950 : Involved in JATO experiments at Wright-Patterson Air base, Dayton Ohio,
xx xxx xxxx : Retired, joined merchant navy.
27 Apr 1977 : Died in Ocala Florida USA.

Examples of documents: Top: MI9 interrogation of Sgt John Pittwood. Right: June 1945 communication of the RNZAF HQ about the whereabouts of the crash and graves of W/O Leslie Lissette.

I. Information about Thomas H. Hubbard.

Thomas H. Hubbard attended North Texas Agricultural College from 1931-1933 and was a member of the Reserve Officers Training Corps where he attained the rank of Cadet Captain and Company Commander. He started a career in military and civilian aviation in 1933. While working in the field of banking, real estate and mortgages, he pursued an interest in flying in his spare time. He first soloed in 1934. He attended the Ryan School of Aeronautics in San Diego, Ca. in 1937. He graduated, gaining a pilot's license as well as an airplane and engine mechanics licence one in May 1938, and in 1937, and obtained licenses in aircraft mechanics and private piloting. He enlisted in the U.S.A.A.C. at San Diego, California, in June of 1938, as a flying cadet and went to Randolph Field, Texas. Hubbard graduated as a Second Lieutenant, U.S. Army Air Corps at Kelly Field, Texas 26 May 1939. After enlisting in the Air Corps at San Diego on 25 June 1938, he started fighter pilot training at Randolph Field in Texas. After graduating at Kelly Field, TX on 26 May 1939, he was assigned to the 20th Pursuit Group at Barksdale Field, LA and flew P-36s. The Group moved to Moffett Field, CA in November 1939. A few weeks later, as the Group was split in two, he joined the 20th Pursuit Squadron of the 35th Pursuit Group at Hamilton Field, CA. Hubbard flew both fighters and bombers in various commands prior to the outbreak of World War II.

The 20th Pursuit left for the Philippine Islands in October 1940 and Hubbard was transferred to the 28th Bomb Squadron, based at Clark Field on Luzon Island. On 7 December 1941, he was at Clark Field, the Philippines with the 28th Bomber Squadron. After spending two months on Bataan, he joined a task force to New Caledonia. He flew 35 missions in P-39 aircraft in the Pacific Theatre. Major Hubbard was awarded the Silver Star for Gallantry in Action while serving in support of the U.S. Marine Corps near Guadalcanal, Solomon Island, during the period October 6-14, 1942, he flew B-10 and B-18 bombers until the Pacific War started. He spent 2 months on Bataan and the Island of Mindanao, then was sent to Australia where he piloted P-40s until he joined a Task Force heading for New Caledonia. There, he

LtCol Tom Hubbard's three Republic P47D Thunderbolt aircraft were
1.) 42-8404 P-47D 354FS, WR-P Lil' Jo, crash landed 5 Nov 1943,
   353FG, repaired.
2.) 42-8444 P-47D 354FS, WR-P Lil' Jo no information about this a/c.
3.) 42-7944 P-47D 353FGHQ, WR-P Lil' Jo.
Lost in this a/c on 13 Nov 1943. He crashed in Holland.

became 67th Fighter Squadron Operations Officer, flying P-40s. After a short period as Commander of the 67th FS, he took a detachment of the Squadron to Guadalcanal in September 1942, participating to the fighting there for two weeks and earned the Silver Star for gallantry in action during this period. Hubbard had a total of 33 missions in New Caledonia, Guadalcanal and elsewhere in the South Pacific, flying P-400s and P-40s.

Upon returning to the US in November 1942, he was Group Training Officer in the 326th Operational Training Group at Wendover Field, where training flights were made on P-47s. Tom Hubbard was assigned to the 355th Fighter Group as Deputy Commander. In May 1943, Hubbard became the Deputy Commander in the 355th Fighter Group and left on mid-June with the Group's advance echelon to the European Theatre of Operations. The 355th FG was assigned to the 8th AF on 6 July 1943, so he again departed for combat, now in the Europe. Soon Hubbard started flying missions with the Group. He was on his 21st mission on 13 November 1943, taking off from Bungay (not from the 355th base of Steeple Morden) in P-47D 42-7944 with his Group escorting 8th AF bombers returning from Bremen when his plane's engine dropped forward in its frame. With his aircraft off balance and the gas and oil lines broken, he got away from the bombers and bailed out at 25,000ft.

After his landing by parachute in Holland, he was helped in his evasion by Dutch, Belgian and French citizens and other Resistance members. Clothed, fed and sheltered in many places, he was led from the Netherlands to Brussels, Belgium, then to the South of France via Paris, Bayonne, Saint-Jean-de-Luz. He crossed into Spain over the Pyrenees mountains with guides and other evaders on 4 June 1944. Once he was safe with his own countrymen has was driven to Madrid in a diplomatic car, and arrived there on 24 June. He was then taken to Gibraltar and flew back from that British base to England on 27 June 1944, landing at Bristol the following day. Colonel Hubbard then served in various military assignments in Europe until 28 June 1951, when he resigned from the USAF to work with the Civil Aeronautics Administration. Colonel Hubbard served with the Civil Aeronautics Administration in the capacities of Air Traffic Controller, Supervisor, and Liaison with US Military Aviation from 28 June 1951 until his subsequent retirement from the Federal Civil Service sector on 31 December 1973. His decorations included the Silver Star, the Distinguished Flying Cross, the Air Medal with Cluster, the Purple Heart, a Distinguished Unit Citation, a Presidential Unit Badge (Navy), the Guadalcanal, and other medals and awards. Colonel Hubbard's great aviation career as an aerial warrior in WWII and as a civilian guardian of U.S. airways brought great distinction to himself, the University of Texas at Arlington, the USAF, and the Civil Aeronautics Administration.

J. Targets on the day the evaders came down.
The last sorties of the five evaders and their aircrew tells us about the dangers they encountered and the fears that were around them. They faced dangers and sometimes endured great perils in a hostile world.

13 November 1943 Bremen – LtCol Hubbard
By the end of 1943, the number of USAAF daylight bombing raids on Germany grew. The 8th Air Force suffered heavy losses in October, beginning with the Marienburg Raid. They were hitting the targets but the accompanying losses were unsustainable, especially on the second Schweinfurt raid on 14th October when they lost 26% of the bombing aircraft. On 13th November they introduced a new tactic when they were accompanied by P-38 Lightning and P-47 Thunderbolt fighters on the 750 mile round trip to Bremen. This was to be the key development in providing the protection that the bombers needed over

Germany. Until then the fighters had only accompanied the bombers out or met them on the return journey. This was a new and little-tested strategy which would not be solved until the arrival of the long range P-51 Mustang at the end of 1943. Mission 130 was aimed at the docks of Bremen. About 270 aircraft detailed to attack. Only 79 of 159 B-17s, 61 of 109 B-24s and 3 of 4 B-17 PFF aircraft hit the port area at Bremen and targets of opportunity in the Kiel-Flensburg area 1120–1145 hours. More than 100 aircraft aborted the mission due to weather; they claimed 20-14-13 Luftwaffe aircraft; 3 B-17s and 13 B-24s lost; 3 B-17s and 3 B-24s damaged beyond repair. 12 B-17s and 10 B-24s damaged, but could be repaired. The number of casualties were 21 KIA, 26 WIA and 162 MIA. The bombers were escorted by 45 P-38s (all the way to the target) and 345 P-47's; they claimed 10-3-6 Luftwaffe aircraft; 7 P-38s and 3 P-47s lost; one of them was P-47D number 42-7944, WR-P of Lt Col Tom Hubbard. Further 2 P-38s damaged beyond repair; 5 P-38s and 2 P-47s damaged but could be repaired. The number of fighter casualties was 9 MIA.

15/16 March 1944 Stuttgart – P/O Barnes and crew

Lancaster III ND530 LE–P for Peter. No.630 Squadron. Take off East Kirby 1912 hrs. Pilot Officer L.A. Barnes (evaded); Sergeant K.A. Walker (evaded); Flying Officer M. Geisler (pow); Sergeant M.E. Gregg (pow); Sergeant G.E. Plowman (pow); Sergeant J.H. Overholt RCAF (killed); Sergeant T.A. Fox (killed). ND530 was shot down by a night fighter, whose first pass killed both air gunners. Abandoned and left to crash at Saint Gilles (Marne) on the west bank of the Ardre River, some 24 kms west of Reims. Sgts Overholt RCAF and Fox are buried at Saint Gilles Church yard. Diversion attacks to Amiens (140 a/c) and Woppy (22 a/c) Raid carried out by 863 aircraft, 617 Lancasters, 230 Halifaxes and 16 Mosquitoes. The German fighter controller split his forces into two parts. Bombers flew a course over France as close as the Swiss border, before turning NE to Stuttgart. This delayed German fighters but during the battle that followed just before reaching Stuttgart, fierce fighting cost the RAF 37 aircraft (27 Lancasters and 10 Halifaxes, 4.3 per cent of the force. Two of the Lancasters landed in Switzerland. Adverse winds delayed to opening of the attack and the same winds may have been the cause of the Pathfinder marking falling back well short of the target, despite the clear skies. Some bombs fell in the town centre but most fell in open country southwest. People killed: 88, 203 wounded.

10 April 1944 USAF Droopsnoot against Gütersloh – Maj Willis

Mission 296: Three forces on fighter-bomber missions; all include P-38 Droopsnoot aircraft: 39 P-38s dispatched to attack Florennes/Juzaine AF, Belgium; no losses or claims. 51 P-38s and 7 P-47s to attack St Dizier, France; primary is cloud covered, 16 P-38s attack Coulommiers AF, France; 2 P-38s lost 1 damaged; 2 pilots MIA; P-47s claim 2-0-1 Luftwaffe a/c on the ground. 28 P-38s and 46 P-47s to bomb Gutersloh AF, Germany: 1 P-38 lost, pilot MIA. (*Willis, HO*). Mission 297: 5 of 5 B-17s drop 2 million leaflets on Lille, Le Mans, Chartres, Reims and Orleans at 2212-2258 hours local without loss. 23 B-24s on Carpetbagger operations.

27 April 1944 USAF Bomber escort and suppression of German fighters – 2Lt Cornett

Mission 323: 486 bombers and 543 fighters dispatched to bomb airfields, marshalling yards and targets of opportunity in France and Belgium; 4 bombers and 4 fighters are lost.168 B-17s dispatched to bomb Nancy/Essay Airfield (103 bomb) and Toul/Croix de Metz landing ground (60 bomb), France; 2 B-17s lost, 33 damaged; 20 airmen MIA. Of 120 B-17s, 98 bomb Le Culot Airfield, 20 bomb Middelkerke / Ostend Airfield, Belgium; 2 B-17s lost, 29 damaged; 1 airman KIA, 20 MIA. Of 198 B-24s, 118 bomb Blainville sur l'Eau marshalling yard and 72 bomb Chalons sur Marne marshalling yard, France; 2 B-24s damaged beyond repair, 22 damaged; casualties 24 KIA, 6 WIA, 1 MIA. Escort provided by 106 P-38s, 283 P-47s and 154 P-51s; they claim 3-0-1 Luftwaffe aircraft in the air and 4-0-5 on the ground; 4 P-47s lost, 2 P-47s and 1 P-51 are damaged; 3 airmen MIA. One of these P-47s is 0-816632. AAF Bottisham. 375th Fighter Squadron 361st Fighter Group. Jack Cornett flew P-47D Thunderbolt, serial number 42-75219, E2-G. His aircraft was hit by Flak while he was strafing Étampes-Mondésir airfield in France on 27 April 1944. He landed near the hamlet of Arrancourt, south of Paris.

03/04 May 1944 Mailly-le-Camp – W/O Lissette and crew

Lancaster III EM F-Freddie, No.207 Squadron. Take off Spilsby 2203 hrs. Warrant Officer L.H. Lissette RNZAF (killed); Sergeant N.J. Stockford (evaded); Flight Sergeant J. Pittwood (evaded); Sergeant L. Wesley (prisoner of war); Sergeant P.N. King (evaded); Sergeant R.T. Emeny (evaded); Sergeant R. Ellis (killed). Badly shot up by a night fighter after bombing the target and shaking off their attacker. Then a second fighter attacked and the Lancaster went down near Chaintreaux (Seine et Marne), 12 kms SE of Nemours. W/O Lissette RNZAF killed. Buried Chaintreaux Communal Cemetery with Sergeant Ellis. Diversion attacks against Mondidier airfield with 84 Lancasters and 8 Mosquitoes, Attacks on Ludwigshafen, Chateaudun, mine laying and SOE mission, in total with 598 aircraft. The raid by 362 aircraft, 346 Lancasters, 16 Mosquitoes. It was a costly raid. The RAF lost 42 Lancasters, 11.6 % of the force. It was found that part of the losses was due to lack of control of the raid. While the marker leader Wing Commander Cheshire ordered the main force to some in and bomb the main force controller Wing Commander Deane, was unable to transmit the order to the aircraft. At that moment US forces broadcasts drowned RAF communications and caused arriving German fighters to kill the bombers. The main attack began when deputy controller Squadron Leader Sparks took over. Some 1,500 tons of bombs were dropped with great accuracy. It caused the destruction of 114 barrack buildings, 47 sheds and ammunition buildings. 102 vehicles and 37 new tanks were destroyed, 218 German soldiers killed and 156 wounded. Squadron Leader Sparks' own Lancaster was shot down but he evaded capture.

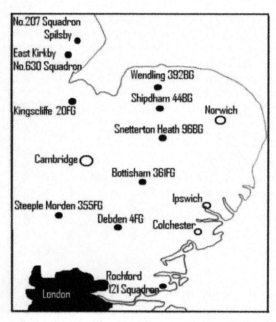

The locations of some airfields mentioned in this book.

Rochford: No.121 Eagle Sqn RAF. P/O Willis.
Debden: 4th FG 1st Lt Willis.
13 November 1943. Shipdham: 44BG Liberator 4207650.
Wendling: 392BG B-24 Liberator 42748.,
Snetterton Heath: 96BG B-24 Liberator 4237830.
Steeple Morden: 355FG. P47D 42-7944.
LtCol Hubbard.
15 March 1944 East Kirkby: No.630 Squadron.
Lancaster ND530 P for Peter. P/O Barnes, F/O Griesler, Sgt Gregg, Sgt Plowman, Sgt Walker, Sgt Fox, Sgt Overholt RCAF.
10 April 1944 Kingscliffe: 20th FG P38J 42-68077 KI-X Major Willis.
27 April 1944 Bottisham: 361st FG P47D 42-75219 E2-G. 2Lt Cornett.
3 May 1944: Spilsby: No.207 Squadron. Lancaster ND556 F for Freddie, W/O Lissette RNZAF, F/S Pittwood, Sgt Emeny, Sgt Stockford, Sgt King, Sgt Ellis, Sgt Wesley.

K. Letters written by relatives and airmen who were shot down over Europe.

'There is nothing worse than to see the lad from the post office walking to the door, handing you the dreaded telegram, mumble something and hurrying away. You take it from him, walk to the living room and open the message with trembling hands, while the rest of the family sat waiting in horror for what you were about to read. 'Deeply regret to inform you that your (husband/son) (name) was reported missing as a result of an air operation on the night of (date).'

Then, there would be total silence, or a scream that cut through the heart like a knife, someone would swear, run out of the house, or just look at the others. My parents told me they will never forget these few minutes. Then, there would be the question 'is he alive and well? Is he badly wounded in a German hospital? Is he a prisoner? Will we see him again one day, healthy, crippled, or will we go to his grave in a foreign country?' These remarks come from one of these family members, who had to accept the loss of a brother. It is amazing to read how the families of a crew supported each other after the news came that answered one or all of the above questions.

It started with a telegram, soon followed by letters giving more information about the airman and if possible, of fellow crewmembers. Then followed a list of belongings of the airman, in this case Sgt. Ken Walker.

CONFIDENTIAL NOTICE

The names of all who lose their lives or are
wounded or reported missing while serving
with the Royal Air Force will appear in the
official casualty lists published from time to
time in the Press.

Any publication of the date, place or
circumstances of a casualty, and particularly
any reference to the unit concerned, might give
valuable information to the enemy, and for
this reason, only the name, rank and Service
number are included in the official lists.

Relatives are particularly requested, in the
national interest, to ensure that any notices
published privately do not disclose the date,
place or circumstances of the casualty, or
the unit.

The Press have been asked to co-operate in
ensuring that no information of value to the
enemy is published.

[OVER

(C50819) 20,000 11/43

The return of the personal belongings always came with the warning not to speak about the missing airman as it was always possible that he had been able to stay out of the hands of the Germans and was hiding with patriots.

127 Uxbridge Road.
Rickmansworth.
Herts.

21/3/44.

Dear Mrs Green.
            I received your
letter & am pleased you wrote,
we share your thoughts & hopes.
I met Barney the Pilot & am
confident he would get them out
of almost anything, my Son told
me often what a fine Pilot he
was, also Ken was a good engineer,
& between them I have every
confidence that we can hope for
the best.
    If you should change your address
let me know & I will do the same,
we must keep in touch, as sometimes
it is such a long time before

one hears.
I know you will pass this on to
Mr & Mrs Walker.
        Yours most Sincerely
        Mr & Mrs Plowman.

Letter of Mr. and Mrs Plowman after the news came that the crew was missing. They refer to Len Barnes as a fine pilot and Ken Walker as a good flight engineer.

122 Upper North St
Poplar E.14

May 9th

Dear Mr Walker
        I feel I must write to
you did you have a letter
from Mrs Gregg to say that
her son Malcolm is prisoner
of war and not wounded
I hope and trust that
we all hear the same
news very soon it gives
you brighter hopes.
    I went to the Red Cross
today with the letter and
they said it will be a
great help to them for all
the parents of the crew
Hoping we will hear something
very soon
        Yours Sincerely
        Mr & Mrs Barnes

122 Upper North St
Poplar E.14

Dear Mr Walker
        Just a few lines to let
you know Mum had the news
this morning to say that
Len is safe and in neutral
country, we have not heard
from himself yet. also we
cannot write direct to him,
Hoping that you will hear
soon from Kenneth and pray
God they are all safe and
they will all be home very
soon.
        Your Sincerly
        J. Barnes

Two letters of the Barnes family to Mr. Walker. In the left one they tell that they have been informed that Malcolm Gregg is a PoW, in the right one they express their joy about the safe return to England of Ken Walker.

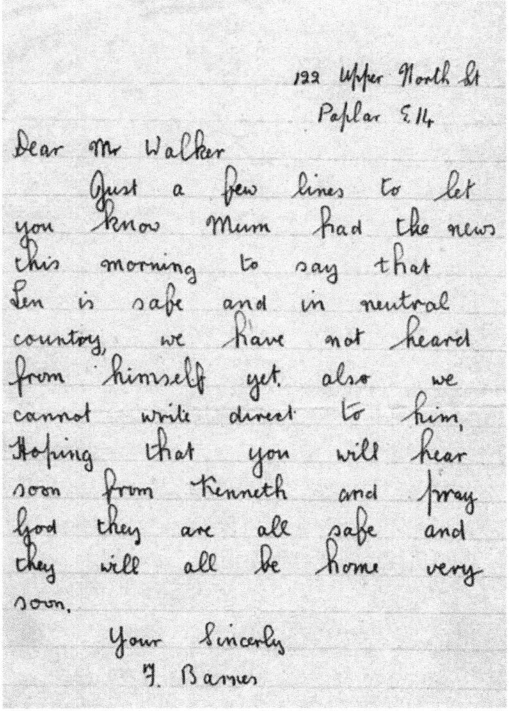

122 Upper North St
Paplar E.14

Dear Mr Walker

Just a few lines to let you know Mum had the news this morning to say that Len is safe and in neutral country, we have not heard from himself yet. also we cannot write direct to him. Hoping that you will hear soon from Kenneth and pray God they are all safe and they will all be home very soon.

Your Sincerly
J. Barnes

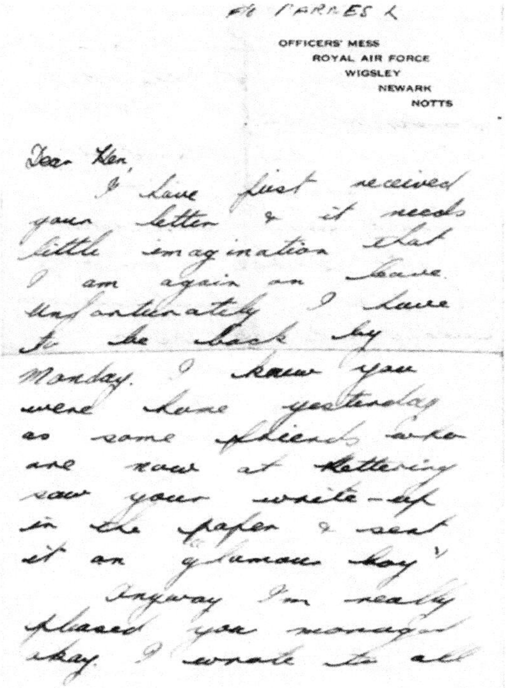

OFFICERS' MESS
ROYAL AIR FORCE
WIGSLEY
NEWARK
NOTTS

Dear Ken,

I have just received your letter & it needs little imagination that I am again on leave. Unfortunately I have to be back by Monday. I knew you were home yesterday as some friends who are now at Kettering saw your write-up in the paper & sent it on "glamour boy". Anyway I'm really pleased you managed okay. I wrote to all

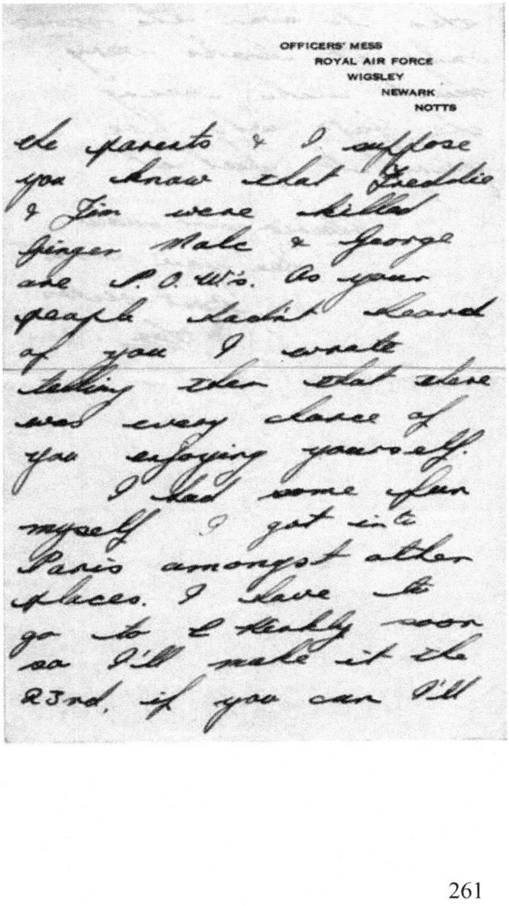

OFFICERS' MESS
ROYAL AIR FORCE
WIGSLEY
NEWARK
NOTTS

the parents & I suppose you know that Freddie & Jim were killed. Ginger Male & George are P.O.W.'s. As your people hadn't heard of you I wrote telling them that there was every chance of you enjoying yourself. I had some fun myself I got into Paris amongst other places. I have to go to bed really soon so I'll make it the 23rd, if you can I'll

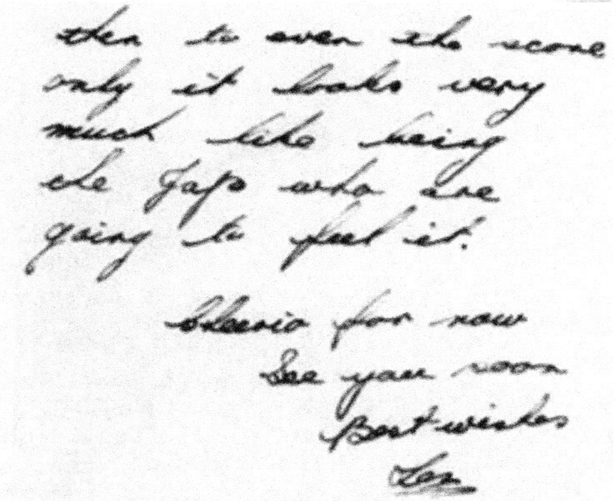

then to even the score only it looks very much like being the Japs who are going to feel it.

Cheerio for now
See you soon
Best wishes
Len

The safe return of Len Barnes was a happy day. Mrs. Barnes wrote a letter to the Walkers, saying how much she hoped Ken would also come home safely. Once Ken was in the United Kingdom his pilot was able to contact him from RAF Wigsley where Len was stationed. In his long letter to Ken, he said that mutual; friends had told him about the safe return of his flight engineer and about the article in the newspaper. He also told that Freddie Fox and Jim Overholt had been killed and that the other three were now in a German prisoner camp. Barnes also remembered the fun he had while hiding in Paris. Barnes was about to be posted to RAF East Kirkby.

TELEPHONE: GERRARD 9234
Exten. 3800
Any communications on the
subject of this letter should
be addressed to:—
THE
UNDER SECRETARY
OF STATE,
and the following number
quoted :—
Your Ref. P.414790/2/44/P.4. Cas. B4.

AIR MINISTRY
(Casualty Branch),
73-77, OXFORD STREET,
12th August 1944. W.1.

Sir,

I am directed to refer to the letters dated 25th
May 1944 and 5th July 1944 from the Department notifying you
that Flying Officer M.Geisler is a prisoner-of-war and Pilot
Officer L.A. Barnes is safe in the United Kingdom and to inform
you that the next-of-kin of Sergeant M.E. Gregg has received
a letter from him stating that he (Sergeant Gregg) is a
prisoner of war.

In addition a report has been received from the
International Red Cross Committee quoting German information
stating that Sergeant G.E.Plowman has been captured. Both
Sergeant Gregg and Sergeant Plowman are members of your
son's crew.

I am once again to extend to you the sincere
sympathy of the Department in your anxiety and to assure you
that you will be notified immediately of any further news
received.

I am, Sir,
Your obedient Servant,
M. Gray.
for Director of Personal Services.

A.H. Walker, Esq.,
1, Glenbank,
Midland Road,
Wellingborough,
Northants.

Here are the photographs that you have requested.
Please excuse the delay but we could not send them sooner.
Here also is a piece of information concerning your relative
and our friend.

The aeroplane crashed some 3 kilometres to the South
of the village, at night, about 2.00 am. The afternoon of
the same day the German soldiers found the bodies of the two
airmen and had the graves dug by the inhabitants of the village.
A few days later a Catholic Priest conducted a funeral service
in memory of the two victims. Certain inhabitants of the
village and a group of partisans (Free French) also assisted.
The ceremony was conducted clandestinely as usual during the
German occupation. The municipality of St. Gilles employ
labour for the up-keep of the graves of your relative and our
friend so that they will not be neglected.

In conclusion please accept this expression of my
sincere good wishes.

Monsieur & Madame R. Coulvier,
51, St. Gilles,
Fismes,
Marne,
FRANCE.

Letters to the parents of Sgt Ken Walker with the news that the pilot Len Barnes had safely returned home and that two other crew members Flying Officer Geisler and Sergeants Gregg and Plowman are prisoners of war. A post war letter sent to the family of Sergeant Fox with information about the crash in which he died.

% MRS. MERCER,
33 WELLINGTON RD,
BLACKPOOL,
LANCS.

Dear Mum & Dad,

As you will see, I am in
a fixed billett. We arrived at Blackpool
from Padgate at on Thursday morning about 11
we are fixed now in private billets and
we have four to six weeks marching
+ other drills in front of us. We only had
10/- at Padgate + that's to last us a
fortnight so I am getting pretty short of
cash already and I am in need of
handkerchiefs too. If you do send anything
will you please put my old green toothbrush
in as it will come in handy for cleaning
buttons. The sea has been a little rough
today, there are a few holiday makers here,
and everything is so bright and gay as
peacetime except blackout.

Tell Doreen I will write to her sometime
when I get time a moment for a few extra stamps.
Give my love to her a tell her I am in at
Blackpool where she got lost on the sands
about six years ago. I hope you are still
getting on alright also Auntie Rob, and still
keeping clear of Jerry.

We have got to go through vaccination +
inoculation yet which will make our arms swell
up + hurt for a day or two.

I don't think there is much chance of
getting home on leave until about February
or March next year because there is a big
course in front of us.

Well, I don't think there is much else
to say, so I shall wait for a letter from
you which will be very welcome.

So cheerio for now, and if you want
to know anything just ask & I will let you
know. Please excuse bad writing but
I had to write this in a hurry as it is
nearly 'lights out'.

With love
from Ken

P.S. Will you mention at the Fitwite Co. that
a letter is on the way as soon as I get time
it will most likely be on the way when
you receive this.
PSS I am in very good billets now so
it is not so bad for me.

Probably the happiest of letters received by Ken Walker's parents. The top one tells them that he has safely arrived in Blackpool to continue his service in the RAF.

All is as it was: billets have been found in a private house with Mrs. Mercer in Blackpool, he needs his 'old green toothbrush, which comes in handy for cleaning buttons', and all is well. He is very busy and has little time to write…

Later Ken was posted to India.

After his stay with the Theveniault family Ken Walker stayed in touch with them after the war. In fact, they became very close and shared many letters which had to be translated for the French. We assume that Ken Walker had picked up enough French to read them without help. The French family however needed the help of an interpreter, a young lady called Suzan.

*une photographie où vous êtes tous
les deux ou tous avec votre père
et Doreen heureuse de connaître votre
famille, si un jour vous venez
en France vous serez reçu avec joie
par tous vos amis, Kenneth il faut
écrire une lettre à Mr Terlet car
il n'en ont reçu qu'une de vous
il ne faut pas les oubliés ils ont
été si bon pour vous
Je termine ma lettre avec espoir
d'avoir bientôt une réponse
Je vous envoie ainsi que mon mari
nos plus douces amitiés pour vous
et votre femme
Bonne santé et Bonne chance à
tous deux
Votre amie de France
Mme Theveniault
Voici l'adresse de M. Vatelot*

*Nous n'avons pas reçu votre lettre
du mois d'août j'espère que
vous recevrez celle-ci avant votre
départ pour les Indes
Mr et Mme Regnier et Mr et Mme
Pioger sont en bonne santé et pense
souvent à vous Mr et Mme Caffinets
vous donne le bonjour
Mes sincères salutations à votre
père ainsi qu'à votre sœur
Pour vous et votre femme nos
plus douces amitiés
Vos amis de France
Mme Theveniault
St Barthelemy par la Ferté Gaucher
Seine et Marne*

Translation: Dear Kenneth, Very happy to have received your letter. Suzan translated for us. Mr. and Mrs. Terlet are also happy to know that you are in good health. It is with pleasure that we learn of your marriage. I wish you and your wife much happiness. We would be happy if you could come and see us both as you intend on your next leave. What a joy for all your friends to see you back in good health and will make Suzan's engagement on July 28 naturally with a very rich young man. Mlle Olivier is to be married soon to be a butcher at the Ferte Gaucher. Not knowing the address of Mme Vatelot who left for Melun now neither is the Vichy occupation agent at the agricultural cooperative, hope to have an address and I will send it to you. Mr. Vatelot is happy that Kenneth has not forgotten his friends in France. We bought a farm for Gilbert 9 km from St Barthelemy and Louisette left, busy on the farm also a lot of work. Tell you to come see us maybe in 1947. I doubt to see you again I would have been happy to know your wife, Kenneth if you have to send me a photograph of you both or all with your father and Doreen happy to know your family, if one day you come to France you will be greeted with joy by all your friends. Kenneth writes a letter to Mrs. Terlet because only one of you has been received so don't forget them, they were so good to you. We did not receive your August letter. I hope you will receive this before you leave for India. Mr and Mrs Regnier and Mr and Mrs Pioger are in good health and often think of you. Mr. and Mrs. Caffinets give you good morning. My sincere greetings to your father as well as to your sister Por you and your wife our sweetest regards. I am finishing my letter with the hope of having a reply soon. I send you and my husband our sweetest regards to you and your wife. Good health in good luck in turn two. Your friend from France Mrs. Theveniault.

'With the greatest possible respect, we give room in this book for those letters, with comment or other information. The war was not fought by soldiers, airmen and sailors, merchant seamen, fire fighters, policemen of wardens. The war was fought in every house that sent a father, son, brother or sister to serve in the fight against evil. With these few letters we want to erect a small monument of words for all those who knew the emotions of loss and of return when the loved ones came home. These are their pages in our book!

Today many of these letters are still in attics and boxes in sheds and garages and run the risk of being thrown away once next generations do no longer grasp the importance of the letters and the emotions expressed in them. We read about fear, sadness, hope and resignation, anger and joy, whatever the news was. 'Your son, brother or father was killed and buried, he is now a prisoner of war, he is still mission in action', and in some cases, like the ones we described in this book 'he is now under allied control, or liberated by allied troops.'

PoW and Concentration camps mentioned in this book.

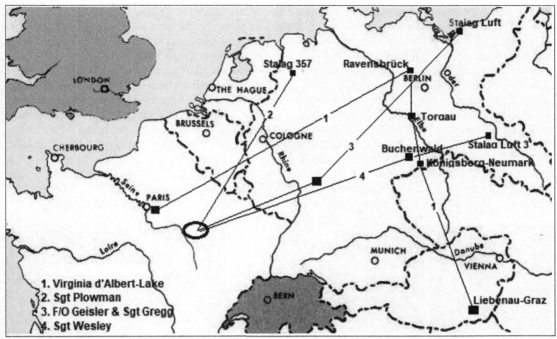

1. Virginia d'Albert-Lake
2. Sgt Plowman
3. F/O Geisler & Sgt Gregg
4. Sgt Wesley

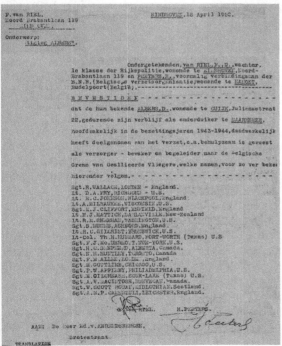

Left: After the war inquiries took place about actions of resistance members. This was done by a policeman with a member of the leadership of the resistance. Dirk Albers was one of these men who being in hiding for the Germans himself actively worked for the local resistance group. He had processed no less than 20 airmen, one of them being LtCol Hubbard. This report was made by Police Sgt 1st Class Van Riel. (HO)

While in a camp the prisoners could follow all kind of classes or indulge in art. Some of them became very accomplished with pencils, at times also working on false documents, stamps or signatures.
This drawing of a P-38 Lightning was made by 2Lt MacArthur in Stalag Luft. (HO)

L. Acknowledgement and bibliography.

It was impossible to write this book without the help of many brave men and women who belonged to the Comète Line and other resistance groups in The Netherlands, Belgium, and France. The help I received from surviving airmen in the United States and Great Britain was essential to be able to tell their story. If it had not been for the patience with which they answered my letters and allowed me to talk with them at length, the construction of the last organised escape to Spain would have been quite impossible. I thank them for photographs, documents, mementoes, and personal recollections from these fearful years. Above all, however, I am grateful to my wife Marjoan and my children Gerdy and Mark-Johan. They were willing to sacrifice family holidays abroad and join me to unknown and sometimes dull places in Belgium, France, and Spain. They know that camping can be very boring indeed. A place of honour is to be reserved for the participants in this book. It is their story and it describes their courage and self-sacrifice. Sadly, since publication of this book, all five travellers have died. Speed Hubbard, Willy Willis, Jack Cornett, Barney Barnes and Curly Emeny were of great help when I researched this book. In telling me about their adventures, they never forgot to mention the many helpers who risked their lives to help them to reach Spain and return home. The names show that people of all backgrounds joined once their country was in need and when total strangers on the run needed help.

One of the many women who never saw their husband again was Mrs. Hanne Bugge from Oslo Norway. Captain Hans Andreas Bugge vanished during a sortie between Iceland and the Faröer, as told in this book. Right: One of the helpers of Walker, Miss Lucienne Dusselier with her German shepherd in La Ferte Gauché.

Our heroes are:

Philippe and Virginia d'Albert-Lake; Father, Mother and the Kuppens brothers. Jef was killed in action in the former Dutch East Indies in 1947; Mysterious 'Hans', who never revealed his identity, but who helped Tom Hubbard to get away and gave me so much information to reconstruct part of his evasion; Dick Alberts; Louis Berinx; Jacques Bolle; brave Miss Yvonne 'Monique' Bienfait, who died in 1993; the Biquets; Luce Carmignac; Pierre Camus; Father Chenu; Léon, Mimi and Christine Coigné; Sir Michael Cresswell; Jean Duschene; Maréchal de Logis-Chef de la Gendarmerie Marcel Dussutour, who allowed Jack Cornett a safe getaway; Henk Eikelboom; Michel Etcheveste: Mr. Evrart; Joke Folmer; the late Go de Greef, the unsurpassed Mother of Comète, who virtually controlled the French-Spanish border and the German officers in Anglet; Paul Hellemans; the Hendrikx family; Mr. l'Heureux; Peter and Mimi v.d.Hurk; Raymond Itterbeek; Henk de Kort; the Lesquilliers; Anna Martens; Pierre Martin; Gaston Matthys; Marthe Mendihara; Ed van de Noorda; Revd and Mrs. an Nooten; Hubert Peeters; Mr le Maire Lucien Pillias; Mrs. Pinard; Frans van Riel; Genevieve Rocher; Marcel Roger; Dr. Salmon; Piet Souren; Lambert Spooren; Miss Terlet; Lucien Tripot and his parents; Dr. Warny; Frans Wijnen; Stewart Willis, the son of Don Willis and Martha McNicoll, Willis' third of four wives. He was frank and honest and had no reservations whatsoever to give a square, fair picture of his father.

Last but not least I thank all who helped me as representatives of archives embassies, government agencies and veterans organisations.

Australia: Hon Stephen Brady; Department of Defence; AM S.D.Evans RAAF CAS; RAFA;
Belgium: J.A.Bolle; J.Bussels; A.Deppé; C.Hoste; R.Itterbeek; Count J.Legrelle; M.Ugueux; W.Verstraeten,
Canada: Marlene Chorpitta; Directorate of History; W.A.B. Douglas; Little Norway Museum; National Defence Headquarters Archives; Royal Norwegian Embassy; Miss B.Wilson.
Finland: LtCol Perrti Nykänen; Eino Ritaranta.
France: Archives Departments de la Marne, Aisne, Seine/Marne; Aube, Yonne, Eure & Loire, Loiret; Association Mailly 3/4 Mai 1944; Philippe & Virginia d'Albert-Lake; Col.Y.Babron; J.Caillot; P. Camus; Luce Carmignac; Lucien Clement; Léon & Mimi Coigné; General Delmas; P.Dubas; Jacueline Dupic; M.Dussutour; M.Etcheveste; J.Hieaux; D.Hubier; Mrs.Jublot; M.Lobry; Mayors of Allainville; Aubeterre; Avant-les-Marcilly; Chalons sur Marne; Courboin; Dommartin-Lettrée; Dravegny; Dreux; Gatinais/Bourgogne; Montigny-le-Guesdier; St Agnan; St Rémy-sous-Barbuisse; Trouans et Villeret; Municipal Libraries of Chalons; Marthe Mendihara; S.Nelis; Lucien Pillias; Gen Poirret; Col Rénault; Col Richard; Maria Sanna; Daniel Sénégas; Lucien Tripot; Robert & Yvonne Lapeyre; Robert de Souza; Jean-Marie le Nours.
Germany: Hans-Ekkehard Bob; Heinz Bardua; Arnold Hackl; Hans Hamann; Rolf Hermichen; Hans Höhler; Erich Pott; Gerhard Schöpfel; Volksbund Deutsche Kriegsgräberfürsorge e.V
Malta: Malta: War Diary; Story of a George Cross; Website maltagc70.com.
Netherlands: Col F.M.Banks USAF; L.F.Berloth; Mrs. Kjersti Busman, LtCol P.G.Cook RA; Mrs.M.E.Coster; H.v.Daal; Col F.B.Gilligan USAF; P.Groenveld; Col W.Hamann USAF; Capt A.Hensher MBE RN; Col A.P.de Jong RNLAF; W.Kock; Capitaine de Vaisseau Jean Lefebvre; Col R.J.Mellody USAF; F.v.Merriënboer; Wg Cdr R.Mudge RAF; LtCol R.Patterson SR; Col A.Ryals USAF; Wg Cdr B.St.Clair RAF; A.C.Timmermans; LtCol M.Woodcock RA; J.Waalwijk; P.Veerman; Cdre A.Viruly KLM; W.Willemsen; staff of the Embassies of the United States, France, Belgium, Great Britain, Spain, Norway, Denmark, Finland;
New Zealand: Shirley Plowman-Grant, Brian Lissette, Air Force Museum New Zealand, Mount Manganui RSA;.NZ Military Archives, National Army Museum, NZ Military Historical Society.
Norway: Maj Gen E. Manshaus; Mrs. Hanne Bugge; Karl Ludvig Bugge; Gro Lobben Brekke; Captain Per Kristen Brekke RNN; Geir Haarr; Colonel A.Steffen-Olsen; Major P.Simonsen; Captain O. Maalen; Knut Arveng; J. Ulrich; Ole R.Bolmann, LtCol A.Krokeide; Prof. O. Riste.
Spain: LtCol Alfredo Chamorro, LtCol Alberto Pirris; José Maria Castroviejo.
United Kingdom: Air Historical Branch; Mrs. Helen Ambrose; Angela Barnes; Leonard and Merville Barnes MBE; Amanda Burrows; M.Bowman; Paul Burbidge; Sqn Ldr K.Butler RAF; Sebastian Cox; John Craft; Mrs.J.Craft; Mrs.K.P.Cummings; Liz Dickson; Patricia Dodd; J.P.McDonald; L.Duncan; P.Elliott; Ronald & Jessie Emeny; Jane Evans; V.Farrugia; Dr.M.Fopp; Roy Fox; R.Freeman; Friends of the Battle Of Britain Monument; Judi Geisler; Peter Gregg; Julie Ingram; Mrs. E.Lucas Harrison; Edward Hines; ACM Sir Lewis Hodges; Kenny John; Hugh Kennard; Denys Laing; National Archives; No.630 Squadron Research Group; RAF Escaping Society; RAF Museum; Lionel Lacey-Johnson; Bryan Morgan; F.F.Lambert; R.C.Wilkinson; J.C.Radford; Jocelyn Sewell; Ken Walker; Mrs.M.West. Stewart K.Willis; John Wood.
United States of America: Air Forces Escape and Evasion Society; American Aviation Historical Society; Air Force Magazine; Everett Atkins; Richard Atkins; 1361st Audio-Visual Squadron; E.Clifton Berry Jr; LtCol Biasi USAF; L.Blanding; Captain C.Blische USAF; D.Booth; H.L.Briggs; C.E. Butzerius; E.Cole; LtCol J.D.Cornett; L.Cornett; Defence Documentation Center; Major U.Drew USAF; J.Eastman; R.Evans; V.J.Ferrari; G.B. Fetrow; G.Fielding; H.Fletcher; G.C.Flitchcraft; R.Frey; Colonel F.B.Gilligan USAF Retd; J.Gray; J.Griffin; V.Haugland; John Hoffmann; Col Thomas H.Hubbard USAF; Gordon W.Hunsberger; Lt Rob Leese USAF; M.Livesay; D.Lynn; B.Mahon; N. Mandell; C.Martin; MPRC Military Personnel Record Center; T.Moore; Mrs.J.F.Mosgrove; Claude & Shirley Murray; National Air & Space Museum; Office of Air Force History; Robert G.Patterson; Ralph K.Patton; Major Joe T.Reams USAFR; Bob Riemenschnieder; R.Rose; MajGen D.H.Ross; A.Rowley; Howard B.Scholten; Secretary of the Air Force/Public Affairs; Heyward C.Spinks; Aubrey C.Stanhope; R.H.Svoboda; L.Sypher; E.D.Taylor; R.Tilley; USAF Historical Research Agency; D.Williams; Patricia J.Willis-Giles; D.A. Young; Joe Durham.

Leslie Lissette as a qualified Sergeant Pilot, front 4th from right.(BL)

Bibliography.
Books Finland: H.Roelfzema: Smeulend Vuur; T.Sorsa: Lentäjan Albumi:Suomen Ilmavoivat.
Books Norway: Lt H.A. Bugge: The 2nd Air Defence Division; Combat report April-June 1940; Lt H. A.Bugge diaries & documents; Hanne Bugge: correspondence & memories of Lt H.A Bugge; G. Haarr: Battle for Norway: April–June 1940; B. Hafsten: Heinkel 115 anvendelse under ntralitetsvakten 1.9.39-9.4.40 og under krigen i Norge 1940; F.Meyer: Haerens og Marinens Flyvapen,1912/45; F.Meyer: Marine flyvere i 1940.
Books Eagle Squadrons: Earl Boebert: The Eagle Squadrons (AAHS Journal 9/1); James Childers: War Eagles; The Story of the Eagle Squadrons; Vern Haugland: The Eagle Squadrons; Yanks in the RAF, 40-42; Vern Haugland: The Eagles' War; The Saga of the Eagle Squadron Pilots, 40-45.
Books Prisoners of War; Escape and Evasion: Virginia d'Albert-Lake: Unpublished Memoirs; C.Andrew: Secret Service; P.Beesley: Very Special Intelligence; J.Bussels: De doodstraf als risico; D. Caskie: The Scottish Pimpernel; O.Clutton-Brook: Footprints on the Sans of Time; A.W.Cooper: Free to Fight Again; E.Cosgrove: The Evaders; D.Darling: Secret Sunday; J.Dominy: The Sergeant Escapers; L.Dumais: Operatie Bonaparte; M.R.D. Foot & J.M.Langley: MI.9; C.Jubault: The extraordinary Adventure of the Forest of Freteval; Sir John Hackett: I was a stranger; T.Kortooms: De Zwarte Plak; A.Neave: Saturday at MI.9; Richard Pape: Boldness be my friend; L.A.Poels and J. Derix: Vriend en Vijand; Colonel Gilbert Rénault: Mission Marathon; Colonel Gilbert Rénault: La Ligne de Démarcation; Réseau Comète (3 vols); Ray Tolliver and Hans Scharff: The Interrogator; Escape and Evasion 1939-1945; M.Smedts: Waarheid en Leugen in het Verzet; F.Visser: De Schakel;

Other books: Heinz Bardua: Stuttgart im Luftkrieg, 1939-1945; B.Bertin and L-M le Nours: Objectif Mailly-le-Camp; M.Bowman: Fields of Little America; M.Bowman: Action Stations; Chaz Bowyer: Bomber Group at War; Paddy Finucane; Fighter Ace; René J. Francillon: USAAF Fighter Units Europe 1942-1945; Roger Freeman: Airfields of the 8th, Then and Now; Roger Freeman: The Mighty 8th; Roger Freeman: The Mighty 8th War Diary; Mike Garbett and Brian Goulding: Lancaster at War 1 and 2; Don Gillison: Royal Australian Air Force 1939-1942; John Herington: Air Power over Europe 1944-1945; E John Herington: Air War against Germany & Italy 1939-1943; Ab Jansen: Sporen aan de hemel (3 vols); Ab Jansen: Gevleugeld verleden; Wg Cdr C.G.Jefford MBE RAF: RAF Squadrons; Wilhelm Johnen: Duell unter den Sternen; William E. Jones: Bomber Intelligence; N. Longmate: The Bombers; The RAF Offensive against Germany, 1939-1945; R. McDowell: Lockheed P-38 Lightning; E.T. Maloney: P-38 Lightning; C.Messenger: Bomber Harris and the Strategic Bomber Offensive, 1939-1945; Martin

Middlebrook & Chris Everitt: The Bomber Command War Diaries; Len Morgan: The P-47 Thunderbolt; Brian Philpott: RAF Bomber Units Europe 1939-1942; Brian Philpott: RAF Bomber Units Europe 1942-1945; Profile Publications: Avro Lancaster, nos.65 and 235; J.D. Rawlings: Fighter squadrons of the Royal Air Force; Dennis Richards and Hillary St. George Saunders: Royal Air Force 1939-1945 (3 vols); Bruce Robertson: Lancaster; the story of a famous bomber; Kenn C. Rust: The 9th Air Force in World War II; Dudley Saward: Bomber Harris; Percy Schramm: Kriegstagebücher des Oberkommandos der Wehrmacht. (8 vols); Jerry Scutts: Luftwaffe Night fighter Units 1939-1945; Christopher Shores: Luftwaffe Fighter Units Europe 1942-1945; Francis Suttill SOE contre Gestapo; Francis J.Suttill Prosper: Major Suttill's French Resistance Network; Gene Turney: The P-38 Lightning; J.J. v.d.Veer: De dag van de Liberator; Walter Verstraeten: Vleugels boven Klein Brabant; A. Viruly: Normandisch Freud; A.Viruly: Kunst en Vliegwerk; Webster & Frankland: The Strategic Air Offensive against Germany 39-45, (4 vols); Wissenschaftliche Rundschau: Gezielter Verrat.

Documents, articles, interviews: ORBs: No.71, 121, 133 (Eagle) Squadrons RAF; ORB: No.207, No. 630 Squadron RAF; ORB: No.61 OTU RAF; RAF Form 414 (Logbook): Squadron Leader H. Kennard DFC; Form 414: P/O Donald K. Willis; RAF Form 414: Maj Donald K. Willis; RAF Form 414: P/O Leonard A. Barnes; HQ VII Bomber Command USAAF: Narrative of Operations, No.130, Bremen 131143; HQ 96BG (Heavy) AAF: Narrative Report of Ops, Bremen 131143; Group History 355FG: Saturday, 131143; Marechaussee: 131143, Report on landing of parachutist; Resistance Questionnaire: LtCol Hubbard; Statement of Witness 141143: Major R.D. Meyers AAC CO 350FS; MACR 1447 of 151143 Hubbard: Major G.J.Dix AAC Ops Officer 355FG; Casualty Questionnaire 1499: LtCol Thomas H. Hubbard; Resistance Questionnaire Mr. Philippe d'Albert-Lake/Comète; MACR. 4409 of 280444 Cornett: 1Lt Genzler USAAF 361FG; Statement of Witness 100444: 1Lt A. Rowley USAAF 20FG; Mission Summary Report: Droop Snoot Gütersloh 55FS/20FG, 10Apr1944; Report on crashed aircraft: Municipal Archives Oud en Nieuw Gastel, Netherlands 100444; Abschuss meldung 993, 230544 (German): Ref. Lt J.D. Cornett; Missing Air Crew Reports: 1551-1554; E&E Report 629: T/S Nicolas Mandell; E&E Report 607: 2Lt Victor J. Ferrari; E&E Report 800: Maj Donald K. Willis; E&E Report 802: LtCol Thomas H. Hubbard; E&E Report 819: 2Lt Jack D. Cornett; ER MI.9/SpG(-)1986, 240644: F/S John Pittwood No.207 Squadron; ER MI.9/Sp G(-)2001, 260644: Sgt Ron Emeny No.207 Squadron; ER MI.9/SpG(-)2000, 260644: P/O Len Barnes No.603 Squadron; BC INRO: No.764: from 1200hrs 14 Mar - 1200hrs 16 Mar 44; Bomber Command SO: 14&15 Mar 1944; Bomber Command SO: 2/3, 3/4, 4/5 Mar 44; Sworn Statement 270444: 1Lt Eugene Cole; Sworn Statement 280444: 1Lt Leroy Sypher; Sworn Statement 280444: Capt. John W.Guckeyson; Telegram 896 290444: Luftwaffe Auswerte Stelle West, Frankfurt, Oberursel; Restricted Telegram 51/30644: US Mil. At. Madrid Col F.D.Sharp; Restricted Telegram 34 260644: Military Liaison Officer AC Gibraltar Col H.W. Forster; RAGO 280644: LtCol T.H. Hubbard HQ 335FG; RAGO 280644: Maj D.K. Willis HQ 67FW; RAGO 300644: Maj D.K.Willis HQ 67FW. RAGO 300644: 2Lt J.D.Cornett 375FS/ 361FG; Statement RNAF 100151: Lt Gen W. Hansteen RNAF; Credentials 180452: Alberts Confirmation F.M.van Riel & H.Peeters: Toledo Blade, Toledo, Ohio, Friday, February 18, 1949. Interview Col Victor J. Ferrari by M.L. Gillette 28th May 1991; the LBJ Library; Article The Navigator's Odyssey, M.L.Gillette; Moosburg online. WWII Forum: Heinkel He-115 Seaplane RAF Special Ops Loss, Malta

Abbreviations and Photo credits:
AB: Amanda Barnes; AC: Amicale Comète; AFeT: Archives Fere en Tardenois; BuA: Bundesarchiv; BG: Bomb Group, BL: Brian Lissette; BS: Bomb Squadron; CCC: Cass City Chronicle; CWGC: Commonwealth War Graves Commission; Dulag Luft: Durchgangslager Luftwaffe (Transit Camp Air Force); E&E: Escape & Evasion; ER: Evasion Report (RAF); ESA: Eagle Squadron Association; Fighter Group: Fighter Group, FS: Fighter Squadron, Finnish Air Force; HO: Hans Onderwater; HQ: Headquarters, INRO: Intelligence Narrative Report of Operations; IWM: Imperial War Museum; KNSM: Koninklijke Nederlandse Scheepvaart Mij; KZ: Konzentrations Lager (Concentration Camp); MA: Militärarchiv; MACR: Missing Air Crew Report, MI.9: Military Intelligence 9; MMMlC: Musée Militaire Mailly le Camp; MoDF: Ministry of Defence Finland; NAC: National Archives Canada; NAUS: National Archives US; NNA: Norwegian Naval Archives; ORB: Operations Record Book; OTU:

Operational Training Unit; RAFM: Royal Air Force Museum; RAGO: Report to Adjutant General's Office, RE; Ron Emeny; RNAF: Royal Norwegian Air Force, FAF: Finnish Air Force; SO: Stalag: Stamm Lager (Main Camp); Summary of Operations; S&S: Stars & Stripes; SOE: Special Operations Executive; UoK: University of Keele; UTAL: University Texas Arlington Libraries; USAFHRC: United States Air Force Historical Research Center.

Other books and articles written by Hans Onderwater MBE

Historic Books:
Mobilisatie, Collaboratie, Liberatie ; de Jaren 1938-1948 in Stadskanaal. (Dutch)
Schetsen uit de Nacht; Barendrecht 1940-1945 (with Jan van Mastrigt). (Dutch)
Reis naar de Horizon; Escape & Evasion in de Tweede Wereldoorlog. (Dutch)
En toen was het stil; de luchtoorlog boven IJsselmonde. (Dutch)
Oorlog rond Hoek van Holland. (Dutch)
Gentlemen in Blue; No.600 (City of London) Squadron. (English)
One of our aircraft is missing… (with Wim Wüst) (Dutch)
Operatie Manna; de voedseldroppings van april/mei 1945. (Dutch)
Operatie Manna/Chowhound; the food drops of April/May 1945. (English)
Memories of a Miracle; Operation Manna/Chowhound. (Dutch and English)
Meer schetsen uit de Nacht; Barendrecht 1945-1950. (Dutch)
Barendrecht; een eeuw in foto's. (Dutch)
Second to None; the History of No.II(Army Co-operation) Squadron RAF 1912-1987.
Second to None; the History of No.II(Army Co-operation) Squadron RAF 1912-2002.
Hereward; Second to None; the History of No.II (Army Co-operation) Squadron RAF 1912-2018.
Kiezen of delen; een oorlogsverhaal uit Barendrecht. (Dutch)
Crossing en oorlogsherinneringen. (Dutch).
A Winged Gunner; the life and times of Air Cdre Andrew James Wray Geddes CBE DSO RAF
Journey to the Horizon; Escape and Evasion (with Brian Lissette)
Onbekende oorlogsverhalen 1940-1945. (Dutch)

Children's Books
Ik wens voor jou… (Dutch)
De Gouden Sleutel van de Verhalenkist. (Dutch)
Een regenboog vol verhalen. (Dutch)

Articles:
Flt Lt Keith Malcolmson RNZAF. (Dutch)
De oorlog van Klein Duimpje. (Dutch)
Tien over toen. (Dutch)
Operatie Manna. (Dutch)
De oorlog van mijn grootvader. (Dutch)
The Arctic Weather War. (Dutch)
His Majesty's Pirates. (Dutch)
The Friendly Occupation; Faroer Island under British rule. (Dutch)
Vier vliegtuig crashes in Barendrecht (Dutch)

About the authors

Hans Onderwater MBE (1946) is a historian, researcher and author from the Netherlands. He was a teacher and a member of the National Reserve Corps of the Royal Netherlands Army for 40 and 30 years respectively. Hans is also the historian of No.II (Army Co-operation) Squadron, the oldest fixed-wing Squadron in the world. He wrote three books about this famous RAF Squadron. As the secretary of the Food & Freedom Foundation Hans was involved in the commemorations of Operations Manna and Chowhound, the Allied food drops over starving Holland in April and May 1945. Hans was secretary of the Netherlands Coastal Defence Museum, governor of the War and Resistance Museum in Rotterdam and chairman of the Documentation Group 40-45. Hans identified several airmen who were buried. He also found the next of kin and arranged for visits to the graves and crash sites of their loved ones. For his research, his many publications and much other work Hans did in the service of the Netherlands, HM Queen Beatrix made him a member of the Order of Oranje-Nassau. In January 2017 HM Queen Elizabeth II of Great Britain honoured with the Most Excellent Order of the British Empire.
Since 1974 he has written 27 books about World War Two, of which a number were also published in English. He also co-operated in the making of a number of documentary films in Canada and the United Kingdom. Hans is married to Marjoan since 1970. They live in Barendrecht, not far from Rotterdam.

Brian Lissette (1941) is a 30 year veteran of the New Zealand Police. He researched the history of his uncle Warrant Officer Leslie Lissette RNZAF for some 20 years. He united descendants of the crew of the Lancasters ND530 and ND556, who reside in Australia, Canada, England and New Zealand. He paid tribute at his uncle's grave in the French town of Chaintreaux, France in 2015. He located Hans Onderwater in 2017 via a Google search. Since then the joined forces to write this book. Brian hosted Hans and his wife Marjoan at his home in February 2020 during their visit to New Zealand. There they decided to work together. This is their first joint project about men who fought, died, endured or evaded capture. It also honours Warrant Officer Leslie Lissette, who gave his life staying at the controls of a burning Lancaster, ensuring the safe descend by parachute of his crew, and Pilot Officer Leonard Barnes who did the same but who escaped death in the cockpit. Brian married Jean in 1967. They reside in Mount Maunganui, New Zealand.

Brian Lisette and Hans Onderwater MBE.

About Nedvision Publishing

Nedvision Publishing is a publishing house of:

- unique books on history, especially World War II and;
- education, especially practice guides for certification and marketing.

Other books published by Nedvision:

- **Arnhem 1944, een historische slag herzien, deel 1: Tanks en Paratroepen,** by Christer Bergström (Dutch)
- **ISO 9001:2015 Gemakkelijk uitgelegd,** by Christof Dahl (Dutch)

Expected in the course of 2021:

- **Arnhem 1944, een historische slag herzien, deel 2: De verloren overwinning,** by Christer Bergström (Dutch)
- **Zoeken naar weten**, by Yehudith Heymans-Gudema (Dutch)
- **A winged gunner; the life and times of Air Cdre Andrew James Wray Geddes CBE DSO RAF,** by Hans Onderwater MBE
- **The Guards of Westerbork,** by Dr. Frank van Riet
- **Stripes of a Zebra,** by Andries van der Wal & Dick van der Zee

If you would like to receive the latest news about our publications, please subscribe to our newsletter or contact us.

Nedvision Publishing
Wagenmakerstraat 9
9403 VC Assen
The Netherlands
T +31 (0)592-749333
E info@nedvision.com

www.nedvision.com

Printed in Great Britain
by Amazon

43734701R00152